THE NEW JERSEY ASSEMBLY, 1738-1775

The Making of a Legislative Community

Michael C. Batinski

UNIVERSITY
PRESS OF
AMERICA

LANHAM • NEW YORK • LONDON

Copyright © 1987 by

University Press of America,® Inc.

4720 Boston Way
Lanham, MD 20706

3 Henrietta Street
London WC2E 8LU England

British Cataloging in Publication Information Available

Library of Congress Cataloging in Publication Data

Batinski, Michael C., 1943-
The New Jersey Assembly, 1738-1775.

Includes bibliographies and index.
1. New Jersey.   Legislature.   General Assembly—
History—18th century.   2. New Jersey—Politics and
government—Colonial period, ca. 1600-1775.   I. Title.
JK83.N5B38   1987   328.749'09   86-28253
ISBN 0-8191-6089-X (alk. paper)

90-10854

to my mother and father

Virginia and Stanley Batinski

Contents

Tables

INTRODUCTION

This study of the New Jersey Assembly applies and clarifies what is emerging as a new conception of the colonial American legislature. "New" and "emerging" might, at first, seem ill-chosen words to discuss a subject that has attracted little attention in recent years. In the two decades since Jack P. Greene completed his study of the southern assemblies, early American historiography has undergone significant revisions, but his analysis of the lower houses has remained essentially intact. That constitutional history of "the rise of representative assemblies" and the accompanying description of an elite that overcame "chaotic factionalism," that provided the talents for leading the house in its "quest for power," and that laid the basis for "political maturity" remain basic themes in colonial history. Some disagreements continue over the degree of success the houses achieved in their "quest for power" or over the relative instability or maturity of that political system. But these seem differences of shading. And, although additional research might resolve these questions, the subject does not attract interest.[1] Nonetheless, a new conception of the legislature is emerging: it is emerging from bits and pieces of seemingly unrelated research and thus needs to be identified and clarified.

As Greene completed The Quest for Power, he identified the direction future legislative studies should take. By choosing to write an "institutional and constitutional" history, he owned that he had produced a partial treatment of the subject and recognized that a full rendering would be achieved only after considering the social and intellectual world of the lawmakers.[2] Since then, these two fields have flourished. Indeed, social and intellectual history seems to have eclipsed political history, and the achievements in these fields have been made without the intent to enhance the study of the legislature. Simply by counting, social historians have provided answers to long-standing questions about who owned what and how many participated in legislative politics. Analysis of society's bottom rungs and of local communities has clarified the social and economic environment that shaped the lawmakers and affected the relationship between themselves and the public. Moreover, recent attention to such commonplace words as "country," "virtue," and "patriotism" has disclosed once unappreciated meanings in the eighteenth-century's vocabulary of political discourse. This intellectual history has not only discovered contents, complexities, European antecedents, and American transformations but in conjunction with social history it has rendered a new perspective, namely, one from the actors' vantage point, of the role of the legislature, the significance of political disagreements and factional disputes, and the meaning of legislation and policy produced by government.

Recent work on the social structure and community life has significant, albeit unintended, implications for understanding the legislature's place within colonial society. First, it has provided the means to map that society into a series of concentric circles with the legislature at the center. At the outer edge were the propertyless and disfranchised. Those males who owned enough to vote made up the second sphere, or the legislative community. And within that sphere was an even smaller one of those who met the property qualification to sit in the legislature. The boundary between the first and second spheres separated the dependent and independent, servant and master, poor and self-sufficient populations. Separation of the electorate from its leadership rested, in part, on legal distinctions among the propertied population. As the eighteenth century progressed and as the local and provincial elite consolidated its positions, the boundary became increasingly difficult to cross. But a bond remained between the two that made for a legislative community. In part, it was expressed in habits of the electorate to defer to this leadership and of the lawmakers to draw their authority to act upon their representative or fiduciary relationship with the electorate. Moreover, this legislative community revealed its nature in its constant efforts to discipline the unruly elements in the third sphere. Second, community studies have disclosed several mappings of a subjective nature. The voters did not share the same estimate of the provincial government's importance. Perhaps a majority was indifferent to the legislature. Deference shaded into indifference. And among those who were concerned perhaps a minority was interested in the constitutional confrontations with the executive, and most of the voters looked to the legislature to resolve local disputes over property or to set policy on the development of waterways or eradication of pests. Finally, these different definitions of the legislature's function carried over into the elite. The lawmakers, like their constituents, set different priorities on the agenda and gave correspondingly different meanings to their task. And, when they spoke of their representative role, they were often imposing a construction of social reality upon an inert constituency.[3]

Simultaneously, intellectual historians have been filling in the contents of these mental maps and have discovered a world view that gave cohesion to this legislative community. That world view contained both traditional communal values and liberal notions of the marketplace. On the one hand, it raised up an ideal of public virtue and selflessness and condemned the predator who used his power, be it in the marketplace or public office, for selfish purposes. On the other hand, these colonists were coming to recognize that the spirit of self-improvement, or self-interest, was the driving force that was transforming the North American wilderness into a garden; and, as they did, so they were coming to accept what would later be known as interest group politics. In sum, they were moving, albeit unwittingly, toward a liberal world view. While this world view did not characterize the thinking of colonists throughout the social order, it did prevail among those who participated in legislative politics. These colonists discussed politics within the framework of these shared attitudes, and they devised policies designed to reconcile the tensions between the modern and traditional and to realize that shared image of the good society. Differences became a matter of shading or style. Those who were most accustomed to the marketplace were also more able to embrace liberal tendencies in policy. In addition, this moral society depended on preserving virtue in government, and the legislature often strove to thwart the corrupt politician's schemes to undermine the constitution. Inevitably, these discussions turned to complex constitutional questions and were couched within an intellectual tradition rich with historical memories and precedents. But those who listened gave different meanings to these debates. While some were familiar with the rich literary tradition of Anglo-American political thought, others were not. Thus, some understood the issues as part of a coherent and formally structured ideology, and others responded from a cluster of attitudes and prejudices.[4]

This social and intellectual history does not repudiate past studies of the colonial legislature, but it does confirm the flatness of the institutional approach and thereby alters the conception of future research. It turns attention from the institution to the actor and from the prominent to all the members including the obscure backbencher. Once the focus is on the institution as it was perceived by the membership, the lawmakers become multifaceted actors, and their understanding requires correspondingly multidimensional psychological explanations. Although historians have rightly attended to the lawmakers' factiousness, preoccupation with that behavior has rendered a one-dimensional portrait of the actors motivated by self-interest. But they were also policy makers, and they acted upon ideas and prejudices as much as calculated pocketbook interest. Moreover, by ignoring the way the actors mapped their political world, set their priorities, and established their expectations of government, historians could focus on those dramatic constitutional questions related to the "quest for power" without considering the commonplace but important social issues that brought so many to the legislature. Not only do social and intellectual historians inspire reconsideration of the legislature, but their work has also progressed to the point that they can no longer neglect this subject. Studies of society "from the bottom up" have proved of immense importance, but even those historians most sympathetic to this approach have also conceded the one-sidedness of looking at the dominated without considering those who did the dominating and the political relationship between the two.[5] So, too, intellectual history advanced on the premise that people cannot do what they cannot conceive. That work has turned full circle to consider the action side of that equation: that is, the role of ideas in society and in the political forum. Perhaps understandably, this work has been especially concerned with the dissemination of ideologies through the social structure, but unfortunately it does not examine political and economic thought in the legislature.[6] Thus, this research points toward the legislature. When the insights and bits and pieces gleaned from nonlegislative studies are assembled, a fresh conception for the legislature begins to emerge. This conception is like a blueprint, however. At best, it suggests what needs to be done and how to proceed. And, like a blueprint, this conception has yet to be executed.

The purpose of this study is to clarify this conception of the colonial legislature and to apply it to a specific institution. It is above all an actor-oriented study: that is, its focus is not on the institution but on its membership. As such, it attends to all the lawmakers--not just the prominent and visible but the backbenchers as well. In turn, the institution is considered as a creation of the members, not of the king or a few leaders. This study examines who the members were in their communities, how they made their livings, what social stations they enjoyed, and how their ethnic and religious identities shaped their political lives. In addition, it seeks to reconstruct their world view and their perceptions of government. In sum, it treats with who they were before they stood for election. Then it explores their reasons for choosing to sit in the legislature and the different ways they interpreted the role of representative. Principally, it focuses on the representatives as law and policy makers. This approach entails consideration of the mundane as well as the dramatic. Finally, it examines how the members worked together as a group, their affiliations and differences, the institutional setting, and the policy-making process. Thus, from the sum of these biographies emerges a group portrait of an elite, the institution it was creating, and the world it was seeking to make.

Anyone familiar with the sources cannot but appreciate the difficulty of such a task. So few personal papers are extant that even the most prominent leaders remain shadowy figures. At best, the researcher must rely on materials found in local records and in genealogical and local history libraries. But, perhaps most frustrating, once the lawmakers enter the house they virtually vanish from sight. The colonial legislature kept its doors closed to the public. The published journals of proceedings do not include debates and only yield a mute record of petitions submitted, resolutions, committee assignments, messages to the governor and council, and a list of the laws passed. An occasional manuscript or printed source will give a fleeting glimpse of some members in agreement or disagreement on a particular issue at a single moment in time. While invaluable, these observations do not provide the continuous and comprehensive record necessary to forge a link between the biographical data and the policy created. Until recently, this problem was endemic to legislative studies no matter the period examined. Computer-assisted roll-call analysis has, however, proved immensely beneficial to this inquiry.[7] This technique has been rarely used in colonial history, in part because most legislatures failed to record such data. Robert Zemsky has made the most significant attempt at roll-call analysis in his study of Massachusetts politics.[8] But, because that legislature recorded an average of one roll call a year, the data remain too sparse to make a satisfactory linkage between individuals and policy. There were, however, other legislatures that left a more complete record. In 1738, for example, the New Jersey Assembly resolved to record roll calls; and by independence it had published over 500 divisions.

This decision to select a single case naturally raises questions of representativeness or uniqueness, especially when that legislature has received less attention than others and is known for its exceptionally volatile politics. Closer examination, however, confirms that political instability and the legislature's institutional immaturity derived from the late date of the province's establishment and that New Jersey's development ran parallel to the histories of the older colonies.

New Jersey became a political entity in 1702 when the crown dissolved the East and West Jersey proprietary governments. The new constitutional arrangement with a governor appointed and instructed by the crown, a Council of royal appointees to advise the governor and sit as an upper house of the legislature, and a House of Assembly elected by the propertied and male population conformed to the prevailing pattern of Anglo-American government. While the Assembly enjoyed the power of the purse and jealously guarded that right from encroachments by the Council and executive, the governor enjoyed countervailing powers. Not only could he call, prorogue, and dissolve the Assembly, but he could employ his patronage powers to create a pliant membership or exercise his veto to check a recalcitrant majority. In the early decades, the

Assembly had not been able to assert itself effectively. Its members were newly arrived men struggling to achieve position and security. Insecurity created politicians who desperately competed for the governor's favor and eyed their colleagues with suspicion. Competition sparked vicious confrontation and left the provincial elite internally divided. And because the first governors held a commission to govern New York and infrequently visited New Jersey, the Assembly met irregularly. Between 1725 and 1738, the house met in only five sessions. But in 1738 when it resolved to begin the practice of recording roll calls, the province received a separate governor, and the legislature began to meet more regularly. Moreover, the leadership was beginning to achieve some security; and, although the sessions sometimes became stormy, they were less volatile than in the earlier decades. In sum, the political system was evolving in the same direction as that of the older and more mature colonies.

This study of New Jersey's legislature is actor-oriented in its focus. And, since its purpose is not simply to enhance a political narrative, its organization requires some explanation. The work is in three parts: the first examines social policy, the second the institution, and the third provincial political and constitutional issues.

The rationale for this structure grew out of the analysis of the assemblymen and the institution which is discussed in the middle section (Chapter Three). New Jersey's assemblymen defined the institution and their roles in different ways. The localist backbencher came to represent his and his neighbors' interests and was concerned principally with social and economic policy that affected his community's life. The provincial politician shared these concerns but in contrast to his backbencher colleague was also active in provincial politics and related constitutional issues. Thus, the legislature attended to two agendas: social policy and provincial politics. In addition, this legislature proved to be by modern standards an immature institution. The legislature was an assemblage of local politicians, and its membership turned over rapidly. It had not created the organizations, either party or faction, to unite the disparate elements, and it had yet to develop the means to socialize the initiate or identify leadership. Indeed, roll-call analysis of the twelve assemblies that met between 1738 and 1775 demonstrated the invertebrate nature of this body. Voting associations were constantly changing. In one assembly, alignments turned on an urban-rural axis; but in the next, sectionalism, economic interest, or religious affiliation would prevail. No association was enduring enough to suggest the presence of legislative organization. While constantly fluctuating relationships might suggest volatility, they also revealed an underlying stability. Voting behavior oscillated between the intensely polarized and the nearly consensual. One assembly would be divided into two clearly defined and antagonistic voting blocs. In the next, these blocs would dissolve, one-time opponents would vote in agreement, and the membership would be drawn toward unanimity. In sum, the differences were myriad but not so profound that they created a permanent division within New Jersey's legislative elite.

The mundane matters of social policy became the focus of the first section (Chapters One and Two) for two reasons: first, the lawmakers were equally interested in these issues and, second, their treatment of this agenda revealed an underlying consensus. The first two chapters treat with the lawmakers' social world, their world view, and the policies they produced. These lawmakers and their constituents thrived in the marketplace; and, though they were coming to accept liberal notions, they were still governed by strong traditional social values. The fusion of the communal and liberal made for a vision of commercial arcadia. This experience and world view created the basis for a legislative community. Disagreements on policy abounded, but voting analysis failed to discover categorical division. Dissent focused on specific measures. It often grew out of personal interest--or the forces of the marketplace. Self-interest itself, however, was an insufficient explanation. The vision of commercial arcadia was fraught with internal tensions, and some lawmakers were more inclined than others to embrace programs for economic improvement. But this behavior suggested the presence of inclination: it was less than ideological, more than interest, and what might be labeled temperament.

This analysis of the lawmakers' social backgrounds, their public policy, and their conceptions of their role in the legislature dictated the decision to postpone the discussion of the provincial political agenda until the last section (Chapters Four to Seven). Not only were those constitutional matters that touched on the house's "quest for power" only one part of the Assembly's business, but, more important, the lawmakers did not all ascribe the same weight to them as have later historians. Moreover, the significance of the ideology that was employed and the depth of the divisions that it provoked could be put in perspective within the context of the previous discussion. The political ideology roused confrontation and the semblance of irreconcilable division. Certainly the participants thought so. The Country ideology moved the lawmaker who came uninterested in constitutional issues and often provoked the normally conservative member to join in extreme opposition to the governor. No doubt, its strength lay in its ability to raise powerful symbols of patriotism and virtue which were deeply embedded in this culture. But the ideology also tended to exaggerate by couching political divisions in manichean terms when in fact the disputants were part of a legislative community. Thus, the ideology was not only powerful but also proved to be ethereal.

A narrative structure was employed in the last chapters to illustrate the workings of this political system--in particular, the role of ideology in this invertebrate institution. The Country ideology was emotionally charged and it was wont to exaggerate, but it also served a function. By creating moods on the floor of the house, it converted lawmakers to positions they normally rejected. When employed by the skillful orator or demagogue, this ideology could frame provincial politics in grand historical terms. It was not just a description that turned on powerful symbols of political virtue; it also contained a script that pitted the patriot against the venal courtier. Once played with the proper staging, actors, and cues, this scenario provided the means to move an otherwise disparate assemblage.

This organization might raise two objections. First, the decision to treat with the institution as a static entity may be necessary to describe the underlying structure of this legislative system, but such an approach also risks distortion by ignoring change. In fact, whenever it seemed important, change has been considered in the text. But, in review of the period, the character of this legislative community did not undergo significant alteration. Moreover, it was strong enough to weather the shock of revolution and to achieve maturity in the first decades of the republic. Second, and most important, this is an elite study. And, because it examines the legislature from the perspective of its members, it might be taken as a recasting of consensus history. My purpose was to portray the lawmakers' world as they described it. Thus, the slave, servant, and vagrant remain shadowy figures who appeared only on those occasions when they violently intruded into that world or when the lawmakers paused to control and discipline that unruly population. Because I have chosen to treat with the lawmakers' world as they understood it, this elite appears to be the progenitor of Louis Hartz's liberal consensus.[9] Recent social history has demonstrated that this world view was not a consensus but a construction of social reality. It was a construction that was shared by this political elite and that gave it consciousness of itself.

It seems inevitable that those who write about colonial American politics feel obliged to establish origins, roots, or foundations of the American political system. In one sense, from the participants' perspective, these lawmakers were establishing the patterns of interest group politics or political pluralism which prevail today. But this explanation is incomplete. In the process of creating this world, they were also hiding an America which, except for an occasional glance from the window of a passing car, remains hidden from the consciousness and conscience of the American polity. The road to the present is not always direct. But research in the Garden State served as a daily reminder of the greenness and wholeness of eighteenth-century New Jersey to be discovered in the libraries and of the glaring contrast between the world those lawmakers enjoyed and that which their heirs had created.

In writing about the politics of eighteenth-century New Jersey, I have often relied upon the words of participants and observers. In quotation I have kept as closely to the original sources as possible. Abbreviations, however, have been spelled out. Spelling and punctuation has been changed only on those occasions when deemed necessary for the sake of the modern reader.

I cannot begin to make adequate acknowledgment of the many debts I have incurred during the process of research. Although separated by distance from the sources during the academic year, I was able to make considerable progress thanks to the librarians of Morris Library at Southern Illinois University, the genealogical division of the St. Louis Public Library, and the staff of the Newberry Library. When I recall the several trips to New Jersey and that region, the librarians and archivists who gave valuable assistance seem countless. I wish to thank the staffs of the state historical societies of New Jersey, New York, Pennsylvania, and Massachusetts, of the libraries at Princeton and Rutgers universities and Glassboro State College, of the New Jersey State Library, of the historical societies of Hunterdon, Gloucester, Burlington, and Cape May counties, of the New England Historical and Genealogical Society, and of the American Antiquarian Society. At this time I wish to make special note of Charles Holliday at Morris Library who gave unending, reliable, and cheerful assistance in the location and acquisition of materials. During my stays in Trenton I was regularly reminded how much William C. Wright has done to encourage research in New Jersey history. One of these research trips was supported by a grant from the New Jersey Historical Commission. Much of the research was computer assisted and could not have proceeded without the support and guidance of Southern Illinois University's academic computing staff.   The generosity and patience of people like Vincent A. Lacey rescued me from countless computer errors.   I came to recognize the significance of a new methodology during my long discussions with Howard W. Allen.   After convincing me, he patiently guided me through my education.   At one critical point in this research when I could not gain immediate access to the sources,   I recruited Virginia Batinski to do research and provide invaluable materials.

While writing, I was able to rely on James B. Murphy, David L. Wilson, John Y. Simon, and Howard Allen for criticism and advice.   I did not always agree, but their comments gave perspective.   Most of all I wish to thank them for their friendship and encouragement.   In the final stages of preparing this manuscript, Susan H. Wilson provided indispensable assistance that made it all less painful.

Throughout the many revisions and typings I was fortunate to depend on the skills of Vera Felts and Frances B. Poirier. And John Jackson, Dean of the College of Liberal Arts, scoured the university coffers and generously provided for the last preparation of this manuscript.

I also wish to thank Rutgers University Press for granting permission to use the map of New Jersey that first appeared in Peter O. Wacker's, Land and People: A Cultural Geography of Preindustrial New Jersey (1975).

The convention of acknowledgment seems an inadequate means to express gratitude for the many acts of generosity, patience, and friendship.   Virginia Hoffman provided all that and more.   Her counsels, although not always heard or heeded, lent perspective.   What I gained is not reflected in the content of the book.   Without her daily gift of friendship, this undertaking would have meant much less.

NOTES

1.   Jack P. Greene, The Quest for Power: The Lower Houses of Assembly in the Southern Royal Colonies, 1689-1776 (Chapel Hill, NC, 1963), 3-47; idem, "Changing Interpretations of Early American Politics," in Ray Allen Billington, ed., The Reinterpretation of Early American History: Essays in Honor of John Edwin Pomfret (San Marino, CA, 1966), 171-72.

2. Greene, Quest for Power, x. Idem, "Changing Interpretations of Early American Politics," 172-75.

3. Kenneth A. Lockridge, "Social Change and the Meaning of the American Revolution," Journal of Social History, VI (Summer, 1973), 403-39; Alfred F. Young, ed., The American Revolution: Explorations in the History of American Radicalism (De Kalb, IL, 1976); Rowland Berthoff and John M. Murrin, "Feudalism, Communalism, and the Yeoman Farmer: The American Revolution Considered as a Social Accident," in Stephen G. Kurtz and James H. Hutson, eds., Essays on the American Revolution (Chapel Hill, NC, 1973), 256-88; the relevant essays in Jack P. Greene and J. R. Pole, eds., Colonial British America: Essays in the New History of the Early Modern Period (Baltimore, 1984); Edward M. Cook, Jr., The Fathers of the Towns: Leadership and Community Structure in Eighteenth-Century New England (Baltimore, 1976); Robert Zemsky, Merchants, Farmers, and River Gods: An Essay on Eighteenth-Century American Politics (Boston, 1971); Michael Zuckerman, Peaceable Kingdoms: New England Towns in the Eighteenth Century (New York, 1970); idem, ed.,Friends and Neighbors: Group Life in America's First Plural Society (Philadelphia, 1982); John B. Kirby, "Early American Politics-- The Search for Ideology: An Historiographical Analysis and Critique of the Concept of 'Deference'," Journal of Politics, XXXII (Nov., 1970), 808-38.

4. Bernard Bailyn, Ideological Origins of the American Revolution (Cambridge, MA, 1967); idem, The Origins of American Politics (New York, 1968); J. G. A. Pocock, Politics, Language and Time: Essays on Political Thought and History (New York, 1971), 80-103; Jack P. Greene, "Political Mimesis: A Consideration of the Historical and Cultural Roots of Legislative Behavior in the British Colonies in the Eighteenth Century," The American Historical Review, LXXV (Dec., 1969), 337-60; J. E. Crowley, This Sheba, Self: The Conceptualization of Economic Life in Eighteenth-Century America (Baltimore, 1974); Richard L. Bushman, From Puritan to Yankee: Character and Social Order in Connecticut, 1690-1765 (Cambridge, MA, 1967); Joyce Appleby, "The Social Origins of American Revolutionary Ideology," The Journal of American History, LXIV (Mar., 1978), 935-58; Joseph Ernst, "Ideology and the Political Economy of Revolution," The Canadian Review of American Studies, IV (Fall, 1973), 137-48.

5. "An Interview with Eric Hobsbawm," Radical History Review, no. 19 (Winter, 1978-79), 127; Linda Gordon, "What Should Women's Historians Do: Politics, Social Theory, and Women's History," Marxist Perspectives, I (Fall, 1978), 128-36;

Elizabeth Fox-Genovese and Eugene D. Genovese, "The Political Crisis of Social History: A Marxian Perspective," Journal of Social History, X (Winter, 1976), 205-20.

    6.   J. G. A. Pocock, "Virtue and Commerce in the Eighteenth Century,"   The Journal of Interdisciplinary History, III (Summer, 1972), 122; Gordon S. Wood, "Rhetoric and Reality in the American Revolution," The William and Mary Quarterly, 3rd Ser., XXIII (Jan., 1966), 3-32.

    7.   Allan G. Bogue, Clio & the Bitch Goddess: Quantification in American Political History (Beverly Hills, CA, 1983), 51-135.

    8. Robert Zemsky, Merchants, Farmers, and River Gods.

    9.   Louis Hartz, The Liberal Tradition in America: An Interpretation of American Political Thought Since the Revolution (New York, 1955).

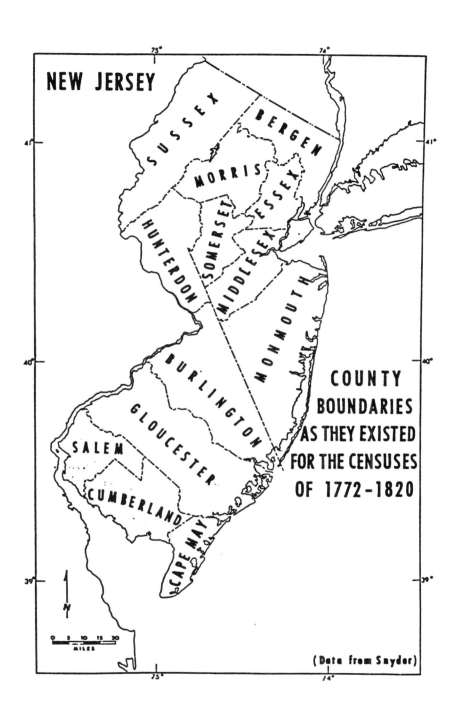

NEW JERSEY

SUSSEX

BERGEN

MORRIS

ESSEX

HUNTERDON

SOMERSET

MIDDLESEX

MONMOUTH

BURLINGTON

GLOUCESTER

SALEM

CUMBERLAND

CAPE MAY

COUNTY
BOUNDARIES
AS THEY EXISTED
FOR THE CENSUSES
OF 1772–1820

(Data from Snyder)

N

0 5 10 15 20
MILES

CHAPTER ONE

THE LEGISLATIVE COMMUNITY, I:
THE VISION OF COMMERCIAL ARCADIA

As Aaron Leaming, Jr., and Jacob Spicer readied their compilation of The Grants, Concessions, and Original Constitutions of the Province of New-Jersey for the press, they paused to reflect on the province's history and to wonder at the "great Rapidity" with which a "savage Wilderness" had been transformed into a "Christian civilized Country." The two assemblymen briefly sketched the outline of that story in their introduction. New Jersey's founding was an event in European expansion, part of that "truly glorious Ambition" that had first inspired Spain's and later England's designs to extend their "Dominions, Commerce, Wealth, and Power beyond the Limits of Europe." Spain's success "could not fail of pointing out a Seat of future Wealth and Grandeur to such an enterprizing aspiring People as the Britons." In contrast to the authority of the Spanish crown, England embarked with a "limitted Government" and needed, instead, to quicken the hearts of Englishmen and stir them from the comforts of home to "dare an untrod Ocean." The Stuart kings thus wisely "hit upon that System which of all others is the most worthy pursuit of a rational Being, namely, the Security of the Religion, Liberties, and Properties of the Adventurers and their latest Posterity."[1]

The lawmakers addressed the reader with the intent not to explicate or elaborate but to evoke a shared historical consciousness. The past recalled--the swarming out of England and the heroic struggle with the wilderness--provided a common identity by which this public understood itself. The eighteenth-century provincial fashioned that story within the context of empire building and portrayed his progenitors as enterprising, self-improving adventurers who, guaranteed of their liberties and properties, embarked on the venture of taming the land. It was a telling that glossed over the founders' religious intents. And by making the dynamic of colonization self-interest, it cast the first generation into the eighteenth century's own entrepreneurial ideal. The province's historian Samuel Smith gave fleeting notice to the founders' religious motivations and told instead a story of land acquisition and settlement. New Ark's convenanter and West Jersey's Quaker utopian became improvers of the land. "Whatever were their motives, they successively encountered the hazards and hardships to which the enterprise was exposed; and, at their own expense, by the blessing of divine providence on their labour, frugality and industry, laid the foundation for the present improvement of

1

territory to the mother country." In the same vein, the legislature recalled the story of hardy self-sufficient, self-improving venturers who transformed the "inhospitable and unknown Wilderness" into a garden. It was a moral world but one worked by Poor Richard.[2]

Jerseymen like Leaming and Spicer absorbed this world view at the hearth, for their own forebears had participated in that history. The first Leaming and Spicer had joined the adventurers who had reshaped the wilderness and turned the land to profit. Both Quakers, they arrived at Cape May at the turn of the century, perhaps drawn as much by the meetinghouse as by the economic opportunities. They prospered, raised themselves to leadership in their newly adopted community, and finally entered the Assembly. Leaming recalled that his father died one of the county's wealthiest. And the son spent his days building upon that inheritance, buying lands, improving them, attending to his crops and herds, cutting timber, and shipping his surplus for export. When he made out his will, he surveyed an estate worth nearly ₤200,000, including properties of several thousand acres, sawmills, and over thirty slaves.[3] The land had yielded its bounty to the Spicers. Jacob was the third in a line of farmer-land speculators. With an acquisitive eye for land, his grandfather had moved from Long Island to Gloucester County and held titles in Monmouth County; his father then removed to Cape May, prospered, and entered the legislature. Jacob extended his holdings to include properties in New York and North Carolina, ventured into fisheries and lumbering, and established himself as a local merchant.[4] For over two decades, he and Leaming represented Cape May County in the legislature.

Jerseymen and visitors wondered at the richness of the landscape, its impressive development, and its promise for growth. The land abounded with farms rich with orchards, fields of grain, and herds of livestock. The ever-industrious farmer improved and prospered: along the Delaware River farmers rapidly erected works to hold back the tide and to drain the fields for cultivation; and, along the streams and rivers that laced the countryside, they constructed mills to process grain and lumber. Thus, one traveler readily affirmed that the province justly deserved its reputation as "the Garden of America."[5] The farmer reaped such bounty that he regularly shipped his surplus, especially grain and meat, along the roads and waterways for sale to foreign markets. Opportunity beckoned everywhere. The forests abounded with timber ready for cutting and export. Deposits of iron and copper promised profit for the venturous Jerseyman.[6]

Impressive as the province was for its progress, it

remained at a primitive state of development. Distinctions between rich and poor found in more advanced societies, even in neighboring colonies, had yet to appear. The young Philip Fithian observed that his native New Jersey lacked the social landmarks of rank and distinction which he discovered in Virginia. In New Jersey, there was a "near approach to an equality of Wealth amongst the Inhabitants," and an easy conversation was maintained between the "high-born, long recorded Families" and "Farmers & Mechanicks." It was a "Spartan Common-Wealth" composed of industrious yeomen, uncorrupted by the luxury that came with the development of trade and commerce.[7] Although farmers engaged in export and some had become merchants, the commercial community remained by comparison with Philadelphia and New York a small part of Jersey society. Thus, the province was "the best poor Man's Country," where, recalled William Moraley, "Almost every Inhabitant, in the Country, have a Plantation."[8]

The picture of an American arcadia worked by independent yeomen was incomplete. In the same breath that Moraley described the yeomen farmers, he observed that they "improve their Lands themselves, with the Assistance both of bought Servants and Negroes." Like Fithian, he glossed over fundamental social divisions and discounted the growing propertyless, bonded, and dependent population. Evidence suggesting social disparity can be found in observations made by contemporaries. While visitors to the Schuyler estate in northern New Jersey focused on the family's social achievement, their descriptions revealed a style of gentility that was achieved and maintained by a laboring class. Benjamin Franklin reported finding "a Deer Park 5 Miles round, fenc'd with Cedar Logs, 5 Logs high." The owners of the Ringwood ironworks had built a furnace, several forges, "a large dwelling-house for the Manager. . ., a new brick house for a store. . ., a large stone house. . .; besides sixteen other log-houses in the woods, for wood cutters and colliers." Leaming's inventory of slaves and servants was, no doubt, large, but the bonded laborer had become commonplace in the homes of the successful farmers.[9]

In fact, the number of Jerseymen who did not fit Fithian's description was growing steadily. The province was experiencing the social transformations common to British North America. Land was becoming scarce: disparities within the propertied class became increasingly apparent, and the landless grew more numerous. One in three males lived without land; and, in Burlington County, this group included half the population. In turn, New Jersey's wealthiest tenth held title to one-third of the land. And the more successful developed their holdings with hired and bonded labor. Slaves constituted 5 percent of the population in the western counties, 12 percent in the eastern counties, and as much as 20 percent in Bergen County.[10]

Recent studies of provincial society have suggested that the world according to Fithian and Spicer was a construction and, equally important, that it was one constructed by the propertied and articulate. That perception held by New Jersey's possessors of the earth, indeed one shared by their counterparts throughout Anglo-America, defined a legislative community. Those who in speaking of their society fixed on the propertied and independent to the exclusion of the lower orders were the same who participated in Assembly politics. Thus, their view became the legislature's definition of the public. It was a political world that by its institutions muted the outsider's voice and barred him from intrusion. The franchise requirement of 100 acres allowed only the propertied to elect representatives and, in fact, excluded between one-fourth and one-half of the adult males. In turn, only the most successful were admitted to the legislature. The qualification stood at Ŀ500 in lands and personal property or 1,000 acres. But only one in ten Jerseymen held over 500 acres. Thus, Governor William Franklin found that the members of the Assembly were "chiefly. . .of independent Fortunes."[11]

Those who possessed the land governed it, and how they governed was determined in part by their attitudes toward the land. They looked upon an arcadic New Jersey and forecast its improvement. Nature's bounty was a commodity to be turned for profit; lands and resources became items for speculation. The legislature was an assemblage of enterprisers, men who lived in the marketplace, speculators in lands, adventurers in ironworks and mills, proprietors of country stores, managers of stage lines and ferries. Commonly they resided in towns and hamlets which served as market centers such as New Brunswick, Raritan Landing, Trenton, Burlington, and Salem. They held land without sentiment: frequently in their wills they instructed their heirs to sell the estate and divide the proceeds among themselves. New Jersey was a stopping place for the venturer to make his fortune. John Low moved from New York to Newark, established himself as a land speculator and merchant, was elected to the Assembly, and then retired to Albany. Charles Read moved from Philadelphia to Burlington, invested in lands and iron furnaces, and ventured into politics. He became a fixture in New Jersey's elite and planned to settle on his country estate and assume the role of gentleman-farmer. But after serving in the Assembly, the Council, and the Supreme Court, he suddenly removed to South Carolina.[12]

It was a world not unlike that discovered by James Lemon in the Pennsylvania counties across the Delaware River, a world

4

peopled by entrepreneurs possessed of a middle-class liberalism. Perhaps, as James Henretta's work has suggested, Lemon has exaggerated the pervasiveness of that eighteenth-century liberalism. The marketplace had not supplanted the traditional, communal, and anticommercial mentality. Rather, the two coexisted, often in tension, with one more pronounced than the other, depending on the sector of society which the historian chooses to examine.[13] Bergen's farmers who were found to live in "natural honesty and artlessness" and in innocence of "documents, seals, signatures, bonds, and other such contracts" may have represented Henretta's traditionalist. But their neighbors, the Dey family, speculated in land and operated stores in the county and New York. Derrick Dey and his son Theunis represented the county. It was the voice of the entrepreneur and not the humble farmer which was heard in the legislature.[14]

This legislative community abounded with visions of the province's future development and expectations "to see Trade and Commerce fflourish." What with its "fine ports" and "fertile lands" that produced an abundance of grain, livestock, timber, and other "Necessaries for Exportation," New Jersey compared favorably to other colonies. And as the author of The Interest of New-Jersey reminded his reader, the economy was "Capable of vast Improvements," especially in trade.[15] The vision was pervasive. In a speculative mood, Jacob Spicer took stock of his linens and calculated the market's potential: "my family consists of 12 in number, including myself" which meant "to an individual £7:3:001/4 annual consumption of foreign produce and manufacture. But perhaps the population in General [may] not live at a proportionate expense with my family. I would suppose their foreign Consumption may stand at £4 to an individual. As the County Consisted of 1100 souls in the year 1746 Since which it has Encreased, then the Consumption of this County of Foreign produce & Manufacture upon that estimate & Supposition will stand at £4400 annually near one half of which will be linens. & it may be observed that I have not included any Salt Articles in the above estimate." Then he proceeded to calculate the annual production of oysters and lumber.[16]

The vision was at once commercial and arcadic. While recognizing self-interest and trade as the twin engines of social improvement, the provincial remained haunted by traditional fears that the two undermined a communal social ethic and replaced a bucolic and morally simple life with the urbane and its accompanying luxuries, vices, and oppressions. While he embraced the modern, he justified his act by adhering to the traditional. To do both required a public policy that governed economic relations among Jerseymen to prevent one from preying on the other and simultaneously channeled the energies

5

of the marketplace outwardly to improve the province's trade relations with its neighbors. What emerged was a brand of "provincial mercantilism" which encouraged development and commerce without sacrificing the collective good. Thus, Samuel Atkinson described the beneficence of trade: "As Providence has order'd it, that not only different Countries but even different Parts of the same Country have their peculiar and most suitable Productions; and that different Men, have Genius's to variety of different Arts and Manufactures: Therefore Commerce or the Exchange of one Commodity or Manufacture for another, is highly convenient and benifical for Mankind."[17]

The Assembly was expected to establish guidelines for daily economic life and for the improvement of this commercial arcadia. It devoted much of its time to the mundane affairs of farming communities, decided disputes between neighbors, and established rules and constructed administrative mechanisms for governing their social relations. How to define a lawful fence, prevent swine from trespassing, recover stray livestock, identify the owner of a cow, prevent stray dogs from destroying cattle and establish a system for compensation, or eradicate pests--these were typical items on the legislative agenda which occupied so much of the assemblyman's time. In addition, the legislature received petitions either requesting permission to erect a bridge over a waterway or to lay out a road or urging grander schemes to establish an adequate medium of exchange to promote the province's trade.[18] Two-thirds of the petitions listed in Table 1.1 focused on economic matters. And the volume increased with each decade. In the first two years of Governor Lewis Morris's administration, the legislature entertained 10 petitions relating to economic matters; fifteen years later, in 1753 and 1754, the number increased to 34; and, in 1768 and 1769, it grew to 147.

Local improvements were a regular subject of deliberation. Jerseymen discovered that by erecting dams and drainage systems they could convert useless marshes into arable and profitable acreage. The owners at Greenwich on Raccoon Creek explained "the great Advantage" they "would reap by stoping the said Creek, in order to make the Marsh useful." Similar projects along such waterways as Ancocas, Newton, Salem, and Woodbury creeks increased rapidly. In turn, they aroused disagreements among neighbors. Drainage systems required a collective effort and could be easily frustrated by one neighbor's negligence. In order to prevent such noncooperation, owners petitioned for recognition as a corporate body empowered to appoint managers, assess its members, and bring delinquents to court. Such undertakings also proved destructive to others: petitions were sent protesting the obstruction of the waterway's navigation. Thus, when the

6

TABLE 1.1
SUBJECTS OF PETITIONS TO THE ASSEMBLY

Biennia (5-year intervals)	Local Improvements (Dams & Mills)	Transportation (Roads & Rivers)	Resources (Game, Fish & Timber)	Court-houses & Barracks	Property (Bounds & Titles)	Debt	Poor Servants Slaves	Economic Development (Trade & Production)	Paper Money	Other	Total	Percentage of All Petitions Sampled
1738-39	4ᵃ (22%)ᵇ	3 (17%)	NP	1 (6%)	NP	NP	NP	NP	1 (6%)	8 (44%)	18	3%
1743-44	1 (3%)	12 (41%)	2 (7%)	NP	1 (3%)	3 (10%)	1 (3%)	1 (3%)	NP	8 (28%)	29	5%
1748-49	NP	9 (24%)	2 (5%)	2 (5%)	6 (16%)	1 (3%)	2 (5%)	NP	NP	16 (42%)	38	6%
1753-54	7 (14%)	6 (12%)	2 (4%)	1 (2%)	1 (2%)	11 (22%)	2 (4%)	NP	4 (8%)	17 (33%)	51	8%
1758-59	3 (4%)	10 (15%)	NP	4 (6%)	3 (4%)	4 (6%)	1 (1%)	NP	NP	43 (63%)	68	11%
1763-64	3 (4%)	13 (17%)	1 (1%)	7 (9%)	8 (11%)	9 (12%)	1 (1%)	2 (3%)	NP	32 (42%)	76	12%
1768-69	6 (3%)	33 (18%)	8 (4%)	2 (1%)	15 (8%)	51 (27%)	NP	22 (12%)	10 (5%)	40 (21%)	187	29%
1773-74	12 (7%)	52 (30%)	2 (1%)	1 (1%)	8 (5%)	19 (11%)	24 (14%)	9 (5%)	6 (3%)	39 (23%)	172	27%
TOTAL	36	138	17	18	42	98	31	35	21	203	639	
Percentage of all petitions sampled	6%	22%	3%	3%	7%	15%	5%	5%	3%	32%		

Note:
a = Number of Petitions during biennium.
b = Percent of Petitions during biennium.
NP = No Petitions.

Assembly recognized such a corporation, it also provided for protection against the destruction of its works.[19]

Regularly the legislature was reminded of colliding interests. The erection of a gristmill that proved beneficial to local farmers in turn intruded upon the livelihoods of their neighbors. Mills owned by Abraham Broca, Samuel Wykoff, and Daniel Hendrickson provided essential services for local farmers, but their construction proved detrimental to navigation and fishing. In response to the "threatenings of some Persons," owners and neighbors appealed to the legislature, explaining the necessity of a bill to protect the mills.[20] According to practice, the Assembly ordered that public notice first be given and then received remonstrances that the mills blocked the waterway and threatened fishing. So, too, a proposal to build a mill at Raritan Landing divided the community between those who relied on the milling services and those who depended on unobstructed navigation rights. In response to these appeals, the legislature established rules regulating the development of such waterworks and requiring the maintenance of clear waterways.[21]

As private venturers improved the province's transportation system, they appealed for special privileges. Matthew Watson had undertaken to establish a ferry at Crosswick's Creek at "extraordinary Expence" and petitioned for the exclusive right to provide that service. In 1769, James Haight explained that he could ferry passengers, livestock, and goods at half the rate charged by his competitors but only if he were granted monopoly rights. Such requests sparked rivalries among venturers, which also embroiled the affected communities. The Assembly noted that Joseph Borden and William Hancock had established a stage line connecting New York and Philadelphia at "a great Expense," but that they were "much annoyed by other Boatmen and Waggoners interferring in the said Business." Two days later, a bill was introduced granting them "an exclusive Right to the said Stage." But, within a week, the Assembly received a rival's plea with supporting petitions from the inhabitants of Burlington that he not be deprived of his livelihood.[22]

These petitions were daily reminders that the enterprising Jerseymen improved but also undermined this mercantile arcadia. The legislature routinely postponed deliberation until the petitioner had given public notice of his intent in order that those affected might respond. The legislature also worked to establish policy for economic development which would encourage improvements without simultaneously intruding on the welfare of others. In response to the growing complaints about obstructed rivers, it enacted that local authorities maintain open navigation of the waterways and ordered that future projects be reviewed by the legislature before their undertaking. So, too, when it established ferries or bridges, it also specified a table of rates to protect the users from exploitation.[23]

Jerseymen were reminded that the wanton use of the province's resources could deplete the province's bounty. The lawmakers heard complaints against unrestrained deer hunting, the use of traps, and the killing of deer out of season and regularly enacted game laws.[24] Also, the legislature considered the deleterious effect of unrestrained lumbering and responded by placing a duty on its export.[25] Along the Raritan and Delaware rivers, fishers realized profits by shipping their catch to the neighboring ports of New York and Philadelphia. The more enterprising constructed networks of traps and nets which threatened to deplete the province's stock. In response to these warnings, the government established prohibitions on the use of traps and regulations on the size of nets.[26]

Enterprising Jerseymen established themselves along trade routes and entertained schemes to encourage commerce and promote their communities as trading centers. The laying out of a road, the establishment of a ferry, the location of a county seat, or the building of a barracks promised profit for these community boosters. Although the selection of a site for the county courthouse was normally a decision that the legislature delegated to the county's freeholders, local rivalries often erupted and prevented agreement. In 1739, the inhabitants of Elizabethtown petitioned that the courthouse and jail be removed from Newark. After fire had consumed the Middlesex courthouse, Perth Amboy contested with the freeholders from the county's outlying communities for the location of the new building. In Cape May, Jacob Spicer determined to remove the courthouse from the neighborhood of Aaron Leaming and successfully organized a petition drive to outflank his colleague. During the last war against the French, the province decided to construct barracks for the quartering of troops. Recognizing the potential of such a project, Princeton petitioned to become a site for one of the barracks.[27]

The improvers of the land agreed that they acted from self-interest and that they did so because they were guaranteed the fruits of their labors. And, since the government functioned primarily for the "Preservation and Protection of their Properties," they expected the legislature to resolve the disputes over title. The task at times required better administration for the recording of deeds and mortgages. On occasion, it meant recognizing a creek as a legal fence or rerouting a road that impinged upon a farmer's property. Some

9

problems seemed to defy solution. When Bergen Town appealed for the right to divide its commons, the legislature entertained petitions and then counter-petitions from rival claimants for nearly a decade. Most troublesome was the long-standing dispute between the East Jersey proprietors and rival land claimants which erupted into violence during the 1740s.[28]

At times, this commercial arcadia seemed overwhelmed by the problem of debtor-creditor relations. The legislator understood the problem intimately. Jacob Spicer recounted in his will how he had "attempted a Trade at Cape May upon publick Spirited Views, and by means thereof. . .sustained Considerable loss, and having otherwise Indulged my Customers with greatest Leneity, so in consequence thereof I remain in Debt to sundry persons."[29] His colleagues' wills also document similar entanglements in debts and credits. Indeed, Assemblyman John Ogden became so enmeshed in a web of debts that he was forced to resign his seat. The number of petitions increased at the end of the provincial period. Debtors prayed for relief: one Abraham Sayre had lingered in prison for nine years for his inability to satisfy his creditors' demands. Creditors, in turn, pressed for reforms to expedite the recovery of what was their due. In response, the legislature regularly reviewed the legal mechanisms: small courts were created for petty cases, procedures were established for the expeditious sale of the debtor's property, and methods for collecting from the absentee debtor were enacted.[30]

While the legislator worked toward realizing his commercial arcadia, the "idle and disorderly persons" intruded upon his world. "Lazy" and "viscious" squatters who lived off the land by hunting and who haunted the taverns did not fit the legislative community's ideal of the industrious "ploughman." Because they "range[d] about the Woods with loose idle Persons" hunting game and sometimes livestock, wasted "Time and Substance in Gaming, Tipling and often Drinking to Excess, to the great Damage, Affliction and Distress of their poor families, and Destruction of themselves," they were a blight upon the New Jersey landscape. Not only did they not fit the model of the virtuous farmer but "the Publick is prejudiced by the Loss of their Labour." The Assembly reacted first by seeking to deprive them of their frolics. No doubt taverns and inns served the public purpose "for the accomodating Strangers, Travellers and other Persons. . .for the dispatch of Business," but the lawmakers lamented that they also fostered "Gaming, Tipling, Drunkeness and other Vices. . .to the Great Scandal of Religion, the Dishonour of God and Impovrishing the Commonwealth." Thus, the legislature established rules for licensing public houses and for prohibiting the sale of liquor in quantities less than one quart. In 1771, it also sought to remove these wastrels from the woods by prohibiting all those who could not meet the franchise requirement from hunting "on the waste and unimproved Lands in this Colony."[31]

No doubt, the lawmakers conceded, there were distinctions to be made among the poor, and there were those who were deserving of compassionate consideration. In fact, they disposed of both--the hapless and deserving as well as the "viscious" and undeserving--in similar fashion. By mid-century, the system of relief administered by the overseers of the poor seemed inadequate to meet the growing number of the poor. "The Inhabitants of this Colony [were] oppressed with great Charges" for undertaking these responsibilities and were convinced that the province was overrun with "disorderly Persons coming from the neighboring Provinces. . .and concealing themselves" until they could establish the residency qualifications for relief. In a series of enactments, the Assembly worked out a system to distinguish the merits of the applicants and verify the worthiness of their claims. Also, the province began the establishment of workhouses. First, the legislature enabled Middlesex County to create such an institution, and later it provided for each community to erect its own. Its purpose was clearly stated--to discipline the idle and to make them productive according to the community's ideal.[32]

The legislator was haunted by the presence of the unruly slave and servant lurking in his home. Servants ran away, and in time of war they sought escape by enlisting in the provincial regiments. On occasion, they rebelled: in Salem County, the Philadelphia newspapers reported, fifteen Irish servants were discovered conspiring "to make an Insurrection in order to seize that County, with an Irish Trooper at their Head." Reports of the rebellious slave roused fears, especially in the northern counties. In Bergen County, the whites rose to arms when slaves burned seven barns in a day. Jerseymen shuddered when they read that Jacob Van Nest of Somerset County was axed to death by his slave but were assured the next week that the murderer had been summarily burned at the stake. The masters attended to the problem with concern and steadily added refinements to the slave codes. During the half century before independence, the legislature prohibited slaves from frequenting taverns, forbade them from meeting in groups larger than five, and created special courts for handling the wrongdoer.[33]

At the end of the provincial period, the legislative community was asked whether slavery was compatible with the society it sought to promote. The criticism came, in part, from a revived Quaker conscience and a heightened prerevolutionary

11

ideology. But the most compelling argument was that dependence on slave labor fostered sloth and, thereby, undermined that public morality and industriousness which was essential for achieving the arcadian dream. One solution was to curb that population's growth by imposing a duty on slave imports. First considered in 1762 and enacted five years later, the measure was justified as a means to encourage industry. Not only would it promote "a Spirit of Industry among the Inhabitants in general" but it would attract "sober, industrious Foreigners." Proposals for manumission, however, met stiff opposition. In response to numerous petitions, chiefly from the Quaker community, the legislature began consideration of a manumission bill. Fears of the rebellious black rose, and those in opposition reminded the lawmakers that freedom was tantamount to license and anarchy. The final bill allowing for the manumission of slaves denied freedmen the right to vote or to testify in court and provided that if found troublesome they would be sold into indentured servitude. The legislature could go no further.[34]

The legislature was expected not only to regulate social relations within its arcadia but also to undertake projects for the fulfillment of its commercial potential. A major impediment was the domination by New York and Philadelphia of the provincial economy. The neighboring merchants exploited Jerseymen by dictating prices and keeping them in debt. Profit accumulated in the pockets of New York's and Philadelphia's merchants, not in New Jersey's own; consequently, currency was rapidly drained from the provincial economy. "New York and Philadelphia. . .run away with their Markets, and maintain always a large ballance against them, which must of necessity keep them low and indigent." This "mean and slavish Trade" must end before New Jersey could realize its potential. Direct trade--both export and import--must be nurtured by the legislature. Such advocates forecast a bright future: lands would increase in value; domestic improvements would flourish; manufactures, mills, and shipyards would spring up across the landscape; and merchants would choose to move to New Jersey. Another exponent of commerce called upon his reader to imagine the prospects: "Would it not truly rejoyce the Hearts of every true Lover and Well wisher of New-Jersey, to see the Tables once fairly turn'd upon [our neighbors], in so much, that Numbers of them would be glad to abandon their Cities and Provinces, and he would think himself happy, that could get a good footing here first."[35]

Lewis Morris commented that Jerseymen would "prohibit the exportation of every one thing they raise to New York; and are so sanguine on this head that they would (if they could) willingly hinder even the carrying of firewood and hay to New

12

York." The author of The Interest of New-Jersey estimated that 100,000 bushels of wheat and considerable quantities of timber were exported along the Raritan annually. Yet Jerseymen did not see the profits justly due them. By placing a duty on these commodities, the legislature could "give the finishing Stroke to that pernicious Trade with our Neighbours." To encourage this project, the legislature prohibited the export of unmilled wheat, timber, and pipestaves. In response to a petition from Middlesex County setting forth "the Hardships this Province at present labours under, for the Want of the Encouragement of Trade," the Assembly found that "the direct Importation of Rum from the. . .West Indies, and such Wines as may be lawfully imported. . .would not only very much contribute toward the Increase of the Trade of this Colony, but would also be a Means of Supporting the Credit of the Currency thereof."[36]

The lawmakers considered proposals for establishing trading companies to advance the mercantile dream. In 1740, they deliberated on a bill to create two companies, one at Perth Amboy and the other at Burlington. To provide the capital, paper money in the amount of ₤40,000 would be issued on loan which would be repaid from the project's profits. In 1770, "Neo Caesariensis" revived the idea and recommended that the legislature establish a company modeled on the East India Company. His proposal was informed by mercantilist thought: "the united company would encourage merchants from different places to settle at Amboy; for in a few years, it may well be supposed, the demand for goods would so far exceed what it does at present, that it would be impossible to supply it out of one store, however large or well filled; which will undoubtedly draw others to open stores there--and give the united company occasion to enlarge their trade still more. Would to heaven these few hints may excite some public spirited persons to push forward a scheme so profitable and patriotic."[37]

Both proposals failed. Although they sparked the mercantilist imagination, they simultaneously awakened the legislative community's ambivalence toward the selfish impulse and its affect upon the communitarian ideal. Government-sponsored trading companies smacked of special privilege, and proposals to regulate the province's export promoted one interest while threatening another. When the advocate of a vigorous mercantile policy reviewed the legislature's record, he despaired, concluding that the law makers' inaction reflected irresponsibility and indifference to the collective good. The criticism seems, in fact, unfounded. If the legislature disappointed the activist, it did so not because it dissented from the mercantilist world view but because it could not reconcile special interests. The task was a delicate one: that is, to construct a coherent economic policy while responding to several and often conflicting interests. Regulation, when passed, for the control of lumbering or for the improvement of the province's flour export roused protests. And, in response, the measure was suspended. But, in review, it is significant not only that there was no sustained argument for an alternative policy but also that the legislature accomplished its task as well as it did.[38]

The legislative community found that through the emission of paper money it could promote the public good and achieve the fulfillment of this commercial arcadia without impinging on special interests. If the Assembly rejected a currency issue designed to benefit a special group of merchants, it readily agreed to an issue that would be distributed by county officials at public loan to the general populace. Such a scheme would promote the commercial dream. Samuel Atkinson unfolded to his fellow Jerseymen an ever-expanding and prosperous New Jersey composed of virtuous and industrious ploughmen. The single impediment lay in the shortage of currency. Without it, interest rates would remain high, and those with capital would prefer to lend rather than purchase land or risk the hazards of trade. Agricultural prices would remain depressed, and laborers and craftsmen would continue to shun the province. This dormancy would become transformed into activity and stagnation into unbounded prosperity, if only the government issued an adequate supply of paper money. Atkinson's case was remarkable for its elaborate and closely reasoned argument, but the sentiment was shared through the legislative community. In response to the prayers of the people in favor of an adequate "Medium of Trade," the legislature made it a cornerstone of policy that the province be supplied with quantities of paper money sufficient to maintain and stimulate the province's commercial life. In 1774, it explained that without a £100,000 emission Jerseymen would be prevented from "extending their Settlements, [and] improving and cultivating their Lands."[39]

In the wake of the last war with France, the legislative community awakened to the vision of commercial arcadia.[40] Governor Franklin found a ready audience when he recommended to the lawmakers that since "Peace is so happily Established," they should turn their minds to the improvement of transportation and the encouragement of manufactures. Schemes abounded. Over half the petitions submitted since 1738 for the improvement of transportation and two-thirds of those regarding the draining of fields and the erection of dams arrived after 1763 (Table 1.1). Among the governor's recommendations that "might prove beneficial to the Colony," the legislature was especially intrigued with and established a system of bounties to be paid on the production of flax, hemp, and silk. In

14

addition, the legislative community attended to proposals for encouraging the production of potash, iron, and wine and others for the improvement of the province's trade by setting controls on the quality of beef, flour, and lumber exports. Of all the proposals for encouraging trade and production since 1738, almost 90 percent arrived during this period. Simultaneously, the legislative community undertook to reform the moral core of this commercial arcadia. In order to encourage industriousness, it sought to discourage slavery and campaigned to control gambling, horseracing, foxhunting, taverns, and the dispensing of liquor.

In review, a world view emerges from the public prints and petitions that record what was expected of government and from the laws enacted in response. It was a way of looking at society which prevailed among the province's propertied and thereby formed the basis of a legislative community. That understanding assumed both spatial and temporal dimensions. When the possessors of the earth spoke of society, the public, or "the People," they meant themselves. When they looked at themselves, they found the self-improving entrepreneur. Temporally, they set their society within a story of unfolding prosperity which began with the first settlers who conquered, took possession, and shaped the land into a garden and which would continue as long as they and their descendants lived secure in those liberties and properties guaranteed to them by the crown and defined in the <u>Grants, Concessions, and Original Constitutions</u>. When they envisioned the province's development, they expected the "ploughman" to enter the marketplace. Yet they did not expect him to discard the traditional or communal virtues. To achieve that balance, or to realize commercial arcadia, required a public policy designed to control and encourage, in sum, to channel the energies of the marketplace. What emerged was a policy of "provincial mercantilism," which the legislature documented in its enactments.

This reconstruction of New Jersey's politics was achieved from a distant vantage point. While the perspective enables a rendering of the whole--the cultural foundations of a legislative community--it does not attend to the specific individual. As a consequence, important dimensions of the picture remained incomplete. First, the world view remains an abstraction, an ideal unconnected to specific personalities. Second, while the world view prevailed, disagreements erupted and sometimes prevented the lawmakers from acting in concert. Indeed, the participants seemed unaware that they acted in a community. What the sources of disagreement were and how deeply they cut into this legislative community requires a second and complementary picture that focuses on the lawmakers' social origins and their responses to public policy.

NOTES

1. Aaron Leaming, [Jr.], and Jacob Spicer, The Grants, Concessions, and Original Constitutions of the Province of New-Jersey (Philadelphia, [1758]), preface.

2. Samuel Smith, The History of the Colony of Nova-Caesaria, or New-Jersey. . .(Burlington, NJ, 1765), xii; Petition of the New Jersey Assembly to George III, May 6, 1768, Larry R. Gerlach, ed., New Jersey in the American Revolution,1763-1783: A Documentary History (Trenton, NJ, 1975), 43. The Testimony of the People Called Quakers, The Pennsylvania Gazette, Feb. 22, 1775, in ibid., 112; Jonathan Elmer, Address to the Inhabitants of Cumberland County, [May, 1775], ibid., 136-38.

3. John E. Stillwell, Historical and Genealogical Miscellany. Data Relating to the Settlement and Settlers of New York and New Jersey, 5 vols. (New York, 1903-32), III, 430-38; "An Appraisal of the Personal Estate of Aaron Leaming, [Sr.]," Apr. 16, 1747, Spicer-Leaming Papers, The Historical Society of Pennsylvania. Also see sketch in Appendix.

4. Manuscript Wills, 253 E, New Jersey State Library.

5. Adam Gordon, "Journal of an Officer Who Traveled in America and the West Indies in 1764 and 1765," in Newton D. Mereness, ed., Travels in the American Colonies (New York, 1916), 413.

6. Thomas Thompson, "A Letter from New Jersey: Monmouth County in the Mid-Eighteenth Century," ed. Fred Shelley, Proceedings of the New Jersey Historical Society, LXXIV (Oct., 1956), 293-303; Patrick M'Robert, A Tour through Part of the North Provinces of North America (Edinburgh, 1776 [1968]), 33-34; Robert Rogers, A Concise Account of North America. . .(London, 1765), 76-78; "Journal of a French Traveler in the Colonies, 1765," The American Historical Review, XXVII (Oct., 1921), 80-81; Alexander Cluny, The American Traveller. . .(Philadelphia, 1770), 60-61; "Diary of Joshua Hempstead," Collections of the New London County Historical Society, I (1901), 527-28; Harry J. Carman, ed., American Husbandry ([London], 1775, [1939]), 98-110; Thomas Pownall, A Topographical Description of. . .Parts of North America

16

(London, 1776), 92-110; Jonathan Belcher to Board of Trade, Dec. 28, 1754, Archives of the State of New Jersey. . ., ed. William A. Whitehead et al. (Newark, 1880-), VIII, pt. 2, 78-86, hereafter cited as N.J.Archs.; Andrew Burnaby, Travels Through the Middle Settlements in North-America, 2nd ed. (Ithaca, NY, 1960 [1775]), 67-74; Lyman Carrier, The Beginnings of Agriculture in America (New York, 1923), 163. Also J. Wood, "Journal (1815) of a Tour to the Northern States," 37-39, University of Virginia.

7. [Philip V. Fithian to John Peck], Aug. 12, 1774, Journal & Letters of Philip Vickers Fithian, 1773-1774: A Plantation Tutor of the Old Dominion, ed. Hunter Dickinson Farish (Williamsburg, VA, 1943), 210.

8. William Moraley, The Unfortunate: or, The Voyage and Adventures of William Moraley. . .(Newcastle, Eng., 1743), 26-27.

9. Ibid., 26; Benjamin Franklin to Jared Eliot, Feb. 13, 1749/50, The Papers of Benjamin Franklin, ed. Leonard W. Labaree et al. (New Haven, 1959-), III, 465-66; The New-York Gazette, Sept. 21, 1772, in N.J.Archs., XXVIII, 246-53. See also Marquis de Chastellux, Travels in North America, in the Years 1780, 1781 and 1782, ed. Howard C. Rice, Jr., 2 vols. (Chapel Hill, NC, 1963), I, 117-18; Pownall, Topographical Description, 97-98; and "Narrative of American Voyages and Travels of Captain William Owen, R. N. and the Settlement of the Island of Campobello in the Bay of Fundy, 1766-1771," ed. Victor Hugo Paltsits, Bulletin of the New York Public Library, XXXV (Mar. and June, 1931), 145-47, 161-62; and Charles S. Boyer, Early Forges & Furnaces in New Jersey (Philadelphia, 1931).

10. Jackson Turner Main, The Social Structure of Revolutionary America (Princeton, NJ, 1965), 25-43; idem, The Sovereign States, 1775-1783 (New York, 1973), 1-66; Dennis P. Ryan, "Landholding, Opportunity, and Mobility in Revolutionary New Jersey," The William and Mary Quarterly, 3rd Ser., XXXVI (Oct., 1979), 571-92; idem, "Six Towns: Continuity and Change in Revolutionary New Jersey, 1770-1792" (Ph.D. diss., New York University, 1974); Ramon S. Powers, "Wealth and Poverty: Economic Base, Social Structure, and Attitudes in Prerevolutionary Pennsylvania, New Jersey and Delaware" (Ph.D. diss., University of Kansas, 1971); Donald J. Mrozek, "Problems of Social History and Patterns of Inheritance in Pre-Revolutionary New Jersey, 1751-1770," The Journal of the Rutgers University Library, XXXVI (Dec., 1972), 1-19; David Alan Bernstein, "New Jersey in the American Revolution: The Establishment of a Government Amid Civil and Military Disorder,

1770-1781" (Ph.D. diss., Rutgers University, 1970), 1-29; Francis D. Pingeon, "Slavery in New Jersey on the Eve of the Revolution," in New Jersey in the American Revolution: Political and Social Conflict. First Annual New Jersey History Symposium (Trenton, NJ, 1970), 41-53; Robert V. Wells, The Population of the British Colonies in America before 1776: A Survey of Census Data (Princeton, 1975), 136. See also James A. Henretta, The Evolution of American Society, 1700-1815: An Interdisciplinary Analysis (Lexington, MA, 1973), 83-107.

11. William Franklin to Earl of Hillsborough, Nov. 23, 1768, N.J.Archs., X, 93. Robert J. Dinkin, Voting in Provincial America: A Study of Elections in the Thirteen Colonies, 1689-1776 (Westport, CT, 1977), 45, 51; Chilton Williamson, American Suffrage. From Property to Suffrage, 1760-1860 (Princeton, 1960), 29; Main, Social Structure, 212; Thomas L. Purvis, "'High-Born, Long-Recorded Families': Social Origins of New Jersey Assemblymen, 1703 to 1776," The William and Mary Quarterly, 3rd Ser., XXXVII (Oct., 1980), 592-615. Also see C. B. MacPherson, The Political Theory of Possessive Individualism: Hobbes to Locke (London, 1962); and William B. Scott, In Pursuit of Happiness: American Conceptions of Property from the Seventeenth to the Twentieth Century (Bloomington, IN, 1977), 5-35.

12. See Appendix.

13. James T. Lemon, The Best Poor Man's Country: A Geographical Study of Early Southeastern Pennsylvania (Baltimore, 1972); idem, "The weakness of place and community in early Pennsylvania," in James R. Gibson, ed., European Settlement and Development in North America: Essays on Geographical Change in Honor and Memory of Andrew Hill Clark (Toronto, 1978), 190-207; James A. Henretta, "Families and Farms: Mentalite in Pre-Industrial America," The William and Mary Quarterly, 3rd Ser., XXXV (Jan. 1978), 3-32; Henretta, Evolution of American Society, 73-117; Michael Merrill, "Cash Is Good to Eat: Self-Sufficiency and Exchange in the Rural Economy of the United States," Radical History Review, IV (Winter, 1977), 42-71; Michael W. Zuckerman's introduction to Friends and Neighbors, 3-25. See also Stephanie Grauman Wolf, Urban Village: Population, Community, and Family Structure in Germantown, Pennsylvania, 1683-1800 (Princeton, NJ, 1976); Robert E. Mutch, "Yeoman and Merchant in Pre-Industrial America: Eighteenth-Century Massachusetts as a Case Study," Societas, VII (Autumn, 1977), 279-302; Robert D. Mitchell, Commercialism and Frontier: Perspectives on the Early Shenandoah Valley (Charlottesville, VA, 1977); Bushman, From Puritan to Yankee; Paul Boyer and Stephen Nissenbaum, Salem Possessed: The Social Origins of Witchcraft (Cambridge, MA,

1974); Carole Shammas, "Consumer Behavior in Colonial America," Social Science History, VI (Winter, 1982), 67-86. Also helpful were J. R. T. Hughes, Social Control in the Colonial American Economy (Charlottesville, VA, 1976); Appleby, "Social Origins of American Revolutionary Ideology." Also Fernand Braudel, Civilization and Capitalism, 15th-18th Century. Vol. I: The Structures of Everyday Life, trans. Sian Reynolds (New York, 1981), 24-25, 444-48.

14. The Journals of Henry Melchior Muhlenberg, trans. Theodore G. Tappert and John W. Doberstein, 3 vols. (Philadelphia, 1942-1958), I, 310; and for the Dey family see Appendix. Also see Ned Landsman, "The Scottish Proprietors and the Planning of East New Jersey," in Zuckerman, Friends and Neighbors, 65-89.

15. Council and Assembly to king, 1738, N.J.Archs., VI, 59; The Interest of New-Jersey Considered, With Regard to Trade and Navigation. . .(Philadelphia, [1743]), 3; "Philo-Patriae," The North American Magazine (Mar., 1758), 51.

16. "Memorandum Book of Jacob Spicer, 1757-1764," Cape May County Historical and Genealogical Magazine, I (1933), no. 3, 164-65.

17. S[amuel] A[tkinson], The Interest of New-Jersey Considered, Modestly enquiring into the Nature and Necessity of a Paper Currency (n.p., 1743), 10; see also New-York Gazette, Mar. 19, 1753. For a general discussion of "provincial mercantilism," see Crowley, This Sheba, Self, 86-91.

18. Carl R. Woodward, "Agricultural Legislation in Colonial New Jersey," Agricultural History, III (Jan., 1929), 15-28. For a review of legislation, see Bernard Bush's introduction to Laws of the Royal Colony of New Jersey, 1703-1745, N.J.Archs., 3rd Ser., II, xxix-xxxviii. For another study of petitions, see Raymond C. Bailey, Popular Influence upon Public Policy: Petitioning in Eighteenth-Century Virginia (Westport, CT, 1979).

19. Petition from Raccoon Creek, Oct. 13, 1744, The Votes and Proceedings of the General Assembly. . ., microfilm at The Library of Congress listed in Lillian A. Hamrick, ed., A Guide to the Microfilm Collection of Early State Records (Washington, DC, 1950), 144-48, and hereafter cited as Votes and Proceedings. Also see petition from Raccoon Creek, Apr. 5, 1758, ibid.; petition from Newton Creek, Jan. 9, 1738/9, ibid.; petitions from Timber Creek, May 16 and 29, 1740, Nov. 7, 1760, ibid.; petitions from Woodbury Creek, Mar. 31, 1758 and Apr. 15, 1768, ibid.; petition from Malago Run, Mar. 12, 1759, ibid.; Act enabling owners of the meadows adjoining to. . ..

Manington Creek to stop out the Tide (1753), Bush, Laws, III, 261-63; Act enabling. . .Lower Sluice Company (1765), ibid., IV, 374-79; Act enabling Owners. . .on English Creek (1771), Samuel Allinson, ed., Acts of the General Assembly of the Province of New-Jersey (Burlington, NJ, 1776), 367; Adolph B. Benson, ed., Peter Kalm's Travels in North America, 2 vols. (New York, 1937), I, 174.

20. Petition from Brocas, Oct. 20 and 24, 1743, Votes and Proceedings; and petition from Benjamin Griggs et al., Nov. 1 and 4, 1743, ibid.

21. Petitions from Raritan Landing, May 28, June 1, 1763, Oct. 10, 1770, Nov. 28, 1771, ibid. Also see petition from Ancocas Creek, Sept. 20, 1762, ibid.; petition from Michael Branin, Mar. 9, 1762, ibid.; petition from Penn's Neck, Dec. 5, 1761, ibid.; Act for the improvement of the Navigation of the South West Branch of the Ancocas Creek (1766), Bush, Laws, IV, 409-11; Act to remove the Obstructions on Assunpink Creek (1774), Allinson, Acts, 466.

22. Petition from Watson, Mar. 8, 1748/9, Votes and Proceedings; petition from Joseph Haight, Oct. 28, 1769, ibid.; petition from Borden and Hancock, Aug. 1 and 3, 1758, ibid.; petition from Daniel Casnor, Aug. 5, 1758, ibid.; petition from Burlington, Aug. 8, 1758, ibid.; petition from Perth Amboy, Aug. 9, 1758, ibid. See also petition from William Atlee, Oct. 28, 1742, ibid.; and petition from William Wilson, Nov. 1, 1744, ibid.

23. Act to preserve the Navigation of the Rivers. . .of New Jersey (1755), Bush, Laws, III, 358-59; Act to lay out a Road on. . .Cohansey Creek. . .and to establish a Ferry (1766), ibid., IV, 407-9; Act for the Regulation of the Rates . . . at Ferries. . .within the Corporation of Perth-Amboy (1771), Allinson, Acts, 364-66; petition of Cortlandt Skinner to W. Franklin, Sept. 15, 1773, Manuscripts, Box I, Governors' Papers, 1720-1789, The New Jersey State Library; petition from Essex and Morris counties, Apr. 27, 1768, Votes and Proceedings.

24. Petition "setting forth, the Inconveniencies attending the Practice of killing Deer," Mar. 16, 1748/9, ibid.; petition from Burlington and Monmouth counties, Oct. 13, 1749, ibid.; petition to Governor and Assembly, 1748/9, Manuscripts, Box I, Governors' Papers, 1720-1789; Act for the Preservation of Deer (1771), Allinson, Acts, 343-47.

25. Petition from Little Egg Harbor, Nov. 8, 1743, Votes and Proceedings; petition from Basking Ridge, Nov. 21, 1748,

ibid.; Act for Preserving of Timber (1743), Bush, Laws, II, 575-78; Peter O. Wacker, Land and People. A Cultural Geography of Preindustrial New Jersey: Origins and Settlement Patterns (New Brunswick, NJ, 1975), 361.

26. Petitions from Hunterdon County, Nov. 4, 1760, Nov. 17, 1773, Votes and Proceedings; petition from Cape May County, Nov. 21, 1763, ibid.; petitions from Burlington, Hunterdon, and Essex counties, April 18, 1768, ibid.; petition from South River, Oct. 12, 1769, ibid.; W. Franklin's Proclamation, Pennsylvania Gazette, Dec. 21, 1769, in N.J.Archs., XXVI, 583-86; Act regulating fishing on the Raritan and South rivers (1766), Bush, Laws, IV, 405-6; Stephanie Smith Toothman, "Trenton, New Jersey, 1719-1779: A Study of Community Growth and Organization" (Ph.D. diss., University of Pennsylvania, 1977), 257-59.

27. Petition from Mr. Ryerson, Dec. 21, Votes and Proceedings; petition from Garret Garretson, Jan. 11, 1738/9, ibid.; petition from Elizabethtown, Feb. 24, 1738/9, ibid.; petition from Newark, June 5, 1740, ibid.; petition from Adrian Bennet, March 25, 1758, ibid.; petition from Cape May County, Mar. 28, 1758, ibid.; petition from Princeton, July 26, 1758, ibid.; petition from Somerset County, Dec. 1, 1761, ibid.; petition from Middlesex County, May 23, 1765, ibid.; "Americus Justitia," The New-York Gazette, Aug. 7, 1766, in N.J.Archs., XXV, 178-83; "A Traveller," The New-York Gazette, June 20, 1768, in ibid., XXVI, 196-97; Wheaton J. Lane, From Indian Trail to Iron Horse: Travel and Transportation in New Jersey, 1620-1860 (Princeton, NJ, 1939), 33- 93; Wacker, Land and People, 378-98.

28. "An Answer to the Council of Proprietors," [Aug., 1747], N.J.Archs., VII, 41. See petitions from Bergen County, Nov. 9, 1743, and Apr. 15, 1768, Votes and Proceedings; petition from Abraham Vanaken, Oct. 14, 1743, ibid.; petition from Elizabethtown, Nov. 9, 1744, ibid.; petition from East Jersey proprietors, Dec. 1, 1748, ibid.; petition from "The Northern Parts of this Province," Mar. 16, 1748/9, ibid.; petition from Hunterdon and Burlington counties, Mar. 16, 1748/9, ibid.; petition from John Conduit, Mar. 18, 1748/9, ibid.; petition from Cape May County, Mar. 28, 1758, ibid.; petition from Chesterfield and Nottingham, Feb. 16, 1764, ibid.; petition from John Stevens, Nov. 9, 1769, ibid.; petition from Middlesex County, Nov. 15, 1773, ibid.; Act for Preserving of Timber (1743), Bush, Laws, II, 575-78; Act for altering one Part of a Six-Rod Road (1758), ibid., III, 597-99; Act for preventing Frauds by Mortgages (1765), ibid., IV, 334-36; The New-York Mercury, Mar. 2, 1767, in N.J.Archs.,

XXV, 302-3; Sackett to Holt, The Pennsylvania Gazette, June 4, 1767, in ibid., 380-81.

29. Manuscript Wills, 253 E.

30. Report from Committee of Grievances, Dec. 3, 1743, Votes and Proceedings; petition from prisoners in Trenton, May 18, 1753, ibid.; petition from Monmouth Grand Jury, Apr. 4, 1758, ibid.; petition from prisoners, Nov. 17, 1763, ibid.; petition from Somerset County, Oct. 14, 1769, ibid.; petition from Abraham Sayer, Feb. 12, 1774, ibid.; Peter J. Coleman, Debtors and Creditors in America: Insolvency, Imprisonment for Debt, and Bankruptcy, 1607-1900 (Madison, WI, 1974), 6-15, 130-34.

31. Act for Regulating Taverns (1739), Bush, Laws, II, 493-98; Act for the Settlement and Relief of the Poor (1758), ibid., III, 599-615; Act for the Preservation of Deer (1771), Allinson, Acts, 343-47; petition from Burlington County, Dec. 7, 1748, Votes and Proceedings. Also see petition from Charles Read and Peter Bard, June 11, 1765, ibid.; petition from Nottingham, Nov. 18, 1748, Manuscripts, Box 12, Legislative Papers, 1724-1755; petition from "sundry persons," 1751, ibid.; Edward Antill to Speaker, May 25, 1763, ibid., Box 42, Legislative Papers, 1746-1863; Act controlling sale of liquor to servants and slaves (1751), Bush, Laws, III, 180-81; Minutes of the Shrewsbury Township Committee, Oct. 6 and 16, 1775, Gerlach, ed., New Jersey in the American Revolution, 148.

32. Act for the Settlement and Relief of the Poor (1758), Bush, Laws, III, 599-615. Also see Act to enable. . . Elizabeth, to build a Poor House (1754), ibid., 288-92; Act for the Settlement and Relief of the Poor (1774), Allinson, Acts, 403-19; The Countryman's Lamentation. . .(Philadelphia, 1762); and Martin W. Stanton, History of Public Poor Relief in New Jersey, 1609-1934 (New York, 1934), 15-27.

33. [Philadelphia], The American Weekly Mercury, Apr. 30-May 7, 1741, June 30-July 7, 1743, Dec. 6-14, 1744; The New-York Mercury, Dec. 25, 1752, Jan. 1, 1753. Also see petition lamenting loss of servants, Oct. 27, 1741, Votes and Proceedings; Act to regulate sale of liquor to servants and slaves (1751), Bush, Laws, III, 180-81; Act to regulate the Trial of Slaves (1768), ibid., IV, 480-81.

34. Act for laying a Duty on the Purchasers of Slaves (1769), ibid., 510-12. See also Act for laying a Duty on the Purchasers of Slaves (1767), ibid., 435-36; Governor Joseph Hardy to Board of Trade, Jan. 20, 1762, N.J.Archs., IX, 345-46; "Amintor," Pennsylvania Gazette, Feb. 2, 1774, in ibid.,

XXIX, 230-34; petitions from Burlington, Monmouth, and Cumberland counties, Nov. 19, 1773, Votes and Proceedings; petition from Perth Amboy, Feb. 14, 1774, ibid.; petition from Monmouth County, Mar. 9, 1774, ibid.; petition from Perth Amboy to Governor Franklin, Jan. 12, 1774, Manuscripts, Box 14, Legislative Papers, 1770-1781; petition from Shrewsbury, Feb. 2, 1774, ibid.; petition from Chesterfield Township, Nov. 9, 1775, ibid.; Pingeon, "Slavery in New Jersey"; Bailyn, Ideological Origins of the American Revolution, 232-46; Winthrop D. Jordan, White over Black: American Attitudes Toward the Negro, 1550-1812 (Chapel Hill, NC, 1968), 269-311.

35. "Philo-Patriae," New American Magazine (Mar., 1758), 51; Interest of New-Jersey, 5, 19. Also see "B. C. Caesaria," New American Magazine (July, 1758), in N.J.Archs., XX, 256-61; petition from Middlesex County, Oct. 13 and 21, 1743, Votes and Proceedings; Lewis Morris to Duke of Newcastle, June 2, 1732, Calendar of State Papers, Colonial Series, American and West Indies (London, 1860-), XXXIX, 135.

36. L. Morris to Board of Trade, Oct. 4, 1733, ibid., XL, 208; Interest of New-Jersey, 10-18; petition from Middlesex County, Oct. 13 and 21, 1743, Votes and Proceedings; Act to encourage the direct Importation of Rum (1743), Bush, Laws, II, 579-81. Also see petition from Middlesex County, June 11, 1740, Manuscripts, Box 12, Legislative Papers, 1724-1755.

37. "Neo Caesariensis," New-York Journal, Oct. 25, 1770, in N.J.Archs.,XXVII, 295-99. Edgar Jacob Fisher, New Jersey as a Royal Province, 1738 to 1776 (New York, 1911), 392-96; petition from Hunterdon County, Jan. 10, 1738[/9], Votes and Proceedings.

38. A Letter to B.G. from one of the Members of Assembly of the Province of New Jersey. . .([Philadelphia, 1739]); petition from Essex County, Apr. 10, 1746, Manuscripts, Box 12, Legislative Papers, 1724-1755; petition from bolters, Feb. 5, 1752, ibid., Box 42; petition from Middlesex County, June 11, 1740, Votes and Proceedings; petition protesting prohibition of rum imports from New England, Jan. 1, 1748, ibid.; petition from Hunterdon County, May 31, 1765, ibid.; Bush, Laws, II, xxxiii-xxxv; Act to lay a Duty upon Wheat (1714), ibid., 130-31; Act for preventing the Waste of Timber (1714), ibid., 131-33; Act to lay a Duty on Wheat (1725), ibid., 331-32; Act to encourage the direct Importation of Rum (1743), ibid., 579-81; Act to prevent the Exportation of unmerchantable Flour (1751), ibid., III, 184-86; Act to. . .lay a Duty upon. . .Pipe and Hogshead Staves exported (1765), ibid., IV, 338-40; Act to prevent the Exportation of unmerchantable Flour (1772), Allinson, Acts, 378-81; Act to regulate the Packing of Beef and

Pork (1774), ibid., 450-53; "Mercator," Pennsylvania Chronicle, Mar. 16, 1767, in N.J.Archs., XXV, 315-16; Woodward, "Agricultural Legislation."

39. A[tkinson], Interest of New-Jersey; petition requesting paper money, May 28, 1753, Votes and Proceedings; Act for striking One Hundred Thousand Pounds (1774), Allinson, Acts, 419-41. Also petition from Northampton, May 30, 1753, Manuscripts, Box 12, Legislative Papers, 1724-1755; petition from "divers Inhabitants," May 28, 1740, Votes and Proceedings; petition from Evesham, May 24, 1753, ibid.; petitions from Middlesex, Monmouth, Somerset, and Morris counties, April 18, 1768, ibid.; petition from Somerset County, Oct. 16, 1769, ibid.; petition from Morris and Somerset counties, Nov. 18, 1773, ibid.; A Modest Vindication of the Late New-Jersey Assembly. . .([Philadelphia], 1745), 10-21; Pennsylvania Gazette, June 4, 1767, in N.J.Archs., XXV, 380-81; Assembly petition to king, Nov. 2, 1753, ibid., VIII, pt. 1, 183-86; Donald L. Kemmerer, "A History of Paper Money in Colonial New Jersey, 1668-1775," Proceedings of the New Jersey Historical Society, LXXIV (April, 1956), 107-44; Theodore Thayer, "The Land-Bank System in the American Colonies," The Journal of Economic History, XIII (Spring, 1953), 145-59.

40. W. Franklin to Council and Assembly, May 22, 1765, N.J.Archs., XVII, 384-87. Also see Middlesex County's petition to governor, Council, and Assembly and its instructions to representatives, Pennsylvania Gazette, Oct. 19, 1769, in ibid., XXVI, 529-33; "To the Farmers of New Jersey," Pennsylvania Gazette, Mar. 1, 1770, in ibid., XXVII, 73-75; "A Jersey Farmer," The New-York Journal, July 16, 1772, in ibid., XXVIII, 192-94; Larry R. Gerlach, Prologue to Independence: New Jersey in the Coming of the American Revolution (New Brunswick, NJ, 1976), 38-41.

CHAPTER TWO

THE LEGISLATIVE COMMUNITY,II:
INTERESTS AND DIVISIONS

When Jacob Spicer met his neighbors, he discerned envy and malice in their hearts. While attending the legislature, he detected the scheming colleague who designed to oppress the weak and unsuspecting. The Jerseyman who envisioned a mercantile arcadia and exhorted the public to undertake a program for that end found his call unheeded and concluded that the province was lacking "public spirit."[1] Perhaps, it seemed, self-interest had wormed too deeply into arcadia. In addition, the province's cultural life seemed so variegated and its political life so contentious that the Jerseyman who participated in legislative politics saw diffusion rather than community and disagreement, even conflict, rather than consensus. The provincial government mirrored those divisions. East and West Jersey, although united in 1702, remained distinct social and political entities. While the West's economic and cultural life was oriented toward Philadelphia, the East's gravitated toward New York. Politicians jealously guarded the principle of sectional parity: that is, that the East and West enjoy equal representation in the Assembly, that the house meet alternately in Perth Amboy in the East and Burlington in the West, and that appointments to the Council be awarded equitably. Nor was either section homogeneous. Each sent an urban delegation, from Burlington and Perth Amboy, and county members, who represented an agrarian interest. Moreover, ethnic and religious differences made for an even more complex social mosaic. Quakers and Baptists prevailed in the West and Presbyterians, Dutch Calvinists, and Anglicans in the East.[2]

While some Jerseymen ascribed the province's divisions to a pervasive stinginess or meanness of the soul, others were wont to see profound social cleavages. The proprietor, after defending his land titles in the courts and against the mob, came to believe that he was besieged by levelers, enemies of government and property, and concluded that a handful of "Wigmen" like himself was outnumbered by "Cap Men." When he discovered the "Mobmen" had gained influence and seats in the lower house, he realized that the last bastion of property and order was the governor's Council.[3] In response, his opponent characterized him as the overlording "courtier" who conspired to enrich himself by oppressing the virtuous "ploughman."[4]

As this investigation tightens its focus on the individual, his economic and social life, and his relations with fellow Jerseymen, it highlights the motifs of division, contention, and conflict. The first turn of the lens discloses an "unstable factionalism" which Bernard Bailyn finds endemic to North American politics. Another turn of the lens confirms Larry Gerlach's impression that New Jersey society was so segmented, its alignments so unstable, that its politics can be described more aptly as "fractional" than "factional."[5] Indeed, what had appeared from a distant vantage point to be a legislative community dissolves into an assemblage of milling interests. The two images--the one of conflict, the other of consensus--are not incompatible but prove to be necessary complements. The one reveals differences and sources of disagreement; the other cautions against exaggerating the distance separating the disputants. The assemblymen found the divisions significant, at times profound. But antagonists once thrust into the melee, no doubt, forget what they have in common. And the provincial acted in a culture which nurtured that impulse to exaggerate. Just as he winced at the implications of an unrestrained marketplace, he abhorred what later generations would accept, even laud, as political pluralism. To countenance either entailed repudiation of the communal ideal. Instead, he tended to explain conflict, which might appear to the modern political scientist as the normal product of interest group politics, as collision between diametrically opposed social orders.

In fact, inspection of the assemblymen confirms not only that they represented the province's wealthy stratum but also that their differences fell within a narrow range. While a landed and commercial interest appeared in the membership lists, the distinction cannot be drawn too sharply. The merchant who owned lands and retreated to his country estate sat beside the farmer who speculated in property, milled his neighbors' grains, and operated a store. The one--more commercial than agrarian--and the other--more agrarian than commercial--represented two extremes of a spectrum. The spectrum was a narrow one bounded by entrepreneurialism, and the differences within it reflected varieties of entrepreneurial behaviors or shadings and balances between land speculating and commercial enterprises. The members were complementary characters making up commercial arcadia. The lawmakers' responses to proposals for promoting the economy confirm that their differences were not categorical but of degree. The voting patterns reveal moments of disagreement but not enduring, dichotomous, or polarized alignments. Instead, they reflect the free play of interest within a legislative community.

The eastern assemblymen--two elected from each of the five counties of Bergen, Monmouth, Middlesex, Essex, and Somerset and from the port of Perth Amboy--represented the section's complex social mosaic and its conflicting interests.[6] Perth Amboy's representatives were easily distinguished from the county members. The differences were, in part, specific. First, Perth Amboy, a commercial center situated at the mouth of the Raritan River, directed its trade toward the back country and out into the Atlantic, but in neither case was it able to compete successfully with the neighboring port of New York. Merchants along the Raritan, at Newark and Elizabethtown, and at the market centers of Woodbridge, Shrewsbury, and Middletown bypassed Perth Amboy in favor of New York. Some had become factors for New York merchants. Perth Amboy's representatives recognized that their port's welfare, indeed survival, depended on severing this network. Second, while the urban legislators spoke for the eastern proprietors, their colleagues from the counties, especially Essex, Middlesex, and Monmouth, represented antiproprietary claimants.[7] But the distinctions transcended interest and included style and taste. Perth Amboy's representatives were urban and Anglican; the county members were agrarian and dissenters; the one was cosmopolitan and the other parochial. That contrast in combination with interest made for a fundamental fissure within the eastern delegations. While the county members shared an antipathy toward Perth Amboy, they also discovered many points of difference among themselves. The towns of Woodbridge, Newark, and Elizabethtown were pockets of New Englanders and were generally Presbyterian. Monmouth County to the south sent as many Quakers as Presbyterians. In the northern county of Bergen and along the Raritan from New Brunswick into Somerset County, the Dutch Reformed were numerous enough to send their own to the legislature.

Perth Amboy's representatives prayed at St. Mary's Church, attended the governing board of the eastern proprietors or owned a share in its interest, formed trading partnerships with each other, and were knit together by marriage and friendship. While their community seemed eclipsed by New York, proximity brought entry into that society and concomitant advantages. Several representatives had resided in the larger port, even had been merchants there, and had married into that province's leading families. In turn, they were familiar with New York's political leaders. Fellow proprietor Lewis Morris had served in both houses of New Jersey's legislature, then removed to New York, entered that

27

Assembly, and became a leading politician and confidant of governors. His friend and fellow proprietor James Alexander sat in the Councils of both provinces. That association enhanced Perth Amboy's position in government. Until 1738, New York's governors held commissions for New Jersey; but, rather than visit and govern directly their lesser charge, they relied on the advice of such as Lewis Morris. Morris returned from London in 1738 having successfully convinced the government to split the commissions and to appoint him governor. Thus, this group had grown accustomed to an easy access to the executive and had been preferred for appointive positions. Furthermore, as Morris's success in London signified, it enjoyed a special connection with English authorities, which set it apart from other Jersey politicians. When Perth Amboy's representatives entered the house, they enjoyed a certain prestige. One of the delegation members was chosen speaker during ten of the twelve assemblies which sat after 1738. The influence of the representatives proved less secure, however, when the house turned to specific policy, especially that which related to the proprietary interest. Concerted efforts to plot election campaigns and to devise legislative strategies were fruitless and only served to remind the group of its isolation and its dependence on the prerogative, the Council, and the Supreme Court.[8]

A member of the Johnston family sat for Perth Amboy in eight of the twelve assemblies held between 1738 and 1775. The founder, Dr. John Johnston, had arrived at the turn of the last century from Scotland to manage his proprietary interest, became a merchant in both New York and Perth Amboy, and served as Perth Amboy's mayor and representative. His sons, Andrew and Lewis, followed his example. Andrew began at the family's business in New York and later established himself in Perth Amboy where he managed a profitable trade with the West Indies, supervised the family's lands, and developed tenant farms. His brother, upon completing his education in Europe, also followed a career in trade, sat on the East Jersey Board of Proprietors, and, in addition, represented the interests of the West Jersey proprietors. Both married into New York's elite: Andrew to a Van Cortlandt and then to a Schuyler and Lewis to a Heathcote. The second generation's political success was comparably impressive. Both Andrew and Lewis sat in the house, and another brother was elevated to the Council. In turn, the sons of all three sat in the legislature. And, by the eve of independence, the Johnstons had married into the families of assemblymen Philip Kearny, Cortlandt Skinner, and Andrew Smyth.

Blood and interest made for a cohesive group. Representative Philip Kearny was the grandson of Lewis Morris.

In addition to venturing in English stock and proprietary claims, he speculated in lands with Lewis Johnston. One child married a Skinner and another a Hude of New Brunswick. His son-in-law Cortlandt Skinner, named after his grandfather Stephen Van Cortlandt, settled in New Jersey after reading for the bar in New York and was soon appointed the province's attorney general. In 1763, he was chosen to represent the port and two years later was selected speaker of the house. For his loyalist sympathies, he claimed that he had lost ₺7,000 in real estate and proprietary rights. James Stevens, another proprietor, plied a profitable trade with the West Indies, invested in copper mines, and speculated in lands with the Johnstons. He married the daughter of James Alexander and after short service in the house was appointed to the Council.

Jealousy and rivalry were present within the group. The Johnstons had on occasion feuded with Lewis Morris and had even sought to block his appointment as governor. When Samuel Nevill arrived from England to manage his proprietary interest, he gained immediate entrance to the group and soon embarked on a public career. After election to the house and then elevation to its speakership, he accepted appointment to the Supreme Court. At times, Robert Hunter Morris, the governor's son, found Nevill's ambitions excessive if not threatening to his own influence in the group. In general, however, the clique retained a common identity and perspective forged by a sense of being besieged by the county majorities.[9]

The faction did find friends among those Middlesex assemblymen who were elected from New Brunswick. Thomas Farmer had been active in both New York and New Jersey society. He married a daughter of New York's Bilop family, pursued trade in New York and Perth Amboy, and finally established himself at New Brunswick where he became active in the town's affairs, was instrumental in securing its charter, and then served as mayor. An ally of Lewis Morris, he first sat in the Assembly in 1710 and was later appointed to the Supreme Court and then to the Council. After a short retirement, perhaps due to mental instability, he returned to the house in 1740. Edward Antill, the son of a New York merchant and purchaser of a share in the eastern proprietary, moved first to Raritan Landing and then to New Brunswick. He was a merchant and a brewer as well as manager of a three-hundred-acre estate worked by slaves. His political fortunes were no doubt aided by marriage to the daughter of Governor Morris: within a year of his election to the house, he was appointed to the county court and four years later to the Council.

Not all New Brunswick's representatives were Anglican. The Hudes were Presbyterians who had first settled at Woodbridge, where Adam was a member of the county court and later was elected to the Assembly. His son James moved to New Brunswick, became a merchant, entered public life, and befriended Lewis Morris. In addition to serving in the legislature, he was the town's mayor, a member of the county court, and finally councilor to the governor. His brother Robert who succeeded him in the legislature also sat on the county court. William Oake was part of the Dutch community that had settled along the Raritan River. Once established at New Brunswick, he opened a tavern and turned to trade sometimes with John Stevens of Perth Amboy. He, too, became the town's mayor and, as a friend of Morris, was appointed justice of the peace.

The Perth Amboy-New Brunswick alliance did not go unchallenged. In the spring of 1749, the Middlesex electors chose John Wetherill who spoke for a different constituency. This South Brunswick Presbyterian owned several tracts of land, including two farms of 100 and 300 acres which he worked with the labor of a half-dozen slaves. When he arrived in the legislature, he proved to be an outspoken opponent of proprietary influence and was elected throughout the remainder of the provincial period.[10] He found support in the transplanted New England town of Woodbridge. For two generations, this community had defended its titles against proprietary claims; and, although it had successfully resolved the issue, it continued to harbor distrust toward the urban clique. This agricultural community had flourished and became a local trading center.[11] Its spokesmen were farmers, slave owners, local traders, and mill owners. Most were Presbyterians such as John Heard, a local miller, his father-in-law James Smith, or their neighbor John Moores, a slave-owning farmer. Shobal Smith represented the town's Quakers. His father and the Fitz-Randolphs had migrated from Massachusetts and became prominent local residents. A prosperous farmer, Shobal, like his father, was elected to the legislature. While these assemblymen actively participated in local affairs as town moderators or on church committees, they failed to gain the governor's notice when it came time to fill the county's civil list.

Monmouth County to the south sent delegations similar in social composition and sentiment to Woodbridge's representatives. Shrewsbury and Middletown, the county's first settlements, had been planted under patents contested by the proprietors and, like Woodbridge, had become by mid-century prosperous market centers.[12] The county's emerging elite was represented most prominently by Robert Lawrence and John Eaton. Lawrence's father settled at Middletown, farmed, and then built a gristmill. This Quaker entrepreneur became a fixture in the community and won election to the legislature and appointments to the county civil list. The son, Robert, removed to Upper Freehold where he was taxed for 375 acres in 1731 and for 976 acres in 1758. In 1743, he entered the legislature and soon proved himself one of Perth Amboy's staunchest opponents. During a career that lasted two decades, he was chosen speaker on two occasions. The Lawrences were part of a kinship network that included other prominent families such as the Hartshornes and the Holmeses. In 1751, James Holmes, a Baptist and a merchant-farmer, joined Lawrence in the Assembly. And, in 1769, Robert Hartshorne, a Quaker merchant and shareholder in the West Jersey proprietorship, was chosen to represent the county. (The Hartshornes were also related to Woodbridge's Quaker leadership.) Lawrence's long-time colleague was John Eaton, a Presbyterian farmer from Shrewsbury who owned lands scattered throughout Monmouth and the neighboring Hunterdon County. This self-styled "yeoman" farmer established an unbroken record of opposition to Perth Amboy's influence which lasted from 1727 until his death in 1750. These representatives faced a mounting challenge. John Anderson, a landowner and deputy surveyor for the proprietors, had been appointed to the county court in 1749 and in 1754 declared his candidacy. He was joined by Edward Taylor, a merchant, who also invested in the eastern proprietorship and in a stage running from New York to Philadelphia. Both were defeated by Holmes and Lawrence. But, in 1763, the electors chose Anderson to succeed Holmes and in the following decade sent Taylor first with Hartshorne and then with Richard Lawrence to the legislature.

Perth Amboy found its staunchest opposition north of Woodbridge and in Essex County. After the English conquest of 1664, New Englanders settled at Newark and Elizabethtown and soon after became embroiled with the proprietors in disputes over the validity and extent of their land claims. Had the Duke of York's grant to the proprietors in London abrogated the one made earlier by his lieutenant in America to the Elizabethtown Associates? Had the proprietors granted Newark the right to buy a single tract from the Indians or had they given the purchasers license for further expansion? And what were the bounds of these grants? The lands in question had come to include all of Essex and parts of the adjacent counties of Somerset and Middlesex. At one level, the issue was between two groups of land-hungry speculators--the New Englanders and the proprietors. At another, it affected the lives of count-less farmers whose security of title depended on the outcome of the question. The uncertainty of title was endemic to other parts of the province. Thus, when agreement could not be reached and when purchasers were harried with expensive law suits and ejectments, rioting erupted in Essex and spread rapidly to other counties.[13]

This controversy, which lasted three generations and was exacerbated by an ingrained Presbyterian antipathy toward the Anglican, made for deep resentments toward Perth Amboy. But an elite was also emerging in Essex society which tended to mollify the expression of that opinion.[14] Newark and Elizabethtown were evolving from agricultural to commercial communities: on their waterfronts could be found grain, meat, and timber which had been transported from the back country and was awaiting export to the West Indies. As if reflecting this transformation, two kinds of leaders emerged: first, the agrarian who harbored an unqualified prejudice toward Perth Amboy but was active principally in local affairs and, second, the county's representatives whose commitment to their community's land claims was tempered by an ambition to enter the inner ranks of the provincial elite. This new leadership was represented by Joseph Bonnell, Stephen Crane, and the Ogdens. Bonnell's father had left Connecticut to settle in Elizabethtown, became one of its principal citizens, and was elected to the East Jersey Assembly. Joseph inherited extensive tracts of land, joined the Presbyterian Church, and became active both in the town's defense of its lands and in its campaign for incorporation. First elected in 1716, he was returned intermittently until 1744. His public career suggested moderation. Although a spokesman for Elizabethtown's interest, he studiously avoided confrontation with the proprietors and earned the confidence of Governor Morris. After accepting his selection as speaker in 1738, the governor made him the town's mayor and a justice of the Supreme Court. Stephen Crane's public life reflects the same expanding horizons. A Presbyterian and a lawyer, he was selected to defend Elizabethtown's claims in London. A confidant of Governor Jonathan Belcher, he received appointments to the county civil list. In 1766, he was sent to the house and five years later was appointed speaker.

In general, the Essex voters deferred to this elite and allowed it to pursue its ambitions in provincial government. Three Ogdens--Josiah and John of Newark and Robert of Elizabethtown--sat in the Assembly between 1738 and 1775. This wealthy family of entrepreneurs had speculated in land, ironworks, and trade. While active in community affairs and in the land disputes, the Ogdens raised suspicions. Some had forsaken their Presbyterian heritage and even initiated the building of an Anglican Church at Newark. While Robert led in Elizabethtown's defense of its lands, a cousin was retained as legal counsel to the board of proprietors. One challenge to this provincial elite came from the Camps and Cranes of Newark (not related to the Elizabethtown Cranes). These Presbyterians busied themselves with farming, with operating their mills, and with local affairs. On occasion, they clashed with the Ogdens but rarely outside town government. Joseph Camp epitomized the localist. When resentments toward the proprietors exploded in the 1740s, he stood for the legislature and won. Perth Amboy knew him as an "open Rioter." Within two years, he returned to his farms and mills and on occasion served as overseer of the poor and a freeholder.[15]

John Low seemed most adept at responding to both segments of this community. The Lows were a family of Reformed Dutch merchants who resided in New York and along the Raritan River. John moved to Newark where he plied a trade which extended at least to Boston. Meanwhile, he invested in lands in the county's northern section. Since his titles were disputed, he joined with fellow speculators, became spokesman in their interest, and negotiated directly with the proprietors. Because his associates were identified with the rioters, the Perth Amboy group concluded that the lawmaker was a "Secret Rioter." The proprietors misunderstood him. Low was determined to protect his investments, and he did capitalize on antiproprietary opinion at the polls. But he also felt uncomfortable with the localists, publicly repudiated their violent acts, and, most important, sought to gain influence in the provincial government. After Governor Morris's death, he began to realize that goal. First, he became a confidant of Governor Belcher and adviser on politics and patronage. Second, he broke with his former allies and forged an alliance with the Ogdens. It puzzled Perth Amboy's leaders that "all the Rioters Should join against John Low, their former head, and that All his. . .opposers should now Chuse him."[16]

The Reformed Dutch communities of Bergen and Somerset remained culturally distinct from the English.[17] Since the first of the century, Bergen's Demarests and Van Buskirks had been accumulating lands and slaves and simultaneously acquiring public offices. David Demarest, who was born of a Huguenot family in New York, arrived in the county in the 1690s. While active in the Dutch Church, he did not forget his origins and continued to read religious books in French. As he increased his properties in Bergen and then Essex counties, he earned public recognition and appointments as sheriff and judge of the county court. In 1738, he was sent to the Assembly with Lawrence Van Buskirk. Although Lutheran, the Van Buskirks had become prominent fixtures in the county's political life. The son of a wealthy landowner and legislator, Lawrence had first entered the Assembly in 1728 and continued to hold that seat until 1751. Near the end of his life, he surveyed his lands

33

and slaves and rejoiced at his "temporal good fortune." He left Ŀ1,400 to his heirs.[18] During the decade they served together, both lawmakers were critical of the Perth Amboy clique, but Van Buskirk's opposition was, in contrast to Demarest's, so uncompromising, indeed disdainful, that he received a single appointment as justice of the peace. The Deys also spoke for that antiproprietary sentiment. After removing from New York, they had bought lands scattered throughout East and West Jersey and New York and set themselves up as local traders. In 1749 and 1751, Derrick was elected to the Assembly. In the meantime, his son Theunis was proving himself capable of managing the family's affairs and had married a Schuyler. Derrick then returned to New York and continued his life in trade. In 1761, Theunis began a legislative career that lasted until independence.[19]

Somerset County seemed the model of commercial arcadia.[20] The county's leading families had been accumulating lands and slaves since the 1680s; their large farms that dotted the landscape produced surpluses that were shipped along the Raritan River; and Raritan Landing had become a thriving trade center. Derrick Van Veghten, like his father, spent his life acquiring land and making improvements. His inventory included several tracts along the Raritan valley, one of twelve hundred acres, and others in Bergen County and New York. His success was apparent. He managed his farms and herds of livestock with a work force of twenty-five slaves and, while choosing to count himself among the county's yeomanry, resided in a two-story brick home. Abraham Van Neste, the son of an assemblyman, milled his neighbors' grains, speculated in lands, and became a local merchant at Millstone. But the most prominent of the county's representatives were Jacob Van Middleswardt and Hendrick Fisher. While sitting on the county court and in the legislature throughout the administrations of Lewis Morris and Jonathan Belcher, Van Middleswardt worked a 650-acre farm with slave labor. Fisher who sat on the county court and was elected regularly to the legislature from 1745 until independence described himself as a "mechanic." But his will suggested much more: in addition to extensive holdings and slaves, he left Ŀ1,065 to be divided among his heirs. And his estate, when evaluated, came to Ŀ4,759.

Quaker influence in the western division was the single most notable factor distinguishing that section's politics from the East. In fact, the Friends exercised political power disproportionate to their numbers. Concentrated in the counties of Burlington, Gloucester, and, to a lesser extent, Salem, they comprised just one-fifth of the division's population. Only Burlington was half Quaker. But the Friends held two-thirds of the division's seats. All Gloucester's representatives, 70 percent from the port and county of Burlington, and half of Salem's attended the meetinghouse. The Baptists were strongest in Salem and Cape May; half of Hunterdon's representatives were Presbyterian; and Anglicans were spread randomly throughout the delegations.[21] Religion aside, life in the West was indistinguishable from the East. While there were fewer slaves in the West, both economies were agricultural and commercial. Trading centers had emerged at the port of Burlington and such lesser depots as Salem on the Delaware River and Cape May Landing on the southern shore. And with the consolidation of wealth, a political elite emerged in each of the counties. The western lawmakers lived in a world of land speculation, commercial agriculture, timbering, and trade and represented interests not unlike those of their eastern counterparts.[22]

The delegations from the ports of Burlington and Perth Amboy came to the legislature with similar interests, social perspectives, and political ambitions. Yet they remained rivals.[23] Both were commercial elites. Burlington had, like Perth Amboy, developed a trade in local agricultural products which it shipped to the West Indies. Its growth was stunted for the same reason as Perth Amboy's--that is, the dominance of a neighboring port, in this case Philadelphia. That proximity had also meant that this elite was absorbed into a larger urban world and had acquired a taste for the cosmopolitan. Burlington's Smiths were related by marriage to the Logans and Pembertons of Philadelphia. The Kinseys were busy in both towns. James Kinsey, the son of Pennsylvania's speaker of the house, attorney general, and chief justice, practiced law in both provinces. After moving to Burlington, he was elected to the house where he quickly established himself as a leading member. Burlington's elite, like Perth Amboy's, aspired toward influence in the provincial government, specifically seats in the Council and access to the executive. And, for this reason, each watched the other with suspicion.[24]

Six Smiths represented the port between 1702 and 1775. The family had joined West Jersey's first planters with shares in the proprietary, rapidly acquired lands, and soon discovered the profits to be made from the West Indian trade. When Richard Smith entered the legislature in 1730, the family's position was secure in Burlington's public life. His father had already sat in the legislature. During Richard's twenty-year service, he also supervised his ships, wharves, and warehouses. And like so many merchants who yearned for gentility, he built a country estate at "Greenhill." When he died in 1750, he left his heirs lands and over £2,000. At the end of his career, his cousin Daniel joined him in the Assembly, and another Smith sat in the Council. The next generation took its place in the legislature. While the family prevailed in Burlington and gained an occasional seat in the Council, its access to the inner circles of power could not match Perth Amboy's. The Smiths needed representation in London and found their spokesman in Richard Partridge, a Friend and the provincial agent. When Governor Morris died in 1746, Partridge provided the necessary connection to London's influential Quakers: he and the Quakers were able to prevent the appointment of Morris's son and then to install an ally, Jonathan Belcher. Although the new governor was not a Quaker, he was Partridge's brother-in-law and had proved sympathetic to the Friends while governor of Massachusetts. Belcher chose Burlington for his home, immediately entered the Smiths' social world, and turned to them for advice on New Jersey politics.

Three-fourths of the port's representatives attended the meetinghouse. Issac Pearson who was known to the community as a silversmith and clockmaker held an interest in the West Jersey proprietorship and ventured in ironworks. After serving as assessor of the poor and on the board of freeholders, he went to the Assembly in 1727 where he sat until 1744. His colleague, John Rodman, had only recently arrived from New York to manage his proprietary interest in the province and lands in Pennsylvania. In 1738, he was appointed to the Council. Rodman's son Thomas married Pearson's daughter and joined his father-in-law at the silver shop. Later, he represented the county and presided at the meetings of the board of western proprietors. The Anglicans who appeared after mid-century held similar interests. The Hewlingses, father and son, were also proprietors and merchants. John Brown Lawrence, a lawyer and landowner, was elected to the house in 1761, became the town's mayor in 1769, and two years later was elevated to the Council.

The most prominent of the Anglicans was Charles Read. His grandfather, after settling in Burlington, removed to Philadelphia. The family prospered in trade and entered the city's elite. Read's father served in the Pennsylvania Council, and his aunts married into the Pemberton and Logan families. The young Read completed his education in England and, after momentarily considering a career in the navy, returned home. Soon he took up residence in Burlington. With unbounded energy, he pursued profit wherever opportunity lured him, be it in timber, land, mills, or ironworks. He embarked on a public career with similar zeal. Although his grandfather had forsaken the meetinghouse, the family continued to enjoy close relations with the Quaker elite. While exploiting that connection, Read simultaneously cultivated Perth Amboy's Anglicans. Thus, he won appointment as provincial secretary and became principal adviser to governors on matters of

36

patronage. He was chosen speaker of the house in his first term and was later appointed councilor and second judge of the Supreme Court.[25]

The typical representative from Burlington County, be he Quaker or Anglican, was an entrepreneur who flourished in the marketplace. This merchant and proprietor ventured widely, and his inventory included such investments as a tannery, brickyard, hattery, ironworks, or mill. William Cooke, a Quaker, sat in the legislature from 1738 to 1754. His father had settled first at Shrewsbury and had been elected to the East Jersey Assembly before he removed to Burlington. Joseph Borden's father, an Anglican, had founded Bordentown. Both assemblymen were merchants. Cooke's estate included five thousand acres and personal property worth Ł3,772. Borden was also one of the county's wealthiest. When operating a stage line from Philadelphia through Bordentown to New York, he took as his partner Perth Amboy's Assemblyman Pontius Steele. His land included several tracts in the county and valuable stands of cedar in Monmouth County, and his estate was evaluated at Ł6,641. While Anthony Sykes, a Quaker, worked his farm in Chesterfield township, he purchased lands throughout the province, including stands of cedar, and operated sawmills. Although Barzilai Newbold, an Anglican, identified himself as a blacksmith in his will, his inventory of lands and his personal property valued at Ł1,437 suggested that he lived in a world not unlike that of his colleagues.

Marriage and friendship bound this Quaker elite together. During the Morris administration, Cooke represented the county with Mahlon Stacy and Thomas Shinn. The Stacys had risen rapidly in West Jersey society. Mahlon's father owned a share in the West Jersey proprietorship, claimed at least 3,500 acres, and engaged in trade with the West Indies. He was elected to the West Jersey Assembly in 1682 and later was appointed to the Council. Mahlon took up residence in Northampton Township where he invested in mills and ironworks with Assemblyman Issac Pearson. His estate was worth Ł1,903. The Shinns had fared as well. Thomas, the son of a substantial farmer, actively speculated in lands and purchased slaves. This prominent member of the meetinghouse also sat on the county court and in 1740 went to the legislature. His daughter married Henry Paxson, who speculated in land while operating a tannery and hattery. In 1754, Paxson began a career in the house which lasted twelve years. His one-time colleague Samuel Stokes counted Gloucester's Hinchmans among his kin.

Gloucester's representatives were Quakers, proprietors, and slaveholding planters. Several families dominated the county's social life: the Hinchmans, Coopers, Mickles, and Clements each sent two to the legislature, or eight of the twelve elected after 1738. Kinship knit these lawmakers together. Joseph Cooper, Jr., and John Mickle who served together from 1738 to 1744 were cousins. Their fathers had laid the families' foundation at Newton Township. Joseph Cooper, Sr., had prospered at Cooper's Creek and was elected to the legislature in 1703. Within months, he was appointed to the Council. His neighbor Archibald Mickle ranked only second behind him in wealth. The bonds between the families were forged when John Mickle, his brother, and his sister married Coopers. In turn, Mickle's son married a Hinchman. Hinchmans married Clements, and the Coopers and Mickles were related to Assemblyman John Ladd.

John Ladd flourished in this commercial-agrarian world and came to be known as "one of the principal Magistrates of Gloucester County." This self-styled "yeoman" resided on a thirteen-hundred-acre estate where he sought to achieve the status of country gentleman. A West Jersey proprietor, he was incessantly acquiring lands, including some tracts as large as 800, 1,000, and 1,500 acres. Some he improved and settled with tenants. In addition, he owned hundreds of acres of timber and cedar swamps, built mills to cut his harvest, and exported lumber and masts. His trade included accounts with Israel Pemberton of Philadelphia. As he prospered, his horizons extended beyond the confines of Gloucester County. While remaining a Quaker, he shed the meetinghouse's strictures on etiquette and social form and entered the world of the provincial elite. During the French and Indian War, he sat in the legislature and consistently supported military appropriations. In recognition of his service, he was elevated after a single term to the Council.[26]

With few exceptions, the southernmost counties--Salem, its offshoot Cumberland which gained representation in 1772, and Cape May--sent Quakers and Baptists to the legislature. The two denominations lived in harmony: in spite of the Baptist clergy's struggle to define its separateness, the congregations invited Quakers to preach; members of both churches lived in close association; and ofttimes their children intermarried.[27] The Sheppards, for example, included Friends and Baptists: Moses, who represented Salem in 1744, had spent his childhood in the meetinghouse, married a Quaker, and later joined the Old Cohansey Baptist Church; John, Cumberland's first representative, remained a Quaker. Salem's Edward Keasby also had been reared a Quaker but joined the Baptist Church. These assemblymen lived like their colleagues throughout the province. They were wealthy landowners like William Hancock who represented Salem County for thirty-three years (1730-1763). Like Leaming and Spicer, they ventured into a variety

38

of enterprises. Issac Sharp's father had come from Ireland to manage his proprietary interest and then returned home. Issac, however, chose to pursue his fortune in Salem where he speculated in land, owned mills, and invested in ironworks. John Sheppard, another wealthy landowner, owned a store, wharf, and ferry at Greenwich. When he died in 1805, he was worth over $4,000. So, too, Nicholas Stillwell, a Cape May Baptist, operated an inn and a ferry and invested in local shipping. The Gibbons were Anglicans. Leonard Gibbon and his brother emigrated from England to Salem, rapidly acquired lands, and built a gristmill on a seven-hundred-acre tract. An active Anglican, he helped found the church at Greenwich. He also gave lands to the local Presbyterian congregation. When elected in 1743, he owned two thousand acres in farms, cattle, and wheat. His nephew Grant became a local merchant and was elected in 1771 and again in 1772.

Hunterdon County, situated to the north of Burlington, deviated most strikingly from the prevailing patterns in the western division. Specifically, its delegations reflected the county's social disharmonies and political rivalries. Migrants from Burlington to the south and from Somerset and Monmouth to the east converged on the county and made for its diversity. The county's representatives included Quakers, Presbyterians, and even a Dutch Calvinist. In turn, its politics was divided between the town of Trenton and the recently settled outlying regions. Trenton, located on the border with Burlington County and on the banks of the Delaware River, had become a commercial center, trading principally with Philadelphia.[28] Its prospering elite, like Burlington's, aspired to remodel the town into a cosmopolitan center. Its influence, however, was challenged by the settlers in the outlying townships. As they increased in numbers, they requested, then demanded, a change in the county seat; and, at the end of the period, they were numerous enough to prevail on election day. Thus, sectional rivalries were intensified by denominational difference; elections were bitterly contested; losers charged their opponents with corruption; and freeholders petitioned for relief from oppressive officials.[29]

Daniel Doughty represented the county's southern orientation. The family had first settled in Burlington County, acquired a share in the western proprietorship, and accumulated extensive holdings in Hunterdon County. Daniel's father was elected to the provincial legislature in 1716. Daniel took up residence in Hunterdon County and was chosen in 1743, 1744, and 1745. He later moved south and represented Burlington County. Benjamin Smith, of Burlington's Smiths, arrived in Trenton in the 1730s, opened a store, invested in mills, and became a local trader. On entering the legislature in

39

1738, he promoted the commercial interests of Burlington and Trenton and defended Governor Morris from his critics. And, as the governor's confidant, he advised on the distribution of patronage in Hunterdon and Burlington counties and promoted his family's political ambitions.[30] His neighbor Samuel Tucker and a partner in Philadelphia conducted a profitable trade in slaves that extended south to the West Indies and north to New England. This venture with his speculations in land yielded returns sufficient to place Tucker at the top of the town's tax list. On his death, he was worth nearly Ⱡ6,000.

But the outlying population was growing. The Middaghs, a Dutch Reform family, had migrated from New York along the Raritan valley, first settling and marrying with the Van Nestes at Somerville in Somerset County and then moving on to Hunterdon County. In 1754, Peter Middagh was elected to the house. In 1768, the county elections were contested bitterly by Trenton's Tucker and John Hart from Hopewell.[31] The Harts were Presbyterians who left Connecticut at the turn of the century and eventually located in Hunterdon County. Hart, a wealthy slave-owning planter and mill owner, had first been elected in 1761 with George Reading, a Presbyterian from Amwell, but was chosen this time with Tucker.

John Emley and William Mott represented the county's divergent interests. William Mott came to the legislature with an intense dislike for the proprietors. His family had first planted in Monmouth County: its lands, however, were disputed by the proprietors, and Gershom, William's father, entered politics in opposition to Lewis Morris. After two years in the legislature, Morris engineered his expulsion. William and his brother moved west to Trenton where they raised wheat and milled grain for export. William entered the legislature in 1743 and during his eleven-year career proved to be one of Perth Amboy's staunchest opponents. His colleague John Emley was, by contrast, an intimate of the Perth Amboy and Burlington communities. The Emleys were prominent Quakers in West Jersey: John's father had served in the West Jersey Assembly and had married one of Burlington's Stacys. From his home in Hunterdon County, John Emley cultivated close ties with the Quaker elite of Burlington and extended his business dealings with the eastern proprietors, especially with Assemblyman John Stevens. His speculation included considerable land in the area: one inventory of his real estate holdings listed 300 acres valued at Ⱡ1,000, 574 at Ⱡ2,009, 141 at Ⱡ600, and 133 at Ⱡ600.

These profiles give substance to two conclusions about this political community: first, a stable political elite was emerging in the province, and, second, the emergence of this leadership spelled the ascendance of an entrepreneurialism in government. This elite's achievement did not match what Philip Fithian witnessed in Virginia. And, no doubt, the province's social demarcations were not so tightly drawn to exclude the newcomer. Henry Young, for example, had been impressed into the British navy, deserted ship while on route to Philadelphia, and made his way to Cape May. Twenty years later, he appeared in the legislature. And John Mehelm had left Ireland for Pennsylvania, tried his hand at teaching school, and soon removed to Hunterdon County. There he practiced law, bought lands, ventured in local trade, operated a mill, and in 1772 stood successfully for election to the legislature. Perhaps the process of elite formation had not kept apace with that of neighboring New York and Pennsylvania, but it pointed in the same direction. In each locale, a few families had prospered and achieved political ascendance, often intermarried, and then transmitted their gains to the next generation. By the time Morris and Sussex counties gained the right to elect their own representatives in 1772, a local elite had emerged not unlike that found in the older counties to the south.[32] Their delegations included substantial farmers such as William Winds and Nathaniel Pettit, the proprietor Joseph Barton, and the self-styled "merchant" Jacob Ford. Ford, in fact, was indistinguishable from his colleagues. After leaving Woodbridge for Morristown, he kept an inn, entered local trade, and won appointment to the local courts. His son-in-law was his colleague from Middlesex County. Indeed, one in five lawmakers was the son of a lawmaker. Five were the sons of councilors. Like Ford, nearly two-thirds were named to the local civil list, and nine were appointed to the Council.

Second, these assemblymen were part of an entrepreneurial elite. Some, like Aaron Leaming, Jr., and John Ladd, chose to identify themselves as "yeomen"; others, like Jacob Ford and Daniel Smith, described themselves as "merchants." The distinction between the commercial and agrarian, however, evaporates on closer examination. New Jersey's self-proclaimed "ploughmen" legislators lived in the marketplace. Their estate records were replete with evidences of debts, credits, and mortgages. They were, in sum, entrepreneurs who speculated in lands; operated gristmills and marketed their product; cut, milled, and exported timber; ventured in ironworks; imported rum; and exported fish. No doubt they were not alike: Jacob Ford and Daniel Smith entered markets of different scale. Disagreements sometimes erupted. But consider, for example, Newark's John Low and Perth Amboy's John Stevens. Both lived in the world of trade and speculation but held conflicting land claims.[33] Theirs was a conflict between entrepreneurs, a product of the marketplace.

This reconstruction of a legislative community remains incomplete, however, until the individual lawmaker is linked to policy. It has discovered, first, the underpinnings of community in a pervasive entrepreneurialism and a prevailing world view and, second, the expression of that community in a legislative record to achieve commercial arcadia. And it has found that differences and disagreements among the representatives were contained within a broad consensus. But the description lacks specificity. While a common experience made for a receptiveness to a world view and its complementary policy, social and economic differences suggest corresponding variations in how that vision was received and how that policy was supported. The interests of proprietors and country members, of inland traders and port merchants, collided. The commercial farmer and merchant ship owner participated in different kinds of markets. Social environments--rural and urban--and religious affiliations--pietist, Calvinist, and Arminian--made for contrasting formative experiences. While evidence suggesting nuances in mentality abounds, a paucity of personal papers frustrates investigation into how experiences translated into opinion and how deeply these variances cut into the consensus. Indeed, the evidence is so fragmentary, in fact mute, that even the possibility of dissent against the prevailing mentality cannot be dismissed. But, if the inner world of the lawmaker is lost, his response to policy proposals is recorded in his votes.

The leap from biographical profile to roll call is a hazardous one.[34] The fragments of biographical data represent the social milieu within which the lawmakers came to think about society and policy. Their votes--recorded moments of behavior--are only observable results of their thoughts, disclosing neither mind nor motive. But roll calls do document patterns of disagreement and agreement, or of support for and opposition to policy, and thereby help to discover how profound the differences were that separated the lawmakers. One roll call, for example, on the question to control the export of flour, reveals a division but by itself gives little clue to whether the "yeas" and "nays" were the result of calculated interest or whether they reflected a general response to the policy of trade regulation. Comparing that single division with others on the same subject, in this case commercial regulation, makes such a distinction possible. And, by comparing the responses to one category of proposals with those toward other topics of social and economic policy, this analysis can determine how deep the divisions, or how comprehensive the alignments, on policy were. In sum, the lawmakers' votes on measures to achieve commercial arcadia reveal whether disagreements arose on specific issues, on categories of issues, or on broad policy.

Roll calls recorded between 1739 and 1751 reveal disagreements between rural and urban lawmakers on government's role in promoting and regulating the economy (Table 2.1, items 1-11).[35] Representatives from Perth Amboy and New Brunswick in the East and Burlington in the West supported a set of proposals to establish two trading companies, to control the export of grain and lumber, to curb the wanton cutting of timber in the eastern division, and to encourage New Jersey's shipping. Opposition to these measures tended to cluster in the counties. The division sprang, in part, from conflicting interests between, for example, the inland trader and port merchant or the proprietor and local lumberman. The split was not always categorical, however. Country representatives, such as William Hancock and David Demarest, endorsed the trading companies. Monmouth's members supported the liquor import bill. Nor was the country member so fixed in his position that he could not change his vote on wine imports. Finally, the dissenters' opposition to legislation controlling the size of bricks suggests that something more than interest, perhaps a response to regulation in general, was at play.

Later roll calls reveal that the differences between urban and country members were not so clearly drawn. The urban delegations were exceptional for their consistent support for bills to define the quality of meat and grain exports and to control the fishing industry (Table 2.2, items 1-6). The country members were, with one exception, distinguished for their inconsistency. Their votes tended to turn on the specific commodity in question, suggesting the presence of interest or pragmatism. Thus, the western counties joined the urban delegations on meat but not on grain. The eastern counties supported the grain and less consistently the meat bill. Similarly, the eastern representatives tended to oppose and the western supported the regulation of fishing. Lawmakers also changed their position on meat exports. And six who voted to defeat a measure to regulate fishing on the Delaware River changed their votes when the bill was reintroduced a week later.

Only two members consistently opposed a bounty on flax, hemp, and mulberry trees (Table 2.2, items 7-11). The urban delegations supported this measure, but their country colleagues qualified their endorsement. Dissent again turned on the specific item in question. In 1765, Hendrick Fisher opposed a bounty on hemp but supported one on flax. Ebenezer Miller supported hemp but not flax. Miller later endorsed the bill containing all three commodities, but Fisher dissented. Ebenezer Keasby had opposed both hemp and flax but supported the final measure, perhaps because it included

TABLE 2.1
ECONOMIC AND SOCIAL ISSUES, 1739–1751

Roll Calls*

ASSEMBLYMEN	1	2	3	4	5	6	7	8	9	10	11	12	13	14	15	16
PerthAmboy																
Johnston,A.		+									+				+	
Johnston,L.	+	+									+				−	
Leonard,S.			+	+		+		+	+			−				+
Nevill,S.		+				+	+			+			+	+		
Steele,P.													+			
Johnston,J.					+											
Stevens,J.					+											
Middlesex(NewBrunswick)																
Antill,E.		+									+				+	
Farmer,T.	+		+			+										
Hude,J.		+									+				+	
Hude,R.	+			+				+	+			−				+
Oake,W.				+				+	+			−				−
Middlesex																
Heard,J.													−	+		
Wetherill,J.					−											
Smith,S.					+											
Essex																
Bonnell,J.			+			+										
Ogden,Jos.											−				+	
Low,J.	−				+		−				−		+	+		
Crane,J.				−			−	−	−		−	+	+	+		−
Camp,J.																
Rolph,J.	+															
Vreeland,G.				−				−	−			+				−
Ogden,R.					+											
Somerset																
Dumont,P.		−									−				+	
VanNeste,G.		−									−				+	
Leonard,T.	+															
VanMiddleswardt,J.	−		−	−	+	−	−	−	−	−		+	+	−		+
VanVeghten,D.			−	−		−	−		−			+				−
Fisher,H.				+		−			−				+	−		
Monmouth																
Eaton,J.	−	−	−	−		+	−	−	−	−	−	+	−	+	+	+
Vandervere,C.	−	−									−				+	
Lawrence,Ro.			−	−	−	+		−	−			+				+
Holmes,J.					−											
Bergen																
Demarest,D.	+		−	−	−		−	−	−	−	−	+	+	+	+	−
VanBuskirk,L.	−		−	−	−		−	−	−	−	−		−	−	+	−
Dey,D.					+											
VanVorst,C.					+											

TABLE 2.1 (Cont.)

ASSEMBLYMEN	1	2	3	4	5	6	7	8	9	10	11	12	13	14	15	16
BurlingtonCity																
Pearson,I.	+	+	+	+		+		+	+		+	+			+	−
Smith,R.	+	+		+		+	−	−	−	−	+	+	+	+	+	+
Smith,D.						−			−				+	+		
Deacon,J.					+											
Burlington																
Cooke,W.	+	−	−	−	+	−	−	−	−	−	+	+	+	+	+	+
Stacy,M.	+	+									+				+	
Shinn,T.						+		−			+					+
Wright,S.						−			−				+	+		
Newbold,B.					−											
Gloucester																
Cooper,J.	−	−	−			−	−	−	−	−	−	+	+		+	+
Mickle,J.		−	−	+		−					−	+			+	+
Hopkins,J.						−			−				∓	+		
Ellis,J.					+											
Hunterdon																
Emley,J.		+			+		−			−	+		+	+	+	
Smith,B.	+															
Peace,J.	+															
Doughty,D.				−			−	−				+				+
Mott,W.				−	−		−	−	−			+	∓	+		−
Salem																
Hancock,W.	+	−	−	−	+	+	−		−	−	−	+	+		+	
Reeves,J.		+									+				+	
Smith,R.	∓															
Gibbon,L.				−		+										
Sheppard,M.				−				−	−			+				+
Wood,R.					+											
Brick,J.							−			−			+			
CapeMay																
Leaming,A.Sr.	−	−									−				−	
Young,H.		−	+				−	−			−	+			−	−
Leaming,A.Jr.	−			−		−			−				+			
Willetts,J.				−		−										
Spicer,J.				−	+		−	−	−	−		+	+			−

*TOPICS OF ROLL-CALLS

1. To establish trading companies (June 12, 1740)

2. To set duty on staves (February 7, 1738/9)

3. To set duty on wheat (November 4, 1743)

4. To encourage and improve manufacture of flour (October 26, 1744)

5. To set standards on flour exports (October 4, 1751)

6. To encourage direct importation of rum and wine (November 10, 1743)

7. To maintain bill for encouraging direct importation of rum and wine (January 8, 1747/8)

8. To prevent timber exports on foreign ships (October 16, 1744)

9. To preserve timber in eastern division (October 31, 1744)

10. To preserve timber in eastern division (January 8, 1747/8)

11. To set standards on bricks (January 23, 1738/9)

12. To issue ₤40,000 bills of credit (October 17, 1744)

13. To issue ₤40,000 bills of credit (April 3 and 16, 1746)

14. To issue ₤40,000 bills of credit (December 8, 1747)

15. To place duty on slave imports (January 23, 1738/9)

16. To place duty on slave imports (October 15, 1744)

When the Assembly voted on the same issue within a short interval, the roll calls were collapsed into a single item. On those occasions some lawmakers changed their position, and both their votes were recorded (∓).

TABLE 2.2
ECONOMIC AND SOCIAL ISSUES
1758-1775

Roll-Calls*

Assemblymen	1	2	3	4	5	6	7	8	9	10	11	12	13	14	15	16	17	18	19	20	21	22	23	24	25	26	27	28	29	30	31	32	33	34	35	36	37
PerthAmboy																																					
Stevens,J.																						+	±	+		+	+	+									
Skinner,C.			+	+			+	+	+				−				+		+																		
Johnston,J.			+	+			+	+	+	+	+	+															+							+			
Johnston,J.L.												−			−	∓	+													+	−			−	+	−	−
Combs,J.	+	+	+							+								+	+	+		+								−	+						
Smyth,A.																						+		+		+	+										
Nevill,S.																						±															
Essex																																					
Ogden,John			−	+	+		+	+	+	+		+			+		+					+		+		−	−	−	−	−					−	−	+
Ogden,R.																						+	∓	+		−	−										
Crane,S.	+	−	−	+					+			+		+	+		+		+		−	−	+					−		+		+	+		−	−	−
Garritse,H.	−	−	−							−				+						−	−	+		−						−	+						
Somerset																																					
Fisher,H.	+	+	+	−	−	+	+	−	−	+	−	+	+	+	+	+	+	+	+	+	+	+	+	±	+	+	−	+	−	+	+	+	+	−	−	−	+
Hoagland,J.				−	−		−	−	−													+	∓	±	+	−	−	−									
VanNeste,A.							+			+		+																									
Berrien,J.		+										+			+	+	+	+												+						−	+
Roy,J.	−	+	+							−			+						−	−	+	+								+	+						
Middlesex																																					
Wetherill,J.	+	+	+	−	−	+	−	−	+	+	−	+		+	+	±	−	−	−	−	−	+	−	+	+	+	−	−	−	+	−	−	−	+	−	−	−
Runyon,R.				−					+			+			+	−	+	−								+				+	+		−	−	−	−	
Dunham,A.																														+							
Moores,J.	+		+							−			+									+								+							
Monmouth																																					
Lawrence,Ro.																						−															
Holmes,J.																						−	−	−		+	+										
Lawrence,Ri.	−	−	−			−	−	−	−	−	−		+	+				+	+	+	+	+				+	+	+		+	+	+					
Hartshorne,R.		+											+		+	+	+	+					±			+	+	+		−	+				+	+	+
Anderson,J.				−	+		+	+	+	+		+														+				−	+					+	
Taylor,E.	−	+	+	+							−		+	+	+	−	−	−	−	−		+								−	−	−	−		−	−	+
Bergen																																					
Vangieson,R.				−	−		−	−	−	+		+										+	+			−	−	−	−						−		
Dey,T.	−		+	−	−		−	−	−	−		−	+	+	+	+	−	−	−	−		−	∓			−	−	−	−	−	+		+	−	−	−	
Demarest,J.	−	+	+	−						−			+	+	+	∓	−	−	−	−	+	−				+	−	−	+		−	−			
Freeland,G.																						+	+														
Morris																																					
Ford,J.	+	+	+							−			+						−	−	+	+								+	+						
Winds,W.	+	+	+							−			+					+	+	+		−								+	+						
Sussex																																					
Pettit,N.	+	−	+				+					+				+	+					−								+	+						
VanHorne,T.	+	−	+				+					+							+	+		+								+							

TABLE 2.2 (Cont.)

Roll-Calls*

Assemblymen	1	2	3	4	5	6	7	8	9	10	11	12	13	14	15	16	17	18	19	20	21	22	23	24	25	26	27	28	29	30	31	32	33	34	35	36	37
BurlingtonCity																																					
Read,C.																						+	+	-	-	+	+	+									
Smith,S.				+			+	+	+					-				-	-	+										-	-				+	+	+
Smith,J.			+									-				-	-	+												-	-				+	+	+
Lawrence,JB			+						+	+												+					+	+					+				
Rodman,T.					+							+																+					+				
Hewlings,A.												+			+	+	+	+												-	-				+	+	+
Hewlings,T.	+		+	+					+					+					+	+	-																
Kinsey,J.		+							+					+					+	+	-												+				
Burlington																																					
Borden,J.				+	+		+	+	+	+												+				+	-	+	+								
Doughty,D.				-	+		-	-	-													-				+	+	+	+				+				
Bullock,J.				+								+			+	+	+													-	+				+	+	+
Paxson,H.	+	+	-	+					+			+	+		+	+	+	+		+		-	-	-						-	-	+	+		+	+	+
Sykes,A.	+	+	-								-			+				+	+	+		+	-										-				
Stokes,A.																																					
Gloucester																																					
Clement,S.Sr.																						-	-	-		+	+										
Clement,S.Jr.						+						-																+					+				
Ladd,J.																						+	+				+		+				+				
Cooper,D.				+	+		+	+	+	+		-										-					+		+				+				
Hinchman,J.	+	-		+							-				+	-		+	+	+	-	-								-	+		-		-	-	+
Price,RF	+	+	-	+							+				+	-		+	+	+		-								-	-	+	-		-	-	+
Salem																																					
Hancock,W.																						-	+	+	+	+	-	+									
Miller,E.			-	+	+		-	+	+	+					-	-	+	+		-		-	-			+	+	+	+	-	+		-		+	+	+
Keasby,E.				+	+		-	-	+	+		-																+					+				
Gibbon,G.	+	+	-								-				+	-																+					
Sharp,I.															+		+													-							+
Holme,B.	+	+	-								-				-				+	+		+											-	-			
CapeMay																																					
Leaming,A.Jr.				-	+				-	+		+	+		-			-		-	-	+	+	+		-	-	-	-	+				+	+	+	+
Stillwell,N.										-		-			-													-							+	+	+
Spicer,J.				+	+		+	+	-													+	+	-													
Hand,J.	+	+	-							+					-			-	-	+	+	+										-	+				
Eldridge,E.	+														-			-	-	+	+	+						+									
Cumberland																																					
Elmer,T.	+	+	-							+					+				+	+	+	+						+	+								
Sheppard,J.	+	+	-							+					-				-	+								+					-	-			
Hunterdon																																					
Hart,J.			-	-	+		+	+	+	+		+	+		+	+	+	+								+	-	+	+	+	+				+	-	-	+
Reading,G.				-	-		+	+	+																	+	-	+	+	+	+		+				
Tucker,S.	+	-	+	+								+	+		+	-	+	+	+	+	+	+								+	+				-	-	+
Mehelm,J.	-	+	-										+					+	+	+		+								+	+						
Yard,J.																					+																
Middagh,P.																						-															

*TOPICS OF ROLL CALLS

1. To regulate meat-packing (September 3, 1772)

2. To regulate meat-packing (February 10, 1774)

3. To inspect grain for export (September 17, 1772)

4. To control oystering (November 21, 1769)

5. To control fishing in the Delaware River (June 6, 1765)

6. To control fishing in the Delaware River (June 12, 1765)

7. To set bounty on flax (May 30, 1765)

8. To set bounty on hemp (May 30, 1765)

9. To set bounty on flax, hemp, and mulberry trees (June 8, 1765)

10. To continue bounties on flax, hemp, and mulberry trees (April 19, 1768)

11. To continue bounty on mulberry trees (August 21, 1772)

12. To issue Ƚ100,000 bills of credit (April 23, 1768)

13. That for the sake of the province's welfare, bills of credit must be legal tender (May 31, 1771)

14. To issue Ƚ100,000 bills of credit (February 26 and March 9, 1774)*

15. To expedite recovery of debts between Ƚ10 and Ƚ50 in inferior courts of common pleas (November 30, 1769)

16. Additional legislation making real estate subject to debt collection and "directing the Sheriff in his Proceedings thereon" (October 25 and 26, 1770)*

17. For relief of insolvents (November 29, 1769)

18. For relief of insolvents (December 9, 1771)

19. To prepare bill for relief of insolvents (February 7, 1775)

20. Additional legislation for relief of insolvents (February 9, 1775)

21. For relief of poor (February 4, 1774)

22. To prevent horseracing and gambling (February 22, 1774)

23. To prevent sale of lottery tickets from other colonies, to prevent gambling, and to revive three of New Jersey's own lotteries (December 1, 3, 1760)

24. To support proposed lotteries (August 3, 1758)*

25. To support proposed lotteries (December 9, 1761; March 5, 6, 1762; September 18, 21, 1762)*

26. To prepare bill preventing importation of slaves (April 2, 1761)

27. Whether duty of slave imports should be set so high to amount to prohibition of such imports (December 3, 1761)

28. To lay duty on slave imports (September 24, 1762)

29. To lay duty on slave imports (June 16, 1767)

30. Additional legislature to appoint commissioners to lay out roads and to establish a fund for such purposes (November 30, 1769)

31. To regulate roads and bridges (October 13, 1770)

32. To regulate roads and bridges (September 18, 1772)

33. To regulate roads and bridges (February 7, 1774)

34. To regulate carriages of burthen (June 16, 1767)

35. To continue bill for regulating carriages (March 22, 1770)

36. To continue regulations on wagon wheels (March 20, 1770)

37. To regulate carriages taken on ferries (November 30, 1769)

*Several votes have been combined and recorded as +.

mulberry trees. Spicer supported hemp and flax but opposed the final version. Nor was the alignment a stable one. The first bill passed by a margin of thirteen to eight. Three years later, Fisher and Rinear Vangieson who had originally opposed the measure endorsed its renewal. Only three remained to object.

Paper money seemed the most discussed and explosive topic of economic policy. The lines were drawn between English determination to restrict colonial emissions and provincial insistence that an adequate medium of exchange was vital to the economy. Within the house, the policy prevailed by majorities of three and sometimes five-to-one (Table 2.1, items 12-14; Table 2.2, items 12-14). And no enduring division on the subject appears from the roll calls. Opponents of one measure supported the next. Hendrick Fisher, for example, opposed one emission for Ŀ40,000 and later supported another for more than twice that amount. Those who disagreed on one bill joined to support another. In the 1740s, the house deliberated on proposals to emit Ŀ40,000. The counties defeated a proposal designed to subsidize trading companies at Perth Amboy and Burlington. But the dissenters who remained in 1744 voted for a general emission. This time, only Perth Amboy and New Brunswick objected. But, in 1746 and 1747, both urban and rural members voted to support another emission by margins of three-to-one or more. The alignments were different during the decade before independence and reflected the presence of sectionalism. The legislature decided that an emission of Ŀ100,000 was imperative for the province's well-being and wrestled with imperial prohibitions against making currency a legal tender. In the East, both urban and country delegations supported the emission with the single distinction that Perth Amboy deferred to the imperial policy regarding legal tender. The western delegations were divided with Gloucester, Salem, and Cape May in opposition, Hunterdon and Burlington counties in support, and the port of Burlington divided. But, on the questions of making the emission legal tender, the western counties joined with their eastern counterparts.

The increased number of roll calls recorded after the French and Indian War enables examination of alignments on other categories of policy such as debt and poverty, public morality, and slavery. The policy toward the debtor and indigent population enjoyed broad support (Table 2.2, items 15-21). By margins of three-to-one, the house passed a bill for the relief of insolvents in 1769 and a bill for relief of the poor in 1774. The voting on debt-related issues reveals continuities: eight of the seventeen who supported the relief act of 1769 supported additional bills, and five opposed both. The pattern of support was broad, not always as unequivocal as Fisher's;

51

but, perhaps more important, dissent was not an irreconcilable position. Indeed, Edward Taylor's nearly categorical dissent seems exceptional. Dissent seemed to fix on specific measures. Of the twenty-two who voted on the debtor relief bill of 1769 and a proposal to expedite the recovery of small debts, fourteen supported both, and only one opposed both. Of the remaining seven, four opposed the debtor relief bill but supported legislation regarding small debts, and the other three supported the first but opposed the latter. A measure to make real estate subject to debt collection proved more divisive. Half of those supporting the debtor relief bill of 1769 opposed this measure. But the dissenter was not always an irreconcilable. Within a day, three switched their votes to pass the real estate bill by a vote of eleven to seven. Comparison of the alignment on this proposal with that on the recovery of small debts reveals again the fragmented nature of dissent. Nine supported both; only one opposed both. The response to the poor law of 1774 reveals not only broad support but fragmented opposition. While those in favor of poor legislation were inclined to support debt relief, the opposition was as inclined to support as to oppose debt legislation.

While seeking to discipline the poor, the legislature undertook measures for reforming public morality by regulating gambling and lotteries (Table 2.2, items 22-25). Indeed, legislation directed at public morality and the poor were complementary efforts to secure the moral foundation of commercial arcadia. And again they won broad support and met a fragmented opposition. Of the twenty-two representatives who voted on bills concerning the poor and gambling, thirteen voted in support of both, and no one opposed both. The remaining split their votes in opposite directions: John Wetherill and Robert Friend Price opposed the poor law but supported restrictions on gambling; John Demarest and Henry Paxson supported the first but opposed the latter. Although the votes on gambling and lotteries are insufficient to describe precisely the alignments, they do reveal denominational differences. The Quaker vote reflected the meetinghouse's strictures against games of chance. With the exception of John Ladd, the Friends tended to oppose all forms of lotteries regardless of their origin or form. Non-Quakers, on the other hand, endorsed a policy to endorse domestic lotteries, if licensed, and to prohibit foreign lotteries but were divided on the question whether to restrict gambling and horseracing.

The discussion of slavery provoked more clearly defined divisions in the legislative community (Table 2.1, items 15-16; Table 2.2, items 26-29). The core of the movement against slavery came from the meetinghouse but was joined by other sectors of New Jersey society. Even while Perth Amboy and

Monmouth were diametrically opposed on general economic issues, they joined to prohibit the importation of slaves. Urban and rural members from both sections, even slave owners such as John Wetherill and John Hart, supported restrictions on imports. Dissent came from a comparably varied bloc including Dutch Reformed and Presbyterian lawmakers of Newark and Elizabethtown and the Cape May delegations in the West.

Between 1739 and 1775, the lawmakers disagreed with each other on proposals for promoting the province's social and economic life, but their differences did not translate into a clearly drawn division across the several categories of policy. The urban members supported the several categories of policy more often than not. Dissent, while coming from the counties, defies easy description.[36] Only shortly, in the 1740s, did it approach a coherence in character which distinguished it from the urban response to policy. In general, it was fragmentary and idiosyncratic. Or it may be best described as a rural tendency. It did not characterize all rural members: some voted with their urban colleagues. Those tending to dissent did not agree among themselves about which policies were objectionable. One type of dissenter, John Wetherill, for example, focused on specific items but did not register unequivocal opposition to a category of policy. The Middlesex representative opposed bounties on certain products, supported others, and even changed his position. This pattern of behavior was a common one and is illustrated in the votes on regulating roads and bridges (Table 2.2, items 30-37). Another and less common type of dissenter opposed an entire category of proposals. Monmouth's Richard Lawrence voted against all bounties. But a legislator's opposition to one category of policy did not translate to another. While rejecting bounties and trade regulations, Lawrence favored revisions in the debt laws and restrictions on slave imports. His colleague Edward Taylor, however, voted in the opposite direction and opposed debtor legislation while supporting trade regulation. While dissent was inconsistent and fell short of an alignment on policy, it was rooted in some counties more than others. The delegations from Cape May, Bergen, and Monmouth tended to cast more negative than positive votes; others like Hunterdon and Burlington were inclined to endorse the legislature's policy. Finally, the character of the dissenter's votes--his ability to favor one facet of policy, such as export regulation, and to endorse another, such as paper currency--suggests that differences within the legislature were not so severe that they undermined this community.

While the different voting records suggest the presence of correspondingly different social backgrounds, biographical information gleaned from such sources as estate inventories and church records yields at best fragmentary clues for making an explanation.[37] Concrete evidence of interest and religion is most easily found; and, no doubt, the one guided voting on commercial policy just as the other played a part in the deliberations on public morality and slavery. But policy did not always touch the lawmaker directly. The western lawmakers were not affected by a proposal to curb the cutting of timber in the eastern division. The urban lawmakers' proclivity to support legislative policy seemed more than the product of the sum of their interests. That record suggests the presence of another dimension that is less tangible than interest and only partially revealed by the biographical fragments. The relationship between residence--or association with a community-- and voting suggests the presence of formative experiences. If life in Perth Amboy bred a distinct form of voting, the rural experience produced an inclination to dissent. And life in some rural communities, such as Bergen County, produced a marked inclination to dissent. The evidence is suggestive yet insufficient to yield a full explanation. Theunis Dey and Jacob Spicer appear to have been two examplars of this commercial arcadic world, but both tended to dissent on social and economic policy. Yet Somerset's "mechanic" lawmaker Hendrick Fisher tended to support the same proposals.

What distinguished the one lawmaker who was disposed to support the legislative policy from his colleague who was inclined to dissent was something more than interest, but less than ideology, or what appears to have been a difference in temperament or disposition. Two types of lawmakers participated in this legislative community: the naysayer or conservative and the yeasayer or activist. The naysayer's conservatism was not ideological. He lived in commercial arcadia and responded to its vision, but with hesitancy. Thus, he was reluctant at times to embrace government programs to improve or regulate commerce or changes in the legal system. That he was inconsistent suggests that his conservatism was temperamental or a cast of mind acquired from his rural experience. That he did not agree with others of the same temperament on what to oppose confirms that his conservatism was less than ideological. The yeasayer could be found throughout the legislative community. By temperament, he was an activist or one who was more willing than his conservative colleague to endorse innovation, to experiment with government projects, or to tamper with the legal system.

This distinction in temperament seems but another manifestation of the differences contained within this legislative community. By joining the commercial and arcadic, this political elite had created a synthesis, albeit an unstable one. Such a fusion was not unique to the province. If Philip Fithian had looked more closely, he might have discovered that beneath that veneer of gentility Virginia's planters were, in fact, entrepreneurs little different than New Jersey's own.[38] While New Jersey's lawmakers took their bread in the marketplace and responded to the projectors of commercial growth, they clung to the communal and bucolic. While entrepreneurs, they chose to identify themselves as a yeomanry. Even the urban merchant dreamed of retreating from the bustle of the countinghouse to the greenness of his country estate. If these lawmakers responded favorably to Samuel Atkinson's Interest of New-Jersey and William Livingston's poetic evocation of "the pleasures of a rural life," they were not in agreement how to strike a balance between the two.[39] And, because some were less comfortable in embracing the modern than others, differences in temperament arose. But it was this synthesis with its tensions which made for a provincial political community.

NOTES

1. "Philopatriae," New American Magazine (Mar., 1758), 51. Spicer's will, Manuscript Wills, 253 E; "Diary of Jacob Spicer, 1755-6," ed. William A. Ellis, Proceedings of the New Jersey Historical Society, LXIII (July, 1945), 175-76; Spicer's address to Assembly, Feb. 22, 1755, Spicer Papers, New Jersey Historical Society.

2. Douglas Greenberg, "The Middle Colonies in Recent American Historiography," The William and Mary Quarterly, 3rd Ser., XXXVI (July, 1979), 396-427; Peter O. Wacker, "New Jersey's Cultural Landscape Before 1800," in Papers Presented at the Second Annual New Jersey History Symposium (Newark, 1971), 35-62; Gerlach, Prologue to Independence, 3-36. See also Thomas Jefferson Wertenbaker, The Founding of American Civilization: The Middle Colonies (New York, 1938); and John E. Pomfret, Colonial New Jersey: A History (New York, 1973), 192-246.

3. James Alexander and Robert Hunter Morris to Ferdinand John Paris, May 30, 1749, N.J.Archs., VII, 262-63. Also R. H. Morris to J. Alexander, July 28, 1747, ibid., VI, 472-73.

4. Assembly petition to king, Oct. 19, 1749, ibid., VII, 351-56; Assembly to Belcher, Feb. 15, 1751, Votes and Proceedings; New-York Weekly Post-Boy, Feb. 17, 1745/6, in N.J.Archs., VI, 292-96; Assembly to L. Morris, May 2, 1745, ibid., XV, 413.

5. Bailyn, Origins of American Politics, 64; Gerlach, Prologue to Independence, 20. Also see Patricia U. Bonomi, "The Middle Colonies: Embryo of the New Political Order," in Alden T. Vaughn and George Athan Billias, eds., Perspectives on Early American History: Essays in Honor of Richard B. Morris (New York, 1973), 63-92.

6. The following discussion of the assemblymen does not attempt to include every member who sat in the legislature between 1738 and 1755. Rather, it seeks to be illustrative. Also, in order to avoid exhaustive references to sources, citations have been limited. For complete list of assemblymen and sources, see Appendix.

7. James H. Levitt, For Want of Trade: Shipping and the New Jersey Ports, 1680-1783 (Newark, NJ, 1981), 13-44, 68-69; Thomas L. Purvis, "Origins and Patterns of Agrarian Unrest in New Jersey, 1735 to 1754," The William and Mary Quarterly, 3rd Ser., XXXIX (Oct., 1982), 600-627; L. Morris to Duke of Newcastle, June 2, 1732, Calendar of State Papers, Colonial Series, XXXIX, 135; L. Morris to Board of Trade, Oct. 4, 1733, ibid., XL, 206-7.

8. R. H. Morris to Alexander, July 28, 1747, N.J.Archs., VI, 472-74; Alexander to John Coxe, May 2, 1748, ibid., VII, 122-24; Alexander to R. H. Morris, April 3, 1751, The Stevens Family Papers, New York-New Jersey Boundary Dispute, reel 24, 355, microfilm at The New Jersey Historical Society, ed. Mirriam V. Studley, Charles F. Cummings, and Thaddeus J. Krom.

9. John Roger McCreary, "Ambition, Interest and Faction: Politics in New Jersey, 1702-1738" (Ph.D. diss., University of Nebraska, 1971), 253-54, 305-15; John Robert Strassburger, "The Origins and Development of the Morris Family in Society and Politics of New York and New Jersey, 1630-1746" (Ph.D. diss., Princeton University, 1976), 204-5, 315-18; R. H. Morris to Alexander, [Feb., 1748], N.J.Archs., VII, 107-10; Samuel Nevill to John Stevens, Mar. 15, 1750/1, Stevens Family Papers, reel 2, 240; James Birket, Some Cursory Remarks. . . (New Haven, CT, 1916), 47-48.

10. R. H. Morris to Alexander, [Feb., 1748], N.J.Archs., VII, 109.

11. Joseph W. Dally, Woodbridge and Vicinity; The Story of a New Jersey Township (New Brunswick, NJ, 1873), 184-99; Ryan, "Six Towns," 16; Alexander to Coxe, Feb. 6, 1748/9,

Paris Papers, X, 52, The New Jersey Historical Society; New-York Gazette, July 29, 1754.

12. George Crawford Beekman, Early Dutch Settlers of Monmouth County, New Jersey (Freehold, NJ, 1901), 54-66; John E. Pomfret, The Province of East New Jersey, 1609-1722 (Princeton, NJ, 1962), 338-39; Ryan, "Six Towns," 16, 30-32.

13. Purvis, "Origins and Patterns of Agrarian Unrest"; Gary S. Horowitz, "New Jersey Land Riots, 1745-1755" (Ph.D. diss., The Ohio State University, 1966).

14. Theodore Thayer, As We Were: The Story of Old Elizabethtown (Elizabeth, NJ, 1964), 14-92; Ryan, "Six Towns," 29-30.

15. Alexander to Coxe, Feb. 6, 1748/9, Paris Papers, X, 52. David Ogden to Alexander, Dec. 12, 1743, Rutherford Collection, New Jersey, 101, The New-York Historical Society; petition of Jonathan Crane, Nov. 16, 23, and 28, 1738, Votes and Proceedings; Records of the Town of Newark. . ., Collections of the New Jersey Historical Society, VI (1864), 131-56.

16. Alexander to R. H. Morris, Apr. 3, 1751, Stevens Family Papers, New York-New Jersey Boundary Dispute, reel 24, 355; Alexander to Coxe, Feb. 6, 1748/9, Paris Papers, X, 52. Alexander to Paris, Dec. 1, 1746, ibid., X, 21; New-York Weekly Post-Boy, Feb. 17, 1745/6, in N.J.Archs., VI, 292-96; "By the Council of Proprietors of the Eastern Division," Mar. 25, 1746, ibid., 315; "Notice of Nathaniel Wheeler and others . . .," Aug. 11, 1746, ibid., 365-67; "An Answer to the Council of Proprietors. . .," ibid., VII, 48; "To his Excellency Jonathan Belcher. . .," 1747, ibid., 63-64; M. Vreelandt to Parker, The New-York Gazette, Mar. 16, 1747, in ibid., XII, 341-46; J. L. to Parker, The New-York Gazette, May 18, 1747, in ibid., 357-59; Belcher to Jacob Wendell, Oct. 5, 1747, Belcher Letterbooks, VIII, 100-101, The Massachusetts Historical Society; and Mar. 18, 1748/9, Votes and Proceedings.

17. Richard W. Lenk, "Hackensack, New Jersey, from Settlement to Suburb, 1686-1804" (Ph.D. diss., New York University, 1968), 7-66. Still helpful despite its philio-pietistic tone is Adrian C. Leiby, The Revolutionary War in the Hackensack Valley: The New Jersey Dutch and the Neutral Ground, 1775-1783 (New Brunswick, NJ, 1962).

18. Journals of Henry Melchior Muhlenberg, I, 284, 327-28.

19. Alexander to Coxe, Feb. 6, 1748/9, Paris Papers, X, 52.

20. Pownall, Topographical Description, 99-100; Kalm, Travels, I, 116-22; Wacker, Land and People, 52; Levitt, For Want of Trade, 41.

21. Wacker, Land and People, 182-83; Gerlach, Prologue to Independence, 20-22.

22. Powers, "Wealth and Poverty," 27-65; Robert T. Trindell, "The Ports of Salem and Greenwich in the Eighteenth Century," New Jersey History, LXXXVI (Winter, 1968), 199-214.

23. Levitt, For Want of Trade, 42-44; Kalm, Travels, I, 321.

24. R. Smith to J. Smith, 19, 6 month, 1747, Smith Family Papers, Chronological Series, II, 266, The Library Company of Philadelphia; R. Smith to J. Smith, 19, second month, 1747, ibid., III, 7; Samuel Smith to J. Smith, 30, 5 month, 1757, John Smith Correspondence, Historical Society of Pennsylvania; John Smith to Richard Partridge, 22, 4 month, 1756, ibid.; Paris to Alexander, Jan. 27, 1746, Statesmen Autograph Collection, The New Jersey Historical Society; Paris to Alexander, Feb. 13, 1746, Paris Papers, X, 20; Alexander to Paris, Apr. 16, 1748, ibid., H, 5; Paris to Alexander, Feb. 10, 1746/7, Rutherford Collection, New Jersey, 121.

25. Belcher to Charles Read, Aug. 1, 1753, Belcher Letterbooks, X, 181-83.

26. W. Franklin to Board of Trade, May 10, 1763, N.J.Archs., IX, 387.

27. Jon Butler, "Power, Authority, and the Origins of American Denominational Order: The English Churches in the Delaware Valley, 1680-1730," Transactions of the American Philosophical Society, LXVIII (1978), 46-47.

28. Wacker, Land and People, 181-84, 408-10; Toothman, "Trenton, New Jersey," 229-43; Kalm, Travels, I, 117.

29. Petitions from Hunterdon County, Oct. 11, 18, and 19, 1743, Oct. 25 and 31, 1744, Votes and Proceedings; disputed Hunterdon election, Oct. 20 and 21, 1743, ibid.; dispute over Hunterdon's courthouse, June 17, 1765, ibid.

30. L. Morris to Benjamin Smith, Jan. 3, 1739[/40], The Papers of Lewis Morris, ed. W. A. Whitehead, Collections of the New Jersey Historical Society, IV (1852), 73-80.

31. Hamilton Schuyler, A History of St. Michael's Church (Princeton, NJ, 1926), 108-9.

32. Theodore Thayer, Colonial and Revolutionary Morris County (Morristown, NJ, 1975), 54-104. See also Bernard Bailyn, "Politics and Social Structure in Virginia," in James Morton Smith, ed., Seventeenth-Century America: Essays in Colonial History (Chapel Hill, NC, 1959), 90-115.

33. Purvis, "Origins and Patterns of Agrarian Unrest"; and for a general discussion Edward Countryman, "'Out of the Bounds of the Law': Northern Land Rioters in the Eighteenth Century," in Young, American Revolution, 39-69.

34. Donald R. Matthews, The Social Background of Political Decision Makers (New York, 1954).

35. Since there were no relevant roll calls after 1751 and not again until 1758, this seemed a logical point to divide the roll calls into two separate tables.

36. Analysis of the divisions was aided by determining each delegation's strength of support for social and economic policies. Each delegation received a policy support score. This score was achieved by counting the total positive and negative votes cast by each delegation, then subtracting the negative from the positive, and finally dividing by the total number of roll calls. The range was from +1.0, which signified absolute support, to -1.0, which signified categorical rejection.

Perth Amboy	.51	Burlington City	.43
Middlesex	.16	Burlington County	.34
New Brunswick	.70	Gloucester	.05
Rest of County	.01	Salem	.14
Monmouth	.00	Cape May	-.17
Essex	.03	Hunterdon	.34
Somerset	.08	Cumberland	.36
Bergen	-.37		
Morris	.55		
Sussex	.60		

See Charles M. Dollar and Richard J. Jensen, Historian's Guide to Statistics:Quantitative Analysis and Historical Research (New York, 1971), 111-16.

37. This discussion was aided by Lee Benson, Turner and Beard: American Historical Writing Reconsidered (New York, 1960), 214-28; and Jackson Turner Main, Political Parties before the Constitution (Chapel Hill, NC, 1973), 32- 33. The emphasis on the temperamental dimension is a departure from that work. Also helpful was A. R. Luria, Cognitive Development: Its Cultural and Social Foundations, trans. Martin Lopez-Morillas and Lynn Solotaroff, ed. Michael Cole (Cambridge, MA, 1976).

38. Aubrey C. Land, "Economic Base and Social Structure: The Northern Chesapeake in the Eighteenth Century," The Journal of Economic History, XXV (Dec., 1965), 639-54.

39. [William Livingston], Philosophic Solitude: or, The Choice of A Rural Life . . . (New York, 1747), 13.

CHAPTER THREE

THE ASSEMBLY: AN INVERTEBRATE INSTITUTION

In June 1768, the freeholders of Somerset County went to the polls and after two days chose Hendrick Fisher as their representative.   Rising to thank his neighbors for "the repeated and distinguishing marks of your sincere respect for my person," he reflected that he had devoted "a considerable part of the appointed number of my days in the public service."   He might have surveyed his life's accomplishments with satisfaction. Fisher had come from Germany as a child and, as a young adult, plunged into his community's life, first in the Reformed Church where he became a deacon and lay preacher and then in politics. In 1740, he was elected to the legislature.   Though dismissed for failure to meet the requirements for naturalization, he returned in 1745 and was now about to begin his eighth term. The election had been conducted with "the greatest coolness and good order."   Indeed, he had stood unchallenged.   Pausing to reflect on the burdens of service, he owned a yearning to spend "the remainder of my moments, in a more inactive, and a retired life."   Yet the solicitations of friends and his worries for "the distressed circumstances of the province" prevailed upon his conscience and persuaded him to remain in the legislature.[1]

Fisher had struck a conventional pose, that of the selfless public servant, but he had not in that fleeting moment revealed what public service meant to him.   Certainly it did not have the same meaning that it had for his one-time colleague Lawrence Van Buskirk.   Bergen County was Van Buskirk's bailiwick.   At maturity, he assumed his family's place in the community, became a pillar of the church, and represented the county in the legislature.   When he looked beyond and at the surrounding English society, his heart welled up in righteous indignation. He returned home from the legislature grumbling at the "worldly gentry" who corrupted the provincial society and at a governor who seemed an avowed atheist.[2]   When attending the house, he sat silently and made little impress on the house proceedings.   A conservative by nature, he regularly voted against proposals to improve the economy.   Fisher, in contrast, extended himself beyond.   He rode the circuit with Reverend Theodore Frelinghuysen and returned home to translate the minister's word into English.   In the legislature, he won recognition as "a man of consequence."   During the 1760s, he regularly presided over the committee of the whole.   In 1765, he represented the province at the Stamp Act Congress; and, in the next decade, he became president of the Provincial Congress.   By temperament, he was an activist and builder.   While in his seventieth year, he promoted the establishment of Queens College and became president of its board of trustees. In the house, he was more open to economic reform or innovation than his naysaying colleague.[3]

The record of Richard Bradbury's public life is meager but in its sparseness revealing. Elected in 1754, he made the journey from Essex's outlying Acquackanonk Township to take his seat at Perth Amboy. For the next five years, he journeyed to Burlington and then to Perth Amboy, sat quietly, and made little impress on the house's proceedings. One-hundred-eight committees were appointed, but he was named to only two--one to inform the governor that the house approved his military requests and another to revise a bill for securing the frontiers. Then, tiring of the burdens of service, he informed the house of his resignation and receded into obscurity. He spent the remainder of his years farming and operating his mill.

James Kinsey seemed immediately at home in the Assembly. His father had presided over Pennsylvania's lower house, and he had grown up listening to political discussion. On election to the New Jersey house, he determined to make his presence felt. Within months, he was shaping house policy and leading it in its dispute with the governor over the robbery of the East Jersey treasury. Two years later, his colleagues sent him to represent the province at the Continental Congress; and, after the Revolution, he presided over the state Supreme Court.

These sketches provoke the historical imagination and thereby guide the strategy for penetrating within the doors of the Assembly. Kinsey and Fisher, Van Buskirk and Bradbury served in different ways, suggesting that they came with different conceptions of the legislative task. Van Buskirk and Bradbury represented a type common to the North American legislatures. This lawmaker was the embodiment of that localist whom William Smith encountered in the New York legislature-- that "plain, illiterate, husbandman, whose views seldom extended farther than to the regulation of highways, the destruction of wolves, wildcats, and foxes, and the advancement of the other little interests of the particular counties, which they were chosen to represent."[4] He came expecting the legislature to attend to the building of a dam, the maintenance of boundaries, or the preservation of game. The volume and content of the petitions sent to the legislature suggest that these expectations were shared by this political community. Indeed, these localist concerns became such an important part of the public business that the house was forced for the sake of efficiency to limit the number of petitions submitted. But the house was called upon to respond to the governor's requests and to imperial policy. Another type of legislator--like Kinsey and Fisher--attended to these matters. His horizons extended beyond his district to include provincial affairs. He spoke for the house's rights and for provincial liberties. Both the localist and provincial assemblyman attended to the interests of his constituents, but the one was less interested in the more remote and sometimes abstract issues of constitutional right than the other.

Both types, the localist and the provincial, were by virtue of their election called upon to attend to both agendas but acted in an invertebrate legislature. Policy was discussed and made in an institutional setting that lacked standing committees or party organizations, in sum, those modern means to socialize the initiate, to provide cues and instructions, or to organize the membership. The localist came with his set of priorities and predispositions, sat quietly as a backbencher, and no matter the length of service remained a localist. In turn, he allowed his colleague who came already concerned with larger issues to become an activist. This was an atomized assemblage composed of members who came with different mental maps and different social orientations but without the means to bring these disparate elements together into an organized policy-making body.[5]

The first step toward discovering the interior of the legislature is the recognition that the participants came with different understandings of public service and played correspondingly different roles. The evidence pointing toward this path of inquiry, that is, toward the interior or subjective world, is simultaneously suggestive and mute. In the absence of personal papers, it is difficult to penetrate and reconstruct Richard Bradbury's interior world in its complexity and richness. He has left only a few bits of information, at best a shadow. Comparison of that shadow outline with those of other lawmakers does, however, reveal important differences. The importance of a legislative seat--the tangible rewards and opportunities--is easily determined. Biographical data and behavior suggest that the lawmakers took these opportunities in different ways. Career lines reveal the scope of the assemblymen's public lives, and their record of participation in the house provides the means for distinguishing the localist from the provincial, the backbencher from the activist. Linking these data together is often hazardous. For example, while lists of appointments reveal differences in the scope of the lawmakers' public lives, the civil lists only document success and not the frustrated ambition of a would-be provincial activist. The nature of the evidence requires an inquiry by indirection and warns against placing every lawmaker in a category. But the shadowy outlines, once reconstructed, and the differences, once appreciated, allow for an understanding of different types of legislators.

Election to the Assembly signified that the lawmaker had arrived at the apex of his community and brought opportunity to render services to his constituents and to himself. In Salem County, Richard Hancock and his neighbors were ever projecting schemes for the draining of marshes, erecting barriers against the tide, and clearing creeks for navigation; and, when they turned to the general court for approval, they expected their representative to shepherd their petitions through the house. Hancock introduced petitions from Cohansie, Mannington, Elsinboro, and Salem creeks, served on committees to review their merits, and then introduced bills approving their projects.[6] Gloucester's freeholders relied on John Ladd, the Coopers, and the Clements to advance their appeals for the right to drain and clear streams along Newton, Timber, and Woodbury creeks.[7] So, too, Bergen's representative David Demarest introduced a bill in response to a petition for a toll bridge over the Hackensack River, and Shobal Smith introduced similar legislation supporting his constituents' petitions.[8]

The "ploughmen" of Essex County and the proprietors of Perth Amboy saw elections as crucial to their interest. Often the cause was less dramatic. The builder of a dam or waterway who provoked protest expected his representative to protect his interest. Sometimes a delegation split. Joseph Cooper and John Mickle disagreed on the building of a bridge at Cooper's Creek, and later David Cooper and Samuel Clement, Sr., differed on a petition to build a bridge over Newton Creek.[9] In 1765, the Hunterdon delegation split on the proposal to remove the courthouse from Trenton. And, two years before, Jacob Spicer, skillfully outmaneuvering his colleague, had the Cape May courthouse relocated in his neighborhood.[10] In Salem County, the question arose whether public fairs be maintained or discontinued. Both parties petitioned the legislature, and each was represented by one of the county's two representatives.[11]

During his stay in the legislature, the lawmaker gained access to the governor. Indeed, he was courted and his advice was sought. And, when he returned home, he was often assured of his influence over his district's civil and military lists. Governor Belcher wrote Leaming and Spicer that their recommendations were sufficient for appointment to the Cape May civil lists. Notwithstanding the objections of the proprietors, John Low was assured that his opinion would be considered when it came time to name Essex County's officials.[12] Such influence secured a local elite's position, sometimes in the most blatant ways. For example, John Hinchman was appointed sheriff of Gloucester County on the eve of the 1754 elections. As presiding officer at the polls, he wielded such influence that, once the votes were counted, the opposition registered its complaint to the Assembly.[13]

These reasons were sufficient to induce Jerseymen to make the trip to the legislature. For some, they remained the principal attraction. Others, however, found opportunity to participate in the administration of provincial matters, sometimes to their own profit. During the imperial wars, the house was called upon to raise troops in defense of the province and to allocate funds for their supply. After approving such requests, it appointed commissioners to administer the purchase of supplies and provided that they receive 5 percent of the amount spent. In 1746, the Assembly turned to its own Hendrick Fisher, John Eaton, Pontius Steele, Jacob Spicer, and John Low to supply the provincial contingent against Canada. During the last war with France, John Stevens, Samuel Nevill, Hendrick Fisher, and Jacob Spicer regularly received such appointments. And, as the house recognized the need to provide quarters for provincial and British troops stationed in the province, it appointed Fisher and Robert Ogden to supply the newly constructed barracks.[14]

For some, election meant admission to other provincial offices. Charles Read served for two terms, his first as speaker, and was then appointed to the Supreme Court and Council. John Ladd sat for a single term during which he distinguished himself by his unremitting support for the administration. Shortly after, he was elevated to the Council. Samuel Smith and John Stevens resigned their seats to take their places in the Council. Governors recommended Edward Antill, Andrew Johnston, James Hude, John Brown Lawrence, and Thomas Leonard. In addition to Read, two other speakers-- Bonnell and Nevill--were appointed to the Supreme Court.

Something less tangible than offices lured some to engage in provincial politics and motivated Leaming and Spicer to spend their spare moments compiling the province's Grants, Concessions, and Original Constitutions. Leaming observed this in Charles Read. On returning from England, Read "determined to enter upon State for which nature seemed to have designed him." He seemed addicted to politics. "Industrious in the most unremitting degree," he climbed rapidly. "No man," Leaming recalled, "knew so well as he how to riggle himself into office." Soon he became principal adviser to governors and "took the whole disposal of all offices" upon himself.[15] English educated, learned in the law, and a political activist, Read stood in marked contrast to Richard Bradbury and his fellow localists. These men were members of the board of freeholders, tax assessors, overseers of the poor, moderators of town meetings, and deacons in the church. They looked to the provincial government to settle local affairs or to secure appointments to the local civil list. Service in the legislature enhanced their position at home. It did not represent opportunity to enter a larger sphere of action. And, thus, they stayed for a short time.

Read and Bradbury were two easily distinguished types. But the differences between the localist and provincial lawmakers were not always so readily apparent until the house began its deliberations. In the course of a session, the house appointed numerous ad hoc committees to draft legislation enabling farmers to stop the tide at Cohansey Creek, to set tax policy, to draft messages to the governor and Council, and to prepare a petition to the king. Committee assignments did not reflect influence in the same sense that membership on a standing committee of a modern legislature might. But, because they were made in the course of deliberations and on an ad hoc basis and because there were so many made--nearly one thousand between 1738 and 1775--they reflect participation (Table 3.1). Counting committees is, no doubt, a crude device, but the results in the extreme ranges reveal the presence of an activist and backbencher. The first and most apparent discovery of this investigation is the marked discrepancies in the number of committee assignments among the members. For example, sixty-nine committees were named in the Sixteenth Assembly (1746-1748), but the members were named to as many as thirty-nine and to as few as four. In the succeeding Assembly, eight received only one assignment. Burlington County's William Cooke was most active with fourteen, but his neighbor Joshua Bispham was one of the least active with three assignments.

In the last Assembly, Fisher and Kinsey appeared on one-third of the 131 committees, while four of their colleagues--Henry Garritse, Azariah Dunham, Jonathan Hand, and Eli Eldridge--were each named to two. The activists' careers illustrate the nature of this institution. Fisher had achieved his importance. During his first term, he had failed to gain recognition or appointment to a single committee; in his second, he became one of the house's more active committeemen; and, by the end of his career, he was one of the most frequently appointed. His achievement does not reflect the presence of a seniority system. Kinsey was a prominent committeeman in his first term. So, too, Robert Lawrence made an immediate imprint on the proceedings and was named to a committee to confer with the governor and another to correspond with the agent in London. But William Mott was appointed to nineteen committees during his eleven-year service, or to 8 percent of the total named. The achievement of Kinsey and Lawrence was the product of interest and the force of personality. Or some like Mott and Garritse preferred the role of backbencher.

TABLE 3.1
PARTICIPATION IN ASSEMBLY PROCEEDINGS
COMMITTEE ASSIGNMENTS AND SPEAKERS*

DISTRICT AND ASSEMBLYMEN**	Assemblies											
	11 (1738-39)	12 (1740-42)	13 (1743-44)	14 (1744)	15 (1745)	16 (1746-48)	17 (1749-51)	18 (1751-54)	19 (1754-60)	20 (1761-68)	21 (1769-71)	22 (1772-75)
Perth Amboy												
Johnston,A.	2	S	S									
Johnston,L.	3	2					3					
Leonard,S.			2	3								
Nevill,S.			1	S	S	S/1	S		S/1	S		
Steele,P.					2	2						
Johnston,J.L.								3	2			
Stevens,J.								2	1	1		
Smyth,A.									1	2		
Johnston,J.										2		
Skinner,C.										S/1	S	S
Johnston,J.											3	
Combs,J.												3
Middlesex												
Antill,E.	1											
Hude,J.	1											
Farmer,T.		1	1		X							
Hude,R.		1		2								
Oake,W.				1								
Kearney,P.						1						
Heard,J.					2	3						
Moores,J.					3							
Smith,J.							3					
Wetherill,J.							2	2	2	2	2	2
Smith,S.								3				
Runyon,R.										3	3	
Dunham,A.												3
Moores,J.												3
Essex												
Bonnell,J.	S		2									
Ogden,J.	1											
Low,J.		2			1	3		3				
Crane,J.					3	3	2					
Camp,J.								3				
Ogden,R.								2	1	2		
DeHart,J.									3			

Note: 1, activist; 2, moderate; 3, backbencher; S, speaker; X, insufficient data.

TABLE 3.1 (Cont.)

DISTRICT AND ASSEMBLYMEN**	11 (1738-39)	12 (1740-42)	13 (1743-44)	14 (1744)	15 (1745)	16 (1746-48)	17 (1749-51)	18 (1751-54)	19 (1754-60)	20 (1761-68)	21 (1769-71)	22 (1772-75)
Ogden,J.									3	2	2	
Crane,S.										3	S/2	S/2
Rolph,J.		3										
Vreeland,G.			3	3								
Bradbury,R.									3			
Garritse,H.												3
Monmouth												
Eaton,J.	2	1	2	1	1	1	1					
Vandervere,C.	3	3										
Lawrence,Ro.			1	1	1	S/1	1	1	S/2			
Holmes,J.							3	3	1	X		
Anderson,J.										3		
Hartsorne,R.											2	
Taylor,R.											3	3
Lawrence,Ri.										2		2
Somerset												
Dumont,P.	3											
VanNeste,E.	3											
Leonard,T.		2										
VanMiddleswardt,J.		3	3	3	3	3	3	3				
VanVeghten,D.			3	3								
Fisher,H.						3	2	1	1	1	1	1
Hoagland,J.									3	3		
VanNeste,A.										3		
Berrien,J.											2	
Roy,J.												3
Bergen												
Demarest,D.	3	2	3	3	3	3						
VanBuskirk,L.	3	3	3	3	3	3	3					
Dey,D.							3	3				
VanVorst,C.								3				
Vangieson,R.									3	3		
Vreeland,G.									3			
Dey,T.										3	3	3
Demarest,J.											3	3
Morris												
Ford,J.												3
Winds,W.												3
Sussex												
Barton,J.												3
Pettit,N.												3

TABLE 3.1 (Cont.)

DISTRICT AND ASSEMBLYMEN**	11 (1738–39)	12 (1740–42)	13 (1743–44)	14 (1744)	15 (1745)	16 (1746–48)	17 (1749–51)	18 (1751–54)	19 (1754–60)	20 (1761–68)	21 (1769–71)	22 (1772–75)
VanHorne,T.												3
BurlingtonCity												
Pearson,I.	2	2	2	2								
Smith,R.	1	1	1	1	1	1	3					
Smith,D.					3	3	3					
Deacon,J.									3			
Read,C.									S	1		
Smith,S.									2	2		
Lawrence,J.B.										2		
Rodman,T.										2		
Hewlings,A.											2	
Smith,J.											2	
Hewlings,T.												3
Kinsey,J.												1
Burlington												
Cook,W.	2	1	1	1	1	1	1	1				
Stacy,W.	2	1										
Shinn,T.		X	3	3								
Wright,S.					3	3						
Bispham,J.								3				
Newbold,B.								2	3			
Stokes,S.									3			
Paxson,H.									2			
Borden,J.										1	2	2
Bullock,J.											3	
Sykes,A.												3
Gloucester												
Cooper,J.	1	1	2	2	3	1	1					
Mickle,J.	3	3	3	3								
Hopkins,E.					3	3						
Hinchman,J.							3					
Mickle,J.							3	3				
Ellis,J.							3					
Clement,S.Sr.									2	3		
Ladd,J.									2			
Clement,S.Jr.										3		
Cooper,D.										2		
Hinchman,J.											2	1
Price,R.F.											2	2
Salem												
Hancock,W.	2	2	3	3	2	2	2	3	2	2		

TABLE 3.1 (Cont.)

DISTRICT AND ASSEMBLYMEN**	11 (1738-39)	12 (1740-42)	13 (1743-44)	14 (1744)	15 (1745)	16 (1746-48)	17 (1749-51)	18 (1751-54)	19 (1754-60)	20 (1761-68)	21 (1769-71)	22 (1772-75)
Reeves,J.	3											
Brick,J.		3				3	3	3				
Gibbon,L.			3									
Smith,R.		X	X									
Sheppard,M.					3							
Wood,R.								3				
Miller,E.									2	3	2	
Keasby,E.										3		
Gibbon,G.											3	2
Sharp,I.											2	
Holme,E.												3
CapeMay												
Leaming,A.Sr.	2	2										
Young,H.	2				3							
Leaming,A.Jr.		3	3		3	2	1	1	2	3	2	
Willets,J.			3									
Spicer,J.					3	3	2	1	2	2		
Stillwell,N.										3	3	
Hand,J.											3	3
Elridge,E.												3
Cumberland												
Elmer,T.												3
Sheppard,J.												2
Hunterdon												
Emley,J.	2					3	3	2				
Smith,B.	2	2										
Peace,J.		3										
Doughty,D.			X	3	3					3		
Mott,W.			X	3	3	3	3	2				
Smith,A.			X									
Middagh,P.									3			
Yard,J.									1			
Hart,J.										3	2	
Reading,G.										2		
Tucker,S.											1	1
Mehelm,J.												2

* This analysis deviates in method from that introduced by Jack P. Greene. ["Foundations of Political Power in the Virginia House of Burgesses, 1720-1776," The William and Mary Quarterly, 3rd ser., XVI (Oct., 1959), 485-506.] In order to identify leaders in the southern legislatures, Greene first distinguished between important and routine committees, gave numerical values to the different categories, and multiplied the value of committee assignments. Introducing this subjective element into the analysis seemed premature. Instead, committees were simply counted. Once the assignments were tabulated, it was clear that some kind of index had to be created to account for the variations in both the number of assignments to the lawmakers and the number of committees created in each assembly. First, the highest ranking member in an assembly was identified and used as a standard. Those who received one-third or less that number of assignments were placed in the lowest category (3); those over that number but less than two-thirds the standard were placed in a middle category (2); and those above were placed in the top rank (1). While this coding system established uniformity of measure from assembly to assembly, problems remained with those who served during only part of a legislature or were chosen speaker and thus were not eligible for appointment to the total number of committees. To give these members a score an artificial number needed to be created. This number was established by determining the rate of participation during the time of eligibility and then projecting that to the assembly's entire lifetime. In some cases, however, the data remained insufficient to make such a projection.

** Some members were identified with two districts. Perth Amboy was part of Middlesex County. Thus, Samuel Nevill who resided in Perth Amboy was elected to the Middlesex delegations in 1743, 1754, and 1761 and to Perth Amboy's in 1744, 1745, 1746, and 1749. Philip Kearney, another resident of the port, was part of the county delegation in 1746. Some members moved. George Vreeland represented Essex from 1743 to 1744 and later Bergen from 1754 to 1760. And Daniel Doughty served for Hunterdon from 1743 to 1745 and in 1761 was elected from Burlington County.

While counting committee assignments reveals the different kinds of participation, the distinction between activist and backbencher becomes clarified when attention turns to the topics of business assigned to the committees. The localist was the backbencher. In addition, he rarely sat on committees that were charged with responding to the governor and imperial authority or with defining provincial policy. Between 1743 and 1745, Daniel Doughty sat on a single committee--one to draft a routine bill of naturalization. When he returned in 1761, he served on twenty committees: six treated with local projects to build waterworks and bridges at Crosswick Creek, Newton, Mannington, Assunpink, and Cape May, one with pesky dogs, and only one with a message to the governor. John Mickle represented Gloucester County from 1738 to 1744. Of the 163 committees named during his tenure, he was included on only four: one on debt legislation, two on road regulation, and one to answer the governor. Lawrence Van Buskirk received a similar set of assignments; he sat on six committees that treated with interest and debt, four with taxation and revenue, two with the registration of deeds, two with the regulation of sheriffs, two with the renewal of the militia act, one with a bill of naturalization, and the rest with proposals to annex part of Essex to Somerset County, to regulate lumbering in the eastern division, and to build a bridge in Bergen County.

The quintessential localist-backbencher came from the Dutch Reformed counties of Somerset and Bergen. With the exception of Fisher, he made little impress on the house's proceedings even if he stayed for several terms. Fisher's colleague John Van Middleswardt sat on the county court and represented Somerset for fourteen years. He was inactive in the house and attended to issues that related directly to his immediate locale such as the regulation of sheriffs and the militia, paper money and debt, the loss of livestock, and deer hunting. Of his twenty-five committee assignments, only one was to address the governor. George and Abraham Van Neste sat on four committees to draft bills to allow the construction of a new jail in Somerset County, to renew the expiring militia act, to limit the squirrel population, and to repair roads at Bedminster. Once Abraham sat on a committee to determine how much the house should pay its printer.

When Fisher entered the house, he sat quietly and was paid no more attention than his neighbor Van Middleswardt. During the Morris administration, a handful of representatives were regularly appointed to committees that conferred with the Council, drafted messages to the governor, instructed the agent, and petitioned the king. These lawmakers included Richard Smith, William Cooke, Robert Lawrence, and John Eaton.

72

Some--Philip Kearny, Jacob Spicer, and John Low--were moderately active in these affairs. In three years, Fisher began to appear on these committees; and, by the beginning of the 1750s, he was one of the most frequently appointed. In those years, the major issues were tax policy, proprietary rights, a nearly empty treasury, and the constitutional relationship among the Assembly, Council, and governor. And Fisher, Cooke, and Lawrence sat on 70 percent of those committees that defined the house policy. A core group of assemblymen who were actively concerned with the governor's recommendations, imperial policy, the house's rights, and provincial liberties could be found in each Assembly. In the last to meet before independence, the house appointed twenty-seven committees to define and explain its position on provincial and imperial affairs: Fisher was named to fifteen, Kinsey to twenty-two, Wetherill to thirteen, and Richard Lawrence to ten. Samuel Tucker and John Hinchman appeared on nine, Henry Paxson on eight, and Stephen Crane on seven.

The localist and provincial lawmakers were not distinguished by how they stood on the public issues but by what importance they gave to the issues or by how they defined the sphere of public service. Sometimes the provincial stood out. Leaming recalled Read's "airs and actions" which were "much after the french manner."[16] But the difference was not between the urbanite and "ploughman." Fisher lived in a world that was an extension of, but not separate from, the localist's. He preferred to consider himself a "mechanick," was self-effacing about his education, and admired the plain style of public speech. When he spoke to his neighbors on that June day about the public service, he and his constituents shared certain concerns. A bridge planned to span Bound Brook required funds, and its promoters had petitioned the legislature for permission to establish a lottery. Those who fished along the Raritan River worried about damages done by mill owners. The county's border with Middlesex required adjustment. Fisher responded to these matters in the legislature. When he spoke of the province's "distressed circumstances," his audience was already mindful of the economic depression and the number of debtors in the county jail. His neighbors had petitioned, urging the government to issue more paper money, and Fisher had argued their cause in the legislature. But Fisher had also entered a larger world than that contained by the bounds of Somerset County. Two months before, he had helped draft a petition to George III reminding him that one of the province's most cherished rights was "the Priviledge of being exempt from any Taxation, but such as is imposed" by its own legislature and remonstrating that "the Duties. . .lately imposed. . .by Parliament, for the sole and express Purpose of raising a Revenue" violated "the Constitution."[17] The localist listened to

Fisher, approved his opinions, but lived in a more confined world than the provincial lawmaker. And, when coming to the legislature, he remained a backbencher whose sights were fixed on local affairs.

A legislature that conducts its business without having developed a system of standing committees or party organization seems by modern standards to be an institutionally invertebrate and immature body.[18] Since the New Jersey Assembly lacked those devices that socialize the initiate, foster identity with an ongoing party or institution, identify leadership, and provide cues and guidance to the membership--since, in sum, it lacked the capacity to breed a sense of group identity among its members--the representatives, in turn, acted principally from those resources--attitudes and perspectives--which they had acquired before entering. While the mature institution can command loyalties unto itself--a sense of "clubbishness"--and thereby has achieved a sense of autonomy or integrity, it has done so by establishing mechanisms or filters that separate it from the outside environment. Or, if the New Jersey Assembly had not achieved that maturity, conversely it remained a representative body accurately reflecting its constituencies. But, for the same reason, it was encumbered when it addressed the public agenda and made policy. Although there were provincial politicians, no provincial political organizations existed to bind them and the localist together. The members brought with them an assortment of identities and interests--country and urban, east and west, proprietor and antiproprietor--which divided them along several axes. The members and their families came from England, Scotland, Ireland, Holland, and Germany, either directly or by way of New York, Pennsylvania, and New England. They prayed at the Anglican (21 percent), Presbyterian (17 percent), Dutch Reformed (13 percent), and Baptist (10 percent) churches and at the Quaker meetinghouse (31 percent). Sometimes these social and economic categories reinforced each other to create a sense of association, and as often they contradicted or cut across each other. This then was a pluralist polity which functioned without the devices for integrating the segments.

The Assembly seemed a gathering of strangers. When the newly elected lawmaker arrived, he recognized his district's other representative and perhaps a relative from a neighboring county. But kinship networks rarely extended beyond the adjacent district.[19] Because the group was small, consisting of twenty-four and after 1772 thirty members, it was possible for him to become familiar with his colleagues in the course of a session. But the lawmaker who was reelected returned to discover that those whom he had learned to trust or oppose were absent and that he was surrounded again by unfamiliar faces. On the average, elections brought a turnover in membership of one-third. Some brought as many as seventeen and eighteen new members. And, in the course of an Assembly, deaths and resignations--on an average of two and in longer assemblies as many as four and once ten--made for even greater instability. It was a group of transients. A quarter of the lawmakers served a year or two and slightly more than half less than five years. There seemed little time to establish enduring working relationships.

Although this was an effervescent body, its members did make judgments of each other, sometimes positive and as often negative. Friend identified Friend; the western member eyed his eastern colleague with suspicion; Anglican harbored prejudice toward Quaker; the proprietor opposed the "rioter"; the urbane member disparaged his "ploughman" colleague's qualifications. While manuscript materials provide fleeting glimpses of such opinions and suggest the presence of factions, they do not reveal the strength or endurance of these associations. Fortunately, the 544 roll calls recorded in the house journals provide the means to aid in this inquiry.

Roll-call analysis clarifies the significance of sectionalism. Contemporaries observed a division between East and West Jersey. Politicians often acted accordingly. But the representatives' voting behavior confirms historians' impressions that these differences did not constitute a strong division.[20] The eastern delegations voted as a bloc on 35 percent of the roll calls.[21] The western members voted together more often, perhaps due to a pervasive Quaker identity, but still on less than half (47 percent) of the roll calls. Furthermore, the roll calls suggest that whatever the differences they did not make for a polarized legislature. Rarely, indeed on only 6 percent of the roll calls, did the sections vote as distinct and opposing blocs on the same question.

Another method for defining legislative associations is simply to determine which members voted together and to place those who agreed on 70 percent of the roll calls in a voting bloc.[22] The blocs or clusters displayed different characteristics in size, level of agreement, and composition and could be distinguished from each other by social composition and their levels of disagreement. Different kinds of blocs appeared: a majority bloc that included nearly all the members, a splinter bloc of only three or four, and a bloc that was equal in size to another. Some blocs tended to have high disagreement scores, and others tended to fuse into each other. Comparison of these voting patterns in twelve assemblies aids in identifying reference points and associations and gauging their relative strength and weakness.

Consider the Eleventh Assembly, which met from October 1738 to March 1739 (Table 3.2). The lawmakers' votes clustered into two distinct blocs. The first (A) was an urban bloc composed of the delegations from Perth Amboy, New Brunswick, Newark, Burlington, and John Emley, a business associate of Burlington's and Perth Amboy's elite. The second bloc (B) included country members, principally Quaker and Dutch Reformed, from both sections. Both blocs were fragile and did not reflect organization or coalition. The urban bloc contained several opposites, if not antagonists, who happened to agree for the moment: Newark's Josiah Ogden disagreed with the Johnstons of Perth Amboy on proprietary rights, and Burlington's Quakers saw Perth Amboy's Anglicans as political rivals. The rural bloc achieved a lower level of agreement which perhaps reflected underlying social differences.

The fragile nature of these voting blocs became apparent during the next four years. While the urban bloc remained intact during the Twelfth Assembly (1740-1742), the rural representatives separated into two clusters (Table 3.3). The one composed principally of western Quakers (B) tended to agree more frequently with the urban representatives than the other (C) which included non-Quakers from both sections. The members of the next Assembly (1743-1744) voted in different clusters (Table 3.4). The urban bloc (A) included Perth Amboy's Leonard and Nevill, New Brunswick's Farmer, and Elizabethtown's Bonnell. With the exception of Bonnell, this bloc assumed an Anglican complexion. The only two rural members to join this cluster were the Anglicans George Vreeland of Essex and Leonard Gibbon of Salem. Burlington's Quakers, Smith and Pearson, were absent and had joined a bloc of rural Quakers and Calvinists, conspicuously Dutch Reformed, from both sections (B).

During the Fourteenth Assembly (1744), the Essex delegation abandoned the urban bloc. George Vreeland voted in slightly more than 50 percent and John Crane in more than 75 percent disagreement with Perth Amboy (Table 3.5). The

TABLE 3.2
VOTING BLOCS
ELEVENTH ASSEMBLY (1738-1739)

Representatives and Denominations

	Representatives and Districts	Johnston,A.(A)	Johnston,L.(A)	Hude(P)	Antill(A)	Pearson(Q)	Smith(Q)	Emley(Q)	Ogden(A)	Demarest(DR)	VanNeste(DR)	Dumont(DR)	Eaton(P)	Vandervere(DR)	Hancock(Q)	Cooke(Q)	Cooper(Q)	Leaming(Q)	VanBuskirk(L)	Mickle(Q)	Stacy(Q)	Young(B?)	Reeves(Q)
A	Johnston,A.(PrthAmby)		100	100	93	87	82	82	81														
	Johnston,L.(PrthAmby)	100		100	92	85	80	80	78														
	Hude,J.(Mddlsx)	100	100		93	86	81	81	80														
	Antill,E.(Mddlsx)	93	92	93		93	87	87	86														
	Pearson,I.(BrlTwn)	87	85	86	93		93	93	80														
	Smith,R.(BrlTwn)	82	80	81	87	93		100	87														
	Emley,J.(Hntrdn)	82	80	81	87	93	100		87														
	Ogden,J.(Essx)	81	78	80	86	80	87	87															
B	Demarest,D.(Brgn)										75	70							70				
	VanNeste,G.(Smrst)									75		92											
	Dumont,P.(Smrst)									70	92			93	75								
	Eaton,J.(Mnmth)													75									
	Vandervere,C.(Mnmth)											93	75		75		87	87	81	80			
	Hancock,W.(Slm)											75		75		76	76	76		75			
	Cooke,W.(BrlCo)														76		76	76	82	81	75		
	Cooper,J.(Glcstr)													87	76	76		76	82	80			
	Leaming,A.Sr.(CpMy)													87	76	76	76		82	71		70	
	VanBuskirk,L.(Brgn)									70				81		82	82	82		80			
	Mickle,J.(Glcstr)													80	75	81	80	71	80				
	Stacy,M.(BrlCo)															75							
	Young,H.(CpMy)																	70					
	Reeves,J.(Slm)																						

Note: A=Anglican; B=Baptist; DR=Dutch Reform; L=Lutheran; P=Presbyterian; and Q=Quaker.

TABLE 3.3
VOTING BLOCS
TWELFTH ASSEMBLY (1740-1742)

Representatives and Denominations

Representatives and Districts	Johnston(A)	Leonard(P)	Hude(P)	Farmer(A)	Smith(Q)	Pearson(Q)	Low(DR)	Rolph(P)	Peace(?)	Mickle(Q)	Cooper(Q)	Smith(Q)	Hancock(Q)	Cooke(Q)	Stacy(Q)	Demarest(DR)	LeamingSr(Q)	LeamingJr(B)	Smith(Q)	VanBuskirk(L)	VanMiddlewardt(DR)	Vandervere(DR)	Eaton(P)
A																							
Johnston,L.(PrthAmby)	100	91	91	91	91	91		83	75														
Leonard,T.(Smrst)	100	100	90	94	84	83	80	84	76	75	75					70							
Hude,R.(Mddlsx)	91	91	94		75	83	80																
Farmer,T.(Mddlsx)	91	90	94		76	86	75	76															
Smith,R.(BrlTwn)	91	84	75	76		84			75														
Pearson,I.(BrlTwn)	91	84	83	86	84								76										
Low,J.(Essx)	84	80	75			75						80											
Rolph,J.(Essx)	83	84	75	76	70																		
Peace,B.(Hntrdn)	75	76	75	76	80	72				70	76	80											
Mickle,J.(Glcstr)		75									91	83				83							
Cooper,J.(Glcstr)		75								75			70	70	70	75							
B																							
Smith,B.(Hntrdn)			76										70	70	70	75							
Hancock,W.(Slm)											80			70	70	75							
Cooke,W.(BrlCo)											83	70	70		75	87							
Stacy,M.(BrlCo)													75	87		95							
Demarest,D.(Brgn)		70											83	75	70	75	81	81					
C																							
Leaming,A.Sr.(CpMy)											75						92	77	76			76	76
Leaming,A.Jr.(CpMy)																	92	84			73	89	70
Smith,R.(Slm)																	77	84		75			
VanBuskirk,L.(Brgn)																	76		73				80
VanMiddleswardt,J.(Srmst)																	76	73	89	75		83	84
Vandervere,C.(Mnmth)																	76	89	75	80	83		78
Eaton,J.(Mnmth)																	76	70	80		84	78	

Note: A=Anglican; B=Baptist; DR=Dutch Reform; L=Lutheran; P=Presbyterian; and Q=Quaker.

TABLE 3.4
VOTING BLOCS
THIRTEENTH ASSEMBLY (1743-1744)

Representatives and Denominations

Representatives and Districts	Leonard(A)	Nevill(A)	Vreeland(A)	Bonnell(P)	Farmer(A)	Gibbon(A)	Leaming(B)	Willets(Q)	Hancock(Q)	Pearson(Q)	Smith(Q)	Cooke(Q)	Shinn(Q)	Cooper(Q)	Mickle(Q)	Doughty(Q)	Mott(B?)	Lawrence(Q)	Eaton(P)	VanMiddlesward(DR)	VanVeghten(DR)	VanBuskirk(L)	Demarest(DR)
A																							
Leonard,S.(PrthAmby)		80	100	90	80																		
Nevill,S.(PrthAmby)	80		100		80	85																	
Vreeland,G.(Essx)	100	100		100	80	100																	
Bonnell,J.(Essx)	90	90	100		90	71																	
Farmer,T.(Mddlsx)	80	80	80	90		71	100																
Gibbon,L.(Slm)	85	100	71	71																100	100	80	100
Leaming,A.Jr.(CpMy)					100																		
Willets,J.(Slm)									83		80	83		75	100	100	100	75		100	100	80	100
B																							
Hancock,W.(Slm)						70	85	83		70	77	80		100	80	80	80	70	80	90	70		80
Pearson,I.(BrlTwn)								70	77		77	100	85	100	100	80	80	88	77	77	75	77	70
Smith,R.(BrlTwn)						80	77	80	77	100		80	85	80	80	80	100	80	100	70	70	88	70
Cooke,W.(BrlCo)						83		83			70		70	85	100	100	80	85	70	100	88	77	70
Shinn,T.(BrlCo)						71	75	75	100	100	85	70		85	85	85	100	80	100	85	88	83	85
Cooper,J.(Glcstr)								100	80	70	77	70	85		100	100	80	70	80	70	77	77	100
Mickle,J.(Glcstr)								100	80	70	77	70	85	100		100	80	70	80	80	77	88	100
Doughty,D.(Hntrdn)								100	80	80	100	80	100	100	100		80	80	80	100	100	75	80
Mott,W.(Huntrdn)								75		100	80	100	100	80	80	80		100	80	75	100	80	70
Lawrence,Ro.(Mnmth)								70	80	88	85	80	85	70	70	70	88		90	70	77	77	88
Eaton,J.(Mnmth)								80	90	77	80	88	80	100	100	80	70	80		80	88	88	77
VanMiddleswardt,J.(Smrst)								100	80	70	85	100	100	80	100	70	80	90	80		77	100	88
VanVeghten,D.(Smrst)								100			77		77	100	100	75		77		77		77	77
VanBuskirk,L.(Brgn)								80		77	83	88	88	75	100	75	100	77	88	88	77		88
Demarest,D.(Brgn)								100	80	70	77	70	85	100	100	80	70	80	100	80	80	100	

Note: A=Anglican; B=Baptist; DR=Dutch Reform; L=Lutheran; P=Presbyterian; and Q=Quaker.

TABLE 3.5
VOTING BLOCS
FOURTEENTH ASSEMBLY (1744)

Representatives and Denominations

Representatives and Districts	Bloc	Lawrence(Q)	VanMiddleswardt(DR)	Cooke(Q)	Cooper(Q)	Sheppard(B)	Smith(Q)	Doughty(Q)	Mott(B?)	Hancock(Q)	Demarest(DR)	VanBuskirk(L)	VanVeghten(DR)	Eaton(P)	Pearson(Q)	Spicer(B)	Crane(P)	Vreeland(A)	Young(B)	Hude(P)	Oake(DR)	Leonard(A)
Lawrence,Ro.(Mnmth)		100																				
VanMiddleswardt,J.(Smrst)		100	100																			
Cooke,W.(BrlCo)		100	100	100																		
Cooper,J.(Glcstr)		100	100	100	100																	
Sheppard,M.(Slm)		100	100	100	100	100																
Smith,R.(BrlTwn)		95	94	94	100	95	95															
Doughty,D.(Hntrdn)		86	83	100	94	86	85	85														
Mott,W.(Hntrdn)	A	91	84	83	84	87	86	73														
Hancock,W.(Slm)	A	90	94	93	94	90	90	85	73	81												
Demarest,D.(Brgn)	A	95	94	94	94	95	90	82	81	90	100											
VanBuskirk,L.(Brgn)	A	95	94	94	94	95	90	81	91	91	100	100										
VanVeghten,D.(Smrst)	A	90	88	88	89	91	85	77	86	90	95	95	95									
Eaton,J.(Mnmth)	A	95	89	88	89	91	90	78	95	81	95	95	82	82								
Pearson,I.(BrlTwn)	A	81	76	76	83	81	86	71	81	85	87	86	80	77	77							
Spicer,J.(CpMy)	A	82	78	77	73	79	77	73	91	72	83	82	78	87	72	72						
Crane,J.(Essx)	A	78	78	88	78	79	72	82	75	81	82	86	70	70	75	75	79					
Vreeland,G.(Essx)	A/B																79					
Young,H.(CpMy)	A/B																					
Hude,R.(Mddlsx)	B																				91	95
Oake,W.(Mddlsx)	B																			91		95
Leonard,S.(PrthAmby)	B																			95	95	

Note: A=Anglican; B=Baptist; DR=Dutch Reform; L=Lutheran; P=Presbyterian; and Q=Quaker.

members from Perth Amboy and New Brunswick had become a small and isolated splinter group (B) arrayed against one large majority bloc (A) which was remarkable for its size, diversity, and cohesion. Sixteen representatives from both sections, urban and rural, Quaker, Dutch Reformed, Presbyterian, and Baptist, voted together. Five voted in complete agreement with each other, and another eight in over 80 percent agreement. Or the entire bloc voted in 88 percent disagreement with the splinter group. Within six years, voting alignments had shifted dramatically: two blocs of equal size and different social complexion had first appeared; each had split; and then diverse elements crystallized to form a large majority bloc set against a small splinter group. Although the same patterns endured in the Fifteenth Assembly (1745), underlying differences in the majority bloc reemerged after the death of Governor Morris.[23]

With the arrival of Governor Belcher, that nearly unanimous opposition to the Perth Amboy faction evaporated, and the lawmakers resumed previous voting habits. In the Sixteenth Assembly, which met from 1746 to 1748 (Table 3.6), one bloc of thirteen members appeared (A). Burlington's Quakers and John Emley joined Perth Amboy. The other seven included four western Quakers and three eastern Calvinists--two from Somerset and one from Middlesex County. The remaining rural members clustered into two small splinter blocs. One composed of three eastern Calvinists and Cape May's Leaming and Spicer (A/B) tended to vote in agreement with the Quakers of the first bloc. Another consisting of Monmouth's Eaton, Hunterdon's Mott, and Bergen's Van Buskirk (C) voted in distinct opposition to the majority bloc. These tendencies appeared again but in somewhat more clarified form in the Seventeenth Assembly (1749-1751). Two well-defined, albeit socially segmented, clusters appeared (Table 3.7). The urban delegations from Burlington and Perth Amboy, three western Quakers, and an eastern Presbyterian formed a highly cohesive bloc (A) with an average agreement of 91 percent. Bloc B formed at a lower level of agreement and included five western representatives--three Quakers and two Baptists--and three eastern Calvinists. Another seven members tended to agree with this bloc but formed a third cluster (C). What distinguished these representatives was their level of disagreement with the Perth Amboy and Burlington delegations. Unlike the members of the second bloc who disagreed with the urban contingent on only 51 percent of the roll calls, these members registered 84 percent disagreement. Second, these members came, with the exception of Hunterdon's Mott, from the eastern counties of Essex, Somerset, Monmouth, and Bergen.

In the Eighteenth Assembly (1751-1754), extreme opposition to the urban bloc dwindled to a small splinter group, and urban affinities emerged more clearly (Table 3.8). Newark's John Low

TABLE 3.6
VOTING BLOCS
SIXTEENTH ASSEMBLY (1746-1748)

Representatives and Denominations

	Representatives and Districts	Nevill(A)	Steele(A)	Kearney(A)	Smith(Q)	Smith(Q)	Heard(P)	Hancock(Q)	Brick(Q)	Emley(Q)	Fisher(DR)	VanMiddlesward(DR)	Cooper(Q)	Cooke(Q)	Low(DR)	Demarest(DR)	Leaming(B)	Crane(P)	Spicer(B)	Wright(Q)	Hopkins(Q)	Eaton(P)	Mott(B?)	VanBuskirk(L)
A	Nevill,S.(PrthAmby)																							
	Steele,P.(PrthAmby)	100																						
	Kearney,P.(Mddlsx)	100	95																					
	Smith,R.(BrlTwn)	87	76	77																				
	Smith,D.(BrlTwn)	86	79	80	96																			
	Heard,J.(Mddlsx)	82		76	85	88																		
	Hancock,W.(Slm)	72	70	70	90	92	78																	
	Brick,J.(Slm)	72		72	80	85	78	83																
	Emley,J.(Hntrdn)	72		80	82	80	72	85	85															
	Fisher,F.(Smrst)	73	80	71	78	85	77	85	96	80														
	VanMiddleswardt,J.(Smrst)			88	71	77	71	82	88	73	88													
	Cooper,J.(Glcstr)	73		77	88	83	82	94	82	84	82	73												
	Cooke,W.(BrlCo)	78	70	77	80	80	75	85	76	78	82	88	88											
	Low,J.(Essx)		73				77	81	85	78	76	79	81	81										
A/B	Demarest,D.(Brgn)										72	73	72	75	75									
	Leaming,A.Jr.(CpMy)								72	77			75	88	80	88								
	Crane,J.(Essx)										76			84	80	80	80							
	Spicer,J.(CpMy)													85	85		85	72						
B	Wright,S.(BrlCo)												73											
	Hopkins,E.(Glcstr)													73			70	70	72	80				
C	Eaton,J.(Mnmth)																						80	90
	Mott,W.(Hntrdn)																			93	80	80		83
	VanBuskirk,L.(Brgn)																				74	90	83	

Note: A=Anglican; B=Baptist; DR=Dutch Reform; L=Lutheran; P=Presbyterian; and Q=Quaker.

TABLE 3.7
VOTING BLOCS
SEVENTEENTH ASSEMBLY (1749–1751)

Representatives and Denominations

Representatives and Districts		Hinchman (Q)	Johnston (A)	Smith,R. (Q)	Smith,D. (Q)	Bispham (Q)	Smith,J. (P)	Hancock (Q)	Brick (Q)	Leaming (B)	Spicer (B)	Cooke (Q)	Dey (DR)	Wetherill (P)	Fisher (DR)	Emley (Q)	Mott (B?)	Crane (P)	Camp (P)	Eaton (P)	Lawrence (Q)	VanMiddleswardt (DR)	VanBuskirk (L)
Hinchman,J.(Glcstr)	A	100	100	100	100	80	100																
Johnston,L.(PrthAmby)		100	85	85	85	83	83	83		71				71									
Smith,R.(BrlTwn)		100	85		100	100																	
Smith,D.(BrlTwn)		100	85	100		100		100															
Bispham,J.(BrlCo)		100	85	100	100		71	85															
Smith,J.(Mddlsx)		80	83			71																	
Hancock,W.(Slm)		100	83	100	100	85	85																
Brick,J.(Slm)	B							85		87	88	100	87	88	77	100		75				71	71
Leaming,A.(CpMy)			83						87		100	88	87	100	88	80		75					71
Spicer,J.(CpMy)			71						88	100		100	88	77	100	83		75	77			71	71
Cooke,W.(BrlCo)								85	100	87	88		88	100	77	100		75	77		75	71	71
Dey,D.(Brgn)									71	88	75	77		88	77	75		75	77		75	74	71
Wetherill,J.(Mddlsx)			71						88	100	100	88	77		83	83	77	74			74	71	71
Fisher,H.(Smrst)									77	87	88	77	88	83		83	77	85	85				85
Emley,J.(Hntrdn)									75	100	80	83	100	75	83		83	75	100	80	100	80	75	100
Mott,W.(Hntrdn)	C												77	83	77	83		75	100	87	87	100	100
Crane,J.(Essx)									71				75	75		75	75		100		85		85
Camp,J.(Essx)									75				77	77			100	100			83	85	71
Eaton,J.(Mnmth)													75			100	87				83	83	100
Lawrence,Ro.(Mnmth)												71	71	74	85	80		85	85	83		80	80
VanMiddleswardt,J.(Smrst)									71	71	71	71	85	71		75	100				71		80
VanBuskirk,L.(Brgn)																100	100	85	71	100	80	80	100

Note: A=Anglican; B=Baptist; DR=Dutch Reform; L=Lutheran; P=Presbyterian; and Q=Quaker.

TABLE 3.8
VOTING BLOCS
EIGHTEENTH ASSEMBLY (1751-1754)

Representatives and Denominations

Representatives and Districts	Stevens(A)	Johnston(A)	Deacon(Q)	Ogden(P)	Low(DR)	Emley(Q)	Hancock(Q)	Mickle(Q)	Wood(Q)	Ellis(Q)	Cooke(Q)	Newbold(A)	Wetherill(P)	Smith(Q)	VanMiddleswardt(DR)	Fisher(DR)	VanVorst(DR)	Leaming(B)	Dey(DR)	Holmes(B)	Lawrence(Q)	Mott(B)
A Stevens,J.(PrthAmby)		95	91	85	78	77	82	86		82	75											
Johnston,J.(PrthAmby)	95		95	89	84	78	85	75		76	72											
Deacon,J.(BrlTwn)	91	95		92	90	88	89	80	80	75	71	78										
Ogden,R.(Essx)	85	89	92		95	83	88	79			72											
Low,J.(Essx)	78	84	90	95		89	90	84		75	73	72										
Emley,J.(Hntrdn)	77	78	88	83	89		84	80		73	72	80										
Hancock,W.(Slm)	82	85	89	88	90	84		80	82			70										
Mickle,W.(Glcstr)	86	75	80	79	84	80	80		76		80	73										
A/B Wood,R.(Slm)			80				82	76					83	81								
Ellis,J.(Glcstr)	82	76	75		75	73																
Cooke,W.(BrlCo)	75	72	71	72	73	72		80				80	70									
Newbold,B.(BrlCo)			78		72	80	70	73			80		80									
B Wetherill,J.(Mddlsx)									83		70	80		77	76	83	94	82	88			
Smith,S.(Mddlsx)									81				77		77	76	87	72	74			
VanMiddleswardt,J.(Smrst)													76	77		91	87	70	87			
Fisher,H.(Smrst)													83	76	91		81	78	85			
VanVorst,C.(Brgn)													94	87	87	81		77	89			71
Leaming,A.Jr.(CpMy)													82	72	70	78	77		73	77	89	
Dey,D.(Brgn)													88	74	87	85	89	73			72	
C Holmes,J.(Mnmth)																		77			89	92
Lawrence,Ro.(Mnmth)																		89	72	89		92
Mott,W.(Hntrdn)																	71			92	92	

Note: A=Anglican; B=Baptist; DR=Dutch Reform; L=Lutheran; P=Presbyterian; and Q=Quaker.

and Elizabethtown's Robert Ogden voted with the urban bloc (A). The three urban delegations achieved 87 percent agreement and were joined by another five rural Quakers, including John Emley. The remaining members, principally from the eastern counties, formed two blocs. The larger of the two (B) tended to fuse with bloc A: while these lawmakers were inclined to concur with the rural Quakers, they were often able to find reason to agree with the urban delegations. Finally, three members disagreed so often with the urban members that they formed a small splinter bloc (C). The Eighteenth Assembly seemed the mirror image of the Fourteenth Assembly: the majority had concurred with one splinter bloc and then with its opposite.

The tendencies for the urban members to agree, for the eastern to disagree with their urban colleagues, especially with Perth Amboy, and for the western to take a moderate position between the two reflect underlying social differences and affinities, but voting in the next four assemblies reveals that those patterns of agreement did not crystallize into permanent voting associations. As the provincial government turned its attention to the last war with France, the lawmakers divided along denominational lines (Table 3.9). In the Nineteenth Assembly (1754-1760), a bloc of fourteen members from both sections (A) voted in nearly 80 percent agreement. What this bloc had in common was that its members were with a single exception Anglican and Calvinist, or not Quaker. The second bloc (B) was less cohesive, achieving an average 68 percent agreement, but with the exception of Wetherill and Newbold it was Quaker and Baptist. The power of religious association may be reflected in the urban delegations from Burlington: while Charles Read voted with the larger bloc, Samuel Smith joined his coreligionists.

It was a fragile and internally divided bloc, but it endured. Wetherill disappeared from this cluster in the next Assembly, and Cape May's Baptists left on the eve of independence. Burlington's Quakers still tended to agree with their urban counterparts. But a western and Quaker bond remained, although at a low level of agreement. Voting alignments were, in part, sectional: western Quakers, Baptists, and Presbyterians tended to agree. But there was also a religious bond. Urban Quakers did not agree with Perth Amboy's leadership as often as before. Indeed, James Kinsey voted consistently with his coreligionists. In addition, Monmouth County's Quakers were more likely to join this bloc than their non-Quaker colleagues.

TABLE 3.9
VOTING BLOCS
NINETEENTH ASSEMBLY (1754-1760)

Representatives and Denominations

Representatives and Districts	Stevens(A)	Johnston(A)	Nevill(A)	Read(A)	Ladd(Q)	DeHart(A)	Ogden(P)	Ogden(A)	Bradbury(A)	Vreeland(A)	Vangieson(DR)	Fisher(DR)	Middagh(DR)	Yard(P)	Smyth(A)	Hoagland(DR)	Stokes(Q)	Wetherill(P)	Holmes(B)	Newbold(A)	Paxson(Q)	Smith(Q)	Clement(Q)	Hancock(Q)	Miller(Q)	Leaming(B)	Spicer(B)
A Stevens,J.(PrthAmby)		97	94	90	85	87	84	84	73	83	74	71	75	83													
Johnston,J.(PrthAmby)	97		95	86	87	88	89	81	76	87	80	80	78	81													
Nevill,S.(Mddsx)	94	95		84	85	81	90	81	82	87	71	71	79	78													
Read,C.(BrlTwn)	90	86	84		90	90	90	90	79	86	71	75	91	82	71												
Ladd,J.(Glcstr)	85	87	85	90		88	76	76	76	87	75	72	80	74	75					100							
DeHart,J.(Essx)	87	88	81	90	88		100	84	91	91	73	70	80	88	85	100				90							
Ogden,R.(Essx)	84	89	90	90	76	100		84	75	94	75	72	77	79	77	100	84			76							
Ogden,J.(Essx)	84	81	81	84	76	84	84		100	100	100	79	82	80	79	76	84	70	82	100	76	90					
Bradbury,R.(Essx)	73	76	82	79	76	91	75	100		79	80	80	74	79	79	82	80				76	90					
Vreeland,G.(Brgn)	83	87	87	86	85	91	94	100	79		78	75	74	77	90		80										
Vangieson,R.(Brgn)	74	80	71	71	82	73	75	100	80	78		82	73	82	77	84	78	72									
Fisher,H.(Smrst)	71	75	72	73	75	70	72	79	80	75	82		73	77	73	80	88										
Middagh,P.(Hntrdn)	75	78	79	91	72	80	77	82	80	74	73	73		77	73	78	73	71	71	70							
Yard,J.(Hntrdn)	83	81	83	90	80	88	77	80	79	77	82	77	77		95	95	71										
A/B Smyth,A.(PrthAmby)								84	79	76	74	80	73	95		95	72	72		100							
Hoagland,J.(Smrst)			80	83	100	72	75	75	82	70	78	88	71	95	95		78	71	70	90	76	72	76	75		78	
B Stokes,S.(BrlCo)				72	76											72						73	73	72			
Wetherill,J.(Middlsx)																		71	71	70			75	75			
Holmes,J.(Mnmth)							100											70	70		90		76	70	88		70
Newbold,B.(BrlCo)					76																90		73	72	78		
Paxson,H.(BrlCo)					90												72						73	73	72	72	
Smith,S.(BrlTwn)																				76	75	72	73	70	78	70	90
Clement,S.(Glcstr)																							80	78	72		
Hancock,W.(Slm)																78				70	90		90	90	83	83	
Miller,E.(Slm)																											
Leaming,A.(CpMy)																											70
Spicer,J.(CpMy)																											

The more cohesive of the two wartime blocs proved to be more segmented and volatile. Its component elements split during the following years, reassembled, and reassembled again in each succeeding assembly. In the Twentieth Assembly (1761-1768), four Anglicans--John Brown Lawrence of Burlington, John Johnston of Perth Amboy, Joseph Borden, a business associate of Perth Amboy's elite, and Newark's John Ogden--and three Presbyterians--Monmouth's John Anderson who was surveyor for the eastern proprietors and the two delegates from Hunterdon County--constituted one voting bloc (Table 3.10, bloc A). John Wetherill dropped from the Quaker bloc (B) to reappear in a third cluster of Dutch Reformed representatives, including Hendrick Fisher (C). In the next Assembly, an urban association had evaporated (Table 3.11). Fisher and his newly elected colleague John Berrien were voting with a delegation of Calvinists from Bergen, Hunterdon, and Essex (A). And John Wetherill with two Baptists from Middlesex and Monmouth counties made up a small splinter group (C).

Analysis of the roll calls recorded in the Twenty-Second Assembly (1772-1775) uncovers four voting blocs (Table 3.12). Quakers constituted the core of one bloc (B), while two others of seven and eight members each reveal the continuing process of segmentation. Calvinists and Anglicans were scattered through three blocs. Middlesex, Monmouth, and Bergen formed one bloc with Cape May (A). Five others--two Friends from Gloucester and Monmouth, a Baptist from Salem, and two Calvinists from Hunterdon County--tended to vote in agreement with this group and the bloc of Quakers (A/B). The other bloc included eight members, six of whom were Calvinists and two Anglicans (C).

Analysis of voting in the twelve assemblies that met between 1738 and 1775 reveals several recurring patterns of behavior. In one type of legislature, the members divided into clearly defined voting blocs. But this behavior took on different forms: a bipolar pattern with two clearly defined blocs of equal size appeared in the Eleventh Assembly; in another, the Eighteenth, three voting clusters emerged with one tending to fuse with another; and, in the Fourteenth Assembly, the members formed one large majority bloc set against a small splinter bloc. These tendencies toward bipolarity and balance, near consensus, and fusion reflect another recurring pattern. In the Sixteenth, Nineteenth, and Twenty-First assemblies, a large majority appeared, but the remaining members failed to form a strong voting cluster among themselves. Or they seemed to splinter off the majority bloc. Even when most members voted in two clusters, some could be found who formed no strong association with either. On considering the entire

TABLE 3.10
VOTING BLOCS
TWENTIETH ASSEMBLY (1761-1768)

Representatives and Denominations

		Lawrence(A)	Borden(A)	Johnston(A)	Ogden(A)	Anderson(P)	Hart(P)	Reading(P)	Miller(Q)	Smith(Q)	Keasby(B)	Leaming(B)	Doughty(Q)	Cooper(Q)	Lawrence(Q)	Wetherill(P)	Fisher(DR)	Hoagland(DR)	Vangieson(DR)	Dey(DR)
A	Lawrence,JB(BrlTwn)		98	90	76	80	74	74	73	86	70									
	Borden,J.(BrlCo)	98		87	80	81	75	71	70	70	86									
	Johnston,J.(PrthAmby)	90	87		84	84	77	76	92											
	Ogden,J.(Essx)	76	80	84		70	80													
	Anderson,J.(Mnmth)	80	81	84	70		74	76	75											
	Hart,J.(Hntrdn)	74	75	77	80	74		76	87											
	Reading,G.(Hntrdn)	74	71	76		76	76		87											
A/B	Miller,E.(Slm)	73	70	92		75	87	87			70									
	Smith,S.(BrlTwn)	86	86																	
	Keasby,E.(Slm)	70							70					77						
B	Leaming,A.(CpMy)																			
	Doughty,D.(BrlCo)													71	76					
	Cooper,D.(Glcstr)										77		71		76					
	Lawrence,Ri.(Mnmth)												76	76						
C	Wetherill,J.(Mddlsx)																72	72	70	70
	Fisher,H.(Smrst)															72		75	76	70
	Hoagland,J.(Brgn)															72	75		74	74
	Vangieson,R.(Brgn)															70	76	74		85
	Dey,T.(Brgn)															70	70	74	85	

Note: A=Anglican; B=Baptist; DR=Dutch Reform; L=Lutheran; P=Presbyterian; and Q=Quaker.

TABLE 3.11
VOTING BLOCS
TWENTY-FIRST ASSEMBLY (1769-1771)

Representatives and Denominations

	Representatives and Districts	Fisher (DR)	Hart (P)	Tucker (P?)	Berrien (P)	Demarest (DR)	Ogden (A)	Crane (P)	Hewlings (A)	Miller (Q)	Price (Q)	Smith (Q)	Johnston (A)	Hinchman (Q)	Bullock (Q)	Paxson (Q)	Hartshorne (Q)	Dey (DR)	Runyon (B)	Wetherill (P)	Taylor (B)	Leaming (B)
A	Fisher,H.(Smrst)																					
	Hart,J.(Hntrdn)	84																				
	Tucker,S.(Hntrdn)	75	70																			
	Berrien,J.(Smrst)	78	75	70																		
	Demarest,J.(Brgn)	73	72		76																	
	Ogden,J.(Essx)	78	82	76	76																	
	Crane,S.(Essx)	75	77	72	74	79	79															
	Hewlings,A.(BrlTwn)							78														
	Miller,E.(Slm)								71													
	Price,RF'(Glcstr)				73				71	71												
	Smith,J.(BrlTwn)				71					71	84											
B	Johnston,J.(PrthAmby)										78	81										
	Hinchman,J.(Glcstr)												81									
	Bullock,J.(BrlCo)													84								
	Paxson,H.(BrlCo)													78	78							
	Hartshorene,R.(Mnmth)												70	70	78	78						
	Dey,T.(Brgn)															71	70					
C	Runyon,R.(Mddlsx)																71					
	Wetherill,J.(Mddlsx)																		80			
	Taylor,E.(Mnmth)																		80	72		
	Leaming,A.(CpMy)																		72	78	78	

Note: A=Anglican; B=Baptist; DR=Dutch Reform; L=Lutheran; P=Presbyterian; and Q=Quaker.

TABLE 3.12
VOTING BLOCS
TWENTY-SECOND ASSEMBLY (1772-1775)

Representatives and Denominations

	Representatives and Districts	Weth(P)	Tay(B)	Dey(DR)	Comb(A)	Moor(P)	Hand(B)	Eld(B)	Tuck(P?)	Meh(P)	Law(Q)	Holm(B)	Pri(Q)	Wind(P)	VanH(DR)	Gib(A)	Kin(Q)	Syk(Q)	Pax(Q)	Hin(Q)	Elm(P)	Shep(Q)	Hew(A)	Fis(DR)	Roy(P)	Dem(DR)	Cran(P)	Gar(DR)	Ford(P)	Pet(A)
A	Wetherill,J.(Mddlsx)																													
	Taylor,E.(Mnmth)	91																												
	Dey,T.(Brgn)		71																											
	Combs,J.(PrthAmby)	83	84	79																										
	Moores,J.(Mddlsx)	85	83	79	88																									
	Hand,J.(CpMy)	78	78	81	75	75																								
	Eldridge,E.(CpMy)	82	78	70	85	85	95																							
A/B	Tucker,S.(Hntrdn)		82		80	86		70																						
	Mehelm,J.(Hntrdn)				71	72		72	74																					
	Lawrence,Ri.(Mnmth)					70			72																					
	Holme,B.(Slm)						70	73	74	72																				
	Price,R.F.(Glcstr)						80	73	72	79		79																		
B	Winds,W.(Mrrs)									70	70	72	72																	
	VanHorne,T.(Sssx)								75	76		72	70	70																
	Gibbon,G.(Slm)													70	73															
	Kinsey,J.(BrlTwn)								89	89		77	89		73	70														
	Sykes,A.(BrlCo)									72			72				72													
	Paxson,J.(BrlCo)								73	73		73	80				74	76												
	Hinchman,J.(Glcstr)								73	73		85	70				75	77	78											
	Elmer,T.(CmbrInd)								82				79				81	74	76	78										
	Sheppard,J.(CmbrInd)								77				85				78	81	80	74	74									
C	Hewlings,T.P.(BrlTwn)																			73				77						80
	Fisher,H.(Smsrt)								71				72				77								85	72		77	85	88
	Roy,J.(Smsrt)																							85		81	78		86	78
	Demarest,J.(Brgn)																							72	81		78	77	80	72
	Crane,S.(Essx)																						80	78	78	77		72	79	78
	Garritse,H.(Essx)																							85	86	80			72	80
	Ford,J.(Mrrs)																							88	78	79	79	72		80
	Pettit,N.(Sssx)																						80	80	72	78	78	78	80	

Parties: DR=Dutch Reform, L=Lutheran, P=Presbyterian, and Q=Quaker.

period, the oscillation between consensus and polarization and the concomitant tendencies toward splintering and fusion seem complements of one another.

The composition of the voting blocs reveals this splintering process. An urban bloc emerged clearly defined and then dissolved. A rural bloc appeared as regularly and as often split into its different components. These elements reassembled in each assembly. Western members exhibited a proclivity to agree but not a strong or lasting one. Quakers and Baptists formed an association, then disagreed. Even antiproprietors were found to agree with Perth Amboy.

This shifting process seems even clearer when following an individual through several assemblies. In succeeding assemblies, John Wetherill voted with a bloc of eastern Calvinists, western Quakers, then with a small group from Bergen and Somerset counties, and later with another from Monmouth County. In the Seventeenth Assembly, Aaron Leaming, Jr., and Hendrick Fisher voted in 87 percent agreement but a decade later disagreed on more than 60 percent of the roll calls. At one point, Fisher and Van Middleswardt achieved 70 percent agreement with Perth Amboy but later disagreed with the same delegation on 60 percent of the roll calls. John Low ranged from 20 percent to 80 percent agreement with the Perth Amboy faction. Or William Cooke of Burlington County voted in 80 percent, but later 40 percent, agreement with Van Buskirk and the Monmouth delegation. That shift meant that Cooke who had once voted in less than 15 percent agreement with the Perth Amboy clique later registered 72 percent agreement.

While the effervescent nature of the voting blocs confirms the absence of political organization, this analysis also reveals on closer examination recurring patterns of agreement which suggest the presence of reference groups. First, the voting underscores the significance of a member's district or a pervasive localism. The delegations from Perth Amboy achieved between 95 and 100 percent agreement and were the most cohesive. On occasion, two members from a district split. In the Sixteenth and again in the Eighteenth assemblies, Mott and Emley agreed on only one in four roll calls; in the Twentieth, Monmouth's Anderson and Lawrence voted in 38 percent agreement, and Burlington County's Doughty and Borden disagreed on over 70 percent of the roll calls. But, of the 147 delegations examined in twelve assemblies, only thirteen pairs of representatives fell below 50 percent agreement. Indeed, the average level of agreement stood at 76 percent.

Second, although the representatives did not identify with organizations extending beyond their districts, their voting also suggests recurring affinities. The delegations of Newark and Elizabethtown, Perth Amboy and New Brunswick, and Burlington and rural members who were intimate with the urban delegations, such as Emley, Borden, and Anderson, tended to support the same policies. That affinity appeared clearly in the Eleventh and Eighteenth assemblies, only partially in the Seventeenth Assembly, and evaporated in the decade before independence. In its inconstancy, this association proved to be less than an organization. In its recurrence, it revealed something shared-- either an affinity to support the same measures or a shared negative response to their rural colleagues.

The urban members, no doubt, also served as a negative reference group to the rural. That response was strongest in the eastern delegations and seemed to focus on Perth Amboy. It was not an enduring reference point, however. Only a small group of assemblymen from Monmouth, Bergen, and Hunterdon counties maintained both high and consistent levels of disagreement with Perth Amboy. David Demarest's record illustrates the fluctuations. At one point, he was in nearly total disagreement with Perth Amboy (92 percent) but later was in nearly 50 percent agreement. Although the proprietors were displeased with the election of Woodbridge's John Heard and James Smith, those representatives concurred with Perth Amboy on more than three in four roll calls. And Fisher was often found voting in the same bloc with Perth Amboy.

Urban-rural antipathies were, no doubt, real and often intense. But they did not translate into either permanent or categorical divisions. Rural majorities regularly chose their speakers from the urban delegations, most often from Perth Amboy. In 1744, Samuel Nevill was the presiding officer, and the Perth Amboy group was defeated on 90 percent of the roll calls. In 1745, the same majority reelected this outspoken advocate of Perth Amboy's interest. And it was only after prolonged debate that the house turned to Robert Lawrence in 1746. But Nevill was returned to the chair the following year. Cortlandt Skinner experienced the same when he presided over a house which devoted its energies almost exclusively to removing his brother from office. Between 1738 and 1775, Lawrence was the only rural member to achieve that position. In that period, Elizabethtown's Joseph Bonnell, Robert Ogden, and Stephen Crane presided for a sum of five years, Burlington's Read for four years, and Perth Amboy's Andrew Johnston, Nevill, and Skinner for a total of twenty-one years.

Religion sometimes surfaced in the voting alignments. The Friends constituted the largest single denomination in the legislature and seemed the closest to a legislative party. Their manners and beliefs set them apart and thereby fostered a sense of group identity. They acted from their egalitarian and pacifist principles when they opposed slavery and the renewal of militia acts. Sometimes they felt besieged: Richard Smith received the governor's proposal that the legislature sponsor a Presbyterian college at Princeton as a scheme to educate and lure the youth from the meetinghouse and eventually to undermine Quaker influence. Certainly Quakers possessed an organizational network: the annual meetings often defined positions on public policy and expected conformity; and Quakers worked with great success at electing their own to the legislature.[24] But group self-consciousness, even the elements of organization, did not translate into a legislative party. The Quaker lawmakers rarely voted as a cohesive bloc. Their doing so during the war years did, no doubt, reflect shared pacifist convictions, but it is equally significant that at that point they achieved such low agreement among themselves. Urban Quakers were as likely to vote with their rural coreligionists as with urban Anglicans. Eastern Quakers were more likely to vote with their Calvinist neighbors in opposition to Perth Amboy than with their western counterparts. Indeed, the western tendency not to vote in extreme disagreement with another bloc suggests a behavior that was as much a function of geography--that is, distance from Perth Amboy--as a Quaker proclivity toward moderation.

Denominational identity was, no doubt, important. Jerseymen identified Quaker and Presbyterian parties. But religion seemed one of several factors that made up the lawmaker's identity and guided his behavior. Membership in the Church of England became a badge that set off the urbane from the rural member and that reinforced the proprietor's opinion of those he brought to court. And, in turn, Calvinist, Dutch Reformed, or Presbyterian association gave added meaning to the rural member's ingrained distrust of the urban Anglican. Urban Calvinists, however, did not make the same of church membership. Although Presbyterian, the Ogdens were more inclined to agree with the Anglicans of Perth Amboy than with their fellow Calvinists. So, too, John Low had as much in common with the proprietors as he did with his coreligionists from Bergen County.

Unwittingly, New Jersey's lawmakers were becoming the creators of modern American politics. Because they came to the legislature representing various social and economic interests and speaking from different perspectives, they were making a pluralist world. Because they had not yet created organizations to encompass and channel the differences and because they seemed to be incessantly shifting their voting associations, theirs remained an unstable form of pluralism. That instability, which often seemed to the Jerseyman to forebode disorder and the breakdown of community, had, in fact, its limits. The

Assembly oscillated between polarity and consensus. The impermanence of voting blocs and the constant reassembling of voting alignments testify to divisiveness but not categorical division and demonstrate how narrow a gulf separated antagonists. Notwithstanding the forces of divisiveness, majorities sometimes grew so large that they achieved near consensus. This equally powerful urge toward consensus is revealed in the voting record of individual legislators. Few, indeed an average of two in each assembly, cast their votes more often for the minority than the majority position, and only half of those who did so dissented on over 60 percent of the roll calls.[25] To return to the modern analogy, if the legislature was not divided into permanent parties, it was similar to a party convention where differences arise, rarely cause a walkout, almost never lead to the creation of a competing party, but lead, instead, to reconciliation.

Because the lawmaker deliberated in an invertebrate legislature which had not established the forms of socializing, guiding, or disciplining its members, or because he considered policy without referring to party, it did not mean that the positions he endorsed were simply the unfiltered reflection of those attitudes which he brought with him from his district or that he was free from influence on the floor of the house. If, for example, the localist had given little thought to an issue or deemed it unimportant, others who found it crucial worked to move him to their persuasion. Influence came from two sources: first, from outside or from the governor who sought to make the representatives amenable to his recommendations and, second, from within or from the lawmakers who worked to influence their peers to endorse or reject a policy.

The provincial fixed upon the governor's power to make appointments, watched as he and a trusted spokesman for the administration distributed favors, and worried that the recipients would compromise their integrity for advancement and profit. Leaming recalled that Charles Read's stature in government circles derived from his role as patronage broker for successive governors.[26] But, as Bernard Bailyn has found, the provincial was prone to exaggerate.[27] Indeed, Leaming conceded that Read's influence, while considerable, was least secure in the lower house. First, the list of appointments at the governor's disposal was too short to build a large clientele. Second, it was especially difficult to maintain a clientele in the lower house. Recommendation to the Council entailed removing a friend from the house, and appointment to a "place of profit" meant that the favored lawmaker was required by law to resign his seat. Third, the governor confronted an entrenched political elite;

and, lest he alienate the province's leading families, he was constrained to maintain them on the civil list even without assurances of their support. Moreover, the provincial's explanation of patronage and its corrupting influence rested upon a crude understanding of human motivation. The governor's favors did not necessarily cause the assemblyman to forsake principle but were often bestowed on those already predisposed to support the administration. John Ladd, for example, was recommended to the Council for services already rendered. Finally, the blatant exercise of patronage provoked charges of corruption and redounded to the governor's disadvantage. As Governor Morris acknowledged, the representative who accepted an appointment risked condemnation and loss of influence with his peers.[28]

On the floor of the house, influence depended on the ability to persuade, the art of conversation, and the skills of the speechmaker. Forensic talents were especially suited to the scene. As Jack Greene has suggested: "With virtually no infrastructure--with no organized parties, factions, clientage systems, or bureaucracy--to serve as basis for mobilizing opinion, leaders had to depend very heavily upon the force of personality and cogency of argument to gain support for their views from within the political community."[29] In this age, leadership was accorded to the orator. It was he who commanded the ability necessary to gain the stranger's attention, to awaken the localist, and to rouse an otherwise atomized body to action.

But, if forensic skills were prerequisite to leadership, their success also depended on the content of argument. Indeed, this matter of political ideology has intruded itself repeatedly, almost insistently, into this discussion of the Assembly's inner life. It is as if this analysis has served to set the stage and introduce the principals in preparation for the reading of a script.

NOTES

1. New-York Gazette, July 4, 1768, in N.J.Archs., XXVI, 208-10. Also The Pennsylvania Chronicle, June 20-27, 1768, in ibid., 194; resolution to disqualify Fisher, Apr. 23, 1740, Votes and Proceedings.

2. Journals of Henry Melchior Muhlenberg, I, 284-85.

3. Jacobus Frelinghuysen, A Clear Demonstration of a Righteous and Ungodly Man. . ., trans. Hendrick Fisher (New York, 1731); "To the Author of a Scandalous Libel," New-York Gazette, May 25, 1772, in N.J.Archs., XXVIII, 147-49; Hugh Hastings and Edward T. Corwin, eds., Ecclesiastical Records of the State of New York, 6 vols. (New York, 1901-1916), III, 2211; T. J. Frelinghuysen to ?, Apr. 22, 1725, ibid., 2305.

4. William Smith, Jr., The History of the Province of New-York, 2 vols., ed. Michael Kammen (Cambridge, MA, 1972), I, 259.

5. The following discussion was aided by a rich literature on legislative studies. Especially helpful were William O. Aydelotte, ed., The History of Parliamentary Behavior (Princeton, NJ, 1977); James David Barber, The Lawmakers: Recruitment and Adaptation to Legislative Life (New Haven, CT, 1965); Frank P. Belloni and Dennis C. Beller, eds., Faction Politics: Political Parties and Factionalism in Comparative Perspective (Santa Barbara, CA, 1978); Allan Kornberg, ed., Legislatures in Comparative Perspective (New York, 1973); Samuel C. Patterson and John C. Wahlke, eds., Comparative Legislative Behavior: Frontiers of Research (New York, 1972); Wahlke et al., The Legislative System: Explorations in Legislative Behavior (New York, 1962).

6. Oct. 5, 1750, Sept. 16, 1751, May 21, 1753, Aug. 4 and 5, 1755, Aug. 8, 1758, Votes and Proceedings.

7. Nov. 1, 1744, Nov. 7 and 8, 1760, Mar. 5, 1762, ibid.; and petitions from Gloucester County, Oct. 12 and 16, 1769, ibid.

8. Oct. 19, 1743, and May 22, 1753, ibid.

9. Oct. 18, 1744, Nov. 7, 1760, Nov. 23 and 24, 1763, ibid.; petition of William Hancock et al., Aug. 4, 1755, ibid.

10. "Americus Justitia," New-York Gazette, Aug. 7, 1766, in N.J.Archs., XXV, 178-83; May 31, June 5, 7, and 11, 1765, Votes and Proceedings; Cape May County petitions, Nov. 21 and 24, 1763, ibid.; Thomas L. Purvis, "The New Jersey Assembly, 1722-1776" (Ph.D. diss., The Johns Hopkins University, 1979), 166-70. Also petition from Elizabethtown, Feb. 24 and 28, 1738/9, Votes and Proceedings.

11. Petitions from Salem County, Nov. 28, 1763, Oct. 12 and 24, 1769, ibid.

12. Belcher to Leaming, Feb. 16, 1754, Belcher

Letterbooks, X, 324; Belcher to Jacob Wendell, Oct. 5, 1747, ibid., VIII, 100-101; Belcher to Read, Aug. 1, 1753, ibid., X, 181-82; Alexander to Coxe, May 2, 1748, N.J.Archs., VII, 123; Alexander to R. H. Morris, [Dec. 19, 1751], ibid., 651.

13. Belcher to Read, Jan. 4, 1754, Belcher Letterbooks, X, 312; petition from Gloucester County, Oct. 3, 10, and 11, 1754, Votes and Proceedings.

14. Act Inlisting. . .Five Hundred Freemen (1746), Bush, Laws, III, 15-21; Act for making. . .Ten Thousand Pounds (1746), ibid., 21-28; Act Inlisting Five Hundred Free Men (1755), ibid., 307-19; Act for making. . .Fifteen Thousand Pounds (1755), ibid., 345-55; Act for building of Barracks (1758), ibid., 556-59; J[ohn] L[ow] to Parker, New-York Gazette, May 18, 1747, in N.J.Archs., XII, 357-59.

15. Aaron Leaming, Jr., Diaries, III (last part of volume), The Historical Society of Pennsylvania. Also see Charles Read to R. H. Morris, July 9, 1748, Robert Morris Papers, Box 2, Rutgers University Library.

16. Aaron Leaming, Jr., Diaries, III (last part of volume).

17. Assembly to king, May 6, 1768, Gerlach, ed., New Jersey in the American Revolution, 42-44. New-York Gazette, July 4, 1768, in N.J.Archs., XXVI, 208-10; Mar. 5, 1762, June 20, 1766, Apr. 16, 21, and 22, 1768, Sept. 11, 1772, Votes and Proceedings; petitions from Somerset County, June 1, 1763, Apr. 15 and 18, 1768, Oct. 12, 1769, Oct. 10, 1770, Nov. 28, 1771, ibid.; Frelinghuysen, A Clear Demonstration, iv-vi.

18. The following discussion was aided by perspective gained from the following: Douglas Price, "Careers and Committees in the American Congress: The Problem of Structural Change," in Aydelotte, History of Parliamentary Behavior, 28-62; Nelson W. Polsby, "The Institutionalization of the U.S. House of Representatives," The American Political Science Review, LXII (Mar., 1968), 144-68; David J. Rothman, Politics and Power: The United States Senate, 1869-1901 (Cambridge, MA, 1966); James Sterling Young, The Washington Community, 1800-1828 (New York, 1966). See also Robert Zemsky, "American Legislative Behavior," American Behavioral Scientist, XVI (May/June, 1973), 675-94; and Donald R. Matthews and James A. Stimson, Yeas and Nays: Normal Decision-Making in the U. S. House of Representatives (New York, 1975).

19. Purvis, "'High-Born, Long-Recorded Families'," 602-3.

20. Main, Political Parties Before the Constitution, 7-8.

21. For a discussion of the method employed, see Lee F. Anderson, Meredith W. Watts, Jr., and Allen R. Wilcox, Legislative Roll-Call Analysis (Evanston, IL, 1966), 31-45, 176-82.

22. Ibid., 59-75, 191-94. Those roll calls that achieved near consensus--that is, more than 90 percent of the membership on one side--were excluded. Also, those members who voted too infrequently to establish a clear voting association also were excluded.

23. Since the Fifteenth Assembly recorded only eleven roll calls and the voting patterns were not unlike those found in the Fourteenth Assembly, the results for that Assembly were not reported.

24. R. Smith to J. Smith, Nov. 23, 1748, Smith Family Papers, chronological series, III; Larry R. Gerlach, "'Quaker' Politics in Eighteenth Century New Jersey: A Documentary Account," The Journal of the Rutgers University Library, XXXIV (Dec., 1970), 1-3.

25. The program PARLOY was used to determine how frequently assemblymen voted with the majority. This program was written by the Division of Academic Computing, Southern Illinois University at Carbondale.

26. Aaron Leaming, Jr., Diaries, III (last part).

27. Bailyn, Origins of American Politics, 59-105.

28. L. Morris to Benjamin Smith, Jan. 3, 1739/40, Papers of Lewis Morris, 73-80; L. Morris to Richard Smith, Feb. 5, 1739/40, ibid., 83; W. Franklin to Earl of Hillsborough, Nov. 23, 1768, N.J.Archs., X, 93.

29. Jack P. Greene, "Character, Persona, and Authority: A Study of Alternative Styles of Leadership in Revolutionary Virginia," in W. Robert Higgins, ed., The Revolutionary War in the South: Power, Conflict, and Leadership. Essays in Honor of John Richard Alden (Durham, NC, 1979), 40.

CHAPTER FOUR

POLITICAL IDEOLOGY:
PRELIMINARY CONSIDERATIONS OF A BRITTLE CONSENSUS

Out of the myriad studies of eighteenth-century politics, three themes emerge that characterize the Anglo-American legislature.[1] First, examination of the membership reveals two types of lawmakers: one whose horizons encompassed province-wide politics and constitutional questions related to the imperial relationship and another whose preoccupations were neighborhood improvements, stray cattle, dams, fences, and pest control. The members worked in an institution devoid of stable political organization or party structure; and, in the conduct of business, each was guided by his own social and economic interest or by local and personal friendship. Alliances were joined, then dissolved, and later reconstituted. The legislature became an arena for unstable and milling factionalism. Second, and seemingly paradoxically, when the focus shifts from the interior to the exterior, or from the individual to the group, the history of the lower house becomes that of an unfolding institutional maturity and a "quest for power": the legislature self-consciously identified itself with the House of Commons; its procedures became formalized; it secured an institutional integrity from the outside interferences of the executive; and it gained powers once claimed by the prerogative. Finally, the legislature expressed an ideological conviction drawn from the English Country tradition. Like parliament's stalwarts who resisted tyranny, the patriot legislators steadfastly, even heroically, defended provincial "rights and liberties" against the corrupt and aggressive courtier who conspired in the governor's anterooms and council chambers to subvert the "ancient constitution" to his selfish ends. These conclusions, while formed principally from the study of other colonies, apply to New Jersey as well. Factionalism and parochialism were rampant. The Assembly was an invertebrate institution. The Country seemed less vocal than in other colonies, perhaps because the province lacked a press, but its sentiments were nonetheless echoed throughout New Jersey politics. The Assembly did not achieve as much in its "quest for power" as, for example, Pennsylvania's lower house, but the dynamic was apparent.

Like other Anglo-American lawmaking bodies, the New Jersey legislature documented in its <u>Votes and Proceedings</u> a "mimetic" impulse to reproduce the forms of the English

99

parliament. In 1738, it acquired a copy of Sir Simonds D'Ewes's journal of the Elizabethan parliaments and instructed its clerk to adopt it as his model. Shortly after, it ordered the acquisition of England's statutes at large since Magna Carta.[2] When the Assembly found that "by an Act of Parliament. . .the Members of the House of Commons first chose their Speaker, and were afterwards qualified in their own House by a Person appointed for the Purpose," the members were "unanimously of Opinion, that they have an undoubted Right to be Qualified in the House, according to the Practice of Parliament in Great-Britain."[3] When deliberating on a member's credentials, the house appointed a committee to inspect both provincial and British laws "relating to Persons disqualified to sit in the House of Commons and General Assembly."[4] And, in 1769, it unanimously agreed to follow the Commons' practice and opened its doors to the public.[5]

Jerseymen agreed that their Assembly, like the House of Commons, was "the Support and Foundation of our Rights and Liberties."[6] The house was entrusted to preserve that birthright brought from England by the first planters and guaranteed by the crown in the Grants, Concessions, and Original Constitutions. On occasion, it mustered specific precedent. Citing the famous ship money case, it concluded that Governor Belcher's claim to interpret the law was unconstitutional.[7] But the principle was such a watchword in provincial politics that in general, when the house claimed the power either to draft money bills or to supervise the spending of public funds, it invoked constitutional right without needing to elaborate or to define what was meant. In sustained crisis, such as that of the 1760s, Jerseymen gave fuller expression to that political consciousness. As the public awakened in response to the "spirit of liberty," Jerseymen reminded their representatives that they were elected "to ye most important of Trusts, Even that of Guardians & Defenders of our Liberties, Privileges, & Property."[8] True to that responsibility, the house took the lead in the province's protests against the crown's disregard for inherited liberties and the constitution.

The Assembly derived its authority to act from its relationship with the public. It was both caretaker of present and future generations' liberties and properties and representative of its constituents' welfare and opinion. Thus, it ordered that its proceedings, its laws, and the compilation by Leaming and Spicer be printed for distribution to the counties. Its members solicited constituency opinion. Routinely, it postponed the final vote on a bill, ordered its printing, and adjourned to measure public sentiment. While considering the bill for establishing trading companies at Perth Amboy and Burlington, the house ordered its printing "for the

100

Consideration of the Members and their Constituents." So, too, it postponed consideration of a petition for a local improvement to give the affected parties opportunity to present their reactions.[9] Leaming and Spicer sought out their neighbor's opinions before returning to the legislature. Leaming appealed to the "Freeholders of the County of Cape May" that "I desire my constituents, or so many of them as can spare the time to meet at the Courthouse the 13th instant at 12 of the clock prepared to give me their advice." Sometimes the freemen could not spare the time. When only "8 or 10" responded to Spicer's call, he reflected on the disappointment in his diary: "I am at a loss to know how to Deport myself. . .agreeable to the General Scope of my Constituents." Nonetheless, the legislators gave legitimacy to their actions by claiming this fiduciary relationship.[10]

The representative's role was crafted from English politics, specifically the Country tradition. The ideal lawmaker was the "perfect Master of what the true Interest of his Country really is" and was governed by the selfless devotion "to serve his Country for the Sake of it." The role was defined by its opposite--the corrupt, self-seeking, and sycophantic "Court Tool" who lurked in this political arcadia. This creature who craved "Promotion" and personal profit "nestled" himself into the favor of governors. His appetites were as insatiable as his principles depraved. "Every fresh Instance of his Wickedness, is a new Argument of his Zeal; and the greater the Roguery of the Servant, the more ardent is the Affection of the Master. He is rewarded according to his Industry, and the Honours conferred upon him, are in Proportion to his wicked Merit." Around the governor and in the Council, these creatures fawned and promised depravity for recognition and profit. The governor who shunned them earned their hatred: because Thomas Boone refrained from selecting favorites or appointing a "prim[e] minister," "The Jersey Courtiers did not Love him." Beware, wrote "Tribunus Populi," the dissembling politician who pretended to place the interest of his country at his heart but, in fact, lusted after power.[11] Thus, politics became a drama in which the pure and simple ploughman legislator contested the venal politician.

The patriot's fears were realized in his own locale, especially when he learned of the governor's most recent appointments to the county's civil and military lists. The sheriff who tampered with elections, the justice of the peace who refused to heed the elected Board of Freeholders, the judge who exacted exorbitant fees--they were common villains lurking in the Country's political world. According to the patriot in Essex County, the proprietors manipulated the courts and the Council to oppress the freemen. According to the freemen of Hunterdon

101

County, a Court favorite received the sheriff's commission, tampered with elections, and oppressed his neighbors.[12] In Burlington, the justices of the peace were charged with levying taxes without consulting the elected Board of Freeholders.[13] Such scandal convinced the lawmakers that sheriffs must reside in the county of their appointment, that they post bond against their good behavior, and that they, as well as other members of the civil list, be governed by a table of fees.[14]

The officer of the court, be he judge, sheriff, or lawyer, burdened the weak and unfortunate with expensive court actions and excessive fees, and the rich, be he creditor or proprietor, harassed the weak with numerous and expensive lawsuits. The "Oppression of some Lawyers" forced the "Plantation Man" to write that while "rioting in Luxury, [they] have acquired Estates, from the Toil and Labour of the Necessitous, whose Cries, I trust, have reach'd the Ruler of Heaven and Earth." Thus, bills of cost must be restrained, he warned, "before the whole Province is sunk in the insatiable Gulph of their Oppression and Avarice."[15] In the wake of the last war for empire, the colonial economy sank into a depression; and, as lawsuits increased, the beleaguered rioted and closed the courts. The Country lamented the act for its intemperance but was quick to note that, as misguided as the rioters were, they reacted from understandable provocation. The best method to prevent such recurrences was to redress the grievance. The outcry against lawyers' greed inspired proposals not only to regulate their fees but to prohibit the nonresident attorney from appearing before the provincial bar. So, too, the legislative community was persuaded that petty cases could be tried effectively and without burdensome cost in small courts and enacted that cases less than Ł15 be heard before a justice of the peace.[16]

The Country imagination was haunted by the fear of military power--not only in the form of a standing army but more immediately by the specter of the overbearing militia officer. The power of the captain to muster freemen for service and periodic training, to fine those who did not attend, and to punish the insubordinate could degenerate into tyranny: the officer's power to fine the absentee freeman encouraged him to become too strict and severe for his own profit and forbode the "impoverishment of the people." Beware, the County warned, against appeals for an invigorated militia system. On the pretext of defense, Jacob Spicer warned his colleagues, the courtier ceaselessly conspired to strengthen the arm of the military. Although not loath to approve a militia bill, the house regularly rebuffed the governor's appeals for a stronger system.[17]

The Assembly itself was vulnerable to corrupting influence. With his power of appointment to the civil and military lists, the governor could construct the mechanisms for influencing and undermining the bastion of virtue and liberty. Since the assemblyman could be enlisted into the governor's faction, the legislature prohibited by law its members from holding "any Office of Profit from the Crown, or from the Governor."[18] The house worried over complaints that the governor's appointee, the sheriff, exercised undue influence at the polling place. Because the governor enjoyed the power to call, prorogue, or dissolve the legislature, he could prevent the lawmakers from undertaking measures which he found obnoxious or he could bargain the threat of adjournment or dissolution for approval of his measures.[19] In response, the Assembly sought to preserve its integrity. Periodically, it pressed for legislation guaranteeing regular elections; and, on occasion, it ventured to dissolve itself. In addition, it sought to regulate its own membership by overseeing disputed elections and by asserting the sole right to accept a colleague's resignation.[20]

Recurrent discussion with the governor and Council over finance led to frequent disputes and caused the house to express its institutional identity. It was a constitutional principle that the Assembly, like the House of Commons, enjoyed the right to initiate money bills. To tax and spend affected the Jerseyman's right of property; and, because the representative enjoyed, in contrast to the appointed governor and councilor, an intimate, indeed fiduciary, relationship with his constituents, he was especially entitled to handle the public's money. Thus, the Assembly stubbornly denied the Council's claims to amend money bills. It explained that it "cannot but set too just a value upon the natural Rights and Priviledges Invested in the representative body of this Province, than to Consent to any alteration in a Bill which so nearly Affects the Priviledges of the people we represent."[21] It extended that right to include control of appropriations; it begrudged the governor and Council a fund to meet contingent expenses while the legislature was not in session; it jealously audited all accounts; it appointed commissioners to supervise the spending of funds for military purposes; and it even asserted the power to appoint the provincial treasurers. With this power of the purse, it exerted control over the governor to make him responsive to the public interest. It withheld treasury supplies, even his salary, in order to press him to approve bills which it deemed vital to the welfare of commercial arcadia.

In response to that public interest, the Assembly pressed for the emission of paper money. It was a popular measure in part because the interest from money issued at loan relieved the public from taxation but also because it was crucial for the maintenance of commerce. During the depression of the 1760s, the province deluged its legislators with petitions decrying "the great Hardships sustained by the People of this Colony, from the Scarcity of Cash."[22] In spite of the popularity of paper money and notwithstanding the arguments that the past emissions had maintained their rate of exchange and that the provincial welfare was contingent on another emission, the governor acted on his instructions to check such measures. In response, the Assembly declined to meet his requests for supplies in the name of provincial poverty. These recurring confrontations reinforced the house's self-image. When Governor Franklin scolded the house for refusing to approve defense appropriations and dismissed its claims of poverty, the legislators replied that he was insensitive to the public interest. "The Reason that your Excellency and we give such different Accounts of the Riches of the Province, is easy to account for: You see nothing but Affluence, we see the Distresses of the People. Therefore we have the best Right to Credit, as we have the best Means for Information."[23]

Frequently, it seemed inevitably, Assembly policy collided with imperial authority. Confrontations on the power of the purse and currency sometimes led to deadlock with the governor. Often the irritant came in the form of rejected bills and the Board of Trade's instructions to the governor. Some, such as the crown's rejection of a poorly drafted bill of naturalization, were minor; others, such as laws to regulate legal fees or to print paper money, were of greater import. The Assembly, however, responded pragmatically and refrained from probing too deeply into the nature of the imperial constitution. Thus, it regularly professed loyalty to the crown and pride in the imperial relationship and fixed its resentments on specific personalities such as the crown's representative, the governor, or native courtiers. If British policy seemed arbitrary, the fault lay with those unprincipled wretches who misrepresented local conditions, gained the ear of the governor, and enjoyed special access to the government in London. The appointment of an agent responsible to the Assembly alone, and not to the Council and governor, became imperative for the maintenance of the provincial welfare.[24]

The Assembly's pragmatic treatment of the imperial relationship was best revealed in its handling of defense issues. The imperial designs against Canada required a colonial contribution in the form of troops and the supply of British forces stationed in the province. While a campaign against the Catholic foe quickened the Protestant imagination and the politicians readily pledged their support for King George, the lawmakers quibbled, even balked, at specific proposals.[25] They were unimpressed with the call to send a delegation to

Albany to confer on a coordinated colonial defense. Although they voted troops for the campaign against Canada, they begrudged the full request. The bargaining of colonial necessities against imperial demands strained relations between the governor and the house. The Assembly declined to vote full requisitions since the province was too poor and exhausted from its patriotic efforts in previous campaigns. When it failed to bend the governor, it concluded that the English had been misinformed about the province's abilities and that they had not heard the voice of the ploughman who best understood the province's prevailing conditions.

Recent investigations into the eighteenth-century's political ideology, inspired notably by J. G. A. Pocock and Bernard Bailyn, have contributed significantly to legislative studies by moving them beyond what seems in retrospect the arid and institutional to an appreciation of the inner world of the lawmakers.[26] In the process of shifting the focus of study from the grand themes of "institutional momentum" and a "quest for power" toward an inquiry into the meaning lawmakers attached to their daily activities, these studies of ideology illuminate as well as point the way for future investigations. The importance of ideas cannot be disputed, and a revival of a crude progressive argument would seem fruitless. The problem for legislative studies is to determine what role these ideas played in the daily world of politics. The ideology, no doubt, was powerful because it explained. But it is also a commonplace that an intellectual system is not always congruent with social reality, and it has been asked how well one constructed in England could transplant to American soil. On examination, it seemed ethereal, even "paranoic."[27] The ideology no doubt motivated. But, by motivating, it roused conflict, framed politics in dichotomous terms, and thereby collided with equally powerful values that disapproved of faction and opposition to authority. When the investigation seeks to link principles with specific actors, the problem becomes more complex. First, the Country claimed to identify an opposition, but research also demonstrates that the Country served as a basis for an emerging political consensus. Furthermore, the attempt to link politicians with principles reveals instead a milling factionalism. Finally, the reconstruction of this ideology comes from a careful reading of the written and printed word. It has discovered intellectual tradition and complexness of thought; but, by so doing, it has provoked questions whether the construction reflects accurately the thinking process of the participants, whether a lawmaker who endorsed the Country message really understood it in that complexity, or whether the participants attached equal importance to the issues.

The patriot explained political life by identifying an opposition and acquired a sense of identity and purpose for action by contrasting himself with his antagonist, the courtier. But the description of the two derived from an English experience; and, as several historians have noted, a Court comparable to the English model cannot be identified in America.[28] In New Jersey, the Perth Amboy clique bore some resemblance to a Court but only a partial one. It was not so distinct in interest or even political persuasion to satisfy the Country's explanation of a polarized polity. Though the interest of ploughman and courtier sometimes collided, both were part of the same legislative community and were more alike than different. Indeed, those labeled as courtiers did not think of themselves as such but accepted their opponent's ideology.

The disagreements within this political community were nonetheless real enough to spark conflict. When confrontation arose, however, the experience provoked discomforts. Political division or faction raised again the specter of self-interest and fears for the communal ideal. When discovered in the marketplace, that motive required regulation; when disclosed in the political arena, it was condemned and shunned. The model of selfless public service was the complement to the ideal of community. Thus, groups that banded together for their special interests--factions--were anathema in this political world. And, just as interest group politics could not be accepted, the idea of loyal opposition was inconceivable. Confrontation with authority represented by the crown or by its servant inspired similar discomforts. Thus, the legislative community strove constantly to assure itself that it was seeking harmony and overcoming discord. To the charge that the Assembly was disrespectful of government, the representatives replied that they "have always esteemed a Harmony & good Agreement with Your Excellency and the Council, to be for the Benefit of the Colony; and from this Disposition have hitherto pass'd over most of the Reflections you have been pleased to cast on our Conduct."[29]

This discomfort could not prevent conflict. Indeed, the provincial found the means to overcome this dissonance, even legitimate his factiousness, and, in the process, exacerbate tensions.[30] Dissonance was overcome once the antagonist was cast into the opprobrious role of conspirator against the community, and the protagonist gathered unto himself those culturally sanctioned attributes which justified his actions. And, by framing provincial politics within such a dramatic explanation, the actor raised the mundane to a high moral plane. In fact, both antagonists sought to create his own scenario or

106

political drama. While the Country patriot sought to impose the role of courtier on the councilor, his opposite responded with an alternative scenario that continued to haunt the Anglo-American imagination. He reminded the house that its behavior was not in the tradition of John Pym but was reminiscent of the republicans and levelers of 1641 who drove the English nation into civil war and anarchy. In this scenario, the virtuous ploughman was recast into the demagogue or "mobocrat." The conflict became one between "Wigmen" and "Cap Men," or the friends of order and the fiends of anarchy.[31] In the exchange, each crafted its script from the same sources and sought to strike at the vulnerability of the other. The Country was reminded of the perils of opposition in an age that cringed at factiousness, and the Court was reminded that it was a selfish interest group in an age that had not yet accepted the legitimacy of interest group politics. Thus, the debate was not between conflicting ideologies but a struggle by each to establish its own scenario. And each in his flight of fantasy infused grand moral purpose into the conflict and thereby heightened tensions.[32]

Perhaps because the Court and Country were, in fact, neither ideologically nor socially distinct, the patriot was vulnerable to his own rhetoric. The assemblyman was charged with corruption and self-seeking. That the lawmakers accepted appointment to the civil list convinced one Jerseyman that the Assembly was packed with "loose and profitless Creatures" who have attached themselves to the province's "great Families" and "thrust themselves into all Company and Business along with their Patrons, sucking and sponging upon them."[33] Another noted that in their lust for power the lawmakers distributed commissions for supplying the military among themselves. Since the confrontation between Court and Country was not between distinct social and ideological groups, the problem for the discerning patriot was to discover the dissembling politician or to spy out the politics of the heart. In response to "Tribunus Populi," a critic revealed him as, in fact, false and signed himself as "Tribunus Populi."[34]

Out of the mundane erupted grand ideological conflict, and as often the fantastic dramaturgy evaporated to disclose commonplace politics. The fragile or effervescent nature of ideological divisions has been noted by historians. Patriots became courtiers and courtiers patriots. Thus, Lewis Morris championed the Country cause in New York but on receipt of his commission to govern New Jersey transformed himself into the Country's epitome of the overlording tyrant. This inconsistency, which Stanley Katz characterizes as ideological brittleness, was endemic to provincial America.[35] Indeed, the effervescent nature of voting associations in the New Jersey Assembly sustains that impression. What appeared to be a

Country-Court dichotomy in one assembly rapidly dissolved in the next.

To discover that the lawmaker was inconstant in his support for the Country is revealing but in itself stands as an observation begging for further explanation. Inconsistency was, no doubt, the product of expediency or interest. But that motive may be considered without denigrating the significance of the politician's professions. Inconsistent behavior, or expediency, signifies motion from one position to another but means little without gauging the degree of difference between the two points or the distance between the two extremes of the political spectrum. In this legislative community where disagreements arose between interests and not social orders, where participants spoke a common political vocabulary, and where a shared ideology explained and motivated but also caused dissonance, the potential for deviation, inconsistency, or motion was great. And, in a world where political party did not command the loyalty of the actors, personal interest, personality, even idiosyncrasy were freely expressed in the political forum. Ideological brittleness and consensus were part of the same. Furthermore, inconsistency suggests another dimension of this polity: that the participants did not give the same priority to the issues or that they did not understand them in the same way. As Joseph Ernst notes, the Country was expressed as an ideology by an articulate leadership, but such "an elaborate, highly-abstracted, intellectualized" system may not represent in its form and structure the political consciousness of all the participants.[36] A distinction needs to be made between ideology and attitude.

Ernst's point is an important one, especially as this analysis turns to the individual's response to the Country. When the lawmakers voted to censure the governor, to appoint an agent, or to deny the crown's request for military appropriations, some were more concerned or had thought longer on the issues than others. One type, the ideologue, had pondered and discussed these questions. Another, the localist, may have agreed with the ideologue, but he had not reflected on the issues and reacted instead from unformed attitudes or prejudices. Both types could be found in England and America. In England, the localist was the English squire who came to parliament grumbling against the foppery of the Court and royal pretensions to power but was preoccupied with affairs of his shire.[37] His counterpart sat in the American legislature. Alongside the lawmaker who couched his thoughts within an intellectual tradition sat the localist who came to promote the building of a dam or road. Unconcerned with the magnitude of the principles at stake and unconscious of the grand historical role he was about to play, this localist attended to the debates and, as tempers rose and the confrontation intensified, was drawn to follow those who gave expression to his feelings. By predisposition, he was inclined toward the Country, but predisposition need not signify ideology. Lewis Morris found him in the Assembly and doubted that he fully understood the issues presented to him. The house messages were, he found, "the sence of the drawers who furnish the words & Paragraphs & may be said to be as little understood as intruding by the greatest part of the Addressors."[38]

Philip Converse's discussion of "belief systems" clarifies this discussion and points the way toward a method of analysis.[39] He distinguishes "belief systems" by their form and structure rather than by their content. In his investigation, he found the ideologue who thinks in large and abstract wholes, sees connections between a broad range of issues, and responds to them as if they are connected. In the New Jersey Assembly, he was the purchaser of Cato's letters, the subscriber to the latest prints, and the author of the house's messages. He responded, in turn, to a broad range of issues as if they were part of a coherent whole. His colleague, who boasted a meager library, who did not commit his opinion to print, who made slight impress on the house's proceedings, and who lingered for a short time, was predisposed to the Country. This lawmaker, who was belittled by some as one of those "mechanicks and ignorant wretches" who dominated the Assembly and by Morris for his intellectual achievement, fits Converse's typology.[40] Unlike the ideologue, he did not appreciate either how the several issues were related to one another or how they fit into a larger ideological whole and responded to them as if they were discrete and specific entities.

It was August 1774, and Stephen Crane was preparing for his journey to Philadelphia. The last eight years seemed prelude to the task he was about to undertake. He had been elected to the legislature in the wake of the Stamp Act crisis-- after his neighbor Robert Ogden had outraged the Sons of Liberty and been forced to resign his seat for refusing to endorse the resolutions of the Stamp Act Congress--and he had arrived in time to celebrate the news of parliament's repeal. But soon he and his colleagues were worrying about other British schemes to tax and regulate the colony. In the winter of 1774, crisis seemed imminent, and the house expected news of further assaults on American liberties. Recognizing the need to respond quickly and the governor's abhorrence of frequent assemblies, the house established a committee to keep informed and to maintain a correspondence with the other American legislatures in the interim between sessions. Crane was appointed to the committee. Shortly after returning home, he received news of George III's decision to punish Massachusetts for its disobediences. Crane worried that parliament's enactments against the port of Boston were harbingers of New Jersey's fate. In June, his constituents gathered at Newark to support the beleaguered Bostonians and chose him as their presiding officer. After condemning parliament's "unconstitutional" and tyrannical acts, the meeting endorsed Massachusetts' call for a Continental Congress to meet in Philadelphia and proposed that representatives from the several counties meet to select the province's delegation. Crane was named one of Essex's representatives; and, six weeks later when the convention assembled at New Brunswick, he was chosen presiding officer. At the end of three days of deliberation, he was named to the congressional delegation. He had accepted a weighty trust--that he work "to obtain relief for an oppressed people," the "redress of our general grievances," and "the re-establishment of the constitutional rights of America on a solid and permanent foundation." While reflecting on his task, he chose to wear a suit of homespun clothing at the Congress. The role he prepared to play was symbolic--a fusion of the Country patriot and the ploughman--and was designed to evoke powerful images and meanings.[41]

The role sprang from a collective imagination. Indeed, Crane discovered that others had chosen the same part. The arcadic ideal and the Country ideology were not only pervasive but they were complementary elements of a single vision of the moral society. At the center stood the ploughman-patriot. Self-sufficient, self-regulating, and self-improving--he set forth in life.[42] Heartened that the fruits of his labors were secure and that his liberties were guaranteed under the constitution, he toiled to make the wilderness into his own. The vision of arcadia and the prospect of unfolding improvements was one of brightness. But, as the ploughman entered society and as he succeeded, he was haunted by dark shadows. The synthesis was fraught with tensions. The energies for realizing arcadia sprang from the marketplace, yet the society that was envisioned remained one built upon an organic ideal. The task of the patriot-ploughman was to act both from self-interest and from a selfless love of country. He worried that self-interest meant selfishness and became greed--that it seemed so often to transform itself into the antithesis of public mindedness. To venture forth in society meant confronting temptations. With trade came luxuries that corrupted and nurtured sloth, self-indulgence, and greed. In his daily encounters, he confronted the predator as merchant, lawyer, and courtier. In the legislature, he saw men who, driven by their passions to exploit and dominate, joined to form factious interest groups. Social life brought intrusions and oppressions. Life in arcadia required diligence and watchfulness--a constancy in defense of one's liberties and a vigilant governance of the market's passions.

The shadows seemed to be growing ever darker and ominous during the decade preceding the Continental Congress. The ploughman-patriot encountered "Villains, Sharpers," and tricksters in the marketplace and courthouse. People had become so corrupted by English fineries and had sunk so deeply in their self-indulgent ways that they became deaf to the patriot's call for reform. It seemed a "Backsliding Age" in which the virtues of self-sufficiency and patriotism had been forgotten, and the patriot had become a Whig-Jeremiah. He warned that English officialdom had come to covet America's bounty and that it conspired to snatch the ploughman's bread from his table and to deprive him of those "constitutional privileges" that were his birthright. But he despaired when he sought to awaken the oppressed and gather them into "the Common Cause of Liberty" against "the Enemies of our happy Constitution." Rather than unity, he discovered that "an Opposition of Measures, a Contradiction of Opinions, Party Spirit, mutual Rancour and Complaints, and every Mark of a divided People are gaining too much Ground." Rather than a rekindled patriotism, he found that those who calculated private gain before, and even at the expense of, the public good were multiplying.[43]

On returning home, Crane reported that the Congress had called upon Americans to join in the continental boycott of British goods and to gather in their communities and establish committees of enforcement. The Association's professed goal was to pressure the English to relent in their tyrannies; but, as Elizabethtown and other communities throughout the province created their committees "to observe the conduct of all persons," the movement took on a larger meaning and became a public crusade for social reformation or an instrument for realizing that long-held vision of a moral economy. Through severing dependencies on English goods, the committees expected the revival of domestic industries. Corrupting luxuries would become unknown, and the spirit of self-sufficiency and improvement would flourish. The movement became an active agency for a public cleansing and an awakening. Crane and the Essex leadership informed the freeholders that success "must, under God, depend on the fidelity of individuals" and that it required a vigilant public that sought out and ostracized those "so lost to a sense of public virtue."[44] In sum, the movement would foster a sense of collectivity, and the communities would purge themselves of the infections of factiousness and discord.

The ploughman-patriot's struggle with the apostate

111

conspirator became, like his earlier confrontations with the courtier, public drama. And, as the resistance movement gained momentum, it provided in symbol and ritual the means for expressing and acting upon impulses that were endemic to this society. The patriot's propensity to speak in manichean and religious terms and to convey a sense of fervor and urgency derived, in part, from his cultural inheritance but also stemmed from deeper inner sources. The dark and ominous which he railed against and which he sought to root out of his community lurked, in fact, within the confines of his soul. Daily social intercourse, routine meetings in the marketplace, became encounters with that other and unaccepted self. When he discovered the "Sharper," he faced the reflection of that part of himself which he struggled to regulate and suppress. To resolve the inner turmoil and quiet the dissonance, he projected that other self, that inner loathsomeness, upon another, made the struggle an outward battle and, as if to dispel lingering doubts, excoriated and attacked viciously. The struggle had brought anguish to Jacob Spicer. He had played the ploughman-patriot well by representing his neighbors for two decades, by preserving their Original Constitutions, and by entering into "a Trade at Cape May upon publick Spirited Views." Yet his neighbors reminded him that by gaining proprietary rights in the county, he had acquired ominous powers over their lives and impinged upon their livelihoods. His assurances did not convince: he was badgered in public with questions; and, in private, he turned the matter over in his mind. The wound festered. He wrote his will not just as bequethal but as apologia. Lest the purchase be "Represented to the prejudice of my memory when the Rubbish of my nature shall sleep in Dust and my Soul (I hope) Inherit the Regions of Bliss," he explained and protested one last time that he had been moved by "publick Utility and self Security."[45] At the same time, he was quick to impugn the motives of others, felt besieged by "Enemies," projected that which he sought to deny in himself upon others, and felt surrounded by those who "did not wish well to my prosperity" and who schemed secretly to "Lessen my Credit."[46] In the process of suppressing and the projecting, private struggles became public and shaped political discourse. Debilitating self-doubts and reminders of one's own factiousness were overcome by fashioning the colleague into the opprobrious role of courtier or leveler, thereby casting him outside community, and simultaneously by presenting one's self as patriot defender of arcadia.

But conflict derived from the same sources that created consensus. In review, legislative community rested on a common social experience and a shared conception of society and government. While pervasive and deep, this consensus contained unresolved tensions and causes for disagreement which made for an acrimonious community. Furthermore, the invertebrate nature of the legislature provided opportunity for, indeed quickened these tendencies toward, harmony and discord. Disagreements came from living in commercial arcadia. In part, they were substantial and came from the rational, calculated pursuit of self-interest in the marketplace. They also sprang from differences in taste or temperament: that is, either the various emphases that were placed on the commercial and arcadic elements in this synthesis or the different priorities that were given to the local and provincial agenda. Often the rational and temperamental complemented each other and were, in turn, reinforced by contrasting rural and urban styles and by religious prejudices. But adoption of this world view meant inner personal tensions. Life in commercial arcadia brought with it daily reminders of the factious and intrusive passions and spurred the call for a vigilant regulation of the self and of the market and government. Because debilitating self-doubts were relieved by projecting them upon society, exaggeration and aggressiveness ensued. The Assembly became the stage for such acting. And, since independence was jealously guarded and faction or party shunned, these inner impulses were given opportunity to be vented freely and without moderating or restraining influence. But influence of another form was exercised. To recruit the stranger and awaken the indifferent required skills of persuasion or conversion--in sum, oratorical or demagogic talents. That skill, if employed successfully, created an approving audience and thereby sustained action but did so by propelling conflict to the level of manichean drama. Yet the same ingredients that caused volatility, dichotomy, and polarity worked to becalm and reconcile. The restraints were within and never quelled. They came not only from the discomforts of conflict and the debilitating tensions of entering into a dichotomous world but also from reading a script that was ethereal and divorced from reality. Furthermore, it was difficult to sustain the scenario in an institution that lacked the formal mechanisms for guiding the initiate and preserving the agenda from one assembly to the next. Thus, polarity dissolved as rapidly as it had appeared; disagreements reemerged for what they were--nuances and variations of a shared world view; and the community moved toward reconciliation and consensus.

Each of the three following chapters extends this discussion by examining the Assembly in a different period. In each period, several issues appeared, became part of an ideological whole, and became a coherent agenda. In the first--from Lewis Morris's arrival to the middle of the Belcher administration--public discussion of the privileges of the house, the control of the public purse, corruption of the civil list, the power of the military, oppression in the courts, public disorders, and tax policy fused into what became a prototypical Court-Country confrontation. A second agenda was defined during the last war with France. Deliberations on the province's contributions to the war, military appropriations, and paper money became intertwined and forced attentions to turn to the imperial relationship. Governor Franklin's arrival marked the opening of the last period. The prevailing issues were of two types: first, the province's efforts to restore health to a depressed economy and the robbery of the East Jersey treasury and, second, the looming imperial crisis. Although the issues did not always converge to form a single package, they did test and strain the Assembly's relationship with the governor and raised questions about opposition, factiousness, and loyalty to authority.

NOTES

1. Bailyn, Origins of American Politics; Greene, Quest for Power, 3-18; idem, "Political Mimesis"; Bonomi, "The Middle Colonies: Embryo of the New Political Order."

2. Nov. 24, 1738, Oct. 15, 1741, Votes and Proceedings. Mary Patterson Clarke, Parliamentary Privilege in the American Colonies (New Haven, CT, 1943).

3. Oct. 10, 1743, Votes and Proceedings.

4. Oct. 5, 1754, ibid.

5. Oct. 12, 1769, Ibid.

6. Advice To the Inhabitants of the Counties of Hunterton [sic] and Morris, (n.p., [1744]). Also see Larry R. Gerlach, "Power to the People: Popular Sovereignty, Republicanism, and the Legislature in Revolutionary New Jersey," in William C. Wright, ed., The Development of the New Jersey Legislature from Colonial Times to the Present (Trenton, NJ, 1976), 7-19.

7. Assembly to Belcher, June 12, 1754, Votes and Proceedings.

8. Gerlach, Prologue to Independence, 117; Gloucester County's instructions to its representatives, Oct. 3, 1769, Gerlach, ed., New Jersey in the American Revolution, 47. Also, "Caesariensis," New-York Gazette, Sept. 12, 1765, in ibid., 10-

12; Essex County Stamp Act Resolves, New-York Gazette, Oct. 31, 1765, in ibid., 18-19.

9. June 12, 1740, Votes and Proceedings. Also Dec. 5, 1743, Nov. 28, 1744, Nov. 24, 1748, ibid.

10. Aaron Leaming, Jr., "To the Freeholders of the County of Cape May," Apr. 4, 1771, Stillwell, Historical and Genealogical Miscellany, III, 437; "Diary of Jacob Spicer," 115. Also, Assembly to Belcher, Mar. 31, 1757, N.J.Archs., XVII, 93-95; petition from Ancocas Creek, Sept. 24, 1762, Votes and Proceedings; Monmouth County's instructions to its representatives, Oct., 1769, Holmes Family Papers, Rutgers University Library.

11. Some Animadversions on a Reply to a Letter from a Gentleman in New-York, to his Friend in Brunswick ([New York], 1750), 3-4; A Reply to a Letter from a Gentleman in New-York, to his Friend in Brunswick ([New York], 1750), 1-7; Leaming Diaries, Mar. 30, 1761, II. Also "To the Freeholders... of New-Jersey," New-York Gazette, Mar. 18, 1751, in N.J.Archs., XIX, 48-50.

12. Petitions from Hunterdon County, Oct. 11, 18-21, 1743, and June 6, 1753, Votes and Proceedings; petition from Gloucester County, Oct. 10, 1754, ibid.

13. Assembly to Belcher, Feb. 21, 1749/50, N.J.Archs., XVI, 222-24; Assembly to Belcher, Feb. 27, 1749/50, Votes and Proceedings. Also Reports from Committee of Grievances, Nov. 19, 1742, and Feb. 9, 1750[/1], ibid.

14. Act to oblige. . .Sheriffs. . .to give Security (1747/8), Bush, Laws, III, 45-48; Act for. . .preventing. . . exorbitant Fees (1747/8), ibid., III, 83-94.

15. "A Plantation Man. . .To the Freeholders," New-York Journal, Oct. 5, 1769, in N.J.Archs., XXVI, 514-16.

16. Assembly to W. Franklin, Mar. 20, 1770, Votes and Proceedings; Assembly petition to king, Oct. 19, 1749, N.J.Archs., VII, 351-56; W. Franklin to Board of Trade, Aug. 8, 1765, ibid., IX, 491. Also "A Letter from a Gentleman in Hunterdon County," New-York Gazette, Mar. 5, 1770, ibid., XXVII, 80-85; "A Tradesman of New-Jersey," The Pennsylvania Chronicle, Sept. 30-Oct. 7, 1771, in ibid., 576-78; "S.T.," The Pennsylvania Gazette, Nov. 14, 1771, ibid., 635-33; New-York Gazette, Feb. 26, 1749/50; Report from Committee of Grievances, Nov. 19, 1742, Votes and Proceedings; Act to prevent Actions of Fifteen Pounds and under (1760), Bush, Laws, IV, 16-17.

17.   A Dialogue between two Gentlemen in New-York. . . relating to the publick Affairs of New-Jersey ([Philadelphia, 1744]); Jacob Spicer's speech to the Assembly, Feb. 22, 1755, Spicer Papers, New Jersey Historical Society;   Hunterdon County's instructions to its representatives, May 28, 1771, N.J. Archs., X, 269-73; petition from Reading Township, Aug. 2, 1758, Votes and Proceedings; petition from Lebanon, Aug. 10, 1758, ibid.; Fisher, New Jersey as a Royal Province, 86, 116, 323, 325.

18.   Act for securing the Freedom of Assemblies (1730), Bush, Laws, II, 399-400.   Petition from Middlesex County, Oct., 1754, Manuscripts, Box 12, Legislative Papers, 1724-1755.

19.   W. Franklin to Earl of Hillsborough, Dec. 27, 1771, N.J.Archs., X, 321-23.

20.   Act for the better Regulating of Elections (1725), Bush, Laws, II, 335-37; Act for the frequent Meeting. . .of the General Assembly (1727/8), ibid., 372; Act for the Septenniel Election of Representatives (1768), ibid., IV, 477-78; Hunterdon County's instructions to its representatives, New- York Gazette, Aug. 12, 1754, in N.J.Archs., XIX, 386-88; L. Morris to Assembly,   July   25,   1740,   Votes   and   Proceedings;   Order regarding John Ogden's resignation, Oct. 23, 1771, ibid.; L. Morris to Board of Trade, Oct. 25, 1740, Papers of Lewis Morris, 123-25.

21.   Assembly to Council, Mar. 16, 1748/9, N.J.Archs., XVI, 201.   Also Assembly to W. Franklin, Apr. 25, 1771, ibid., X, 252-56; Assembly to Council, Feb. 22, 1749/50, Votes and Proceedings; Assembly to Belcher, June 6, 1751, ibid.; Letter to B. G.; The Note-maker noted, and the Observer observed upon. . . ([Philadelphia, 1743]), 11-13; and Fisher, New Jersey as a Royal Province, 101-70, passim.

22.   Petition from Somerset County, Oct. 16, 1769, Votes and Proceedings.   Also petition from Burlington County, Oct. 30, 1769, ibid.

23.   Assembly to W. Franklin, Apr. 25, 1771, N.J.Archs., X, 256.   Also Assembly to W. Franklin, Nov. 26, 1763, Votes and Proceedings.

24.   Aaron Leaming, Jr., to "Dear & worthy Gentlemen," May 26, 1771, Leaming Papers, Stewart Collection, Glassboro State College, NJ; Assembly to Belcher, Feb. 22, 1749/50, N.J.Archs., XVI, 215; Assembly to W. Franklin, Apr. 25, 1771, ibid., X, 251-56.

25. For a general discussion, Fisher, New Jersey as a Royal Province, 319-59.

26. Bailyn, Origins of American Politics; Pocock, Politics, Language and Time, 80-147. Also Wood, "Rhetoric and Reality in the American Revolution."

27. See David Brion Davis, ed., The Fear of Conspiracy: Images of Un-American Subversion from the Revolution to the Present (Ithaca, NY, 1971), 23-28, passim.

28. Paul Lucas, "A Note on the Comparative Study of the Structure of Politics in Mid-Eighteenth-Century Britain and Its American Colonies," The William and Mary Quarterly, 3rd Ser., XXVIII (Apr., 1971), 301-9; Richard L. Bushman's review of Bailyn, Origins of American Politics, ibid., XXV (Apr., 1968), 284-86; idem, "Corruption and Power in Provincial America," in Library of Congress Symposia on the American Revolution: The Development of a Revolutionary Mentality (Washington, DC, 1972), 63-91; J. G. A. Pocock, The Machiavellian Moment: Florentine Political Thought and the Atlantic Republican Tradition (Princeton, NJ, 1975), 506-26.

29. Assembly to Belcher, June 14, 1754, N.J.Archs., XVI, 463. Also Modest Vindication of the Late New-Jersey Assembly, 32. And for a general discussion, see Richard Hofstadter, The Idea of a Party System: The Rise of Legitimate Opposition in the United States, 1780-1840 (Berkeley, CA, 1969), 1-39.

30. Helpful in the following discussion were Victor Turner, Dramas, Fields, and Metaphors: Symbolic Action in Human Society (Ithaca, NY, 1974); Erving Goffman, Frame Analysis: An Essay on the Organization of Experience (Cambridge, MA, 1974). Also helpful were Clifford Geertz, "Ideology as a Cultural System," in David E. Apter, ed., Ideology and Discontent (New York, 1964), 47-76; Murray Edelman, The Symbolic Uses of Politics (Urbana, IL, 1964); and Ferdinand Mount, The Theatre of Politics (London, 1972).

31. Alexander to R. H. Morris, May 30, 1749, N.J.Archs., VII, 262-63.

32. L. Morris to Assembly, Nov. 25, 1742, N.J.Archs., XV, 268-79; Assembly to king, Oct. 19, 1749, ibid., VII, 351-56; Assembly to Council, Feb. 20, 1750/1, ibid., XVI, 271-73; Council to Belcher, Oct. 22, 1751, ibid., 340-41; L. Morris to Board of Trade, June 10, 1743, Papers of Lewis Morris, 162; L. Morris to Samuel Nevill, Sept. 26, 1745, ibid., 270; Alexander to Paris, Oct. 25, 1754, Paris Papers, I, 40.

33. New-York Weekly Journal, May 11, 1741, Oct. 26, Nov. 3, 4, and 7, 1769, Votes and Proceedings. Also Purvis, "'High-Born, Long-Recorded Families'," 603-4.

34. Alexander Miles, New-York Gazette, Feb. 16, 1747, in N.J.Archs., XII, 331-36; Reply to a Letter from a Gentleman in New-York, 8.

35. Stanley Katz, "The Politics of Law in Colonial America: Controversies over Chancery Courts and Equity Law in the Eighteenth Century," Perspectives in American History, V (1971), 257-84.

36. Ernst, "Ideology and the Political Economy of Revolution," 143-44. Also idem, "'Ideology' and an Economic Interpretation of the Revolution," in Young, American Revolution: Explorations in the History of American Radicalism, 161-69.

37. Conrad Russell, Parliaments and English Politics, 1621-1629 (Oxford, 1979); J. H. Hexter's review of ibid., New York Review of Books, Dec. 18, 1980, 58-61; Derek Hirst, "Court, Country, and Politics before 1629," in Kevin Sharpe, ed., Faction and Parliament: Essays on Early Stuart History (Oxford, 1978), 105-37.

38. L. Morris to Sir Charles Wager, May 10, 1739, Papers of Lewis Morris, 41. Also L. Morris to Board of Trade, Oct. 4, 1739, ibid., 61; and W. Franklin to Samuel Smith, Aug. 24, 1772, Samuel Smith Papers, Rutgers University Library.

39. Philip E. Converse, "The Nature of Belief Systems in Mass Politics," in Apter, Ideology and Discontent, 206-61.

40. Carl Bridenbaugh, ed., Gentleman's Progress: The Itinerarium of Dr. Alexander Hamilton, 1744 (Chapel Hill, NC, 1948), 31.

41. New-York Gazette, Oct. 31, 1765, in Gerlach, ed., New Jersey in the American Revolution, 19-20; Essex County resolution, June 11, 1774, ibid., 69-72; Resolution of Provincial Congress, [July 23, 1774], ibid., 76-77; Assembly resolutions, Feb. 8, 1774, Votes and Proceedings; Richard Smith Diary, Paul H. Smith, ed., Letters of Delegates to Congress, 1774-1789 (Washington, DC, 1976-), II, 17.

42. The fourth chapter of R. H. Tawney, Religion and the Rise of Capitalism: A Historical Study (London, 1926) remains one of the most insightful discussions of this psyche.

118

43. "At a Meeting of the Freeholders. . .of Essex," New-York Journal, June 7, 1770, in N.J.Archs., XXVII, 169-72; "To the Printer," New-York Journal, Sept. 20, 1770, in ibid., 244-46; J. Borden "to J. L., J. R., & J. L.," New-York Journal, Sept. 27, 1770, in ibid., 255-56; "Cethegus," New-York Gazette, Oct. 8, 1770, in Gerlach, ed., New Jersey in the American Revolution, 57-59. Also Aaron Leaming, Jr., to his constituents, May 26, 1771, ibid., 61- 64. For a general discussion, see Crowley, This Sheba, Self, 125-46; and Edmund S. Morgan, "The Puritan Ethic and the American Revolution," The William and Mary Quarterly, 3rd Ser., XXIV (Jan., 1967), 3-43.

44. Stephen Crane et al. to Freeholders, New-York Gazette, Dec. 5, 1774, in Gerlach, ed., New Jersey in the American Revolution, 95-97.

45. Spicer's will, Manuscript Wills, 253 E.

46. Spicer, "Diary," 175-76. Also Spicer, "Memorandum Book," 165-68, 184; and "Diaries of Aaron Leaming," ed. Lewis T. Stevens, The Cape May County Magazine of History and Genealogy, I (June, 1932), 73.

CHAPTER FIVE

THE COUNTRY VERSUS COURT, 1738-1752:
A PROTOTYPICAL CONFRONTATION

The venal courtier conspiring to undermine provincial liberties, the selfless Country patriot staunchly defending the provincial constitution--this cast of characters and an accompanying script flourished in the American polity. Periodically, the personalities and issues converged; a province's political life became transformed into a reenactment of historical constitutional conflicts; memories of Stuart tyrannies, of struggles to preserve the rights of parliament, of the confrontation of 1641, and of the Civil War informed the discussions and elevated the mundane world of the colonial politician into a grand historical drama.[1] Such a prototypical confrontation occurred shortly after the appointment of Governor Lewis Morris. The Assembly constructed an agenda of issues, informed the public of a Court, and sustained an ideologically coherent package throughout the Morris administration and the first half of the Belcher administration. Then the drama evaporated as quickly as it had erupted.[2]

Morris arrived confident of his administration's success. As sometime resident and former assemblyman, he was intimate with the province's politics. And, because he had secured the separation of New Jersey from New York's executive, he expected gratitude and support from the legislature. In its first message, the house congratulated the governor. "His Knowledge of the Nature and Constitution of this Province" and "his great Skill in Affairs of Government, which we more than once have had Experience of" were well known. "If His Inclinations and Endeavours to promote our Welfare, bear any Proportion to His Abilities (which we have no Reason to doubt)," he was "every way qualified to render us a happy and flourishing People."[3] Some already doubted his motives: his reputation as a proprietor and past quarrels in the legislature had not been forgotten. A motion to thank Morris for securing the province's own governor and to vote him a cash reward for his efforts sparked a heated and prolonged debate. The voice of the Country could be heard; lawmakers warned that Morris was assembling a Court of favorites. One member noted the "continu'd Promises and Threat'nings from the Court Party": unless "the Governour was pleas'd," it warned, he would remove "Good Officers" from the county civil lists and replace them with "others not so agreeable to the People." Three members buckled under the pressure, and the house approved a grant to the governor.[4]

The Country, however, did come to prevail. The governor's irascible personality, his friends, and the issues he raised worked together to create the stage and script for enacting a prototypical Country drama. The eastern proprietors under the leadership of Lewis Morris and his ally James Alexander had been aggressively asserting their claims and prosecuting their opponents in the courts. That Alexander, a New York resident, sat on the Council and that Morris appointed his son Robert Hunter to the Council and then to the Supreme Court smacked of a Court conspiracy to turn government to private ends. The upper house of the legislature had fallen into the control of members who sat on the East Jersey Council of proprietors. Constitutional precedent and form were violated.[5] The Assembly reminded Morris that recommendations to the Council be made to give equal representation to both sections and, moreover, that the appointees "Reside so near each Part [of the province], as that they may have some real Acquaintance with every Part of the Government under their Care." But what the house deemed inviolate principles the governor dismissed as royal indulgences that could be suspended. For the sake of efficiency, he insisted that his advisers reside within an easy ride of his residence.[6] The Country also noted that the Court penetrated into local government: the civil lists were being filled with the governor's friends, and such "Leaches" and "Sluggish Creatures" had penetrated the legislative chamber itself.[7]

When Morris proposed reforms, he exacerbated suspicions. Noting the inconvenience of meeting alternately at Perth Amboy and Burlington, he recommended that a single capital be established and that the legislature provide funds for government buildings as well as for the governor's mansion. In preparation for this change, he took up residence at Trenton. In addition, he stressed that the militia system required reform and repeatedly pressed for a "more Useful and effectual" system. Specifically, he and the Council sought to expand the powers of militia officers to require the Jerseyman's attendance at the county muster and to establish a provincial cavalry.[8]

The house readily renewed the militia act but balked at Morris's demands. The Country raised the specter of tyranny, specifically of militia officers extracting fines and lording over the helpless yeoman. "The evil Tendency of a strict" militia meant the expansion of corruption: the officer, the governor's appointee, would seize goods for nonattendance, would cast those guilty only of "Poverty" into jail, and would influence elections. Applauding the lawmakers for resisting Morris's proposals, one pamphleteer concluded that if they had concurred with the governor "their Behaviour might richly have meritted the Curses of the Publick to latest Posterity."[9]

The Assembly not only resisted but also seized the initiative. The house found that eight of Hunterdon County's justices of the peace had violated the legally prescribed procedures for choosing the county's loan officer and then addressed the governor requesting that he either remove or prosecute his appointees. Morris responded before dissolving the house with a message reprimanding it for impinging on the executive prerogative.[10] Also, the house discovered that the rich were harassing the poor with expensive lawsuits and passed regulations preventing small cases involving less than ₤15 from being taken to the Supreme Court. Since lawyers and the governor's appointees on the local courts lorded over the public by extorting extravagant fees, the Assembly pressed for the establishment of a table to regulate fees. The sheriff received special notice: the house sent up legislation requiring that an appointee post bond for good service and that he serve for no more than three years. Finally, in order to protect the integrity of the house from the executive's manipulation, it passed a septennial act. Morris rejected each of these items in the house's agenda.[11]

Opposition to the proprietors' claims finally erupted into rioting first at Newark and then spread into neighboring counties. Morris warned that unless he were given additional powers to meet the crisis the "Infection" would spread and become "Rebellion." Specifically, he pressed the house to augment his powers under the militia act.[12] The Assembly replied that it responded to lawless actions with "Abhorrence" but was hesitant to heed the governor's recommendations. The oppressions of the proprietors had forced some misguided farmers to riot. Moreover, it would not allow the governor to use this crisis as a pretext for forcing acceptance of his militia reforms. Thus, it replied that the governor already enjoyed the powers sufficient to quell the disturbances. And, finally, it took the opportunity to remind Morris that he had countenanced the lawbreaking by Hunterdon's justices of the peace and thus set an example: "common People will follow the Example of their Superiors, and hope for the like Impunity."[13]

The public welfare required an issue of paper money. Not only did an adequate supply of currency stimulate commercial life, assured numerous contributors to the public prints, but the interest collected from paper money issued at loan had supplied the treasury with enough funds to relieve the public of taxes. Thus, the Assembly pressed for an issue of ₤40,000. While rejecting the proposal to establish two private banks, it regularly passed a general issue. The idea was popular.

Indeed, the Council concurred with the Assembly on the project. The governor himself was not categorically opposed to paper money; but, because he was bound by his instructions, he steadfastly opposed the legislature's demands. In the legislative chamber, this conflict demonstrated once again the governor's callous disregard for the public welfare.[14]

Regularly, the Country's disputes with Morris and his allies turned on the constitutional principles related to the power of the purse. Whether the Council had the right to amend money bills and whether the governor and Council should be granted an exigency fund to meet unexpected expenses arising while the Assembly was in recess were questions raised in the first sessions. Notwithstanding the governor's censure, the Country replied that these were "natural Rights" preserved in the English constitution and warned the public that the "ancient principal Pillars of the Constitution" were shaken by the Council's aggressive and passionate lust for power. Both parties recognized the significance of the treasury issue. Morris did not miss the mark when he accused the lower house of coercing him by withholding a supply act and his salary on condition that he accede to its demands. "What these gentlemen [of the house] Call proposing I call'd threat'ning. That if I did not pass such bills as they sent up, they would not support, or as they call it, grant a support for the Government."[15] The house made it clear that the amount it voted for an official's salary was proportionate to its estimation of his service to the public. In light of complaints that the justices of the Supreme Court, most notoriously Robert Hunter Morris, were negligent in their duties, the Assembly discovered that voting a low salary was the only effective means to bridle that behavior.[16]

The legislative sessions became short and stormy. Dissolutions were prompt. In 1744, the Assembly granted the governor half his normal salary, promising the remainder on condition that he meet its demands to allow an issue of paper money and approve legislation to reform the courts and civil list. He refused and then dissolved the Assembly. The newly elected legislature denied him the entire sum. In addition, Morris pressed in vain for riot legislation. And, finally, he called the legislature to Trenton. The governor claimed sickness. The house saw calculated insult and intrusion on its rights and privileges. In April 1745, after a heated and unproductive session, the Assembly answered the governor's rebuke: "We are the third Assembly your Excellency hath met with in these Ten months last past, from which we have learnt rather to expect Dissolutions than Laws."[17]

Out of the prolonged confrontation, two positions emerged with each accusing the other of undermining the constitution.

According to the Country, the patriot yeoman stood resolute in the defense of provincial liberties against an overweening Court. In turn, the governor and his allies witnessed the dissolution of social order and the disruption of the constituticn. Court reform, argued the Country, was the responsibility of the legislature; the governor replied that the house was intruding beyond its boundaries and that justice should be achieved by the courts themselves. That the Assembly did nothing to stop the rioting belied its professions and demonstrated sympathy with the mob and republicanism. That the governor and Council sought a riot act confirmed the lawmakers' suspicion that the Court was grasping for the means to trample on the people's liberties. Memories of Stuart tyranny haunted the imagination of the Country. In the governor's circle, the events of 1641 and the specter of Oliver Cromwell shaped its understanding.[18]

The announcement of Morris's death in the spring of 1746 brought with it a change in the tone of political discourse. In the interim, while the province awaited news of the next appointment, the executive devolved upon the senior member of the Council. John Hamilton, a proprietor like Morris, recommended that the Assembly somehow take action against the rioting but, unlike his predecessor, did not indulge in histrionics or insulting exchanges. After a year's respite, and when Governor Jonathan Belcher arrived, rioting continued unabated, and the Assembly still had refused to act. In addition, the treasury would soon be emptied unless taxes were raised, and the discussions of taxation raised the issue of rates on unimproved lands owned by proprietors. Belcher made it his principle to avoid factional involvement, keep the contending parties guessing, and thereby force them to come to a settlement among themselves. He had come as a stranger: a native of Boston and former governor of Massachusetts and New Hampshire, he had spent three years in London seeking another commission. He had hoped for a better appointment than New Jersey; but, after fruitless and humiliating waiting in the anterooms of power, he accepted the opportunity. Likening himself to an exile, the aging governor arrived in the "wilds of Nova Caesarea" resolved to make the best of his stay and to avoid factionalism.[19]

The change in governors seemed to influence relations between the Council and Assembly and to bring about an agreement on the riot issue. To the upper house's demands for a riot bill, the lower responded with a call for clemency. In 1748, both agreed on a pardon act in exchange for a riot act. The agreement proved ineffective, however. The offer of clemency went ignored, and bands of farmers rescued their friends from jail. The proprietors were alarmed as the rioters seemed to grow stronger: the antiproprietors were constructing their own government, taxing themselves, meeting in convocations with sympathizers as far afield as Cape May, and sending their spokesmen to the legislature. In addition, rumors spread that they planned a march on the capital while the legislature was in session. Admitting that the compromise had failed, Belcher returned to the legislature asking for additional legislation. But the representatives would make no further concessions and voted by a margin of fifteen to three that the government already had powers sufficient to restore order in the province.[20]

First by its harassment of farmers in the courts and then by its opposition to the tax bills, the proprietary interest in the Council revealed its "sinister Views" and its proclivity for "Injustice and Opression" to the assemblymen.[21] The government was no longer able to meet its expenses from the interest collected on bills of credit, and the legislature began to consider a system of taxation. The critical problem was a method of evaluation--whether or not to tax the proprietors for their unimproved lands at the same rate as improved lands. The two houses came to an impasse. Between 1748 and 1751, the Assembly passed six bills, but none could meet the Council's approval. The upper house returned each with its amendments to protect proprietary interests, and, in response, the lower house denied the other's claims to alter money bills. In frustration, the governor dissolved the Assembly in 1751, called for new elections, and, laying aside his promise to himself that he stand above partisan entanglements, worked to place friendly representatives in the new house.[22] His efforts seemed for naught. In October, the Assembly passed the usual tax bill with only two dissenting votes from the Perth Amboy delegation. When the Council returned the bill with its usual amendments, the Assembly tore them from its original version and returned them without comment. Then venturing to bypass the usual constitutional process, it voted to send its bill directly to the governor for his approval. Belcher was at first tempted to join in the stratagem and reconsidered only when prevailed upon by Councilor Alexander. Then reversing himself, he indignantly scolded the house and adjourned it. Belcher despaired of a successful resolution to the issue. Yet, in January, the house met again and to the governor's surprise passed a bill that proved acceptable to the Council. That "short session," Belcher rejoiced, "has turned out the best of any since my Arrival."[23]

Roll-call analysis at once clarifies the interior life of the legislature and by doing so offers a different impression than that gained from the house's messages and the public prints. From the exterior, the representatives seemed ideologically

126

divided over the Country's agenda. Their votes resembled such a division; but, in contrast to the rhetoric, they did not reveal a hard, fast, or categorical split between Court and Country (Tables 5.1 through 5.3). Those who disagreed on one question did not divide in the same way on another item of the agenda. Support for the Country fluctuated radically: for example, the members voted by a margin of ten-to-one that the governor's salary be withheld pending compliance with their demands, but later only one-in-ten voted against a tax bill that complied with the Council's position. Categorical support or opposition to the several items of the agenda was exceptional. Instead, the majority left mixed records. Furthermore, although the house produced and maintained an ideologically coherent agenda for over a decade, its achievement did not reflect the ability of one clearly defined group to dominate the proceedings. Indeed, the votes provided more detailed evidence of the inchoate and volatile nature of the Assembly.

The fluctuating support for the Country suggests gradations of opinion. Understanding these shades of differences requires a method other than simply counting how frequently the members voted for or against the Country--or one that attends to the content of the votes and illuminates the specific issues or points of disagreement which distinguished one assemblyman from his colleague. To do this, a scale was constructed by ordering the roll calls from those that gained the greatest to those that gained the least margin of support for the Country. Then the representatives were ranked in descending order from those who gave the most to those who gave the least frequent support for the Country. The votes when laid out produced a pattern of group behavior and not only enabled identification of extreme and moderate members but also provided the means for understanding which issues provoked different responses.[24]

This method of analysis yielded significant conclusions. First, it revealed an underlying group behavior. The voting records reproduced the assumption behind the scales: that is, that the several items of the scale provoked varying degrees of difficulty for the members and that they were intellectually related. Each member responded in such a way that a point could be drawn in his record dividing his "yea" from "nay" votes. Thus, while their records were different, they responded to the scale of questions in a similar way as if they were connected. The emergent pattern with the "yea" votes clustering toward the upper left and the "nays" toward the lower right reflected a group response and confirmed that the agenda was, in fact, an intellectually coherent whole. Second, the distance from one end of the spectrum to the other was narrow. Only a small segment of the membership established

TABLE 5.1
COUNTRY-COURT DIVISIONS
1738–1744

Roll-Calls*

Assemblymen and Districts	1	2	3	4	5	6	7	8	9	10	11	12	13	14	15	16	17	18	19	20	21	22
Eaton,J.(Mnmth)	+	+	+	+	+	+	+	+	+	+	+	+	+	+	+	+	+	+	+	−	+	−
Lawrence,Ro.(Mnmth)		+	+	+					+						+							
Mott,W.(Hntrdn)		+	+	+					+						+							
VanBuskirk,L.(Brgn)	+		+	+	+	−	+	+	+	+	+	+	+	+	+	+	+	+	+	−	+	−
Cooke,W.(BrlCo)	+	+	+	+	+	+	+	+	+	+	+	+	+	+	+	+	−	+	+	+	+	+
Stacy,M.(BrlCo)	+		+									+	+	+		+		+	−		−	+
VanNeste,G.(Smrst)					+		+	+		+	+				−					−		
VanMiddleswardt,J.(Smrst)	+	+	+	+		+			+				+	+	−		−				+	
VenVeghten,D.(Smrst)			+	+					+						−							
Doughty,D.(Hntrdn)		+	+	+					+						−							
Willets,J.(CpMy)		+	+	+											−							
Hancock,W.(Slm)	+	+	+	+	+	+	+	−	+	+	+	−	−	−	−	−				+	+	+
Vandervere,C.(Mnmth)	+			+	+	+	+		+		+	−	+		−	+	−	−		−	+	−
Leaming,A.Sr.(CpMy)	+			+	−	+	+		+	+	+		−	−	−		−	−	−			
Mickle,J.(Glcstr)		+	+	+	+		+	+	+	+	+	−		−	−	−				+	+	+
Cooper,J.(Glcstr)	+	+	+	+	+	+	+	+	+	+	+	−	−	−	−	−				+	+	+
Brick,J.(Slm)						+									−							−
Shinn,T.(BrlCo)		+	+	+											−							+
Demarest,D.(Brgn)	+	+	+	+	+	+	+	−	+	−	−	−	+	+	−	−	−	+		−		+
Low,J.(Essx)	+					+							−	−						+	+	
Peace,J.(Hntrdn)	+					−							−	−						+	+	
Dumont,P.(Smrst)				+		+	−		+		+									−	−	−
Leonard,T.(Smrst)						+							−	−						+	+	
Rolph,J.(Essx)	+					+							−	−						+	−	
Smith,R.(Slm)	+														−							
Gibbon,L.(Slm)									−					−								
Reeves,J.(Slm)					+		+	−		−	−	−					−			+		
Young,H.(CpMy)					+		+	−		−	−	−					+			−		
Hude,R.(Mddlsx)	+					+							−	−			−	−	−	+	+	
Leaming,A.Jr.(CpMy)	+	+	−	−		+							−	−			−	−	−	−	−	
Farmer,T.(Mddlsx)	+	+	−	−		−							−				−	−		−	−	+
Smith,B.(Hntrdn)	+					−	−	−							−		−	+		+	+	
Hude,J.(Mddlsx)				−	−	−		−	−	−	−	−			−					−		
Antill,E.(Mddlsx)				−	−		−	−	−	−					−					−		
Leonard,S.(PrthAmby)		−	−	−					−						−							
Johnston,L.(PrthAmby)	−					−	−	−							−	−				−	+	
Johnston,A.(PrthAmby)						−	−	−							−					−		
Nevill,S.(Mddlsx)		−	−	−					−						−							
Emley,J.(Hntrdn)						−	−	−		−	−	−					−			+		
Ogden,J.(Essx)						−	−	−		−	−	−					−					
Bonnell,J.(Essx)		−	−	−		−	−	−	−						−							
Vreeland,G.(Essx)		−	−	−		−	−	−							−							
Pearson,I.(BrlTwn)	−	+	+	+	−	−	−	−	+	−	−	−	+	−	+	−	−	−	−	+	+	+
Smith,R.(BrlTwn)	−	+	+	+	−	−	−	−	+	−	−	−	−	−	−	−	−	−	−	+	+	+

128

*TOPICS OF ROLL CALLS**

1. Not to confer with the Council on its amendments to bill for regulating sheriff appointments (June 11, 1740)

2. To approve address to the governor refusing his request for a revised militia act (June 27, 1744)

3. To approve the committee report that the militia act is sufficient (June 26, 1744)

4. To reject the Council's militia bill (July 2, 1744)

5. To withhold appropriation for securing a separate governor (December 15, 1738)

6. To approve measure for regulating fees (November 10, 1742)

7. Not to grant Lewis Morris a "sum of money for the expense of procuring a distinct governor" (December 15, 1738)

8. To allow Governor Morris Ⱡ300 instead of Ⱡ500 for securing a separate governor (February 3, 1738/9)

9. To pay chief justice Ⱡ100 instead of Ⱡ150 (December 3, 1743)

10. Not to acknowledge Morris's efforts for securing a separate governor (February 3, 1738/9)

11. Not to pay Morris Ⱡ500 for securing a separate governor (Feburary 3, 1738/9)

12. Not to pass a support bill (February 15, 1738/9)

13. Not to pay the second justice of the Supreme Court Ⱡ30 (October 22, 1741)

14. Not to pay the third justice of the Supreme Court Ⱡ20 (September 23, 1741)

15. To pay the governor Ⱡ800 instead of Ⱡ1000 (December 3, 1743)

16. Not to confer with the Council on support bill (March 3, 1738/9)

17. Not to pass a support bill (November 17, 1742)

18. Not to pay the chief justice Ⱡ200 (October 22, 1741)

19. Not to pay the third justice of the Supreme Court Ⱡ30 (October 22, 1741)

129

20. Not to pass the militia bill (January 25, 1738/9)

21. To pass a bill requiring sheriffs to give security (June 3, 1740)

22. To appoint an agent in London (November 17, 1742)

** In order to establish consistency in the scales, the wording of several motions needed to be inverted. Consider items 3 and 4: the original wording of 3 was to approve a committee report on the militia, but the wording of item 4 was to approve the Council's militia bill. Those who voted "yea" on the first were recorded in the house journal to vote "nay" on the second roll call. In fact, the one roll call is the reflection of the other. And for the sake of consistency, the votes of the second roll call were recoded to read "yea" (+) in the scale and the wording of the motion was corresponding inverted.

TABLE 5.2
COUNTRY-COURT DIVISIONS
1744-1745

Roll-Calls*

ssemblymen and istricts	1	2	3	4	5	6	7	8	9	10	11	12	13	14	15	16	17	18	19	20	21	22	23	24	25	26	27
ton,J.(Mnmth)		+	+	+	+	+	+		+	+	+	+	+	+	+	+	+	+	+	+	+	+	+	+	+	+	−
wrence,Ro.(Mnmth)	+	+	+	+	+	+	+	+	+	+	+	+	+	+	+	+	+	+	+	+	+	+	+	+	+	+	−
nBuskirk,L.(Brgn)	+	+		+	+	+	+	+	+	+	+	+	+	+	+	+	+	+	+	+	+	+	+	+	+	+	+
nVeghten,D.(Smrst)		+	+		+	+		+	+				+	+	−	+	+	+	+		+	+					
nMiddleswardt,J.(Smrst)	+	+	+	+	+	+		+	+	+	+	+								+	+	+	+	+		+	+
w,J.(Essx)	+						+				+		+	+										+	+	+
ott,W.(Hntrdn)	+	+	+	+	+	+	+	+	+	+	+	+	+	+	+	+	+	+	+	+	+	+	+	+	+	+	−
ith,R.(BrlTwn)	+	+	+	+	+	+	+	+	+	+	+	+	+	+	+	+	+	+	+	+	+	+	+	+	+	+	+
arson,I.(BrlTwn)		+	+		+	+			+	+					+	+	+	+	+		+	+	+	+			
ith,D.(BrlTwn)	+					+	+					+															
oke,W.(BrlCo)	+	+	+	+	+	+		+		+	+	+	+	+	+	+	+	+	+					+	+	+
ight,S.(BrlCo)	+			+			+	+			+	+	+	+										+	+	−
inn,T.(BrlCo)		+	+																								
pkins,E.(Glcstr)	+			+			+	+			+	+	+	+										+	+	+
oper,J.(Glcstr)		+	+	+	+	+			+	+		+	+	+	+	+	+	+				+	+	+			+
ckle,J.(Glcstr)		+	+																								
eppard,M.(Slm)		+	+		+	+		+	+				+	+	+	+	+	+	+	+	+						
marest,D.(Brgn)	+	+	+	+	+			+	+		+	+	+	+	+	+	+	+	+	+	+	+	−	+			+
ncock,W.(Slm)	+	+	+	+	+	+	+	+	+	+	+	+	+	+	+	+	+	+	+	+	+	+	−			−	−
ick,J.(Slm)	+			+	+		+		+	+														+	−		+
aming,A.Jr.(CpMy)	+		+		+	+		+	+	+	+													−	−		+
cer,J.(CpMy)	+	+	+	+	+	+		+	+	+	+	+	+	+	+	+	+	+	−	+	+	+	−	−	−		+
ughty,D.(Hntrdn)	+		+	+	+	+			+	+		+	+	+	+		+	+	+	−	+	+	−		−	+	+
ane,J.(Essx)	+	+	+	+	+	+	+	+	+	+	+	+	+	+	−	+	+	+	−	+	−	−	+	−		+	+
eeland,G.(Essx)		+	+		+	+		+	+						+	−	−	−	+	−	−	−			−	−	+
her,H.(Smrst)	+			+			+	+			+	−	−											−	−		+
ung,H.(CpMy)		+	+		+	+		+	−						−	−			−	−							
rmer,T.(Mddlsx)			+									−															
ores,J.(Mddlsx)	+					+				−		−	−											−	−		+
ard,J.(Mddlsx)	−		−			−	−				−	−	−											−	−		−
de,J.(Mddlsx)		−	−		−	−		−	−			−	−	−													
ke,W.(Mddlsx)		−	−		−	−		−	−			−	−	−													
ele,P.(PrthAmby)	−			−	−		−	−		−		−	−	−										−	−		+
onard,S.(PrthAmby)		−	−		−	−		−	−			−	−	−	−	−	−	−	−	−	−						

131

*TOPICS OF ROLL CALLS**

1. To print Governor Morris's letter to the speaker, which reprimands the house for printing its address to him before it was delivered (May 24, 1745)

2. To approve bill emitting Ł40,000 in paper money (October 9, 1744)

3. To pass bill emitting Ł40,000 in paper money (October 17, 1744)

4. That Governor Morris's decision to move the Assembly to Trenton is a grievance (October 18, 1745)

5. That commissioners of the Loan Office were chosen illegally and that the justices of the peace of Hunterdon County are guilty of violating the law (November 9, 1744)

6. To approve remonstrance to Governor Morris that Hunterdon County's justices of the peace have violated the law (November 9, 1744)

7. To send message to the governor accusing him of needlessly provoking controversy and insulting the house and reminding him that his support will be suspended until he approves legislation approved by the house (May 28, 1745)

8. To approve message to the governor reminding him that the house expects approval of bills for paper money, regulating sheriffs, and preventing small cases from being brought to the Supreme Court before it will approve his support (May 30, 1745)

9. To reject the Council's amendments to the militia bill (November 27, 1744)

10. To send message to the governor noting the illegal acts by Hunterdon County's justices of the peace (November 10, 1744)

11. To approve message to the governor accusing him of provoking needless controversy and answering his attacks on the house (April 18, 1745)

12. To approve message to the governor accusing him of heeding lying councilors, lamenting his opposition to the militia bill, refusing to grant powres for responding to the Newark riot, and reminding him that his salary will be withheld (October 3, 1745)

13. To pay the governor Ł500 instead of Ł1000 (April 30, 1745)

14. To pass support bill which withholds the governor's salary (May 1, 1745)

15. To pay councilors three instead of six shillings per diem (November 24, 1744)

16. To pay the governor Ł500 instead of Ł1000 (November 24, 1744)

17. To cut the chief justice's salary to Ł50 (November 24, 1744)

18. To pay the second and third justices of the Supreme Court Ł20 instead of Ł30 (November 24, 1744)

19. To pay the representatives three shillings per diem instead of nothing (November 24, 1744)

20. To pass a militia bill (October 26, 1744)

21. Not to confer with the Council on the militia bill (November 28, 1744)

22. Not to pass bill for support of the government (November 27, 1744)

23. To decline proposals to alter the militia bill (November 27, 1744)

24. Not to confer with the Council on bill preventing cases involving less than Ł15 from introduction to the Supreme Court (November 20, 1744)

25. To accept the committee report that the province defer its support for the war effort (April 26, 1745)

26. To cut the chief justice's salary to Ł50 (April 30, 1745)

27. Not to pay the representatives six shillings per diem (April 30, 1745)

** In order to establish consistency in the scales, the wording of several motions needed to be inverted. See note for Table 5.1 for further explanation.

TABLE 5.3
COUNTRY-COURT DIVISIONS
1746-1754

Roll-Calls*

Assemblymen and Districts	1	2	3	4	5	6	7	8	9	10	11	12	13	14	15	16	17	18	19	20	21	22	23	24	25	26	27	28	29	30	31	32	33	34	35	36	37	38	39	40	41	42	43	44	45	46	47	48	49	50
Eaton,J.(Mnmth)	+	+																																															-	+
Lawrence,Ro.(Mnmth)				+	+	+	+	+	+	+	+	+	+	+	+	+	+	+	+	+	+	+	+	+	+	+	+	+	+	+	+	+	+	+	+	+	+	+	+	+	+	+	+	+	+	-	-	-		
Holmes,J.(Mnmth)			+																																							+	+	+	+	+	+	+	+	+
Mott,W.(Hntrdn)	+	+	+						+						+	+	+	+	+	+																													-	+
VanBuskirk,L.(Brgn)	+	+	+		+	+	+	+	+	+	+	+		+	+	+	+	+	+									+		+	+										+	+	+	+	+	+		+	-	-
VanVorst,C.(Brgn)															-	+	+	+	+	+	+	+	+	+	+							+			+	+										+				
Smith,S.(Mddlsx)															-	+	+	+	+	+								+	+	+	-	+											-	-	-	-	-	-	-	-
Hopkins,E.(Glcestr)	+	+			+	+	+	+	+	+	+	+		+	+	+					+	+								+	+					+	-											-	+
Wright,S.(BrlCo)	+	+			+	+	+	+	+	+	+	+									-							+	+							-											-	+	+
Crane,J.(Essx)	+	+			+	+	+	+	+	+	+	+									+	+						-	-	+						-											-	+	+
Low,J.(Essx)	+	+			+	+	+	+	+	+	+	+				-					+	+				+		+	+							-											-	+	+
Camp,J.(Essx)			+	+		+	+	+					+								-	+									-					-												-	+
Dey,D.(Brgn)			+	+		+	+	+			+																																							
Demarest,D.(Brgn)	+	+			-	-	+	+	+	+	+	+	+	+	+	+	+	+	+	+	+	+			+	+			-						+														+
Spicer,J.(CpMy)	+	+					+	+	+	-	+				+	+	+	+	+		+					-									+													+	+
Leaming,A.Jr.(CpMy)	+	+			+	+	+	+	+	+	+	+			+	+	+	+			+					-				+					+														+
Wetherill,J.(Mddlsx)			+						+		+				+	+	+	+			+				-	-				-																			
VanMiddlewardt,J.(Smrst)	+	+			+	+	+	+	+	+	-	-	-	-	-	-	-	-	-	-	-	-			+	+			-	+	+	+			+												+	+
Fisher,H.(Smrst)	+	+			+	+	+	+	+	-	-	-	-	-	-	-	-	-	-	-					+	+			+	+	+				-												-	+
Mickle,W.(Glcstr)										-	-	-	+	+	+	+	+	+			-								+	+																		-	+
Wood,R.(Slm)			+																						+																								
Cooke,W.(BrlCo)	+	+			+	+	+	+	+	+	+	+			+	+	+	+	-	-	-	-			+	+			-	+	+				-												+	+
Brick,J.(Slm)	+	+			+	+	+	+	+	+	-	+			+	+	+	+	-	-	-	-							-	-	-				-												+	+
Hancock,W.(Slm)	+	+			+	+	+	+	-	+	-	+									-	-			+				-						-													
Emley,J.(Hntrdn)	+	+			+	+	+	+	-	-	-	-									-	-			+				-	-	-				-												+	+
Cooper,J.(Glcstr)	+	+			+	+	+	+			+										-								-																		-	+
Hinchman,J.(Glcestr)															+	+																																	
Ellis,J.(Glcstr)															+	+														-																			
Heard,J.(Mddlsx)	+	+			+	+	-	-																	-	-	+			-					-						-							-	+
Smith,R.(BrlTwn)	+	+			+	+	-	-	-	-	-	-									-	-			-	-				-					-						-	-						+	+
Smith,D.(BrlTwn)	+	+			+	+	-	-	-	-	-	-									-	-								-					-						-	-						+	+
Newbold,J.(BrlCo)			+								+				-	+									-	-	+																						
Deacon,J.(BrlTwn)			+												-	+									-																								
Bispham,J.(BrlCo)									-																-																								
Smith,J.(Mddlsx)			+	+					-																-																								
Ogden,R.(Essx)				+																																													
Nevill,S.(PrthAmby)	-	-										-																						-					-							-			+	+
Johnston,L.(PrthAmby)	-				-	-						-																		-																-			+	+
Steele,P.(PrthAmby)	-				-	-			+																					-																-				+
Johnston,J.(PrthAmby)																														-									-							-				
Kearney,P.(Mddlsx)	-	-			-	-	-	-																						-									-							-				

*TOPICS OF ROLL CALLS**

1. To send message to Governor Morris that the Assembly will not pay his salary until he approves its bill (May 7, 1746)

2. Not to grant Governor Morris's estate back salaries (December 17, 1747)

3. Not to pay the Morris estate (October 11, 1749)

4. To pass an uncompromised support and tax bill (October 15, 1751)

5. That additional riot legislation is not needed (December 7, 1748)

6. To reaffirm house position that additional riot legislation is not needed (December 8, 1748)

7. To reject the Council's riot legislation (May 1, 1746)

8. To approve the message to Governor Belcher that the Assembly has done all that is possible to stop the riots (March 25, 1749)

9. To send a message to Governor Belcher accusing the Council of subverting the constitution and preventing the supply of the treasury (February 22, 1751)

10. To grant Ŀ60, not Ŀ100, for Governor Belcher's house rent (December 2, 1748)

11. Not to confer with the Council on its amendments to tax bill (February 10, 1748)

12. To send a message to Governor Belcher that the Council is to blame for instigating riots (March 4, 1749)

13. To pay Ŀ25 instead of Ŀ30 to second and third justices of the Supreme Court (October 15, 1746)

14. To print a bill for preventing riots (May 1, 1746)

15. To pay the attorney general Ŀ30 instead of Ŀ40 (December 2, 1748)

16. To send a message to Governor Belcher asserting the Assembly's constitutional right to set method for supplying the treasury (June 4, 1751)

17. To set tax assessments at a high level (October 12, 1751)

18. To send a tax bill directly to Governor Belcher rather than to the Council (October 21, 1751)

19. To print a house resolution that sending the tax bill directly to the governor was constitutionally correct (October 23, 1751)

20. That the Assembly has the constitutional right to bypass the Council on tax bill (October 22, 1751)

21. To approve amendment on tax bill regarding assessments on unimproved lands (Feburary 7, 1752)

22. To set tax assessments at a high level (February 6, 1752)

23. To inform Governor Morris that the house will not pay his salary unless he approves its bills (May 7, 1746)

24. To pay the chief justice Ŀ50 instead of Ŀ100 (October 15, 1746)

25. To reject an amendment related to the assessment of land values (February 6, 1752)

26. To reject an amendment on land values (February 7, 1752)

27. To accept an amendment on land value assessments (February 7, 1752)

28. To pay the chief justice Ŀ50 instead of Ŀ100 (October 7, 1749)

29. To pay Governor Belcher Ŀ800 instead of Ŀ1000 (October 7, 1749)

30. To pay the chief justice Ŀ50 instead of Ŀ100 (December 2, 1748)

31. To pay Governor Morris's house rent (December 17, 1747)

32. Not to support a compromise on the tax bill (February 7, 1752)

33. To amend the tax bill (June 15, 1754)

34. To send tax bill directly to Governor Belcher rather than to the Council (February 8, 1752)

35. Not to support compromise tax bill (February 8, 1752)

36. Not to pay the attorney general (October 15, 1746)

37. To pay Governor Belcher Ŀ800 instead of Ŀ1000 (December 2, 1748)

38. Not to support the government (December 19, 1747)

39. To pay Governor Belcher Ŀ800 instead of Ŀ1000 (December 2, 1748)

40. Not to support the government (December 5, 1748)

41. Not to support the government (October 9, 1749)

42. To pay Governor Belcher Ł800 instead of Ł1000 (February 6, 1752)

43. To pay Governor Belcher Ł800 instead of Ł1000 (May 31, 1753)

44. To pay Governor Belcher Ł800 instead of Ł1000 (June 15, 1754)

45. To pay Governor Belcher Ł800 instead of Ł1000 (June 1, 1751)

46. Not to pass a riot bill (February 13, 1748)

47. Not to support a compromise tax bill (June 15, 1754)

48. Not to support a compromise tax bill (June 18, 1754)

49. In support of a bill emitting Ł40,000 in bills of credit (April 3, 1746)

50. In support of a bill emitting Ł40,000 in bills of credit (December 8, 1747)

** In order to establish consistency in the scales, the wording of several motions needed to be inverted. See note for Table 5.1 for further explanation.

and maintained an undeviating record over time. Instead, the majority was capable of agreeing with one extreme and then the other. Third, closer examination of the individual records revealed that the lawmakers often changed their position on the same issue. Furthermore, while the house explicitly connected several components of the agenda in its messages, some members separated them into separate segments and supported one and not another. These behavior patterns suggested something other than moderation in the rational sense and pointed instead to extrarational dimensions such as intellectual tension or discomfort, changes in mood, and different levels of abstraction. Fourth, the roll calls documented sequences of behavior over time and changes in mood. Members not only changed their position on specific items but made extreme and categorical shifts on the entire agenda. For example, in 1744, the house was considering far more radical motions than what had been introduced in previous assemblies. Yet those who had been reluctant or incapable of embracing the more moderate motions were now adopting even more extreme alternatives.

Between 1738 and 1754, two small segments of the house membership voted consistently at the extreme ends of the scales. At one end, the Perth Amboy clique voted consistently in support of the governor, for an invigorated militia and riot legislation, in defense of the proprietary interest, against messages condemning the governors or the Council, for all support bills, and for high salaries. It did not always vote alone. The representatives, especially from the port of Burlington and a few from the counties, tended to agree with that position. What distinguished Perth Amboy's representatives was that, unlike Richard Smith and Issac Pearson, they did not deviate. Moreover, the delegation's record reflected a strong sense of group identity: with the exception of Nevill, the port's representatives did not stay long, but the rate of turnover did not affect the delegation's record. No doubt its stand was born of interest and even a sense of being besieged by the rural majorities. But the consistency was more than the product of narrow economic calculations of a factious interest group. Belcher's appointment had roused concerns in the proprietary circle that it had lost exclusive access to power. It jealously attended to reports that the governor was consulting with such rivals as John Low and Richard Smith. Indeed, proprietors openly confronted the governor at the Council table.[25] But, in the house, these urban representatives who were once in and now out of power continued to support the governor as consistently as they had during the Morris administration.

When the proprietors discussed their opposition, they fixed their attention on Woodbridge and Newark. Yet the roll calls disclose that it was not Newark's John Low but Bergen's

Lawrence Van Buskirk who consistently voted in disagreement with Perth Amboy. Between 1738 and 1751, Van Buskirk defined a die-hard Country position: only once, on a motion to regulate fees, did he agree with Perth Amboy. He and a splinter of the membership consistently endorsed every message critical of both governors and the Council, opposed changing the militia system and the passage of riot legislation, rejected any tax bill that made concessions to the proprietary interest, attempted to reduce salaries, and finally voted against every government support bill. These die-hard lawmakers were found principally among the Monmouth representatives: John Eaton, Robert Lawrence, and James Holmes. William Mott remembered his father who represented Monmouth County and who had opposed Lewis Morris. Since then, he had removed to Hunterdon County; but, when he entered the Assembly in 1743, he joined in voting with his former neighbors.

David Demarest agreed as often as he disagreed with his neighbor Lawrence Van Buskirk. The majority of the representatives voted somewhere between the two ends of the scale. What distinguished them from the Country diehard was their voting on salaries and the government's support. They found it easier to oppose militia reform, to reject the governor's pleas for riot legislation, and to challenge the proprietary interest on tax bills than to cut salaries or to deny the government's supply. When Hendrick Fisher entered the Assembly, he joined in reprimanding Governor Morris for heeding the advice of lying "Informers" and courtiers in the Council, for obstructing the public welfare, and for violating the liberties of the people and the privileges of the house, but he also preferred to maintain high salaries for the governor and his son.[26] In the next two assemblies, he and William Hancock resisted attempts to augment the governor's powers to quell the rioting, but they both voted with Perth Amboy to pay salaries and to pass a general support bill. Of course, there were differences of opinion, gradations of opinion, among the majority. Hancock and John Heard, for example, were more likely than not to agree with Perth Amboy. On the other hand, there were some like Fisher, Demarest, and Spicer who voted in the center of the scale. Finally, there were those like Hopkins and Wright who appeared closest to the die-hard end of the scale.

The lawmakers were not choosing between irreconcilable positions. When voting on salaries, they were usually not deciding whether to grant or deny an official his income but how much to allow him. And the low alternative (only slightly less than the high amount) seemed a symbolic gesture of disapproval. In the course of their deliberations, the lawmakers came to make fine distinctions and were seeking a common basis for agreement.

Opposition to the militia bills came from two sources: one denominational or Quaker and the other a reluctance to empower the militia officers. Quaker opposition was predictable but not always firm: sometimes a Friend did support a militia bill, and it was not uncommon for one to abstain from voting. Non-Quakers agreed on the necessity of a militia bill but disagreed over its provisions. But the lines were not clearly drawn. A member could support one version and not another. In the fall of 1744, Crane and Vreeland were not completely satisfied with the house bill but approved its passage. Nor did they approve the Council's amendments. But they also approved motions to reconsider the bill and to confer with the Council on its revision. Riot legislation initially met with the majority's disapproval, but later roll calls demonstrated that only a handful of diehards were uncompromising and that most could approve some form of legislation. Representatives Wright and Fisher approved a riot bill but later rejected motions for additional legislation. Demarest rejected a Council bill and, after supporting the house bill, went on to press for additional legislation. John Heard, who confronted the rioters at his doorstep, supported the Council's bill but later rejected motions to augment the house riot bill.[27]

The lawmakers regularly found themselves on common ground. Those voting at opposite ends of the scale--the Country diehard and Perth Amboy's so-called courtier--came to agree on measures for regulating the behavior of sheriffs and for emitting additional paper money. Sometimes during the deliberations on taxation, the chances for reconciliation seemed remote. Hancock and Fisher, for example, approved the house bill that made no concession to the proprietors' interest and refused to confer with the Council. When the house prepared messages stating its position accusing the upper house of selfish disregard for the public welfare and of subverting the constitution, Fisher voted his approval, but Hancock joined with the Perth Amboy delegation in dissent. Finally, both members joined to support a compromise bill. Only a splinter group of three diehards--Lawrence, Holmes, and Mott--and Bergen's Cornelius Van Vorst opposed sending the bill to the Council.

Because the lawmakers conducted their business without reference or loyalty to party organization and because their differences did not translate into irreconcilable ideologies, they were able to resolve their disagreements and move toward a central ground. But the absence of party had another effect. As the number of issues increased, incongruities appeared between the agenda and voting behavior.[28] An item, although intellectually congruent with the agenda, produced unexpected responses. That is, the votes did not conform to the scale, and the members responded as if it were unrelated to the others.

140

As the Assembly constructed its agenda in confrontation with the governor and Council, it entertained a proposal to appoint an agent to represent its position at Whitehall and to defend its actions against Morris's charges. The question also introduced a constitutional debate whether the appointment could be made by the house alone or whether it required the assent of the governor and Council. Yet the division bore little resemblance to the alignments on the whole agenda. The governor's staunchest critics tended to oppose the measure; those at the opposite end of the scale tended to approve; and the remaining rural members in the middle cast their votes in a manner which bore little resemblance to the scale of roll calls.

In general, the lawmakers responded to the several issues of the agenda as if they were congruent or scalar. Those opposed to an invigorated militia also were testy about riot legislation and responded to the tax issue in a similar manner. But, on closer examination, the scales revealed something other than degrees of opinion. While the cutting points in individual records between "yea" and "nay" votes served as an indication of moderation, they also suggested that some members established an association or linkage between related items of the agenda and others did not. The differences between this coherent and segmented pattern emerged in the votes on salaries. Salary votes were a barometer of opinion: those inclined toward low allowances were most inclined to support the Country opposition. The house made the connection explicit: "every Man," it reminded Governor Morris, "ought to be rewarded according to his Works."[29] The standard applied to the governor's appointees and allies as well. During the stormy session of 1744, the house voted on allowances for its members and the councilors. Those members in opposition to the government voted to pay low per diem allowances to the councilors, and the small splinter of dissenters replied by proposing that the assemblymen be paid nothing for their services and that the councilors be compensated double what was approved. Although the house identified the governor and his allies as coconspirators, lawmakers registered their disapproval of some but not others. While the drafters of the house messages identified a Court, some of their colleagues focused on specific personalities--the governor, but not his son. David Demarest, for example, voted for high and low salaries for Lewis and Robert Hunter Morris and for Jonathan Belcher. And, during the session of 1745, five members split their votes on the governor and chief justice.

Demarest had also shifted his position on thanking the governor for getting final separation from New York. But changes on specific measures were not uncommon. Some voting records revealed much more dramatic, even categorical, motion.

141

John Low began his career as a moderate who approved reform of the civil list as well as high salaries and the support bill. In the Fifteenth Assembly (1745), he took a more extreme position by not only condemning the governor for violating provincial liberties and provoking deadlock between the branches of government but also by cutting the governor's salary and then denying him anything until he mended his ways. By the end of the decade, the Newark representative returned to supporting the government and was even voting with Perth Amboy: he approved riot legislation; on the tax issue, he refused to embrace the house's constitutional arguments and finally endorsed concessions to the proprietary interest. William Cooke's change was dramatic. When entering the house in 1738, the representative from Burlington County adopted Van Buskirk's die-hard position. At that time, his neighbor Richard Smith was voting with Perth Amboy. In the sessions of 1744 and 1745, Smith swung to the opposite position and voted with Cooke in categorical opposition to the government. Smith, however, soon resumed his previous voting habits in the last session to meet with Morris. But Cooke also proved to be no diehard. After eight years of voting at the extreme end of the scale, he moved toward a moderate position: while unsympathetic to pleas for additional riot legislation, he approved high salaries for Chief Justice Morris and the governor and supported compromise tax legislation.

If the lawmakers had taken their cues from either Samuel Nevill or Lawrence Van Buskirk, they would have divided along clearly defined ideological and social lines, and the alignments would have reproduced the descriptions rendered by Jerseymen themselves. Instead, the majority proved the two lawmakers exceptional. The scale analysis discovered that most members refrained from either extreme or that they tended to vote in a manner which might be labeled moderate. This method, because it disclosed patterned responses to a coherent agenda, tended to focus attention on a single dimension--the rational. Evidence also points toward the extrarational. Voting on the Country agenda bears a resemblance to the responses to the socioeconomic agenda. In neither case were the members deliberating on ideological alternatives. To raise up the image of a Court was hyperbolic, if not fantastic. And, in both cases, representatives segregated related, even complementary, elements from each other and changed their positions on identical questions. Moreover, the profiles of assemblymen, including the record of their participation in the house proceedings, pointed to differences in temperament and style. Consider again Nevill and Van Buskirk. Their differences were something more than rational. The Bergen lawmaker was just as unbending in his opposition to the province's "worldly gentry" as he was disapproving of measures enabling the government to achieve economic improvement. The speaker, on the other hand, embraced measures for domestic improvement as consistently as he opposed the Country's attack on the government. Van Buskirk, the diehard and naysayer, was also a backbencher who did not participate in the drafting of messages and legislation. Rather than defining policy alternatives, he reacted to an agenda that was the creation of others. In contrast, Nevill, who was once an English journalist and who later edited The New American Magazine, entered the house already familiar with the constitutional questions and their historical antecedents. On entrance, he achieved recognition as an activist, was soon after chosen speaker, and later became a justice on the Supreme Court.

Both Van Buskirk and Robert Lawrence were diehards and naysayers. But Lawrence, a lawyer, also resembled Nevill in that he was a house activist and sometimes speaker. Because representatives supported the same measures did not necessarily mean they attached the same meaning to their votes. Several psychological dimensions, both rational and extrarational, contributed to the voting. And they did not always combine in the same way. Cooke participated actively in the house's business and supported economic reforms. But, during the Morris years, he joined with the die-hard opposition. And later he shifted to a moderate position. Something more than the sum of biographical information explains why Fisher in contrast to his colleagues of similar social origins emerged as an activist and a moderate on both agendas. But the contrasting profiles suggested the presence of several factors. The meaning of an individual's voting record was not reflected in the bills and messages he approved and disapproved. The lawmakers came from different paths to approve the same measures. They came with different intellectual horizons--some localist and some provincial. While some plunged into the house proceedings, other remained passive observers. In turn, they did not give the same priority to the agenda. And some understood and discussed the issues as part of a coherent ideological system, while their colleagues responded from cultural prejudice or temperament. So, too, some voted from prejudice or negative feelings toward colleagues rather than from a full understanding of the content of the issues. These factors combined, not always perfectly but sufficiently, so that a typology of lawmakers may be sketched.

The Country was as much temperament as ideology, as much a cluster of attitudes or prejudices rooted in a social experience, as it was an abstract intellectual tradition. Its embodiment was the testy representative who came to the Assembly guided by a stubborn independence and a wariness toward the provincial government. He was that plain and virtuous ploughman lawmaker who received appointments to local office as his due or as recognition of his achievements but not with a sense of reciprocity or binding obligation to the governor. Lewis Morris made his appointments in the hope that he could bind these independents to his administration; but, in return for granting commissions to representatives Mott, Van Buskirk, and Cooke, he received their unbending opposition. Most lawmakers had received appointment to the civil lists. In 1744, when the majority came to an impasse with the governor and only five refused to cut his salary, two in every three members had received appointments from the governor's office.[30] The Country member arrived already leary of the provincial government and predisposed to reject motions empowering it with the means for promoting the economy.[31] And it was the same temperament that readied him to join in efforts to restrain the governor's powers over elections and the civil and military lists.

This temperament, born of a common social experience, brought with it a common receptivity to the rhetoric of the Country. It was a temperament that was both rural and conservative. First, it was both rural and localist. It was found in the member who came concerned about the building of a bridge or a dispute over its maintenance or about a mill and its affect on navigation rights. While expecting the Assembly to aid in his or his neighbors' affairs, he had paid little attention to provincial affairs, especially those affecting the "ancient constitution." Second, his conservatism fell short of the systematic but was a collection of prejudices and predispositions against the provincial government. The prejudices that prodded him to reject economic reform also led him to support attempts to limit the governor's powers. He need not attend to ideological argument to support the Country agenda. Memory of recent sheriff appointments in his county was reason enough to support reform of the civil list. And meeting provincial officialdom and its allies pricked rural and dissenting prejudices against the urban and Anglican. And, in turn, the rhetoric of the Country was appealing because it evoked images of himself as the virtuous ploughman patriot. Another type of lawmaker shared these attitudes but also gave them ideological expression. He was the member who made provincial affairs his concern, drafted messages stating the house's position, and contributed to the construction of the house agenda. His horizons stretched out both spatially and temporally to include the last century of Anglo-American constitutional and political history. In sum, he entered the world of print, translated his prejudices into formal abstract thought, and constructed a coherent and articulate agenda.

As a blend of prejudices and ideology, the Country was multifaceted. Thus, majorities responded to the agenda along a spectrum from extreme to moderate support for the Country. The scales not only reflected differences in considered belief but also served as a barometer of rural prejudices. So, too, the vocabulary evoked different meanings. There was broad agreement that the courtier was someone to be disdained and opposed. Opposition lifted the mundane world of provincial politics to the level of grand historical drama. Morris and his henchmen were burrowing deeply into the body politic: they held the executive, prevailed in the Council, and, with the aid of a sycophantic following, were extending their influences into the counties. The infection seemed systemic to some. Others, however, fixed their sights more narrowly and upon specific malefactors. Thus, when opportunity came to withhold approval of public services, they focused on one but not another member of the Court. And, when the Country bloc was the largest and most aggressive (Table 3.5), a majority chose to reinstate Samuel Nevill as presiding officer. The governor made a difference. After Morris's death, the Country continued its attack on his Court, which remained entrenched in the Council; but, without his presence, it could not sustain the majorities or the offensive it had once achieved.

The Country was strong because it was a fusion of temperament and ideology. As such, it became an agent binding an assemblage of strangers together into an opposition. But prejudices had to be powerful enough to overcome the discomforts that came with opposition. Thus, no matter the principles at stake, the Assembly found it most difficult to exercise the power of the purse. Few Country patriots countenanced withholding support from the government. Most, even after weeks of disagreeing with the governor, voted him his full salary. And those in dissent proposed that his salary be reduced from £1,000 to £800. In 1745, Country sentiment ran high and seemed to overcome inhibitions. The majority voted in extreme opposition and with the die-hard Country. But the mood could not be sustained. A year later all but one returned; and, although the issues remained, many rural members resumed their moderate voting habits.

The lawmaker who voted against the Country was not a courtier. He drew from the same pool of attitudes as his opponent but gave them different emphasis. In contrast to his rural and localist colleague, he came to the Assembly with an urban and provincial perspective. This member was at home with the provincial elite; friends and relatives sat in the Council; he dined with governors; and he attended to London politics. He did not share the rural lawmaker's jaundiced opinion of the government. And, just as he was by temperament disposed to embrace reforms empowering government to promote a well-regulated economy, so, too, he was disinclined to join the

Country opposition. On the floor of the house, he not only acted upon previously acquired attitudes but was also reacting to his rural colleagues. Temperamental differences were quickened by contrasting cultural styles and sometimes reinforced by competing economic interests. If he shied from opposition, he did so in reaction to individuals and not in repudiation of the principles they espoused. For Perth Amboy's delegates, taste and interest combined to create a sense of being besieged. According to Nevill, he confronted dissembling patriots acting upon ill-disguised selfish motives or gullible lawmakers who were duped by demagogic rhetoric.[32] Burlington's urban politicians came with a similar perspective; and, under normal conditions, they voted with Perth Amboy. But they did not feel so endangered, and they also harbored their own jealousies and suspicions of their eastern counterparts. Thus, when Country tempers ran high in 1744 and 1745, Smith and Pearson were swept up for the moment and voted with the opposition. But this was only a temporary lapse from their normal behavior; and, already in the first session of 1746, they were endorsing efforts to achieve an agreement with Governor Morris. So, too, but for its own reasons, Essex's urban elite distrusted the eastern proprietors. But, significantly, John Low, who had invested deeply in the antiproprietary claims, did not generalize from that interest to join the die-hard opposition. Rather, pocketbook issues served to deflect him from an urban voting record. In 1751, he was joined by Robert Ogden who had also been engaged in antiproprietary suits. In that legislature, both members voted with the urban bloc.

Personal interest, cultural prejudice, and temperament reinforced each other, creating a kind of glue binding together the active and indifferent lawmaker so that members, regardless of their priorities or their understanding of the issues, came together to support an agenda. These factors made for differences and in tandem were powerful enough to create divisiveness and ongoing divisions which to the participants seemed profound. But the antagonisms were contained and blunted by shared social and cultural origins. Even the extremes remained within a legislative community. Thus, while differences and disagreements bred antagonisms and opposition, they were restrained by discomfort with factiousness and discord. Since disagreements fell short of the ideological, the divisions were neither categorical nor hard and fast. Lawmakers who voted on opposite ends of the spectrum found themselves in agreement on regulating sheriffs, the appointment of an agency, or paper money.

Finally, the members, as they moved from one extreme to another, toward disagreement and then toward agreement, were

146

influenced by the environment within the Assembly. That influence did not come from institutional loyalty such as party. Although strangers often unaccustomed to working with each other, they reacted to one another, and their reactions created a mood that affected and shaped their behavior. The sessions of 1744 and 1745 registered a collective change in mood. Members once reluctant to diminish the governor's salary were suddenly able to hold the governor in ransom and to suspend support for the provincial government. The division came to approximate categorical division--but not for long. Soon they reversed themselves. This oscillation, or motion over time, can best be understood by returning to the narrative itself.

Not only did Lewis Morris raise issues that were sure to provoke, he did so in a way that was almost intended to rouse an opposition. His insistence on militia reform and his proposals to dissolve the distinction between East and West Jersey and build a new capital, the manner in which he called, adjourned, and dissolved assemblies, and his insulting messages pricked basic prejudices and roused latent suspicions. He indulged in controversy and seemed to thrive on disputation. Despite his resolves to the contrary, he could not let go an issue and indulged in ever longer and more insulting exchanges and ever more elaborate legal arguments. If the backbencher did not heed the content of his messages, he could not but note the taunting style. Three years after Morris's death, the house considered whether to attend to the payment of his salary that remained in arrears. Because Morris's "Memory must be precious to his Family," it concluded that it would be better that that time be "buried in perpetual Oblivion." And, although it did not wish "to rake into the Ashes of the dead," the house concluded that for the sake of "the Publick Welfare" and "in duty to their Constituents" it must give explanation for its refusal. It then gave a detailed accounting of how Morris had acted "in direct Contradiction" of the law, "refused to do the Duties of Government" and abused "the Powers of Government," how his messages were so "filled with Invectives," and how he bore "unreasonable resentment" against the Assembly.[33]

Morris had provided the staging and rendered the first reading of a script laid within the Country ideology. He allowed himself to be cast in the opprobrious role of despot who defiled the constitution and abused his trust and power. In turn, he gave the house the opportunity to play a heroic role. In this script, opposition to a governor who condemned the people's liberties became heroic, indeed a sacred trust. When Morris addressed the assemblymen as "Ignorant and Malicious men," lacking in "Virtue and Honour," he roused historic memories and

147

pricked prejudices. Once he called them "Ideots." The house replied by recasting itself in mirror image of the governor's insult. The lawmakers protested that they were "Ploughmen," not "Ideots." They were simple but virtuous defenders of liberty. In contrast to their "Courtly" opponents who possessed more "Polite Education and perhaps less sincerity," they boasted a love of "Plainness and Truth."[34]

The confrontation, thus framed as a Country scenario replete with heroes and miscreants, gathered a direction and momentum of its own. Regardless of the members' original priorities or their historical understanding, a majority was caught up by the mood. As prejudices were quickened, fears of contention and predispositions toward moderation were cast aside. By 1744, the house and governor were at deadlock. Those who voted to hold the governor ransom had once shunned messages of milder reproof. The Assembly had shifted to a more radical position but not because of a significant change in membership. Indeed, the elections of 1744, 1745, and 1746 had brought fewer changes than previous ones. Rather, it was the shaping experience of legislative service that impelled a majority to deny Morris its cooperation against the rioting in Essex County.

At this point, the Country majority appeared to be large and cohesive. Yet, because it was built upon a mood, it was unstable; and, because it had ventured beyond the member's normal limits, it was fragile. It rested on the reading of a script which exaggerated and also competed with another powerful script. Perth Amboy politicians read a script, both equally powerful and increasingly plausible, which recast the patriots as selfish, factious demagogues bent on plunging the province into civil war and anarchy. They were levelers, blindly following, as Morris believed, "the example of the parliament of 1641."[35] This alternative script which pitted unbridled passion against reason and order also was an exaggeration. But Perth Amboy could give a credible reading. News of rioting and the spread of disorders set the stage. The cues were being delivered. And a successful reading raised discomforts in the Country. To keep the Country scenario intact required the proper cues, the staging, the credibility sufficient to overcome the dissonance evoked by Perth Amboy and the rioters.

Morris provided the cues necessary for maintaining the Country scenario. His friends regretted his excesses, his ability to turn the assemblymen into an uncompromising opposition.[36] Even at the height of confrontation, opportunity for settlement appeared, but Morris refused to seize it. In the winter of 1746, Morris met with a new Assembly. Although only

148

one new member had been elected, the lawmakers were ready to lay aside their antagonisms. According to cluster bloc analysis, the polarized voting patterns that had prevailed in the previous two years evaporated during this session. Fourteen members, including ploughman and urban delegates, agreed to offer the governor his salary only if he would consent to the emission of £40,000 in paper money. The governor curtly refused, and that afternoon twenty members resolved that they could not support the government. Only three from Perth Amboy dissented. The earlier pattern had reappeared. But two days later Lewis Morris died.

For the next fourteen months, the province waited for a new governor. In the interim, the Assembly met intermittently and accomplished little. Although the rioting continued, it declined to respond. But the Assembly had conducted its business without indulging in histrionics. When Governor Belcher arrived, he failed to play the role or provide the cues for renewing the Country scenario. In contrast to his predecessor, he was uninterested in constitutional disputes and was resolved to enjoy a quiet administration. He made it a guiding principle that he stand apart from factional entanglements and that he open his government to all parties. Indebted to the Quakers for his appointment, he took up residence in Burlington and established cordial and intimate relations with the Smiths. Simultaneously, he sought to establish good relations with both eastern proprietors and their opponents. His heeding the advice of John Low raised suspicions in Perth Amboy.[37] But the town's representatives seemed unaffected and continued to support the government as they had in the past. Quickly, the polarized voting patterns dissolved (Table 3.6). At the end of his first session, Belcher signed nineteen bills, promised to support a petition to the king requesting permission for another emission of paper money, and received in return the full salary of £1,000. "There has been," he congratulated himself, "a considerable harmony among the several Branches of the Legislature to the passing of many good Laws for the better peace and good order of the province for the Future. Not only the Body of the People but the general Assemble treat me with much Respect and have granted me as large a support as they have ever given."[38]

Fundamental differences remained unresolved, however. Robert Hunter Morris harbored resentments toward the governor, became convinced that Belcher had secretly befriended the rioters, and provoked a confrontation in the Council.[39] The Country still faced councilors who, acting from private motives, oppressed the province's yeomanry and blocked the passage of a tax bill. But the riots had raised discomforts. With Governor Morris, the choice had become whether to augment the powers of an arbitrary executive or to tolerate the disorders. His actions--the role he played--had roused such fears and animosities that they overrode doubts. So the house had voted by a margin of sixteen to six to reject the Council's riot bill. It was an uncomfortable position for Burlington's urban delegation: Richard Smith who had been voting with the opposition dissented and joined with Perth Amboy. The Country script continued to be read but with less dramatic affect. The membership moved away from the extreme and toward a middle ground. So, in 1748, the house agreed to endorse riot legislation if coupled with a pardon bill. Only Van Buskirk and Mott dissented. The house could not be moved beyond that compromise even after Belcher returned reporting that the rioters ignored offers of a pardon. With only two proprietors and Bergen's Demarest dissenting, it noted that no additional legislation was required. Repeatedly, the house refused to heed Belcher's appeals. When it did so, the majority did not act in unison. Antiproprietary sentiment was waning: Nevill was restored to the speaker's chair. Western Quakers, less affected by the proprietors, declined to join with the majority. The Country was strongest in the eastern counties and in Cape May.

The salient issue was taxation. The discussions turned on three questions. Two--whether proprietary investment in unimproved lands be assessed at a lower rate than improved holdings and whether the Council had the right to amend money bills--fused to make the subject an extension of the debates on riot legislation. In February 1748, the house voted by a margin of twelve to five not to consult with the Council on a tax bill. Eleven of the twelve rejected Belcher's pleas for additional riot legislation. But the third question--could the house deny the government a revenue--pulled the discussions in an opposite direction. Normally, all but a few lawmakers found it most difficult to cut salaries or to oppose passage of a supply bill. These twelve lawmakers were a disparate lot, including six from the eastern counties, five from the western, and one from the port of Burlington. They did not constitute a voting bloc: seven voted in more than and five in less than 50 percent agreement with Perth Amboy. They included Daniel Smith, who disagreed with the Country agenda on 85 percent of the roll calls, as well as the diehard Lawrence Van Buskirk. John Low opposed conferring with the Council; but, during the course of the Assembly, he agreed with the proprietors on 50 percent of all roll calls. Moreover, he disagreed with the Country agenda two-thirds of the time.

Tax assessment could be discussed within two frameworks-- as either an antiproprietary and Country issue or as a practical question of supplying the treasury. Which of the two prevailed depended on prejudice and emotional appeal as much as on cogency of argument. And, in this invertebrate legislature, the membership could be moved in both directions. Alignments were unstable and the discussions volatile. At one point, Perth Amboy believed that it had persuaded a third of the members "by private Conversation" to support a "Just valuation of Lands" but in the course of floor debate saw its gains evaporate. At another time, a committee drafted a bill that promised to meet the Council's criterion; but, when reported to the floor, "The Confusion" grew so great "and the Noise so astonishing, that the Member who brought the Bill into the House. . .was so scared and terrified, that he voted against that very Bill of which he had been one of the Compilers!" The reversal caused the observer to reflect: "No one can imagine the Influence that one busy, talkative Man, (though void of Sense) may gain over the rest of the House; especially over those who weigh Words more than Reason."[40]

During the winter of 1751, the Assembly concluded that the treasury could not be supplied. "Friendly Communication" with the Council was "cut off," it informed the governor. The blame clearly lay with the upper house. To concede to its demands would be betrayal of a trust the people had lodged in their representatives. The councilors acted from unpublic motives. The "railing language" of their "false and scandalous" messages could not disguise that they were "rich men" who possessed "so many large Tracts of Land liable to be taken an account of, for future Taxation." "Had the Gentlemen less Estate, especially in Lands, 'tis probable they might have assented to some one of the seven Bills sent them for Concurrence by this House." Their claiming the right to amend tax bills was an attempt "to invade the Rights and Privileges" of the people. To concede to their demands would abrogate the principle that the people "be Taxed According to their own Consent" and by their elected representatives. "This would be a manifest violation of the Subjects Liberty in the Disposal of their own Property, inconsistent with the Natural Freedom of Mankind, destructive of the very Notion of Property and repugnant to our happy Constitution."[41] So, by a vote of fifteen to three, the house concluded that the treasury remain empty and that it would be a fruitless exercise to consider another bill. Belcher agreed and then dissolved the Assembly.

The governor believed that he could effect a change in the house membership by appealing to the electorate. In his election proclamation, Belcher reviewed the Assembly's record of irresponsibility but refused to believe that "the withholding the Support of Government, is agreeable to the Sentiments of the good People of this Province, or for their Credit or real Interest."[42] At first, when the new house convened at Perth Amboy, his tactic seemed to work. Ten new representatives

151

were elected. The house recognized that no government salaries had been paid for two years and approved the payment of those arrears from funds to be raised from a tax bill "which shall be hereafter made." Then it approved a bill that outlined the procedures for making tax assessments. While claiming that the bill was "of the Same Tenor" as previous legislation, it added a critical "Declaratory Clause to Discover our Intent of taxing Lands hereafter according to value in Quantity and Quality between limitted sums to be hereafter fixed." This concession was a significant first step, and the Council agreed that "with the Provisoe and Explanation now Added" it could endorse the bill's passage.[43]

Yet, in the autumn session, the lawmakers reversed their course. As they began to move beyond procedure and toward the drafting of a tax bill, Country prejudices resurfaced and the old scenario was replayed--this time with even more dramatic results. The deliberations turned on defining precisely those limited sums of land assessments and also on a method for collecting from absentee landholders. On the amount of assessment, the members divided along a rural-urban line. All but two from Perth Amboy agreed to send the supply and tax bill up to the Council. The Council found the bill "repugnant": the tax burden fell most heavily on the large holder of unimproved lands and thus made "void" the previously endorsed principle that assessment would be made according to both "Quantity and Quality." Within a week, it returned the bill with its amendments. The house responded by tearing the amendments from the bill and returning them to the Council without comment. Then it ventured into new territory. By a vote of twelve to eight, it chose to send the bill directly to the governor. The speaker was appalled and registered his dissent in the house journals. The Council found the move "Unprecedented" unless, it suggested, the Assembly was taking its cue from the parliament that "Voted Kings and Lords useless." Belcher despaired: "I have rarely observed. . .that dissolutions of Assemblies have brot others together better disposed, bono-publico."[44]

The aggressive act was a symptom of the Country's brittleness. It was as if this staging of high drama was necessary to keep the discussion focused on Country issues and to overcome the need for resolution. Already the western counties were reluctant to support the venture. After a three-month adjournment, the house met again in the winter of 1752 and moved rapidly toward resolving its disagreements with the Council. First, a majority changed its position on assessments. Five western representatives changed their position, so that the western division, except for Mott and the absent Leaming and Spicer, joined with the urban bloc. On the matter of

152

collections, the membership rapidly changed its position. At first, the urban bloc and two western lawmakers voted in the minority. But, after two days of discussion, all the western members, except for Mott, had joined with the urban bloc. The eastern members were in the minority. When the house turned to vote on the whole bill, the eastern members, first Fisher and Dey then Smith and Van Middleswardt, began to defect. Finally, only a handful--Lawrence, Holmes, Mott, and Van Vorst--voted against this compromise tax bill. As if in symbolic gesture, these four and Dey voted to send this bill to the governor and bypass the Council.

Because taxation could be discussed within two frameworks, the lawmakers oscillated between extremes. In the fall session, they discussed taxation as part of the Country agenda: those who proposed to place high assessments on land speculators also voted to send the supply bill directly to the governor. But few were impervious to the need for supplying the treasury, and the majority could lay aside differences for the sake of a settlement. For example, Deacon, Low, and Ogden joined with Perth Amboy on assessments, and Leaming and Fisher took the opposite position. But all five approved both tax bills. Strength of conviction varied among the members. Although the western members had voted with their antiproprietary colleagues, they were the first to abandon that position for the sake of a settlement. The same applied to the eastern counties. Shobal Smith of Middlesex County opposed the proprietary interest on assessments and voted to bypass the Council. But, during the winter session of 1752, he shifted to support the compromise tax bill and declined endorsing a motion to send the bill to the governor. Although defeated, the Country position was not silenced. In 1754, Smith joined with four others to reverse the method of collecting from absentee landholders. But, on final passage of that bill, only two--Holmes and Mott--voted in the negative.

Legislative sessions were volatile. Assemblymen acted upon those prejudices and suspicions which they brought with them. Because the language they employed was so morally charged and the descriptions of issues and personalities so exaggerated, even manichean, debate often served to exacerbate differences. Lewis Morris described one session: "there grew So great a rancour among the members that they Shun'd the conversation of Each other Out of the house, and could not preserve the rules of common decency in it descending to downright Scolding, giving the lye, threat'ning to Spit in the faces & were (as I am inform'd) often very nigh getting together by the Ears."[45] From a modern perspective, that volatility was a sign of institutional immaturity, the absence of restraining institutions, or the lack of established norms of behavior. But it was also the sign of an organizing principle. In this assemblage of strangers, communication and persuasion required dramatic appeal. The floor drama did not transform lawmakers into something they were not, but it focused their attitudes and prejudices. The playing of a Country script replete with patriots and courtiers set the framework for the building of majorities. And the successful enactment of that script galvanized an otherwise inchoate body and provided the energy for creating and maintaining an agenda.

Because the Country-Court division evaporated into what it really was did not mean that the principles espoused were ethereal and unimportant. They continued to influence, perhaps less dramatically, house proceedings through the remainder of Belcher's administration. A recurring issue was the matter of appointments to the civil list. The Assembly found the governor was appointing nonresidents as sheriffs in violation of the law. The commissioning of "arbitrary and despotick Officers" was "so destructive to the Liberties of the People" that the Assembly felt charged to confront the governor. The debate entered the constitutional realm with the governor reprimanding the house for presuming to interpret the law and the house citing seventeenth-century English precedent to justify its actions.[46] In addition, the house balked when the governor summoned it to his residence, now at Elizabethtown. Rather than break precedent, it asked to be adjourned. When charged with treating the governor disrespectfully, the Assembly issued its parting barb: "In What Manner Your Excellency has exerted Your Publick and Private Interest for the good of the Inhabitants of this Province, We are at a Loss to know."[47] Meanwhile, the focus of public debate was turning toward a new agenda of issues related to the war with France, the province's contribution to the military effort, and the house's relationship to royal government.

NOTES

1. T. H. Breen, The Character of the Good Ruler: A Study of Puritan Political Ideas in New England, 1630-1730 (New Haven, CT, 1970), 203-69; Paul S. Boyer, "Borrowed Rhetoric: The Massachusetts Excise Controversy of 1754," The William and Mary Quarterly, 3rd Ser., XXI (July, 1964), 328-51; Robert M. Weir, "'The Harmony We Were Famous For': An Interpretation of Pre-Revolutionary South Carolina Politics," ibid., XXVI (Oct.,

1969), 473-501; Patricia U. Bonomi, A Factious People: Politics and Society in Colonial New York (New York, 1971), 103-39, 279-86; and Bailyn, Origins of American Politics.

2. For a general account of these years, see Donald L. Kemmerer, Path to Freedom: The Struggle for Self-Government in Colonial New Jersey, 1703-1776 (Princeton, NJ, 1940), 154-236. Fisher, New Jersey as a Royal Province remains useful; in addition to his account of the Morris and Belcher administrations (101-57), also see his sections on land conflicts (171-209) and the financial system (273-318).

3. Assembly to L. Morris, Dec. 16, 1738, Votes and Proceedings. Also see L. Morris to Board of Trade, Sept. 11, 1738, N.J.Archs., VI, 56; Addresses from Perth Amboy, Burlington, and New Brunswick to L. Morris, New-York Weekly Journal, Sept. 18, 1738; Address from Monmouth to L. Morris, Pennsylvania Gazette, Sept. 28-Oct. 5, 1738. For biography of Lewis Morris, see Eugene R. Sheridan, Lewis Morris, 1671-1746: A Study in Early American Politics (Syracuse, 1981), but also see Strassburger, "Origins and Development of the Morris Family."

4. Letter to B. G. Also L. Morris to Assembly, Jan. 31, 1738[/9], Votes and Proceedings; L. Morris to Assembly, Dec. 7, 1743, ibid.; L. Morris to Sir Charles Wager, May 10, 1739, N.J.Archs., VI, 65.

5. Letter to B. G. And Advice to the Inhabitants of Hunterton [sic] and Morris Counties; Assembly to Council, Dec. 5, 1744, N.J.Archs., XV, 377-80.

6. Assembly to L. Morris, Dec. 16, 1738, Votes and Proceedings. L. Morris to Assembly, Jan. 31, 1738[/9], ibid. Also petition from Western Division, Oct. 23, 1751, ibid.; L. Morris to Duke of Newcastle, Oct. 18, 1740, N.J.Archs., VI, 109-10.

7. New-York Weekly Journal, May 11, 1741.

8. L. Morris to Council and Assembly, Oct. 3, 1741, N.J.Archs., XV, 200-204. L. Morris to Council and Assembly, Nov. 15, 1738, ibid., 8-9; Modest Vindication of the Late New-Jersey Assembly, 28-29.

9. Dialogue between two Gentlemen, 2-7. And Assembly to L. Morris, June 27, 1744, N.J.Archs., XV, 326-27; Modest Vindication of the Late New-Jersey Assembly, 28-29.

10. Assembly to L. Morris, Nov. 15, 1744, N.J.Archs.,

XV, 355-58; L. Morris to Assembly, [Dec. 8, 1744], Votes and Proceedings; Assembly to L. Morris, Mar. 13, 1745/6, ibid.

11. Reports of Committee of Grievances, Nov. 10-19, 1742, ibid.; Modest Vindication of the Late New-Jersey Assembly, 6-8, 26-27; Note-maker noted; Council resolution, June 4, 1740, N.J.Archs., XV, 152; L. Morris to Assembly, Dec. 7, 1743, ibid., 312-14; L. Morris to Board of Trade, Oct. 25, 1740, Morris Papers, 124; L. Morris to Board of Trade, Dec. 15, 1742, ibid., 152.

12. L. Morris to Assembly, Sept. 28, 1745, Votes and Proceedings. Horowitz, "New Jersey Land Riots"; Steven G. Greiert, "The Earl of Halifax and the Land Riots in New Jersey, 1748-1753," New Jersey History, XCIX (Spring-Summer, 1981), 13-31.

13. Assembly to L. Morris, Oct. 3, 1745, N.J.Archs., VI, 250.

14. Assembly to L. Morris, May 30, 1745, Votes and Proceedings; L. Morris to Duke of Newcastle, Oct. 22, 1745, Morris Papers, 284.

15. Letter to B. G.; L. Morris to Board of Trade, Jan. 28, 1744[/5], Morris Papers, 216. L. Morris to Board of Trade, Aug. 16, 1741, ibid., 136-37; Assembly to Council, Feb. 24, 1738/9, N.J.Archs., XV, 50-51; L. Morris to Council and Assembly, Apr. 5, 1745, ibid., 403-4; Assembly to L. Morris, Oct. 9, 1741, Votes and Proceedings; Assembly to L. Morris, Oct. 19, 1743, ibid.

16. Nov. 13, 1742, ibid.

17. Assembly to L. Morris, May 2, 1745, N.J.Archs., XV, 417. Assembly to L. Morris, Oct. 3, 1745, ibid., VI, 246; Assembly to L. Morris, May 25, 1745, Votes and Proceedings; Assembly to L. Morris, May 30, 1745, ibid.; Assembly to L. Morris, Aug. 21, 1745, ibid.; L. Morris to Speaker, Aug. 23, 1745, ibid.; Assembly to Council, Aug. 23, 1745, ibid.; Assembly to Council, Oct. 8, 1745, ibid.; Council to Assembly, Oct. 11, 1745, ibid.; Assembly resolutions, Oct. 14, 1745, Morris Papers, 276.

18. L. Morris to Council and Assembly, Apr. 16, 1740, Votes and Proceedings; L. Morris to Assembly, Sept. 28, 1745, ibid.; L. Morris to Assembly, Dec. 10, 1743, N.J.Archs., XV, 315-21; L. Morris to Council and Assembly, Apr. 5, 1745, ibid., 395-408; Assembly to L. Morris, Oct. 3, 1745, ibid.,246-51; L. Morris to Assembly, Oct. 18, 1745, ibid., 251-65; Assembly to

Belcher, Oct. 5, 1749, ibid., VII, 336-43; Assembly to king, Oct. 19, 1749, ibid., 351-56; "A Brief State of Facts. . .," ibid., 207-26.

19. Belcher to J. Belcher, Sept. 17, 1747, Letterbooks, VIII, 43-44; Belcher to Garvan, Sept. 18, 1747, ibid., 53.

20. Alexander to Paris, Apr. 27, 1747, Paris Papers, X, 32; "A Brief State of Facts. . .," N.J.Archs., VII, 207-26; Council to Belcher, Aug. 22, 1747, ibid., 24; Belcher to Council and Assembly, Dec. 3, 1748, ibid., XVI, 25-26; Assembly to Belcher, Dec. 9, 1748, ibid., 42-44; Assembly to Belcher, Mar. 7, 1749, ibid., 122-25; Report of Board of Trade, June 1, 1750, ibid., VII, 484.

21. Assembly petition to king, Oct. 19, 1749, ibid., 355; Assembly to Belcher, Feb. 15, 1750[/1], Votes and Proceedings. Also New-York Gazette, Feb. 26, 1749/50, Jan. 21, 1750/1; "To the Freeholders of New Jersey," New-York Gazette, Mar. 11, 1750[/1], in N.J.Archs., XIX, 34-48; "J. N.," New-York Gazette, Mar. 25, 1751, in ibid., 53-59; "A-n.," New-York Gazette, Jan. 21, 1751, in ibid., 13-20; New-York Gazette, Nov. 11, 1751, in ibid., 106-12; Richard Smith, Jr., to R. Partridge, Dec. 20, 1749, ibid., VII, 366-68; Some Animadversions, 3-5; A Letter from a Gentleman in New-York, to his Friend in Brunswick ([New York, 1750]); A Reply to a Letter from a Gentleman in New-York.

22. Council to Assembly, Oct. 8, 1750, Votes and Proceedings; Assembly to Council, Feb. 14, 1750/1, N.J.Archs., XVI, 254-58; Assembly to Council, Feb. 22, 1750/1, ibid., 271-73; Belcher to Council and Assembly, May 21, 1751, ibid., 291-92; Assembly to Belcher, June 6, 1751, ibid., 300-302; Belcher to Woodruffe, Feb. 25, 1750/1, Letterbooks, IX, 105-6.

23. Belcher to Col. Brattle, Feb. 22, 1752, ibid., 359. Council to Assembly, Oct. 21, 1751, N.J.Archs., XVI, 337-38; Assembly to Council, Oct. 22, 1751, ibid., 339-41; Alexander to R. H. Morris, Oct. 27, 1751, ibid., VII, 627.

24. See Anderson, Legislative Roll-Call Analysis, 89-121. But the procedure employed in this study was a modified version of that scaling technique. See Aage R. Clausen and Richard B. Cheyney, "A Comparative Analysis of Senate House Voting on Economic and Welfare Policy, 1953-1964," The American Political Science Review, LXIV (Mar., 1970), 138-52. Also see Clausen, How Congressmen Decide: A Policy Focus (New York, 1973).

25. Alexander to Coxe, May 2, 1748, N.J.Archs., VII, 123; Coxe to Alexander, May 30, 1748, ibid., 127; Alexander to Coxe, Dec. 31, 1748, ibid., 204-5.

26. Assembly to L. Morris, Oct. 3, 1745, ibid., VI, 246-51.

27. Affidavit of William Gilman, Feb. 15, 1748/9, ibid., VII, 231.

28. See Samuel C. Patterson, "Dimensions of Voting Behavior in a One-Party State Legislature," Public Opinion Quarterly, XXVI (Summer, 1962), 185-200; Joan Wells Coward, Kentucky in the New Republic: The Process of Constitution Making (Lexington, KY, 1979), 132-33.

29. Assembly to L. Morris, Oct. 3, 1745, N.J.Archs., VI, 249.

30. L. Morris to B. Smith, Jan. 3, 1739[/40], Morris Papers, 80; L. Morris to R. Smith, Feb. 5, 1739[/40], ibid., 82-83.

31. There is a rough but discernible relationship between voting behaviors on the agenda of Country-Court issues and on the agenda of social and economic issues. Although the roll calls on the two agendas do not achieve scalar relationship by empirical standards, there is a tendency for the extreme Country to adopt a naysaying position on social and economic questions. In turn, those most inclined to support the governors also tended to approve social and economic reforms. Consider the members listed in Table 5.1, and compare the third at each end of the list. Those most for the Country position received a median policy support score of -.3, and the third at the opposite end of the scale received a median positive score of .7. So, too, in Table 5.3, the Country achieved a -.3 score, and the other third recorded a median positive score of .1. See Tables 2.1 and 2.2 and explanatory note p 59, n. 36.

32. Nevill to Alexander, Nov. 10, 1744, Rutherford Collection, New Jersey, 108; Nevill's speech to the Assembly, New-York Post-Boy, May 19 and 26, 1746, in N.J.Archs., VI, 323-48. Also R. H. Morris to Alexander, July 28, 1747, ibid., 471-74; Alexander and R. H. Morris to Paris, May 30, 1749, ibid., VII, 262-63.

33. Assembly to Belcher, Oct. 5, 1749, ibid., 336-43.

34. L. Morris to Assembly, Nov. 25, 1742, ibid., XV, 273-

78; L. Morris to Council and Assembly, Apr. 5, 1745, ibid., 394-408; Assembly to L. Morris, May 2, 1745, ibid., 410-18. Also L. Morris to Assembly, May 2, 1745, ibid., 418-37; Assembly to L. Morris, Oct. 3, 1745, ibid., VI, 246-51; L. Morris to Assembly, Oct. 18, 1745, ibid., 251-66; R. Smith to John Smith, [1743?], Smith Family Papers, chronological series, II, 3; L. Morris to Duke of Newcastle, Jan. 28, 1744/5, Morris Papers, 227-28.

35.   L. Morris to Board of Trade, June 10, 1743, ibid., 162. L. Morris to Board of Trade, Oct. 4, 1739, ibid., 61; L. Morris to Board of Trade, Jan. 28, 1744/5, ibid., 216-17; Alexander and R. H. Morris to Paris, May 30, 1749, N.J.Archs., VII, 262-63.

36.   P. Collinson to Alexander, Oct. 14, 1747, Rutherford Collection, IV, 81; Smith, History of the Colony of Nova-Caesaria, 428-30; A Pocket Commentary of the first Settling of New-Jersey. . .(New York, 1759), 19.

37.   Matthias Hatfield and Stephen Crane to Dr. Avery, Mar. 7, 1747/8, Miscellaneous Manuscripts, Princeton University Library.

38.   Belcher to Sergeant, Feb. 23, 1747/8, Letterbooks, VIII, 253.

39.   Memorandum of Council meeting, Dec. 16, 1748, N.J.Archs., VII, 183-84; Councilors to Belcher, Dec. 22, 1748, ibid., 185-88.   Coxe to Alexander, May 30, 1748, ibid., 127; Alexander to Paris, Dec. 1, 1746, Paris Papers, X, 21; Paris to Alexander, Feb. 10, 1746[/7], Rutherford Collection, New Jersey, 121; Alexander to R. H. Morris, Nov. 30, 1749, Morris Papers, III.

40.   Alexander to [R. H. Morris], Oct. 10, 1750, Stevens Family Papers, New York Boundary Dispute, A; "To the Freeholders of New Jersey," New-York Gazette, Mar. 11, 1751, in N.J.Archs., XIX, 41-42, 47.

41.   Assembly to Belcher, Feb. 22, 1750[/1], Votes and Proceedings; Assembly to Council, Feb. 22, 1750/1, N.J.Archs., XVI, 272-73; Assembly to Council, Feb. 14, 1750/1, ibid., 255-56.

42.   Belcher's election proclamation, New-York Gazette, Mar. 4, 1751, in ibid., XIX, 30-32.

43. Act for the Support of the Government (1751), Bush, Laws, III, 169; Assembly to Belcher, June 6, 1751, N.J.Archs., XVI, 301; Council to Belcher, June 6, 1751, ibid., 309.

44. Council to Assembly, Oct. 22, 1751, ibid., 343; Council to Belcher, Oct. 22, 1751, ibid., 341; Belcher to Oliver, May 4, 1751, Letterbooks, IX, 123.

45. L. Morris to Sir Charles Wager, May 10, 1739, N.J.Archs., VI, 61-62.

46. Assembly to Belcher, June 12, 1754, Votes and Proceedings. Belcher to Assembly, Feb. 21, 1750[/1], ibid.; Belcher to Assembly, Feb. 12, 1752, ibid.; Belcher to Morris, June 17, 1754, Letterbooks, X, 408; Belcher to Assembly, June 21, 1754, N.J.Archs., XVI, 474-77.

47. Assembly to Belcher, June 14, 1754, ibid., 462-65. Assembly to Belcher, Mar. 31, 1757, ibid., XVII, 93-95; Assembly to Belcher, June 6, 1753, Votes and Proceedings; Belcher to Assembly, June 8, 1753, ibid.; Assembly to Belcher, June 12, 1754, ibid.

CHAPTER SIX

THE WAR YEARS, 1754-1763: PATRIOTISM AND DISSENT

In the autumn of 1754, Governor Belcher directed the representatives' attention to "the Bold and unwarrantable Incroachments of the French (with their Indians) upon His Majestys Lands." Though the danger might seem distant, he reminded the lawmakers that the fate of all loyal subjects of his majesty was at stake. "The present Melancholy Situation of many of our Neighbours requires your speedy and human Regard towards them; Nor must you. . .imagine Yourselves Exempted from these cruelties and barbarities; No! if there be not an Effectual Stop put to them you must Soon Expect the Enemy on your Own Borders." Repeatedly, the aging governor summoned the Assembly to rally it against the French and Indians. The war was a crusade to preserve Protestantism and the traditions of British liberty in North America. The stakes were obvious: "Whether his Majesty is to Maintain his Just Rights and Dominions in North America, and His Subjects their Religion, Liberties and Properties; or Whether the Perfidious French with their Savage Allies, are to go on in their Cruel Murders and Depredations, and finally Drive the Kings good People into the Sea." Victory was imperative: "Carthago est Delenda" became the watchword of his administration.[1]

The call sparked the provincial imagination. From the pulpit, Aaron Burr prodded his congregation and the general public to rally to the cause. He noted that some hardened their hearts and supported "stingy Provisions for Defence." "Had we but the Spirit of our brave Ancestors, who cheerfully ventured their Lives, and resigned all the Comforts thereof, in an howling Wilderness, that they might hand down to us the inestimable Privileges we now enjoy: Were we, I say, animated. . .with the same ardent Desire of leaving them inviolate to our Posterity;-- did but the noble Ardor kindle from Breast to Breast, I doubt not, by the Smiles of Heaven, we should soon make our Enemies flee before us, and again sit quietly under our Vines and Fig-trees, and eat the Good of the Land."[2] Once rumors flashed through the province that the French had landed at Salem. Recurring troubles on the frontier caused a steady flow of petitions to the legislature, requesting aid against the local and invading Indians.[3]

Between 1754 and 1763, the Assembly was convened principally to attend to the war. Each spring the lawmakers listened as the governor described the next campaign against the enemy in Canada or in the Ohio valley and then called for a

161

contingent of volunteers. The task raised several problems: how many troops could the province raise, how much should they be paid, how long should they serve, whether servants could be enlisted, whether the provincial regiments might be drawn from standing militia companies, and finally whether the province should join in the crusade. Also, the Assembly was compelled to consider its own defenses: how to treat with the Indians within the province, how to construct a perimeter of defense, and whether to augment the powers of the militia officers. The discussions turned to costs and inevitably focused on paper money. In addition, the quartering of English troops in the province roused localist antagonisms. And the English efforts to forge a union among the northern provinces raised concerns for the province's autonomy. Together these topics became the essence of a political agenda that dominated the Assembly for nearly a decade.[4]

The cause was just. The legislature readily affirmed its loyalty to the crown and its support for the war. Implementation also forced the lawmakers to confront the implications of living within the imperial system and specifically roused localist prejudices, fears for the provincial constitution, and dread of the military. British requisitions drained the province's resources. After reviewing the heavy losses at Fort Oswego and the mounting debt, the lawmakers were reluctant to join the next year's campaign. Although they had "Conven'd from Hearts deeply sensible of the Necessity of assisting in the Common Cause," they found that "our Distress'd Circumstances in several Respects, one of which is the Scarcity of Money" and another is "the Large Number of Voluntiers who have already been raised in this Government. . .and many voluntiers in the Provincial Services, which with the Loss of our Forces and Stores at Oswego adds to our Difficulties" prevented the province from acting according to its patriotic impulse.[5]

For the Quaker lawmakers, the war provoked a crisis of conscience. The Society of Friends stated its position: "with Respect to the Commotions and Stirrings of the Powers of the Earth at this Time near us, we are desirous that none of us may be moved thereat."[6] Traditionally, that counsel had come to mean that Quakers would not support war directly by bearing arms in a campaign, but for many it did not exclude the granting of funds for such purposes as long as Quakers were not engaged in their administration. At mid-century, however, reformers were pressing for a stricter standard. To act according to conscience brought additional discomforts for the assemblymen. By habit they were not inclined to take a categorical stand against the government. Moreover, some had come to recognize the futility of opposing the war. Not only were they a minority incapable of influencing the outcome but

162

they also stood to pay a political price for resisting the war effort. By acting according to conscience, they made themselves vulnerable to criticism. Legislation was being prepared in England to expel Quakers from the colonial legislatures. Friends saw several alternatives, one of which was to withdraw from public life at least for the war's duration. Some Friends did so, but these were members of the Pennsylvania legislature. None resigned in New Jersey. But by keeping their seats they remained in a dilemma. Torn between conscience and pragmatism, the Quakers adopted several positions. One was to oppose military measures: dissenting votes came principally from the Quaker lawmakers. Another was to acquiesce to political reality by assenting to bills for raising and supplying provincial troops. And a third response was to abstain.

While the Assembly professed its support for the war, its contribution fell short of what the crown and some patriots expected. From Governor Belcher's perspective, patriotism had succumbed to niggardliness and an incessant carping over constitutional principles. Another imperial enthusiast censured the Assembly in the public prints. Writing from New York, Archibald Kennedy captured the purpose of the war: "As France has hitherto, by the Means of Great-Britain chiefly, been prevented from enslaving the World and Mankind, they are become of Course our implacable and most inveterate Enemies." Yet he had discovered that the New Jersey legislature was insensitive to patriotic appeal. The lawmakers "at this very critical Point of Time treat the Decrees of Heaven, and the King, with great Contempt!" The glaring discrepancy between profession and action could not but displease English authority. Did the lawmakers believe that their empty professions of loyalty could "protect them from his Majesty's Displeasure" or the censure of parliament?[7]

The Assembly's restrained support for English military ventures was in character with its earlier stands. Governor Morris had twice requested that provincial troops be raised, first in 1740 against Spanish Carthagena and later in 1745 against the French at Louisburg. Both times the house procrastinated. After repeated reminders, it responded but voted support on terms objectionable to the governor. The provincial contingent was to be supplied by diverting previously allocated funds, and these funds were to be spent by commissioners appointed by the Assembly. The method was unconstitutional, Morris and his Council objected. Since the money had originally been designated for routine government expenses, a special tax should be raised for this extraordinary expenditure. Moreover, the Assembly assumed unwarranted control of treasury funds. But the house refused to concede and forced acceptance of its version. Shortly after Morris's death, the crown called upon the province to join an expedition against Canada and promised reimbursement for the incurred expenses. After the house submitted a statement of expenses, William Shirley, the Governor of Massachusetts, persuaded the government in England to honor less than half the amount. When Shirley called for troops against Crown Point in 1748, the Assembly lauded the effort but pled that the provincial treasury was so depleted that it could not bear the burden of another campaign.[8]

During the last war for empire, the house focused its attention almost exclusively on military affairs. What had caused only an intermittent dispute came to set the tone of legislative politics. And, as the house clarified its position, tensions with imperial authority became exacerbated. The English regularly expected the colonies to supply troops for their expeditions against Canada and determined as well to direct the method for financing. New Jersey learned that it could not issue paper money as legal tender, that the issues must be redeemed within five years, and that the governor and Council must have control over the spending of treasury funds. The two issues--the military and finances--were clearly joined in 1754 when Governor Belcher informed the Assembly of a campaign against the French in the Ohio valley. The house voted to support the campaign but three days later attached to that resolve the provision that the provincial contingent be supported from a Ƚ70,000 emission. Since the bill established this paper currency as a legal tender and placed control of its spending in the hands of the Assembly, it clearly challenged English policy. The year before, the Assembly had petitioned the crown for permission to issue Ƚ60,000 and had just received news that the Privy Council had rejected its application. Now the house sought to bargain its contribution to the war effort for compliance with its financial policy. As Governor Belcher concluded, there was little hope for New Jersey's participation in the war until the currency issue was resolved.[9]

Each year Belcher and his successors presented the imperial campaign plan, and each time the Assembly responded by pleading that poverty and the lack of currency prevented the province from acting according to its patriotic desires. The Assembly could be cajoled to raise a contingent, often less than requested, and always with a paper money emission. For example, in 1755 it voted to raise 500 troops who would be supplied from a Ƚ15,000 emission. Soon after, it received news that the Privy Council had rejected the Ƚ70,000 emission, and in return the Assembly rejected the governor's call for additional troops. In 1756, it did not respond to the British commander's appeal for a contingent, and in 1757 it granted half his request.

The next year it agreed to raise 1000 volunteers but with an issue of £50,000 to be withdrawn after 1774.[10]

When Governor Francis Bernard arrived in 1758, he quickly recognized that strict adherence to English currency policy jeopardized the war effort. His instructions must be revised, he wrote the Board of Trade. If not, "I shall not be able to support his Majesties service in the manner I shall desire & ought to do without a breach of my Instructions. And I shall be sorry to be reduced to the alternative of either being indifferent to his Majesties Service or disobedient to his commands." Before receiving his revised instructions, he had approved a military supply of another £50,000 to be granted in legal tender and redeemed after five years. He reiterated his position: although agreeing with the Board's policy, he concluded that the exigencies of war required lenity. "In time of war & for the service (as we hope) of the last campaign, I thought the augmenting his Majestys forces my first duty &, if in so doing I only followed the steps of my predecessor, I trusted that I should be justified in it."[11]

Imperial policy pricked localist sensibilities in many ways. The Assembly was not just reluctant to participate in military ventures beyond its frontiers. When invited to join in Indian conferences, the house responded that it had never participated in the past and saw no reason to now. When called to send a delegation to confer with representatives of the other northern colonies at Albany and devise a coordinated defense, the house concluded that such a scheme threatened the constitution and voted not to participate. When presented with the Albany Congress's plan of union, the house expressed its criticism: "things in it, which if carried into Practice would affect our Constitution in its very Vitals and for that reason we hope and believe, they will never be Countenanced by a British Legislature."[12]

Nor was the legislature always eager to support the governors' recommendations for securing the province's own frontiers. Settlers in the northern counties petitioned the government that they lay exposed to raiding parties. But governors and lawmakers could not agree on what was a sufficient defense. Once the lawmakers agreed with Governor Belcher to station a force of 250 on the frontier; but, shortly after, they demanded that he dismiss 100 of the troops at once "and the Remainder of them also as Soon as it can be done with Safety to the Inhabitants." Belcher condemned the resolution as irresponsible and refused to cooperate. When Francis Bernard arrived, he discovered that only fifty troops were stationed on the northern frontier. Since the force proved incapable of defending the province from numerous raiding parties, Bernard proposed that the borders be protected by a permanent line of forts and regular patrols of troops and dogs. Again the lawmakers responded to the crisis with caution. They agreed to raise 150 troops and to support the project with an emission of Ƚ 10,000 in legal tender. Although the force was half of what he recommended and the funding violated his instructions, the governor had no recourse but to accept.[13]

Thus, parochial jealousy of imperial intents, frugality, and an urgent need for paper money governed the Assembly's response to the war effort and worked to mute its Anglo-American patriotism. The war provoked contradictory feelings: as a crusade against French tyranny, it stirred the patriot to defend Anglo-American liberties, but it also raised up the ever larger and foreboding image of military power. The exigencies of war were not enough to overcome ingrained suspicions of the governor's recommendation to reform and strengthen the militia system. As it had during the Morris years, the Assembly balked at proposals to increase the penalties for absence from militia musters and to grant the governor the power to raise and move troops in time of an emergency. Although recruiting officers failed to meet their quotas for the expeditionary forces, the Assembly declined to allow for "draughting or detaching out of the Militia" the troops necessary to complete the contingent. The wartime experience clarified deep-seated fears. The Assembly responded to a general outcry in the legislative community against the recruitment of servants. Petitioners charged that some military officers inflicted excessive punishments and "cruel Usage" upon their neighbors and that others pocketed funds meant for the service of the soldiers. Moreover, British troops stationed in New Jersey were quartered in private homes. At the end of one winter, the house received petitions claiming damages to homes and abuses to civilians. Princeton requested relief: "Although many of your Petitioners are poor, have small houses and numerous families, with not more than one room, they have yet been obliged to entertain sometimes ten, twelve, or fifteen Soldiers for a night." Finally, the lawmakers responded by constructing barracks for the military.[14]

The Assembly kept a vigilant eye on traditional constitutional principles and jealously guarded its integrity and independence from executive dictation. At the opening of the war, Governor Belcher urged the house to follow the example set by other colonies and the Council and exact an oath binding its members to keep secret their deliberations on war policy. While "justly sensible of the great Necessity of keeping the Operations of His Majesty's Forces a Secret," the house balked at what appeared to be executive intrusion into its own affairs. After refusing to comply with the governor's recommendation, it

166

explained that it would investigate any breach of security and discipline indiscretion with "the severest Censure."[15] In the interim between Governor Belcher's death in August 1757 and Francis Bernard's arrival a year later, Council President John Reading assumed the executive. Sick and aging, Reading summoned the Assembly and sent a message from his bedside in Trenton urging action against "the Distressed Situation of the Frontiers" and suggesting that it adjourn to Trenton. The Assembly declined as it had with Governor Morris: "[we] assert our Right in the strongest Manner; lest a continued Suspension of an unalienable Privilege, should hereafter prompt future Governors to repeat the Precedent, of calling their Assemblies to unconstitutional Places, to the great Prejudice of the Publick Good."[16]

During the war years, the Assembly established its claims to control the treasury. An Assembly committee oversaw the disposal of public funds, and commissioners appointed by the house supervised the purchase of military supplies. The practice set a dangerous precedent, observed Governor Bernard, for it broke down "the legal Distinctions of the Regal and Popular Rights" and thus imperiled the health of "the British Constitution." His successor, Thomas Boone, reminded the lawmakers that their recent practices "with regard to the Disposal and Issuing of Publick Money" was a gross "Deviation from the Principles of the Constitution." The Assembly believed it was "capable of a better Construction" of the issue. It denied that it had "the least Inclination" to violate constitutional principle by encroaching "on the known Rights of any other Branch of the Legislature." While affirming that it was "truly sensible, that the Body Politick may be distempered as well as the natural Body, and that it can only be kept in Order, by preserving to the Crown and the People, the true and exact constitutional Rights of each," the house concluded that it was acting only according to time-honored precedent and vowed that it would "steadily and inviolably adhere to the Preservation of the Privileges of our House, and Liberties of our Constituents, and conscienciously transmit these inviolable Blessings to our Posterity without Dimunition." For the sake of the war effort, the governors had to concede the issue.[17]

The years of war roused contradictory attitudes toward the imperial relationship. On the one hand, patriotism stirred the Assembly to "Discharge our Duty to Our King & Country," while on the other hand, English authority became an irritant and an adversary. Although the patriot's task was to support the war, it was also his duty to serve his constituents. Often the two seemed irreconcilable. The Assembly wrestled with the contradiction without achieving resolution. But in the process it forged a policy that reflected the patriot's often antagonistic

167

beliefs. First, the Assembly did, notwithstanding its critics' accusations, contribute to the war effort. Though exasperated at times, Governor Bernard had cause to congratulate the house for its "unanimity" and "dispatch" in the discharge of its duties. Second, it often seemed to make its contribution grudgingly. When it did so, it acted from practical and ideological reasons. The legislature's patriotism caused it to consider the welfare and liberties of its constituents. It became conscious of how heavily the war bore upon the province. Heavy losses in battle and the mounting expenses of war had sapped the province of the means to meet English requirements. And whatever contribution was to be made could come only if it were tied to paper currency. But such a decision only provoked confrontation with royal authority. The Assembly pled the province's case but seemingly to no avail. English requisitions remained impossible to meet, and the currency policy seemed unrealistic and burdensome. Assemblymen came to suspect that the English were either insensitive to the province's hardships or were misinformed. In this and other ways, they were reminded of the empire's presence. British troops and their overbearing officers caused resentments and conflict. So, too, debates over military powers, the proposed plan of union, and the power of the purse quickened concerns for provincial rights and liberties. Localist prejudices and Country sensibilities were roused but had not yet hardened. Rather, they merged with ingrained loyalties to make for frustrated patriotism. Thus, Lawrence Henry Gipson reviewed New Jersey's role in the war and concluded that "in proportion to its population. . .both in the prompt appropriation of money and in the equally prompt raising of troops for the general service, the record of the colony was praiseworthy and in many respects contrasts with that of Pennsylvania and the provinces to the south."[18]

The Nineteenth Assembly, which met from 1754 to 1760 and attended principally to the war, recorded more roll calls than any of its predecessors. Although promising such complete documentation on the divisions over military policy, the roll calls also pose problems endemic to this kind of analysis. First, the questions were posed after deliberation and compromise, so it is difficult to make important distinctions between representatives who voted alike. For example, in 1756, Governor Belcher called upon the house to raise 750 troops "for His Majestys Service in the Insuing Campaign."[19] After considering the request, the Assembly voted approval of one-third that number. But the roll call does not distinguish between the members who approved the lesser number and those who initially supported the governor's proposal but later compromised for the sake of the war effort. Second, the Assembly's stand on military matters was multidimensional and most often came from a fusing of recruitments with paper money. It is difficult to isolate the separate elements. There were roll calls to raise troops, but too few focused exclusively on currency. Most often, the lawmakers voted on measures to approve both. The evidence does not identify the member who notwithstanding his reservations on currency voted his approval of the whole measure.

Nevertheless, roll-call data do clarify the legislators' response to the war. Preliminary observations confirm, first, that this was an atomized body. The election of 1754 brought eleven new members to the house; only one in three had served more than one term; and, during the next six years, four replacements were added to the list. Not only was this a gathering of strangers, but it also lacked factional organization. The war created voting patterns that were different than previous alignments. This time the divisions tended to turn on denominational and sectional axes with Calvinists and Anglicans, principally from the eastern division, supporting the province's war effort and Baptists and Quakers, principally from the West, dissenting. Delegations that had usually opposed each other-- such as Perth Amboy and Bergen County--came to agree on the war. In turn, the Quakers, although recognized for their organizational talents, achieved only the barest semblance of group cohesion (Table 3.9). Second, disagreements did not make for a polarized legislature. Even though divisions turned on matters of principle, they did not translate into categorical or irreconcilable positions. Conscience played its part among the Quakers, but their behavior fell short of the meetinghouse's strictures. In general, the distance separating the dissenter from the prowar member was slight. If one acted from Anglo-American patriotism, he also shared the dissenter's suspicion of English policy. Both balked at English demands; the difference was only a matter of degree. Finally, notwithstanding the differences of opinion and the invertebrate nature of this institution, the bonds of community were strong enough to enable these lawmakers to work remarkably well toward a coherent policy.

A diverse group supported the Assembly's military position. One element was the province's urban and provincial elite (Table 6.1). These representatives--including Anglicans John Stevens, Charles Read, and Jacob DeHart, Presbyterian Robert Ogden, and the Quaker John Ladd--gave consistent support to the war effort. On occasion, they voted for even greater expenditures than what the majority could countenance. In 1755, they voted for a Ł1000 rather than a Ł500 grant to supply English forces, and later they endorsed raising a 600 rather than a 500 troop contingent. These members were also inclined to approve an oath of secrecy, revision of the militia law increasing the

169

TABLE 6.1
WARTIME DIVISIONS
1754–1760

Roll-Calls*

Assemblymen and Districts	1	2	3	4	5	6	7	8	9	10	11	12	13	14	15	16	17	18	19	20	21	22	23	24	25	26	27	28	29	30	31	32	33	34	35	36	37	38	39	40	41	42	43	44	45	46	47	48	49	50	51	52	53	54	55	56
Stevens,J.(PrthAmby)	+	+	+	+	−	+	+	+	+	+	+	+	+	+	+	+	+	+	+	+	+	+	+	+	+	+	+	+	+	+	+	+	+	+	+	+	+	+	+	+	+	+	+	+	+	+	+	+	+	+	+	+	+	+	+	+
Nevill,S.(Mddlsx)	+	+	+	+	−																																							+	+	+	+	+	+	+	+	+	+	+	+	+
Johnston,J.(PrthAmby)	+	+	+	+		+		+	+	+	+	+	+	+	+	+	+	+	+	+	+	+	+	+	+	+	+	+	+	#	#	+	+	+	+	+	+	+	+	+	+	+	+	+	+	+	+	+	+	+	+	+	+	+	+	+
Smyth,A.(PrthAmby)								+																														+						+	+			+	+								
Vreeland,G.(Brgn)	+	+	+	+		+	+	+	+	+	+	+	+	+	+	+	+	+	+	+	+	+	+	+	+	+	+	+	+	+	+	+	+	+	+	+	+	+	+		+	+	+		+	+	+	−	+	+	+	+	+	+	+	+
Ogden,R.(Essx)						+	+											+	+																		+	+	+		+	+	+		+	+	+				+	+	+	+		+	+
Ogden,J.(Essx)							+																																		+	+														
DeHart,J.(Essx)	+	+	+			+	+	+	+	+	+	+	+	+	+	+	+	+	+	+	+	+	+	+	+	+	+	+	+	+	#	+	+	+	+	+	+	+	+	+	+	+	+	+	+	+	+	+		+	+	+	+	+	+	+
Yard,J.(Hntrdn)	+	+	+	+		+	+	+	+	+	+	+	+	+	+	+	+	+	+	+	+	+	+	+	+	+	+	+	+	+	+	+	+	+	+	+	+	+	+	+	+	+	+	+	+	+	+	+	+	+	+	+	+	+	+	+
Read,C.(BrlTwn)	+	+	+			+	+	+	+	+	+	+	+	+	+	+	+	−	+	+	+	+	−	+	−	+		#	#	+	+	+	+	+	+	+	+	−	+	+	+	+	+	+	+	+	+	−	+	+	+	+	+	+	+	+
Ladd,J.(Glcstr)	+	+	+	+		+	+	+	+	+	+	+	+	+	+	+	+	+	+	+	+	+	+	+	+	−	+	+	+	#	#	+	+	+	+	+	+	+	+	+	+	+	+	+	+	+	+	+	+	+	+	+	+	+	+	+
Bradbury,R.(Essx)	+	+	+	+		+	+	+	+	+	+	+	+	+	+	+	+	+	+	+	+	+	−	+	+	−	−	+	+	#	+	+	+	+	+	+	+	+	+	+	+	+	+	+	+	+	+	+	−	−	+	+	+	+	+	+
Vangieson,R.(Brgn)	+	+	+	+		+	+	+	+	+	+	+	+	+	+	+	+	+	+	+	+	−	+	−	−	+	−	−	#	#	#	+	+	+	+	+	−	+	+	+	+	−	−	−	+	+	+	+	−	+	−	+	+	+	−	+
Fisher,H.(Smrst)	+	+	+	+		+	+	+	+	+	+	+	+	+	−	+	+	+	+	+	+	−	+	+	+	−	+	+	#	#	#	+	+	+	+	+	+	+	+	+	−	+	+	+	+	−	+	+	+	+	+	+	+	+	−	+
Middagh,P.(Hntrdn)	+	+	+	+		+	+	+	+	+	+	+	+	+	−	+	+	−	+	−	+	+	+	+	+	+	+	+	#	#	#	+	+	+	+	+	+	+	+	+	−	+	−	+	+	+	+	+	−	+	+	+	+	+	−	+
Hoagland,J.(Smrst)	+	+	+	+		+	+	+	+	+	+	+	+	+	−	+	+	+	+	+	+	+	+	+	+	+	+	+	#	#	#	+	+	+	+	+	+	+	+	+	−	+	+	+	+	−	+	+	+	+	+	+	+	+	−	+
Wetherill,J.(Mddlsx)	+	+	+	+		+	+	+	+	+	+	+	−	+	−	+	−	+	−	−	+	−	+	−	+	−	+	+	#	#	#	#	+	+	+	+	+	+	+	+	−	+	+	+	+	−	+	−	−	−	−	−	+	+	−	+
Hancock,W.(Slm)	+	+	+	+		+	+	+	+	+	+	+	−	−	−	+	−	−	−	−	−	−	−	−	−	−	−	−	+	#	#	+	+	+	−	−	+	−	+	+	−	+	+	+	+	+	+	+	+	+	+	+	+	+	+	+
Paxson,H.(BrlCo)	+	+	+	+		+	+	+	+	+	+	+	−	−	−	+	−	−	−	−	−	−	−	−	−	−	−	−	−	#			+	+	−	−	−	+	−	−	−	+	+	+	+	+	+	+	+	+	+	+	+	+	+	+
Newbold,B.(BrlCo)	+	+	+	+		+	+	+	+	−	−	−																		#						−	−	−	−	−	−	+	+	+	+	+	+	+	+	+	+	+	+	+	+	+
Smith,S.(BrlTwn)	+	+	+						−	−																					#			+	−	−	−	−	−	−	−	−	+	+	+	+	+	+	−	+	+	+	+	+	+	+
Miller,E.(Slm)	+	+		+	+		+		+					−												+	+	+	#		#	#	+	−	+	−	−	−	−	−	−	−	−	−	−	+	+	+	−	+	+	+	+	+	+	+
Stokes,S.(BrlCo)	+	+	+					−	−	−																			#												−	−	−	−	−	−	−	−	−	++	+	−	−	−	+	+
Holmes,J.(Mnmth)	+	+	+	−	−			+	+	+	−	−	−	−	−	−	−	−	−	−	−	−	−	−	+	+	+	#	−	#	#	#	−	#	#	−	−	−	−	−	+	+	+	+	+	+	+	+	−	+	−	+	−	+	+	+
Clement,S.Sr.(Glcstr)	+		+	+			−															−	−	−	−	+	+	#	−	#	−	−	−	−	−	−	−	−	+	+	−	+	+	−	+	+	+	−	+	−	+	+	+	+	+
Leaming,A.Jr.(CpMy)	+	−	−	−	−			−														−	−	−	−	−	−	#	#	#	#	#	−	#	#	−	−	−	−	−	+	+	+	+	+	+	+	+	−	+	+	+	+	+	+	+
Spicer,J.(CpMy)	−	−	−	−	−			−	−	−			−							−		−	−	−	−	−	−	#	#	#	#	#	−	#	#	−	−	−	−	−	+	+	+	+	+	+	+	+	−	+	+	+	+	+	+	+

Note: #, compromise position.

*TOPICS OF ROLL CALLS**

1. To approve "Plan of Operation" presented by the governor to build forts near Crown Point (April 9, 1755)

2. To provide for the transport and supply of English troops transported through the province (February 25, 1755)

3. To aid the king in driving the French from the Ohio valley (October 8, 1754)

4. That the Ł15,000 to be issued be redeemed by provincial taxes of Ł5,000 a year beginning in two years (April 9, 1755)

5. To pass a bill preventing supplies from being transported to the enemy (August 18, 1755)

6. To pass a bill for the raising of 1000 volunteers for the coming campaign (March 14, 1759)

7. To pass a bill for the raising of 100 volunteers (March 24, 1760)

8. To issue Ł15,000 for the supply of troops (May 25, 1756)

9. To issue Ł17,500 (May 29, 1756)

10. To issue Ł10,000 (December 22, 1755)

11. To pass a bill for the raising of 500 troops, erecting forts at Crown Point, and issuing Ł15,000 (April 17, 1755)

12. To pass a bill empowering commissioners to supply each company (April 24, 1755)

13. To accept the offer of "some gentlemen" to buy arms at cost providing the legislature will repay them (August 19, 1755)

14. To allow commissioners funds for raising troops (April 23, 1755)

15. To issue Ł30,000 for military purposes (October 18, 1757)

16. To raise 100 troops for frontier defense (September 13, 1757)

17. To revise the militia law (May 31 and June 2, 1757)

18. To raise 250 troops to join with New York and Pennsylvania against the Indians (March 10 and 12, 1756)

19. To raise more troops (March 31, 1758)

20. To revise the militia law (August 12, 1755)

21. To approve the governor's proposal that the militia should be used in an emergency (May 27, 1757)

22. To pay captains for expenses while enlisting troops (April 19, 1755)

23. To raise 500 troops (March 30, 1757)

24. To allow the drafting of troops (March 26, 1757)

25. That the members of the Assembly will take an oath to keep military affairs secret (April 8, 1755)

26. To allow Governor Bernard funds for travel during war (August 1, 1758)

27. That the issue of Ь50,000 be redeemed in five years instead of ten years (March 28, 1758)

28. To supply English troops with Ь1000 rather than Ь500 or nothing (February 25, 1755)

29. To raise and supply 600 troops rather than 500 or none (March 16, 1757)

30. To pay each volunteer 30 shillings rather than 20 shillings or nothing (March 28, 1758)

31. To pay each volunteer 15 shillings rather than 10 (May 30, 1757)

32. To grant Ь12 bounty to each volunteer rather than a lesser amount or none (March 28, 1758)

33. To raise a force of 1000 rather than one of 500 or none (March 28, 1758)

34. To purchase 2000 stand of arms rather than 1500 or none (August 24, 1757)

35. To supply forces by issuing Ь15,000 rather than Ь12,000 or nothing (April 9, 1755)

36. To raise 500 troops rather than 400 or none (April 9, 1755)

37. To pay Governor Bernard Ь1000 instead of Ь800 (August 1, 1758)

38. To pay Governor Belcher Ь1000 instead of Ь800 (March 19, 1757)

39. To pay the attorney general Ь30 instead of Ь20 (August 1, 1758)

40. To pass a bill for the support of the government (November 25, 1760)

41. To pay Governor Belcher Ŀ1000 instead of Ŀ800 (May 26, 1756)

42. To pay Governor Belcher's rent (May 26, 1756)

43. To pay President Reading Ŀ500 (October 13, 1757)

44. To pass bill for the support of the government (August 8, 1758)

45. To support the commander in chief (October 21, 1757)

46. To pay the chief justice Ŀ100 instead of Ŀ50 (March 19, 1757)

47. To pay the chief justice (November 19, 1760)

48. To pay Governor Boone for travel expenses (November 19, 1760)

49. To hold the Assembly at Perth Amboy and not at Elizabethtown (May 24, 1756)

50. To pay expenses for negotiating with the Indians (August 8, 1758)

51. To advance Ŀ1600 for the purchase of Indian lands rather than Ŀ1500 or nothing (August 11, 1758)

52. To support a bill for the purchase of Indian lands (August 11, 1758)

53. To pass a bill for the purchase of Indian lands (August 12, 1758)

54. To use public funds for settling Indians at Brothertown (November 12, 1760)

55. In support of a bill for the purchase of Indian lands (November 22, 1760)

56. To pass a bill for the purchase of Indian lands (November 25, 1760)

** In order to establish consistency in the scales, the wording of several motions needed to be inverted. See note for Table 5.1 for further explanation.

governor's military power, and a tight currency policy. Their record did not differ markedly from that of many rural representatives. Joseph Yard of Hunterdon County and George Vreeland of Bergen County were two of the most steadfast supporters of the war effort. But there were others, such as house careerist Hendrick Fisher and his backbencher neighbor John Hoagland, who tended to express their reservations. Although the two Somerset representatives did vote for the war effort, they, unlike Perth Amboy's John Stevens, were more sensitive to the provincial hardships. Thus, they were inclined to support the war with fewer troops and smaller budgets than the governor requested. And, in defiance of English policy that paper money be redeemed within five years, they voted to extend that period to ten years. So, too, they rejected the governor's recommendations for an oath of secrecy and a conscription law.

Dissent was multifaceted, springing from sensitivity to the province's poverty, frugality, a testiness toward the royal prerogative, as well as pacifism. In general, it did not assume that consistency found in the prowar bloc. Rather, it might best be described as a cluster of tendencies. If some acted from frugality, their inclination to begrudge the government was not an unbreakable maxim. At times, dissent was the expression of localist prejudices and whiggish principles, but it never hardened into the die-hard position found in the Morris years. So, too, pacifism seemed more a principle to guide but not dictate Quaker behavior.

It was not the Quakers but three Baptists--Leaming and Spicer of Cape May and James Holmes of Monmouth County--who registered the most extreme statement against the war. Holmes was following in the tradition of his predecessors from Monmouth County. On entering the house in 1751, he consistently refused to make concessions to the proprietary interest in the Council on tax policy. And, during the war years, he voted with few exceptions against contributing to the war effort. His was an unusual record because he was also the only lawmaker to vote consistently against high salaries and bills for the support of the government. By contrast, the Cape May delegation had come to its position slowly.[20] When Leaming and Spicer first entered the house, they had voted a moderate Country position. Shortly, during the last volatile meetings with Governor Morris, had they joined with the diehards. During these years, they had not opposed the governor's call for joining English military campaigns. But gradually they had begun to shift their position. During the first half of the Belcher administration, they rejected proposals for additional riot legislation, the Council's claims to amend money bills, and compromises on tax policy. When the last war for empire began, they were voting

174

with James Holmes. It is important, however, to note the limits of the Baptists' opposition. Their records suggest that they acted out of concern for the costs of the war but not from criticism of the war itself. Thus, when the house considered three alternatives--a high appropriation, a modest one, or none at all--they took the middle ground.

For some time, Quaker politicians had been struggling to reconcile their conscience with public life. Their pacifist stand had made them vulnerable to critics who were ready to call for their expulsion from public office. Some began to bend to political expediency. While they remained united against militia acts, they could not agree on provincial contributions to the war efforts. In 1746, only four representatives--all Friends--had opposed raising troops against French Canada. But another three acceded to the venture. Then, in 1754, most of the Quaker legislators joined with the majority to approve a resolution that New Jersey unite with other colonies against the French. By the 1750s, reformers in the meetinghouse were bearing witness against the backslider. The evidences of declension abounded. Some were arming themselves against the enemy, and it was a Quaker who counseled Governor Bernard on frontier fortifications. Thus, the Quaker who took a seat in the legislature exposed himself to the criticism of both Quakers and non-Quakers. Yet none of the eight Assemblymen resigned their seats. They responded to the military agenda in a variety of ways. While they tended to dissent, some voted for supplies for English and provincial troops, the erection of forts at Crown Point, and the raising of troops. Some, when given the opportunity, chose to abstain, but some did not. And, though the times were difficult, seven Friends stood successfully for election to the legislature in 1761.[21]

Consider the two extremes in Quaker behavior: John Ladd and Samuel Clement, Sr., both of Gloucester County. Ladd, the ubiquitous entrepreneur, was firmly entrenched in local politics and also moved easily with the provincial elite. Already he had forsaken the Friends' attitude toward simplicity. When he entered the Assembly, partly with the aid of Charles Read's allies, he became one of the house's most steady supporters of the war effort. Of thirty-one roll calls, he dissented only twice. Soon he won the governor's attention and was appointed to the Council. Clement, like Ladd, was a land speculator and mill owner. Unlike his neighbor, he was a localist. And, although he did not adhere to the meetinghouse's strictures against owning slaves, he did register his disapproval of the war on 90 percent of the roll calls.

It was a time of stress for the Quaker lawmakers. Even Clement had on occasion approved military appropriations. At the war's beginning, Samuel Smith of the port of Burlington approved aiding the English campaign to drive the French from the Ohio valley. The following year, however, he was regularly casting his vote against military measures. William Hancock took a different course. For example, when Smith opposed a Ł 30,000 grant for military services, the representative from Salem gave his approval. His record hardly fits the pacifist standard. At home, he had urged his sons to arm themselves in the event of an enemy invasion. In the Assembly, he voted to raise and supply troops for the English campaigns. In 1759, the house excused the Quaker members from voting on a bill to raise 1000 volunteers for that year's campaign. Hancock declined the opportunity to abstain and instead voted to pass the measure.[22] Indeed, he dissented on only half the military votes.

While New Jersey's lawmakers disagreed over the military agenda, they also shared many attitudes. First, the crusade against Catholic France stirred powerful emotions throughout the legislative community. A diverse bloc of lawmakers joined in support of the war effort. Indeed, lawmakers who normally distrusted each other and disagreed on other matters of the public agenda came together to form a remarkably cohesive voting bloc. Nor was the dissenter impervious to the cause. At times, the legislature approached unanimity. For example, twenty members including many dissenters supported and only two opposed a resolution to aid expelling the French from the Ohio valley. In turn, dissent was not only less cohesive, it also fell short of categorically opposing the war. Second, dissenters were not alone in their concern for the province's welfare and its rights and liberties. Assemblymen and even councilors could agree that New Jersey needed paper money. Legislators at both ends of the scale sought to protect the value of currency emissions and supported their quick redemption. So, too, the lawmakers jealously guarded provincial liberties from the prerogative. Supporters of the war also found it difficult to grant the governor increased military power, to allow troops to be drafted for military service, or to accept the governor's proposal to take an oath of secrecy. In sum, the legislators shared a dilemma: how to reconcile Anglo-American loyalties with New Jersey's interests. Even membership in the meetinghouse could not make the Quakers immune to these concerns. While their dissent was rooted in religious principle, their support for war measures and their propensity to approve frugal appropriations suggest that they shared the attitudes held by the general legislative community. Thus, what emerged from the house as policy was an amalgam of often contradictory attitudes.

Jacob Spicer's role in the house deliberations helps to gauge the distances separating the membership. His voting

176

record was exceptional. He was only one of two representatives to oppose the military expedition to the Ohio valley. On the floor of the house, he bluntly questioned whether the French had intruded upon English territory and wondered whether the disagreement between the two crowns could be settled peacefully. While conceding that the British interest must be protected, he was unimpressed by British appeals to expel the French from the continent. In addition, he counseled that in the event of war the province should devote its resources to its own defense. Perhaps the frontier provinces were exposed to the enemy. Yet they seemed reluctant to defend themselves. Why then, he asked, should the province lend support? New Jersey lay exposed to marauding enemy from the sea. To expend the province's limited resources elsewhere would be gross negligence, he reminded his colleagues. "If we Should weaken [the colony] by applying the people's strength & Substance to the Security of remote possessions, shou'd we not be guilty of a Sort of State Infidelity, and render curselves an Easier prey to the Attacks of a foreign power?" For the same reason, he expressed his "Zealous" opposition to the Albany Plan of Union. "Will not this Colony be bro't in for their Quota in Support of the Frontiers tho not so much Effected in point of Danger as Many if any of the Northern Colonies?"[23]

Spicer focused his attention on English authority, specifically the crown. Had not, he reminded his colleagues, the crown denied the colonists' request for paper money? The instruction to prohibit emissions as legal tender had a "Natural Tendency to discourage Borrowers and Lessen the Credit of the money" and thereby worked against the provincial welfare. Royal policy even threatened provincial liberties. On learning that London wanted a permanent fund to pay the governor, he warned that the provincial constitution was in peril. If the governor were "not subject to annual appropriations," he would enjoy "a Dangerous Independency unsafe to the Liberties of the People. For the purse strings are known to be the Grand check we have upon our Superiours." The king, he continued, acted as if unconcerned by his duties to his subjects. The province's promised reimbursement for past war expenditures had yet to be paid. Thus, invoking the precedent of the House of Commons, he called upon the Assembly to demand a quid pro quo: paper money for military support. "Have not the parliament of Great Britain often taken advantage of the Necessities of the Crown to obtain Important Service for the Nation? And is it not reasonable so to do, when the Crown witholds necessary Acts of Government from the Subject?"[24]

After years of public service, Spicer had come to view provincial government with a jaundiced eye. Governor Belcher, he was convinced, secretly worked against the Assembly petitions for paper money emissions. Military affairs were linked to ongoing tensions between the Country and the Court. Speaking against a bill to establish a standing force on the frontiers, he warned the house that the danger had been exaggerated and then reminded his colleagues that certain Jerseymen in their midst had been conspiring for some time to expand the government's military powers. These plotters would use, even fabricate, an emergency to achieve that end. Ten years earlier, when rioting had broken out, the disorders had furnished "a Pretext to the Court Interest to Labour for the accomplishment of that Scheme." Now they were concocting another emergency to achieve the same end.[25]

At the end of a day's exhortation, Spicer reflected in the privacy of his diary on his inability to awaken his colleagues. He stood alone, like a provincial Laocoon. Often he was outvoted by great majorities. Even, he lamented, "my pacifist gentlemen" voted "contrary to my expectations." His consistent dissent gave him reason to sense his isolation, but his voting record exaggerates the distance separating him from the other members. His arguments did strike responsive chords in the house. His arguments for tying paper money to war appropriations, his resentments of imperial policy, and his suspicions of executive power differed from others only in degree. Finally, the house's position reflected the same concerns. Moreover, Spicer had come to play an important role in the Assembly. Not only did he routinely sit on important committees to consider the Albany Plan, instruct the provincial agent in London, supply troops, and petition for bills of credit, but he also became the conscience of the house. He played the Country patriot to a receptive audience. When chosen commissioner to supply the provincial troops, he requested that his commission be reduced. And it was during this period that his colleagues delegated to him the responsibility for compiling New Jersey's Grants, Concessions, and Original Constitutions.[26]

The spectrum of opinion was narrow. John Wetherill of Middlesex County agreed as often with Spicer and the dissenters as he did with the prowar bloc. At the outset of the war, he joined in the decisions to aid the campaign against the French in the Ohio region, fortify Crown Point, raise a contingent of 500 troops, and supply English and provincial forces. Four years later, he voted to recruit 1000 volunteers for the coming campaigns. His patriotism, however, did not blind him to his constituents' hardships. He often chose a frugal position by either reducing or opposing provincial contributions. Sensitive to the growing financial burdens of the war, he preferred to extend the time for redeeming currency emissions. And, like Spicer, he opposed measures to revise the militia system, expand the governor's military powers, and to establish military conscription. His record, in short, came close to William Hancock's. And although he tended to dissent more often than representatives Fisher and Middagh, their differences were slight.

On the one hand, the assemblymen were grappling with important principles which, in turn, provoked continuing disagreements. But on the other hand, their disagreements did not harden into polarized or irreconcilable blocs. This was because they were not only disagreeing with each other but were also struggling with their own internal conflicts. How they responded to these shared dilemmas, which position they gravitated toward, depended upon rational consideration of the principles at stake and just as importantly on temperament. And, as their treatment of Indian policy reveals, there was always room for agreement.

Although New Jersey's frontier crisis was not as serious as New York's, the government regularly received reports of Indians descending upon exposed settlements and of skirmishes with the native Delawares. A garrisoned frontier and offensive ventures seemed sufficient to treat with the Indians from outside. As for the natives, the government recognized that a peaceful and lasting settlement required resolution of all disputed land claims. In 1758, Governor Bernard negotiated an agreement by which the government would buy disputed land claims and purchase a 3000 acre reservation in Burlington County for the resettlement of the native Indians.[27]

It was the Assembly's task to provide the money for the land purchases. The voting alignments on the enabling bill bear a resemblance to the divisions on the general military agenda. That is, the "nay" votes tended to be cast by those who usually dissented. But support came from all sections of the community. Spicer and Stevens, who rarely agreed, steadily supported the Indian policy. Moreover, the majority was able to answer objections to the bill. On August 11, the house read the bill for a second time and voted approval by only one vote. Those in opposition were three regular dissenters and five others who were more approving of the war effort. The next day, however, the bill was revised to the satisfaction of four of its critics. Only Wetherill, Holmes, Hancock, and Miller opposed the bill's final passage.

In sum, the wartime voting alignments did not fit previous and later patterns. Yet that behavior also illustrates other recurring patterns of fragmentation and cohesion. Clearly this was an invertebrate body. Voting blocs were not the product of organization. Those in support of the house war policy included strangers and even antagonists. This bloc would disintegrate in the next Assembly (Tables 3.9 and 3.10). Although the Quakers had a reputation for organization, they were not able to achieve anything approximating unity on the war. Indeed, the lawmakers seemed to approach the wartime agenda from different vantage points, weighing in their own way patriotism, domestic concerns, and whiggish and pacifist principles. But there was also an underlying pattern of community, perhaps best understood as shared dilemmas which came from efforts to reconcile English loyalties with domestic needs and concomitant conflicts with imperial authority. Thus, rather than split into two irreconcilable camps, the lawmakers shared enough to work together. And while principles affected their decisions, the lawmakers--even Quakers and patriot enthusiasts--could work together pragmatically. And the policy that finally emerged from their deliberations reflects the strength of community.

A new legislature was elected in 1761, two years before the war ended. In its first sessions, this Assembly treated with the usual military questions. The members divided the way they had in the earlier legislature, and the policy they agreed upon provoked the same disagreements with the governor. But they were also beginning to attend to a new agenda: a postwar depression, new and troublesome imperial policies, and, concomitantly, domestic disturbances and a politically aroused public. During the following decade, English policy created tensions ever more difficult to resolve, attitudes began to harden, and the legislative community confronted revolutionary crisis.

NOTES

1. Belcher to Council and Assembly, Oct. 3, 1754, N.J.Archs., XVI, 481-83; Belcher to Council and Assembly, Mar. 9, 1756, ibid., XVII, 6-7; Belcher to Sir John St. Clair, Sept. 3, 1755, ibid., VIII, pt. 2, 133. Also Belcher to Assembly, Aug. 1, 1755, ibid., 121-22; Belcher's proclamation of fast day, New-York Mercury, Apr. 12, 1756, in ibid., XX, 20-22.

2. Aaron Burr, A Discourse . . . on Account of the late Encroachments of the French (New York, 1755), 39-41. John F. Berens, Providence & Patriotism in Early America, 1640-1815 (Charlottesville, VA, 1978) 32-50; Alan Heimert, Religion and

the American Mind: From the Great Awakening to the Revolution (Cambridge, MA, 1966).

3. Petition of frontier inhabitants, Feb. 17, 1757, Manuscripts, I, Governors' Papers, 1720-1789; Abraham Van Campen to Belcher, Apr. 25, 1757, ibid.; petition from Sussex County, Apr. 27, 1757, ibid.; petition from Sussex County, Mar. 31, 1758, Votes and Proceedings; petition from Cape May, Apr. 11, 1758, ibid.

4. For general surveys of the period, see Kemmerer, Path to Freedom, 237-74; Fisher, New Jersey as a Royal Province, 158-67, 319-59. Also Alan Rogers, Empire and Liberty: American Resistance to British Authority, 1755-1763 (Berkeley, CA, 1974); Bernhard Knollenberg, Origin of the American Revolution, 1759-1766 (New York, 1960).

5. Assembly to Belcher, Mar. 31, 1757, N.J.Archs., XVII, 93-94. Assembly to Belcher, June 3, 1757, ibid., 109-12.

6. Society of Friends, An Epistle . . . ([Philadelphia, 1755]), 3. Richard Bauman, For the Reputation of Truth: Politics, Religion, and Conflict Among the Pennsylvania Quakers, 1750-1800 (Baltimore, MD, 1971); Sydney V. James, A People Among Peoples: Quaker Benevolence in Eighteenth-Century America (Cambridge, MA, 1963); Jack D. Marietta, "Wealth, War and Religion: The Perfecting of Quaker Asceticism, 1740-1783," Church History, XLIII (June, 1974), 230-41; Rufus M. Jones, The Quakers in the American Colonies (London, 1911), 393; L. Morris to Governor Clinton, Dec. 13, 1745, Morris Papers, 289.

7. [Archibald Kennedy], Serious Considerations on the Present State of the Affairs of the Northern Colonies (New York, 1754), 3, 22. Belcher to Assembly, Apr. 29, 1754, Votes and Proceedings.

8. Fisher, New Jersey as a Royal Province, 110-11; Kemmerer, Path to Freedom, 177-78.

9. Belcher to Partridge, July 2, 1754, Letterbooks, X, 417; Assembly resolution, Oct. 11, 1754, Votes and Proceedings; Assembly petition to king, Oct. 17, 1754, ibid.; Belcher to Board of Trade, Nov. 26, 1754, N.J.Archs., VIII, pt. 2, 73-74; Belcher to Thomas Robinson, Dec. 17, 1754, ibid., 77.

10. Spicer, "Diary," 97-100; Belcher to Assembly, Mar. 28, 1757, Votes and Proceedings; Assembly to Belcher, Mar. 28, 1757, ibid.; Assembly to Francis Bernard, Mar. 10, 1759, ibid.; Assembly to Belcher, Mar. 31, 1757, N.J.Archs., XVII, 93-95.

11. Bernard to Board of Trade, Aug. 31, 1758, ibid., IX, 136; Bernard to Board of Trade, Mar. 30, 1759, ibid., 171. Assembly to Bernard, Aug. 9, 1758, Votes and Proceedings; Bernard to Assembly, Mar. 19, 1760, ibid. See Edward McM. Larrabee's sketch of Bernard in The Governors of New Jersey, 1664-1974: Biographical Essays, ed. Paul A. Stellhorn and Michael J. Birkner (Trenton, NJ, 1982), 62-65. And for Bernard's successors Thomas Boone (1760-1761) and Josiah Hardy (1761-1763), see sketches by Larry R. Gerlach and James Kirby Martin in ibid., 65-72.

12. Assembly to Belcher, Oct. 21, 1754, N.J.Archs., XVI, 492. Assembly to Belcher, Nov. 14, 1755, ibid., 562-64.

13. Assembly to Belcher, July 24, 1756, ibid., XVII, 47. Belcher to Council and Assembly, Dec. 16, 1755, ibid., VIII, pt. 2, 193-94; Bernard to Board of Trade, June 20, 1758, ibid., IX, 116-20; Belcher to Assembly, July 26, 1756, Votes and Proceedings.

14. Belcher to Assembly, Mar. 26, 1757, ibid.; petition from Reading Township, Aug. 2, 1758, ibid.; petition from Princeton quoted in John Shy, "Quartering His Majesty's Forces in New Jersey," Proceedings of the New Jersey Historical Society, LXXVIII (Apr., 1960), 85. Petition from Trenton, Dec. 23, 1756, Votes and Proceedings; testimony of Assemblyman Joseph Yard, Dec. 24, 1756, ibid.; Assembly to Belcher, June 3, 1757, ibid.; Belcher to Assembly, June 3, 1757, ibid.; petition from Middlesex County, Mar. 31, 1758, ibid.; petition from Lebanon, Aug. 10, 1758, ibid.; Assembly to Bernard, Mar. 10, 1759, ibid.; and the extraordinary account in John Recker's petition, May 27, 1763, ibid.; Assembly to Belcher, July 24, 1756, N.J.Archs., XVII, 45-47; Belcher to Council and Assembly, Mar. 26, 1757, ibid., 91-92; Belcher to Council and Assembly, Aug. 20, 1757, ibid., 113-15; J. Alan Rogers, "Colonial Opposition to the Quartering of Troops During the French and Indian War," Military Affairs, XXXIV (Feb., 1970), 7-11.

15. Assembly to Belcher, Apr. 8, 1755, Votes and Proceedings. Belcher to Assembly, Feb. 26, 1755, N.J.Archs., VIII, pt. 2, 93.

16. President John Reading to Council and Assembly, Oct. 13, 1757, ibid., XVII, 143; Assembly to Reading, Oct. 18, 1757, Votes and Proceedings.

17. Bernard to Assembly, Mar. 25, 1760, ibid.; Thomas Boone to Council and Assembly, Oct. 30, 1760, ibid.; Assembly to Boone, Nov. 21, 1760, ibid.; Assembly to Bernard, Mar. 25,

1760, ibid. Bernard to Board of Trade, Mar. 29, 1760, N.J.Archs., IX, 225; Alexander's opinion before Council, Mar. 1, 1755, ibid., XVI, 520-21.

18. Assembly to Belcher, June 3, 1757, ibid., XVII, 111; Bernard to Council and Assembly, Mar. 15, 1759, ibid., 218; Lawrence Henry Gipson, The British Empire Before the American Revolution, 15 vols. (New York, 1949), VII, 308-9. Assembly to Reading, Apr. 17, 1758, N.J.Archs., XVII, 165-67; Leaming to "Dear & worthy Gentlemen," May 26, 1771, Gerlach, ed., New Jersey in the American Revolution, 61-63.

19. Belcher to Council and Assembly, Mar. 9, 1756, N.J.Archs., XVII, 7.

20. April 26, 1745, Votes and Proceedings.

21. June 25, 1746, ibid.; Bernard to Board of Trade, June 20, 1758, N.J.Archs., IX, 118; Bernard to Board of Trade, Mar. 21, 1759, ibid., 169; Kemmerer, Path to Freedom, 84.

22. Carl Raymond Woodward, Ploughs and Politicks: Charles Read of New Jersey and His Notes on Agriculture, 1715-1774 (New Brunswick, NJ, 1941), 166-67; Mar. 14, 1759, Votes and Proceedings.

23. Transcript of Spicer's address in Anthony Nicolosi, "Colonial Particularism and Political Rights: Jacob Spicer II on Aid to Virginia, 1754," New Jersey History, LXXXVIII (Summer, 1970), 78; Spicer, "Diary," 40. Spicer's notes on speech to Assembly, Feb. 22, 1755, Spicer Papers; Spicer to Partridge, Feb. 9, 1755, ibid.

24. Nicolosi, "Colonial Particularism," 82-83, 87. Spicer, "Diary," 49, 82.

25. Spicer's notes on speech to Assembly, Feb. 22, 1755, Spicer Papers.

26. Nicolosi, "Colonial Particularism," 88. Spicer, "Diary," 82.

27. C. A. Weslager, The Delaware Indians: A History (New Brunswick, NJ, 1972), 265-71.

CHAPTER SEVEN

CRISIS IN ARCADIA, 1761-1775:
THE LEGISLATIVE COMMUNITY TESTED

The war was prelude to a series of crises for the Assembly and its constituency. The issues were familiar: paper money and debt, the support of government, its officials and the military, and Assembly rights and the prerogative. But the legislature deliberated in an atmosphere of mounting urgency. Post-war depression required the lawmaker's attention: debtors' pleas for relief grew louder, finally erupting into violence, and proposals for reviving and improving the economy abounded. Simultaneously, English authority became more intrusive, first as it impeded the legislature's ability to respond to the economic crisis and, second, as it imposed new taxes on the province. In turn, the legislature watched a once inert public awaken to the crises. Together, the representatives and their constituents came to sense that the issues joined and to share forebodings that arcadia--its rights, liberties, and well-being-- was imperiled. But political awakening forced a new and special problem upon the legislature: that is, how it related to the community. As patriot ploughmen joined in organized opposition to what seemed a corrupt and tyrannous conspiracy, resistance began to assume its own momentum. The legislature was ignored. Increasingly unable to channel the patriot's fervor and actions, it was losing its claim to represent and speak for the province. Thus, concomitant with the erosion of English loyalties, the legislature was grappling with its own legitimacy crisis.[1]

After the war, the public became more actively concerned about the legislature. At the beginning of the Morris administration, the Assembly had received only eighteen petitions; but, in the sessions of 1763 and 1764, it read seventy-six. And five years later the number had increased again to 187 (Table 1.1). In response to the mounting workload, the Assembly ruled that it could consider only those petitions submitted during the first ten days of a session. The list of subscribers grew as well. Usually a petition had been signed by a handful of private individuals and local magistrates, but now some included as many as 200 and even 400 subscribers. The Sons of Liberty was the first sign of even broader political involvements. During the following decade, Jerseymen met in their communities to protest English policies by legal and extralegal means and in the process came to form county and then provincial associations. Once petitions had expressed the need of a particular locality. Suddenly province-wide petition drives were undertaken, and the petitions from several counties came to duplicate each other in content and even expression. The Assembly acted in the same spirit. It ordered that its doors be opened so that "all Persons may, if they think proper, be present at any publick Debate, under the same Rules and Orders observed in the House of Commons." And, in the same vein, it recorded more roll calls in its printed minutes than it had before: during the decade of 1738 to 1747 the Votes and Proceedings listed 110 and in the ten years before independence 197 divisions.[2]

The legislative community was preoccupied with the provincial depression. During the war, the province had prospered, but military spending had ceased, currency drained from the province, and prices fell. The once thriving ploughman became the desperate and embittered debtor. In March 1767, the Morris County court heard 100 debt-related suits and in December twice that number. Hardly a day passed without the legislature receiving petitions from the debtor and insolvent. The Assembly was pressed to issue paper money, reduce interest rates, and regulate court costs and legal fees. Legal expenses would be reduced if only the Assembly directed that small cases be heard before local magistrates. Jerseymen witnessing the "Multiplicity" and "the great Expence of Law-Suits" cried out against lawyers who were enriching themselves by their "Extortions in the Bills of Cost." These "Serpents" were "living upon the Ruins of the Poor"; like "Leaches," they were "sucking out our very Hearts Blood." Action must be taken against this "Oppression. . .while some little Property remains as yet out of their Reach." While some petitioned, others grew impatient. The injustices caused one patriot to "cry out to you my Countrymen." "Rouse, Rouse!. . . . Remember the saying of Solomon of old, that Oppression maketh a wise Man mad; stand together and forbid them Practicing in our Court, and rid the County of such Barbarity, and turn them out of the County." First in Monmouth and then in Essex County the ploughmen assembled at the courthouse and prevented the attorneys from conducting their business.[3]

"The Deplorable Condition of the Province. . .occasioned by the great Scarcity of Money, Decay of Trade, Multitude of Law Suits" pressed upon the Assembly, but its actions did not match public expectations. Although paper money remained a perennial favorite, the Assembly was restrained by imperial policy. During the war, the government had issued Ł350,000 and had done so by bargaining the province's needs against English military requirements. Now in peacetime, it resolved to issue another Ł100,000 at loan but discovered that Whitehall was obdurate and could not be budged from its conservative fiscal policy. When the Assembly turned to debt reform, however, it chose to respond cautiously. It acted only after the rioters had closed the courts in Monmouth County. While endorsing legislation to regulate cases of small debt, it refrained from regulating lawyers and, in fact, established the means for the expeditious sale of debtors' property.[4]

Proposals for advancing and realizing mercantile arcadia flourished. In the midst of the war, "B. C. Caesaria" predicted that once New Jersey had realized its productive potential it could extricate itself from its bondage to the New York and Philadelphia merchant. Specifically, he advised the government to encourage woolen and linen production. With peace, the enthusiasm for economic improvements grew. Governor William Franklin addressed a receptive audience at the end of the war when he urged the legislature to improve the economy and trade. Bounties might be placed on flax, hemp, silk, and wines; the arteries of commerce--roads and ferries--needed improvement. Jerseymen advanced schemes to encourage beef production and the establishment of trading companies. And the Assembly responded by regulating the quality of meat and grain exports, by setting bounties on flax, hemp, and silk, and by controlling the fishing industry. During the post-war decade, it passed more legislation for domestic improvements, such as roads and ferries, than it had in previous years.[5]

The province would realize that vision of mercantile arcadia if it promoted public morality. The "careful, pious Life. . . makes good Common-wealthmen"; the "sordid, careless, negligent Life," the "bad Common-wealthmen." The voice for moral reform grew louder. Jerseymen looked to the government to regulate drinking, gaming, racing, and foxhunting. Sometimes the issue triggered disagreements: would a lottery stimulate civic improvements or would it undermine provincial character? Slavery became the principal issue in this debate. The petitions for and against the institution abounded. For some Jerseymen, slave labor was requisite to prosperity. For others, it nurtured the slothful and indolent.[6]

But Jerseymen alone were not defining the public agenda. While attending to the province's moral economy, they came to sense that English policy boded ill for the colonies. Already sensitive to the imperial presence during the war, the legislative community watched as England sought to reform its administration, revive the executive prerogative, and extend parliament's authority over the colonies. As Governor Bernard had warned, concessions made in war, the unconstitutional aggrandizement of legislative powers, would no longer be tolerated "when the times were more settled."[7] The Currency and Quartering Acts of 1764 and 1765 aggravated long-standing disputes. Whitehall's decision to secure an independent judiciary and a permanent salary for the governor raised fears for the provincial constitution. The Stamp Act and then the Townsend Duties introduced new topics for concern. Together, English decisions spelled an unsettling reformation and inspired fears that an English conspiracy was being devised to undermine American rights and liberties.

Governor William Franklin spoke for that English authority. The fourth governor to arrive in the six years after Belcher's death, Franklin ended a period of instability in the executive office. When he addressed the legislature in the spring of 1763, he seemed at first poorly suited for the task. The illegitimate son of Pennsylvania's agent Benjamin Franklin, he had earned the reputation of a rake. He had no administrative experience and owed his commission to his father's influence. Yet he quickly dispelled doubts and proved an able representative of the crown in a period of mounting political crisis. Drawing on his acquaintance with Pennsylvania politics, he skillfully managed his relationship with New Jersey's lawmakers sometimes by bargaining and oftentimes by persuasion. Although he lost control of his temper at times, he, unlike Lewis Morris, managed to avoid needless and prolonged confrontation. In his twelve years as governor, he demonstrated diligence in the pursuit of his duty and concern for the province's welfare. Thus, in a time of mounting crisis he earned and maintained general public support.[8]

The currency question tested Franklin's skill at mediating between a legislature which was convinced that the provincial welfare depended on an emission of ₤100,000 at loan and his superiors in London who were determined to restrict what they deemed an irresponsible addiction to paper money in the colonies. The issue turned on the Currency Act's prohibition of currencies issued as legal tender. In 1768, Franklin refused his assent to the Assembly scheme but, sympathetic with its argument, wrote requesting permission to accept a revised version on condition that it met the legal tender requirement. The house thanked him for his efforts and in its next proposal conceded that the money not be counted as legal tender in the discharge of debts but that it be allowed for the payment of taxes. Convinced that the bill would receive London's approval, Franklin wrote to his superiors recommending its acceptance. When informed, however, that the Board of Trade remained unimpressed by his arguments, he was dismayed and humiliated. Though his efforts to negotiate a settlement had been for naught, failure did not translate into political liability. The Assembly thanked him for his good offices but declined to reconsider the matter. "Unless the said Bills of Credit are a

LEGAL TENDER in the Loan Offices," it explained, "they will not answer the good Purposes desired." While the Assembly continued to receive pleas of Jerseymen for paper money, it stubbornly refused to reconsider the issue for the next three years. In 1774, English policy seemed to relax; and, on the governor's advice, it passed an issue which met with English approval.[9]

After the expulsion of the French from Canada, English troops remained stationed in New Jersey, and the province was called upon to provide for their supply and quartering. The house responded reluctantly and with niggardly appropriations. Later, it refused to vote any support. The troops pricked Anglo-American sensibilities regarding the presence of a standing army, and occasionally confrontations between the military and civilians reinforced that loathing. In addition, English demands rankled the lawmakers. When they complied, they did not adhere to the letter of the Quartering Act which required a precise enumeration of the supplies granted. The legislature continued to bargain English needs against its demands for paper money. In September 1770, Franklin summoned the house to inform it, first, that the second loan office scheme had failed London's approval and, second, that English troops required provisions. The house expressed its disappointment and ignored the request for a military supply. "However," Franklin recounted, "upon my talking the Affair over in private with some of the leading Members, and representing the ill Consequences that would probably ensue to the Province from their Refusal," he convinced enough members to approve a supply for the immediate future.[10] The funds ran out shortly, and Franklin reopened the subject. But the legislature could not be budged this time. Tempers flared, and each accused the other of distortion and misrepresentation. According to the governor, the province could bear this expense. To refuse could only be constructed as disloyalty. By the house's lights, the representatives of the people, not the governor, could best determine what their constituents could afford. Franklin's arithmetic was faulty: where he found "Affluence" the lawmakers found "Distresses." Franklin could not abide such "Railing," adjourned the Assembly, and recalled it within a month but to no avail. According to Aaron Leaming, the confrontation was the gravest he had witnessed during his three decades of service. Within months, however, the issue was fortuitously resolved when the troops were withdrawn. When they reappeared for short stays in transit, the Assembly readily granted supplies.[11]

The governor and the legislature continued long-standing debates over the civil list. Specifically, the issue turned on the establishment of a permanent salary, the amount to be paid

189

officials, and the control of appointments. Neither party gained a clear victory. Franklin quickly realized the futility of advocating a permanent salary. But, from the outset of his administration, he pressed for higher salaries. His argument that current salaries were insufficient to support the dignity of government made a slight impact on lawmakers. By a narrow margin, they voted to raise salaries, in the governor's case by £200. But they were impervious to his later appeals for additional amounts. Even when he warned that the king might assume the responsibility, the legislature remained indifferent.[12] Franklin gained concessions on occasion. Sometimes, as on the appointment of the provincial agent to London, the victory was symbolic. When the question first arose whether the house alone or all three branches of government should make the selection, Franklin was dubious that precedent could be reversed and that the house would concede the point. Yet he prevailed upon the Assembly to allow the Council and the executive to participate in the choice. But as he privately admitted, he had gained little of substance since the house maintained control of the agent's salary. On another occasion, the legislature relinquished real power. During the debates over the military, it surrendered the authority to appoint barracks commissioners to the governor.[13] The most volatile dispute focused on the appointment of the treasurer of East Jersey. In the wake of the robbery of the eastern treasury, the house launched its investigation and concluded that the incumbent Stephen Skinner should be removed for incompetence. Once Skinner resigned his post, the Assembly successfully blocked Franklin's choice for the vacancy and forced its favorite upon him.

On review, Governor Franklin skillfully employed the limited resources of his office in the conduct of his relations with the Assembly, but paradoxically his methods, notwithstanding their immediate success, redounded to raise fears of executive corruption and to rouse the legislature in defense of its integrity. He might avoid collision with the house by promoting such pet projects as paper money. But, when his responsibility to the crown forced him toward confrontation, he grappled with the limitations of his office. Without the patronage sufficient to enlist a loyal following in the house, he had to rely on the art of persuasion and to employ his powers to summon, adjourn, and dissolve the legislature. Often "private Conferences," even intimations that intransigence risked the displeasure of the crown and perhaps drastic reprisals, worked to change a lawmaker's vote. A favorite tactic was to employ the power of adjournment. At the opening of a session, Governor Franklin allowed the representatives to advance their favorite schemes before broaching a controversial subject. Then, in private, he suggested that unless they acceded to his recommendations he would prorogue them before completing their pet projects.[14] At times, he refrained from summoning the legislature. So, too, he chose to avoid the risk of calling elections.

Such tactics worked to rouse the Country's suspicions. During the Stamp Act crisis, the house at first responded cautiously to Massachusetts's call for an intercolonial congress. Within hours of adjournment, it resolved against "Connecting" with the other colonies. In the succeeding weeks, however, support for participation mounted. Despite the urging of assemblymen, Franklin refused to reconvene the legislature. So twelve representatives met in caucus at Perth Amboy and selected a delegation to represent the province at the congress. Finally, in November 1765, the governor summoned the legislature but kept it just long enough to scold it for its unprecedented action. The house did not meet again until the next June and after the Stamp Act had been repealed.[15] The episode smacked of executive manipulation. The legislators charged that Speaker Robert Ogden had, when he first received Massachusetts's letter, welcomed the congress but had buckled under the governor's pressure and that he had then postponed revealing the letter to the house until the last moment and when most of the representatives had gone home. Thus, the representatives had no recourse but to meet in an extralegal "Convention."[16] Franklin was learning that frequent sessions only gave opportunity to the opposition and that frequent elections only stirred the populace. Thus, at a time when the legislative community was awakening, he reversed what had been the practice of calling the house twice a year. Sometimes he prorogued the Assembly as long as eighteen months. So, too, he called only two elections during his twelve years in office. The Assembly protested that it should meet more often than to grant periodic supplies to the government. Since "Dissolutions of the General Assembly at proper Periods, tend greatly to secure the Liberty of the People" and "a long Continuance of Assemblies may endanger that Liberty," it pressed for frequent and regular elections.[17] But Franklin jealously guarded his power over the Assembly. When the house received John Ogden's resignation in June 1770, it forwarded its request to the governor that he call for an election in Essex County. This procedure was customary, but Franklin spied a dangerous precedent. By allowing one representative to resign, he would be unable to prevent the entire legislature from following suit and thereby force the governor to call for general elections. The issue was hotly contested until Franklin appointed Ogden to an "Office of Profit" and thus made him legally ineligible to hold his seat.[18]

By protecting its integrity from executive manipulation, the Assembly was also defending its place within provincial society as the guardian of the public's rights. During these years, attentions turned toward English policies, especially those enacted by parliament. And the central issue turned on the House of Commons's presumption that it could levy taxes on the American colonies. From the Stamp Act crisis to its last meeting in December of 1775, the house played a traditional role as bastion of the public's rights, this time against parliament's misdeeds. Jerseymen, it maintained, enjoyed the rights of Englishmen--one of which was the right to hold property. Accordingly, the people relinquished their property by consent and through their representatives. Since the colonies were not represented in the English legislature, parliament had no constitutional right to levy taxes on America. No matter the form of taxation, be it the Stamp Act or the Townsend Duties, the principle remained the same. Even London's conciliatory proposal that the American legislatures devise their own methods of raising taxes for the support of imperial expenses did not alter the issue. In sum, the Assembly was groping toward what would later be known as dominion status with the several legislatures of the empire, both American and English, enjoying equal status and owing a common allegiance to the king.[19]

While its efforts pointed toward a redefinition of the imperial relationship, the house self-consciously assumed a conservative role and explicitly defined its purpose as protector of "ancient" constitutional forms and of its constituents' English birthrights. During its last meeting, it protested Governor Franklin's charge that it was flirting with independence and resolved that all avenues be explored toward "restoring the Union between the Colonies and Great-Britain upon constitutional Principles." Yet the crises of a decade were transforming the mood of the legislative community and thereby creating an inner "logic of rebellion." The voice of the Country grew louder and shriller. The quartering of English troops in the province and parliament's several schemes to tax without representation confirmed that London was devising a multipronged assault on American liberties. Jerseymen stood to lose not only the right of property but also a free press and trial by jury.[20] Aaron Leaming reflected with his constituents on English intentions: during the last war "General Officers and other Gentlemen of Rank" came to America, learned to envy its prosperity, and "grew jealous that we Should in time rival England itself." Concluding "That Too much Liberty had made us too rich," they undertook to impose taxes and quarter troops in the province. Assemblyman Joseph Borden interpreted England's several attempts at taxation--the Stamp Act, Townsend Duties, and the Tea Act--as elements of a single conspiracy. Parliament devised each of these taxes so that they would fall lightly on the colonists. But its purpose was not so much to raise revenue as it was to accustom Americans to paying taxes without representation. Once this had been accomplished, the rates

192

would become heavier. "The Scheme is more for Posterity than for present Profit to the Ministry." Although "we are to be taxed [in] our Lives but small," "our Children" can expect to pay on "not only Paint, Glass, &c. but their very Stock and block, even to their Heads." As Jerseymen learned of English tyrannies in neighboring colonies, they awakened to a common American cause. And, as their calls to protect the constitution grew more urgent, resistance to tyranny assumed its own momentum that propelled the legislative community toward rebellion.[21]

These were perilous times. While the provincial resisted parliament's tyrannous intentions, he sought to check public immoralities and promote the ideal of commercial arcadia. The two movements became intertwined.[22] Renewed interest in the moral economy--the discussions of slavery and gambling--had awakened the ploughmen to slothfulness and corruption. English policies worked to make him more sensitive to the danger, especially when he discovered his venal neighbor conspiring to betray the cause of liberty for selfish motives. So, too, the provincial was already preoccupied with domestic improvements and industry and seized upon nonimportation as the opportunity to resist English taxation and to stimulate local manufactures. Thus, the ploughman found himself encircled by enemies both from outside and at home. The designing minister in London had his counterpart in arcadia. The villainous trader became the apostate to liberty. According to the indebted farmer, the enemy of liberty and the predatory lawyer were the same. Thus, the patriot movement was a crusade to uproot and purge the corrupt from arcadia. And these concerns, once fused, sparked New Jersey's political awakening with a sense of urgency.

While sharing these attitudes, the legislature was also confronting a crisis of its own. At the beginning of the imperial crisis, it assumed its accustomed role as representative of its constituents and caretaker of their rights. The public's response at once reinforced and challenged that role. As communities were roused to defend their "long-enjoyed, boasted and invaluable Liberties and Privileges," they encouraged their representatives. "The Eyes of the People are Fixed Upon you Viewing you in the Crisis of time, as Instruments of Protection and Preservation of our Rights and Liberties, and Expect Such a Conduct from you as Becomes Persons Animated with a. . .Spirit of Liberty." But the awakening also brought unsettling transformations in provincial politics. Beginning with the Stamp Act crisis, communities were devising stratagems to resist English tyranny, establishing networks of communication, and constructing first county and later provincial organizations. Committees of inspection enforced boycotts against English imports and disciplined or intimidated "those vile Miscreants, who have violated their so often plighted Faith."[23] With this grassroots mobilization, new faces appeared in the leadership of the protest movement. From the legislative chamber, the changes often seemed foreboding. The lawmakers were no longer able to control and direct the politics of protest, and its violence often chilled this political elite. Even one of its own, Essex County's Robert Ogden, suffered at the hands of the Sons of Liberty for refusing to endorse the resolves of the Stamp Act Congress. While the Assembly struggled to maintain control, it discovered that Governor Franklin's practice of long adjournments frustrated the attempt. By 1775, a provincial congress had emerged to lead the resistance movement and assume the responsibilities of government.

The deepening crisis and a transforming electorate did not, in fact, radically alter the social composition of the legislature. Although public indignation had driven Robert Ogden to resign, the Essex electors chose Stephen Crane, another of Elizabethtown's elite, to represent the county. In 1768, they re-elected Crane and John Ogden, Robert's cousin. Four years later, they favored Crane again but also turned to Henry Garritse, a Dutch Reform ploughman from a northern township. This elite's ability to endure was not unique. With a single exception, the proprietary clique prevailed at Perth Amboy. In the counties, entrenched families--the Coopers of Gloucester, the Gibbons of Salem, the Van Nestes of Somerset, and the Lawrences of Monmouth--continued to be elected. Newcomers appeared in the Assembly but not at an unusual rate. The denominational composition of the membership began to change: the number of Baptists and Anglicans increased. But these alterations did not make for radical change. In the port of Burlington, for example, the Smiths shared office with such Anglicans as Abraham and Thomas Hewlings, both of whom held West Jersey proprietary interests. So, too, the presiding officers of the house reflected continuity. Cortlandt Skinner of Perth Amboy succeeded Robert Ogden in 1765; and, except for one short interlude when he was replaced by Stephen Crane, he sat in the speaker's chair until the dissolution of royal government in 1775.

The membership rotated at a rapid rate but not significantly greater than in earlier years. Between 1738 and 1754, seventy-seven representatives sat in eight assemblies. In a comparable period, 1761 to 1775, only three assemblies were elected and a total of sixty-five representatives were chosen.[24] Incumbents were returned at a normal rate: sixteen in 1761, twelve in 1769, and fourteen in 1772. It is difficult to ascribe

194

the slight decrease in incumbency to dramatic political change. The mundane cannot be overlooked. The lifetime of each Assembly was longer, and many may have chosen not to return. Of the sixteen incumbents returned in 1761, six were still sitting in that Assembly's last session of 1768: seven had died; two were promoted to the Council; and only Robert Ogden had resigned. In 1772, incumbents were outnumbered, but this change was because six representatives came from the new counties of Morris, Sussex, and Cumberland.

The Assembly remained a gathering of local elites, and much of its business continued to focus on parochial concerns and mundane rivalries. Petitions requesting assistance in the draining of a field, the maintenance of a waterway, or the building of a bridge outnumbered those that addressed provincial and imperial affairs. Often the house attended to old conflicts of interests. Eastern proprietors continued to protect their lands from their long-standing opponents. During the Stamp Act crisis, the legislature deliberated on the placement of the Middlesex and Hunterdon county courthouses. The representatives divided along familiar lines. The urban members from Newark, Perth Amboy, and Burlington voted to keep the Middlesex courthouse at Perth Amboy and Hunterdon's at Trenton; the members from Middlesex, Monmouth, Somerset, and Bergen counties supported removal; and the western delegations split. In part, the division reflected the play of local interest, but the issue also stirred antiurban predispositions and antiproprietary sentiments.

But the legislature did address a provincial agenda and a looming political crisis. It did so as an institutionally invertebrate body--an assemblage of milling interests and divergent membership. Governor Franklin's observation that "There are no Parties existing in the Province" is confirmed by cluster bloc analysis (Tables 3.10 to 3.12).[25] The voting patterns reveal affinities among urban members, tendencies for rural members of similar denominational identity to agree, traditional antagonisms, and an underlying base for consensus. While tending to polarize, voting associations remained loose, often did not achieve high levels of agreement, and, finally, did not reflect the presence of organization. Long-standing associations--for example, among the members from Middlesex and Monmouth counties and among the urban representatives from Perth Amboy, Newark, and Burlington--continued in these three assemblies. Perhaps the most enduring was the Quaker-Baptist bloc, but it was also achieved at low levels of agreement. Voting blocs also included strangers and even opposites. Thus, Cape May's Baptists and Middlesex's Presbyterians voted in over 80 percent agreement in the last assembly. Often voting associations split apart: the Dutch

Reform members tended to vote together in one assembly and divide in the next. Some lawmakers continued to cast their votes in such a random fashion that they failed to appear in any voting bloc. Although voting association reflected shared attitudes, these associations had not yet translated into effective organization. Finally, these voting patterns reflect both polarizing tendencies and their weakness or, equally significant, the enduring strength of a consensus.

In sum, New Jersey's legislature had not changed. The lawmakers who attended to the imperial crisis were the same kinds of men who had first met with Lewis Morris in 1738. As a decision-making body, it exhibited the same traits of instability and stability. On the one hand, it was a body of strangers lacking in organization, an assemblage of fragmented and unstable voting associations. There was little continuity in leadership. Of the twenty-four representatives who attended to the Stamp Act in 1765, ten had sat with Governor Belcher. Yet, five years later, only four remained. And by 1775 one in six had sat during the Stamp Act crisis. On the other hand, the membership shared, not always consciously, attitudes and perspectives which enabled it to work toward agreement.

So, too, the assemblymen responded to the agenda of issues as they had in earlier decades. The roll calls on military appropriations, to support the government and pay its officials, for debt relief, riot legislation, and paper money, and on relations with the governor and imperial authority bear some resemblance to the cluster blocs, but they also highlight flexibility (Tables 7.1 to 7.3). First, members were not fixed on a certain position. Just as they shifted their positions on bounties for flax and hemp, so, too, they changed on the salary and military questions. Within two days, three members moved from opposing to accepting requests for support to English troops. Theunis Dey supported military appropriations in the early 1760s but by the end of the decade had shifted to the opposition. Within two years, four lawmakers switched their votes on the governor's salary. And Stephen Crane and John Hinchman voted with the majority to approve debt legislation but later joined with the minority against additional legislation. Finally, alignments on one category of policy were not reflected in another. For example, in the Twentieth and Twenty-First assemblies, voting on the military and salaries did not correspond to the divisions on paper money, riot legislation, the agent, or domestic improvements. The patterns confirm that policy was constructed by different combinations of assemblymen or that no single group defined the house's position on the public agenda. Differences that rose from principle, social experiences, mundane antagonisms and suspicions, and even

DIVISIONS ON THE PUBLIC AGENDA
1761-1768

Roll-Calls*

Assemblymen and Districts	1	2	3	4	5	6	7	8	9	10	11	12	13	14	15	16	17	18	19	20	21	22	23	24	25	26	27	28	29	30
Lawrence,Ri.(Mnmth)	-	-	-	-	-			-	-	-	-	-	-	-	-	-	-	-	-	-	-	+	+	-	+	-	+	+	-	+
Holmes,J.(Mnmth)	-	-			-	-	+	-																		+	+		-	
Doughty,D.(BrlCo)						-	-	-		-					-	-	-					-		-	+	-		+	-	+
Clement,S.Sr.(Glcstr)	-	-	-	-	-	-	-	-	-	-	-	+			-	-	-	-	-	-	-	+			+	-		+		+
Wetherill,J.(Mddlsx)	-	-	-	-	-	-	+	-	-	-	-	-			-	-	-	+	+	+	-	+	+		+	-	+	-	+/-	+
Runyon,R.(Mddlsx)								-							-	-	-	+	-	+		+				-			+/-	+
Cooper,D.(Glcstr)	-							-	-	+			+		+	+	+	-	+	+	+	+	-	+	+	-		+	+/-	+
Spicer,J.(CpMy)	-	-						-					-													-			+/-	-
Leaming,A.Jr.(CpMy)	+	-											+		-	+	+	-	+	+	+	+	-	-	-	+	-	-	+/-	+
Stillwell,N.(CpMy)								-	+						+	+	+	+	+	+	+		-	+	-	+	-	-	+/-	+
Miller,E.(Slm)	+							-	+			+	-	+	+	+	+	+	+	+	+	+		-	+	+	-			
Hancock,W.(Slm)	-	+						-				+					+					+	+	+	+	+			+	+
Keasby,E.(Slm)			-	-	-										+	+	+	+	+	+			-		+	-			+/-	+
Rodman,T.(BrlTwn)	+	+	+	+	+	+	+	+	+	+	+	+	+		+	+	+	+	+	+	+	+	+		+	+	+	+	+	+
Smith,S.(BrlTwn)	+	+	+	+	+	+	+	+	+	+	+	+	+		+	+	+	+	+	+	+		+	-		+/-	-		+	
Fisher,F.(Smrst)	+	+	+	+	+	+	+			+			+	+	+	+	+	+	+	+	+	+	+			++/-	-	+	+/-	+
VanNeste,A.(Smrst)								-																+		-			+/-	
Hoagland,J.(Smrst)	+	-	+	+	+	+	+	-		-			+		+	+	+	+	+	+	+	+	+		-	+	-	+	+/-	+
Vangieson,R.(Brgn)	+	+	+	+	+	+	+	+	-	+	+	+	+		+	+	+	+	-	+	+		+		-	+/-	-	-	+/-	+
Dey,T.(Brgn)	+	+	+	+	+	+	+	+	+	+	+	+	+		+	+	+	+	+	+	+			+	-	-	-	+	+	+
Reading,G.(Hntrdn)	+	+	+	+	+	+	+	-	+	+	+	-	-		+	+	+	+	+	+	+	+	+			-		+	+	+
Hart,J.(Hntrdn)	+	+	+	+	+	+	+	+	+	+	+	-	+		+	+	+	+	+	+	+		+	+	-	+	-	+	+	+
Ogden,J.(Essx)	+	+	+	+	+			+	+	+	+	+	+		+	+	+	+	+	+	+		+	+		+++	+	+	+	+
Ogden,R.(Essx)	+	+	+	+	+	+	+	+		+	+	+			+	+	+	+	+	+	+							+		
Crane,S.(Essx)															+	+	+	+	+	+	+		+		+	+/-	+	+	+	+
Anderson,J.(Mnmth)	+	+	+					+	-	+	+				+	+	+	+	+	+	+		+	+		++/-	+	-		+
Nevill,S.(Mddlsx)								+																						
Johnston,J.(PrthAmby)			+	+	+				+	+			+		+	+	+	+	+	+	+	+	+	+	+	++	+	+	+	+
Smyth,A.(PrthAmby)	+	+						+		+			+		+	+	+	+	+		+								+	+
Skinner,C.(PrthAmby)			+	+	+								+	+			+													
Stevens,J.(PrthAmby)	+	+			+	+	+	+	+	+	+	+	+		+	+	+	+	+	+	+	+		+	+	++			+	+
Lawrence,J.R.(BrlTwn)	-	+	+	+	+	+	+	+	+	+	+	+	+		+	+	+	+	+	+	+	+	-	+	+	++++		+	+	+
Porden,J.(BrlCo)	+	-	+	+	+			+	+	+	+	+	+		+	+	+	+	+	+	+	+		+	+	++++		+	+	+

*TOPICS OF ROLL CALLS**

1. To approve bill for raising 600 volunteers (April 3, 1761)

2. To grant Governor Josiah Hardy Ŀ500 to cover travel expenses during war (December 5, 1761)

3. To approve appointment of commissioner for raising troops (February 16, 1764)

4. To extend assistance to New York against Indians (February 23, 1764)

5. To approve bill for raising volunteers (February 23, 1764)

6. To grant Ŀ1602 for military expenses (April 27, 1762)

7. To approve bill for completing the provincial regiment (March 8, 1762)

8. To add Ŀ25 to Justice Nevill's salary (December 5, 1761)

9. To pay Governor William Franklin Ŀ1200 rather than Ŀ1100 or Ŀ1000 (May 30, 1763)

10. to pay Chief Justice Robert Hunter Morris Ŀ150 rather than Ŀ100 (May 30, 1763)

11. To pay Justice Nevill Ŀ50 rather than Ŀ40 or Ŀ25 (May 30, 1763)

12. To pay Justice Charles Read Ŀ50 rather than Ŀ40 or Ŀ25 (May 30, 1763)

13. To continue Governor Hardy's salary (December 3, 1761)

14. To pay Governor Franklin Ŀ1200 rather than Ŀ1000 (June 5, 1765)

15. To pay Chief Justice Frederick Smyth Ŀ150 rather than Ŀ100 (June 18, 1766)

16. To pay Governor Franklin Ŀ1200 rather than Ŀ1000 (February 18, 1764)

17. To pay Governor Franklin Ŀ1200 rather than Ŀ1000 (June 19, 1767)

18. To pay Chief Justice Smyth Ŀ150 rather than Ŀ100 (June 19, 1767).

19. To pay Governor Franklin Ŀ1200 rather than Ŀ1000 (June 19, 1766)

20. To pay Governor Franklin Ŀ1200 rather than Ŀ1000 (June 3, 1768)

21. To pay Chief Justice Smyth Ŀ150 rather than Ŀ100 (May 3, 1768).

22. To pass a support bill (December 7, 1761)

23. To approve the bill for emitting £100,000 (April 23, 1768)

24. To distribute arms purchased by the government to the inhabitants (December 10, 1761)

25. To support the provincial agent (June 19, 1767)

26. Not to remove the Middlesex County courthouse from Perth Amboy and the Hunterdon County courthouse from Trenton (May 31; June 5, 7, 11, 14, and 17, 1765)***

27. To set a duty on slave imports (April 3, 1761, September 24, 1762, and June 16, 1767)***

28. To pass a bill preventing horse racing and gaming (December 4, 1761)

29. To set bounties on flax, hemp, and mulberry trees (May 30, 1765; June 8, 1765; April 19, 1768; and August 21, 1772)***

30. To approve address to the king (June 20, 1766)

** In order to establish consistency in the scales, the wording of several motions needed to be inverted. See note for Table 5.1 for further explanation.

*** Several votes have been combined and recorded as +.

TABLE 7.2

DIVISIONS ON THE PUBLIC AGENDA
1769–1771

Roll-Calls*

Assemblymen and Districts	1	2	3	4	5	6	7	8	9	10	11	12	13	14	15	16	17	18	19	20	21	22	23	24	25	26	27	28	29	30	31	32	33	34
Taylor,E.(Mnmth)	-	-	-	-	-	-	-	-	-	-	-	-	-	+	-	+	+	-	-	-	+	+	+	-	-	-	-	+	+	-	-	-	-	-
Hartshorne,R.(Mnmth)	-	-	-	-	-	-	-	-	-	+	+	-	-	-	-	+	+	-	+	-	+	+	+	-	-	+	+	+	+	+	+	+	+	-
Paxson,H.(BrlCo)	-	-	-	-	-	-	-	-	-	+	+	+	-	-	+	+	+	-	+	-	+	+	+	-	-	+	+	+	+	+	+	+	-	-
Dey,T.(Brgm)	-	-	-	-	-	-	-	-	-	+	+	+	-	-	-	-	+	-	-	-	+	+	+	+	+	+	+	+	+	+	-	-	-	-
Hinchman,J.(Glcstr)	-	+	+	+	+	-	-	+	+	+	-	-	-	-	+	+	+	-	+	-	+	+	+	+	+	+	+	+	-	+	+	+	+	+
Miller,E.(Slm)	-	-	-	-	-	-	-	+	+	+	-	-	-	-	-	+	+	-	+	+	-	-	-	+	+	+	+	+	-	-	+	-	-	-
Sharp,I.(Slm)													+		-	+	+	-		+						+	+	+	+	+			+	-
Gibbon,H.(Slm)	-	-																																
Leaming,A.Jr.(CpMy)	-	-	-	-	-	-	-	+		+	+	+	-	-	-	+	-	-	+	-	+		+	+	-	+	+	+	+	-			-	-
Hand,J.(CpMy)					-	-	-	-		-		+		+		-		+	-	+		+	+	+	-	+	+	+	+	-	-		-	-
Stillwell,N.(CpMy)														+										+	+			+			+			-
Runyon,R.(Mddlsx)	-	-	-	-	-	-	+	-	-	+	+	-	-	+	+	-	-	-	-	-	-	-	-	+	-	-	-	+		+	-	-	+	-
Wetherill,J.(Mddlsx)	-	-	-	-	-	-	+	-	-	+	+	-	-	+	+	+	-	-	-	-	-	-	+	-	-	-	-	+	+	+	-	-	-	-
Ogden,J.(Essx)	-	-	-	-	+	+	-	-	-	-	-	+	+	+	+	+	+	+	+	+	+	+	+	+	+	+	+	+	+	+	+	+	+	-
Crane,S.(Essx)	-	-	-	-	+	-	-	-	-	-	-	+	+	+	-	+	+	+	+	+	+	+	+	+	+	+	+	+	+	+	+	+	+	-
Hart,J.(Hntrdn)	-	-	-	-	+	+	+	-	+	+	+	+	+	+	-	-	+	+	+	+	+	+	+	+	+	+	+	+	+	+	+	+	+	-
Tucker,S.(Hntrdn)	-	-	+	+	-	-	+	+	+	+	+	+	+	+	+	+	+	+	+	+	+	+	-	+	+	+	+	+	+	+	+	+	+	-
Demarest,J.(Brgm)	-	-	-	-	+	+	+	+	+	+	+	+	+	+	-	+	+	+	+	+	+	+	+	+	+	+	+	+	-	+	+	+	-	-
Fisher,H.(Smrst)	-	-	-	+	+	+	+	+	+	+	+	+	-	-	+	+	+	+	+	+	+	+	+	+	+	+	+	+	+	+	+	+	+	-
Berrien,J.(Smrst)	-	-	-	+	+	+	+	+	+	+	+	+	-	-	+	+	+	+	+	+	+	+	+	+	+	+	+	+	+	+	+	+	+	-
Price,R.F.(Glcstr)	-	-	-	-	+	+	-	+	+	+	+	+	-	-	+	+	+	+	+	+	+	+	+	-	-	+	+	+	+	+	+	+	-	-
Hewlings,A.(BrlTwn)	-	+	+	-	+	+	+	+	+	+	+	-	-	-	+	+	+	+	+	+	+	+	+	+	+	+	+	+	+	+	+	+	-	+
Bullock,J.(BrlCo)	+	+	+	+	-	+	+	+	+	+	+	-	-	-	+	+	+	+	+	+	-	-	-	+	+	+	+	+	+	+	+	+	-	+
Smith,J.(BrlTwn)	+	+	+	+	+	+	+	+	+	+	+	-	-	-	+	+	+	+	+	+	+	-	+	+	+	+	+	+	-	-	+	+	+	+
Johnston,J.L.(PrthAmby)	-	+	+	+	-	+	+	+	+	+	+	+	+	+	-	+	+	+	+	+	-	-	-	+	+	+	+	-	-	-	-	+	+	+
Skinner,C.(PrthAmby)	+	+	+	+	+	+	+	+	+	+	+	+	+	+	-	+	+	+	+	+	+	+	+	+	+	+	+	+	+	+	+	+	+	+

*TOPICS OF ROLL CALLS**

1. That the province is able to provide for English troops (April 19, 1771)

2. That the province is able to provide for English troops (April 20, 1771)

3. That the province has the funds to provide for English troops (May 31, 1771)

4. To support Governor Franklin's request for additional supplies to the treasury (December 21, 1771)

5. To pay part of General Thomas Gage's accounts (December 10, 1771)

6. That the province can pay requisition requests for English troops (December 16, 1771)

7. That the province can grant "some allowance" for English troops (October 23, 1770)

8. That the province can allow "something" for English trcops (December 20, 1771)

9. That the province can pay no more than Ŀ500 for the supply of English troops (October 25, 1770)

10. To pass a bill granting Ŀ500 for English troops (October 26, 1770)

11. To grant Ŀ318 for English troops (December 20, 1771)

12. To grant Ŀ122 to provincial delegation to Fort Stanwix (December 1, 1769)

13. To approve a militia bill (November 29, 1771)

14. to approve a new militia bill (March 17, 1770)

15. To pay Justice John Berrien Ŀ75 rather than Ŀ50 (November 8, 1769)

16. To pay Justice Charles Read Ŀ75 rather than Ŀ50 (November 8, 1769)

17. To pay Justice Frederick Smyth Ŀ150 rather than Ŀ100 (November 8, 1769)

18. To pay Justice Smyth Ŀ150 rather than Ŀ100 (October 19, 1770)

19. To pay Governor Franklin Ŀ1200 rather than Ŀ1000 (December 11, 1771)

20. To pay Justice Smyth £150 rather than £100 (December 11, 1771)

21. To pay Governor Franklin £1200 rather than £1000 (November 8, 1769)

22. To pay Governor Franklin £1200 rather than £1000 (October 19, 1770)

23. To pay Justice Read £75 rather than £50 (December 11, 1771)

24. Not to support bill for annual elections (March 22, 1770)

25. To support Governor Franklin's position that John Ogden's resignation is not legal (April 26, 1771)

26. To approve the conduct of the Monmouth County authorities in suppressing recent riot (March 27, 1770)

27. To pass a riot bill (March 17, 23, and 26, 1770)

28. To pass a bill for relief of insolvents (November 29, 1769)

29. To pass a bill for the quick recovery of debts (November 30, 1769)

30. To approve a bill subjecting real estate to the payment of debts (October 25 and 26, 1770)***

31. To pass an additional bill for the relief of insolvents (March 24, 1770)

32. To pass a bill for the relief of insolvents (December 9, 1771)

33. To approve a bill regulating attorneys (December 1, 1769)

34. In support of £100,000 emission of paper money provided that the currency is not a legal tender (May 31, 1771)

** In order to establish consistency in the scales, the wording of several motions needed to be inverted. See note for Table 5.1 for further explanation.

*** Several votes have been combined and recorded as +.

TABLE 7.3
DIVISIONS ON THE PUBLIC AGENDA
1772–1775

Roll-Calls*

Assemblymen and Districts	1	2	3	4	5	6	7	8	9	10	11	12	13	14	15	16	17	18	19	20	21	22	23	24	25	26	27	28	29	30	31	32	33	34	35	36	37	38	39	40	41	42	43	44	45	46	47	48	49	50	51	52	53	54	55
Crane,S.(Essx)	+	+	+	+	+	+	+	+	+	+	+	+	+	+	+	+	+	+	+	+	+	+	+	+	+	+	+	+	-	+	-	+	-	+	+	-	+	+	+	+	+	+	+	+	+	+	+	+	-	-	-	+	-	+	-
Fisher,H.(Smrst)	+	+	+	+	-	+	+	+	+	+	+	+	+	+	+	+	+	+	+	+	+	+	+	+	+	+	+	+	-	+	+	+	+	+	+	-	+	+	+	+	+	+	+	+	+	+	+	+	-	-	-	-	-	+	+
Roy,J.(Smrst)	+	+	+	+	+	+	+	+	+	+	+	+	+	+	+	+	+	+	+	+	+	+	+	+	+	+	+	+	+	+	+	+	+	+	+	+	+	+	+	+	+	+	+	+	+	+	+	+	-	-	-	-	-	+	+
Ford,J.(Mrrs)	+	+	+	+	+	+	+	+	+	+	+	+	+	+	+	+	+	+	+	+	+	+	+	+	+	+	+	+	+	+	+	+	+	+	+	+	+	+	+	+	+	+	+	+	+	+	+	+	-	-	-	-	-	+	+
VanHorne,T.(Sssx)	+	+						+	+		+														+	+																	-	-	+	+	-								
Pettit,N.(Sssx)	+	+	+	+	+	+	+	+	+																																													
Barton,J.(Sssx)																	+	+	+																											-					-		+
Demarest,J.(Brgn)	+	+	+	+	-	-	+	+	+	+	+	+	+	+	+	+	+	+	+	+	+	+	+	+	+	-	-	-	-	-	-	-	-	-	+	+	+	+	+	-	+	+	-	+	+	-	-	+	-	-	-	-	+	+	+
Elmer,T.(Cmbrlnd)	+	+	+	+	+	+	+	+	+	+	+	+	+	+	+	+	+	+	+	+	+	+	+	-	-	-	-	-	-	-	-	-	-	+	+	+	+	+	+	+	+	+	+	+	+	-	+	+	-	-	+	+	+	+	+
Gibbon,G.(Slm)	+	+			-	+	-	+	+	+	+	+	-	+	+	+	+	+	+	+	+	-	-	-	-	-	-	-	-	-	-	-	-	+	+	+	+	-	+		+	+	-	+	+	-	-	-	-	-	-	-	-	-	-
Mehelm,J.(Hntrdn)	-	-	+	+	+	+	+	+	+	+	+	+	+	+	+	+	+	+	+	+	+	-	-	-	-	-	-	-	-	-	-	-	-	+	+	+	+	+	+	+	+	-	+	+	-	-	+	-	-	-	-	+	+	+	+
Kinsey,J.(BrlTwn)	-	-	+	+	+	+	+	+	+	+	+	+	+	+	+	+	+	+	+	+	+	-	-	-	-	-	-	-	-	-	-	-	-	+	+	+	+	+	+	+	+	-	+	+	-	+	+	+	-	+	+	+	+	+	+
Hewlings,T.(BrlTwn)	-	-	+	+	+	+	+	+	+	+	+	+	+	+	+	+	+	+	+	+	+	-	-	-	-	-	-	-	-	-	-	-	-	+	+	+	+	+	+	+	+	-	+	+	-	+	+	+	-	+	+	+	+	+	+
Paxson,H.(BrlCo)	-	-	+	+	+	+	+	+	+		-								+																			-					-	-	+	+	-					-			-
Hinchman,J.(Glcstr)	-	-	-	-			-	-		+	+	+		+	+	+	+	+	+	+	+	+	-	-	-	-	-	-	+	+	+	-	-	-	-	-	-	-	-	-	-	+	+	+	-	+	+	+	+	+	+	+	-	-	-
Price,R.F.(Glcstr)	-	-	-	-			-	+	+	+	+			+	+	+	+	+	+	+	+	+	-	-	-	-	-	-	+	+	+	-	-	-	-	-	-	-	-	-	-	+	+	+	-	+	+	+	+	+	+				
Holme,B.(Slm)	-	-					-	-	+		+			-	-	+	+	+	+	+	+		-	-	+	+	-	-	+	+	+	+	+	+	+			+	+			+	+	+	-	+	+					-			
Sheppard,J.(Cmbrlnd)			-	-			-	-	-			+	+				-	+	+	+	+	+	-	-	-	-	+	+			+											-	-	+	-	+	+					-	+	+
Dey,T.(Brgn)	+	+	+	+	+	+	+	+	+	+	+	+	+	+	+	+	+	+	+	+	+	+	-	-	-	-	+	+	+	+	+	+	+	+	+	+	+	+	+	+	+	+	+	+	+	-	+	+	-	-	-	+	+	+	+
Garritse,H.(Essx)	+	+	+	+	-	+	+	+	+	+	+	-	+	+	-	-	+	+	+	+	+	+	-	-	-	-	+	+	+	+	+	+	+	+	+	+	+	+	+	+	+	+	+	+	+	-	+	+	-	-	-	+	+	+	+
Winds,W.(Mrrs)	+	+	+	+	-	-	+	-	-	-	-	-	-	+	+	-	-	-	-	-	-	-	-	-	-	-	+	+	+	+	+	+	+	-	-	+	+	-	-	-	-	-	+	-	+	-	+	-	-	-	-	+	-	+	-
Sykes,A.(BrlCo)	+	+	+	+	-	-	-	-	-	-	-	-	-	-	-	-	+	+	+	-	-	-	-	-	-	-	+	+	+	+	+	+	+	-	-	-	-	-	-	-	-	+	-	+	-	+	-	+	-	-	-	-	-	+	-
Tucker,S.(Hntrdn)	-	-	-	-	-	-	-	-	-	-	-	-	-	-	-	-	-	+	-	-	-	-	-	-	-	-	+	+	+	+	+	+	+	+	+	-	-	-	-	-	-	-	+	-	-	-	-	+	-	+	-	-	-	+	-
Eldridge,E.(CpMy)	-	-	-	-	-	-	-	-	-	-	-	-	-	+	+	-	+	-	+	+	-	-	-	-	-	+	-	-	+	+	+																	+	+						
Hand,J.(CpMy)	-	-	-	-	-	-	-	-	-	-	-	-	-	-	-	-	-	-	-	-	-	-	-	-	-	+	+	-	+	+	+						+		-		+	+	-	+	+	-	+	+							
Moores,J.(Mddlsx)	-	-	-	-	-	-	-	-	-	-	-	-	-	-	-	-	-	-	-	-	-	-	+	+	+	+	-	-	-	-	-	+	+	+	+	-	-	-	-	-	-	-	-	-	-	-	-	+	-	-	-	-	-	-	-
Wetherill,J.(Mddlsx)	-	-	-	-	-	-	-	-	-	-	-	-	-	-	-	-	-	-	-	-	-	-	-	+	+	+	+	-	-	-	-	+	+	-	-	-	-	-	-	-	-	-	-	-	-	-	-	-	-	-	-	-	-	-	-
Dunham,A.(Mddlsx)	-	-	-	-	-	-	-	-	-	-	-	-	-	-	-	-	-	-	-	-	-	-	-	-	-	-	-	-	-	-	-	-	-	-	-	-	-	-	-	-	-	-	-	-	-	-	-	-	+						
Combs,J.(PrthAmby)	-	-	-	-	-	-	-	-	-	-	-	-	-	-	-	-	-	-	-	-	-	-	-	-	-	-	-	-	-	-	-	-	-	-	-	-	-	-	-	-	-	-	-	-	-	-	-	-	-	-	-	-	-	+	-
Lawrence,Ri.(Mnmth)	-	-	-	-	-	-	-	-	-	-	-	-	-	-	-	-	-	-	-	-	-	-	-	-	-	+	+	-	-	+	+	+	+	+	+	-	-	-	-	-	-	-	-	-	-	-	-	-	-	-	-	-	-	+	-
Taylor,E.(Mnmth)	-	-	-	-	-	-	-	-	+	-	-	-	-	-	-	-	-	-	-	-	-	-	-	-	-	-	+	-	+	+	+	+	+	+	+	-	-	-	-	-	-	-	-	-	-	-	-	-	-	-	-	-	-	+	-

*TOPICS OF ROLL CALLS**

1. To pay councilors eight shillings a day instead of six (March 3, 1774)

2. To pay assemblymen eight shillings a day instead of six (March 3, 1774)

3. To pay councilors eight shillings a day instead of six (February 6, 1775)

4. To pay assemblymen eight shillings a day instead of six (February 6, 1775)

5. To pay Justice David Ogden Ł150 instead of Ł100 (March 2, 1774)

6. To pay Justice Richard Stockton Ł150 instead of Ł100 (March 2, 1774)

7. To pay Attorney General Skinner Ł40 instead of Ł30 (March 2, 1774)

8. To pay Justice Read Ł100 instead of Ł75 or Ł80 (September 12, 1772)

9. To pay Justice Ogden Ł100 instead of Ł75 or Ł80 (September 12, 1772)

10. To pay Justice Ogden Ł150 instead of Ł100 (February 6, 1775)

11. To pay Justice Stockton Ł150 instead of Ł100 (February 6, 1775)

12. To pay Attorney General Skinner Ł40 instead of Ł30 (February 6, 1775)

13. To pay Governor Franklin Ł1200 instead of Ł1000 (September 12, 1772)

14. To pay Justice Ogden Ł150 instead of Ł100 (November 29, 1775)

15. To pay Justice Stockton Ł150 instead of Ł100 (November 29, 1775)

16. To pay councilors eight shillings instead of six (November 29, 1775)

17. To pay assemblymen eight shillings instead of six (November 29, 1775)

18. To pay Governor Franklin Ł1200 instead of Ł1000 (March 2, 1774)

19. To pay Attorney General Skinner Ł40 instead of Ł30 (November 29, 1775)

20. To pay Governor Franklin Ł1200 instead of Ł1000 (February 6, 1775)

21. To pay Governor Franklin Ł1200 instead of Ł1000 (November 29, 1775)

22. To provide for the repair of barracks (November 23, 1775)

23. To empower commissioners with the care of the barracks (December 4, 1775)

24. To grant governor Ŀ300 for repair of barracks and supply of king's troops (August 28, 1775)

25. To supply troops quartered in barracks (December 18, 1773)

26. To consider petitions for paper money (September 15, 1772)

27. To prepare a bill for issuing Ŀ100,000 (February 26, 1774)

28. To prepare a bill for issuing Ŀ100,000 (March 9, 1774)

29. To approve additional legislation for relief of insolvents (February 8, 1775)

30. To pass additional legislation for relief of insolvents (February 9, 1775)

31. To pass a bill for "the Settlement and Relief of the Poor" (February 4, 1774)

32. To approve the Council's bill for regulating doctors (September 18, 1772)

33. To reject a motion to request more information on the treasury robbery from the governor (November 16, 1773)

34. To reject a motion "that the Affair of the Robbery of the Eastern Treasury, mentioned in His Excellency's Speech, has not yet been brought to light" (December 18, 1773)

35. Not to print a report on the robbery (December 18, 1773)

36. To reject a resolution that the Eastern Treasurer had not taken proper care of the funds in his charge (February 19, 1774)

37. To reject a message to governor condemning him for his insulting language and asserting the house's right to appoint the treasurer (September 25, 1772)

38. To reject a motion calling for prosecution of the Eastern Treasurer (September 26, 1772)

39. To reject a motion that the house should investigate the present state of the eastern treasury (November 30, 1773)

40. To reject a message to the governor calling for Stephen Skinner's removal (December 21, 1773)

41. Not to receive the committee report on the eastern treasury (February 19, 1774)

42. To reject resolutions that Stephen Skinner should not be trusted with public funds, that the Assembly can no longer place money in his trust, that Skinner's "Continuance in Office. . .is much to the Dissatisfaction of the good People of this Colony," that Skinner should be removed from office and his continuance "tends to the Prejudice of his Majesty's Service," that the governor is responsible for Skinner's continuance in office, and that a petition be sent to the king for redress (February 19, 1774).

43. To reject a message to the governor calling for prosecution of the treasurer (March 2, 1774)

44. To reject a message to governor calling for Skinner's removal (February 9, 1774)

45. To reject an address to governor calling for Skinner's removal (September 17, 1772)

46. That the Assembly should answer the governor's message which contradicted its position on the robbery (September 26, 1772)

47. To receive Skinner's account (September 8, 1772)

48. To reject a message to the governor calling for legal opinions he made reference to on February 14 (February 15, 1774)

49. To reject Kinsey's motion for drafting legislation for securing the treasury (February 9, 1775)

50. Not to consider the governor's correspondence with Lord Dartmouth (May 20, 1775)

51. To reject a motion that two of the three remaining delegates to the Continental Congress could represent the province (November 22, 1775)

52. To reject an address to the governor which condemns parliament's latest position (November 25, 1775)

53. To reject a motion that the speaker must sign a petition to the king (February 13, 1775)

54. To reject a message to the governor calling for a dissolution of the Assembly (Nov. 30, 1775)

55. To allow the speaker to record his dissent in the house minutes (February 13, 1775)

** In order to establish consistency in the scales, the wording of several motions needed to be inverted. See note for Table 5.1 for further explanation.

temperament were not powerful enough to create a deep fissure in the institution.

Throughout this period, the Assembly treated with military matters, first with continuing support for the war effort, later with the supply of English troops quartered in the province, and, finally, with the maintenance and repair of the barracks. The divisions continued along the lines set in the previous Assembly with dissent coming from the western division and from Middlesex and Monmouth counties in the East. That the sources of opposition were Quaker, Baptist, and Presbyterian suggests that the motives were a mixture of both religious and secular principles. The Quaker delegations still could not agree on how to respond. While Samuel Clement, Sr., consistently opposed raising volunteers and paying military expenses, many Friends regularly chose to abstain. John Hinchman and Ebenezer Miller were inconsistent and voted for and against supplying troops. And some, following the example of former Assemblyman John Ladd, regularly approved the administration's requests. In the Twenty-First Assembly, Robert Friend Price of Gloucester approved 57 percent of the military proposals, and Joseph Smith of Burlington voted 78 percent approval on the same roll calls. And, by the 1770s, Friends such as James Kinsey regularly voted for the maintenance of the provincial barracks. On review, dissent was inspired by other motives than pacifist conscience. Edward Taylor, a Monmouth Baptist, and John Wetherill, Middlesex's Presbyterian representative, in fact, registered a stronger record of opposition than did Ebenezer Miller. Finally, dissent was clearly not a product of organization. For example, Wetherill voted in 70 percent agreement with Hendrick Fisher and the Dutch Reform members in the Twentieth Assembly. Yet Wetherill's colleagues supported the province's military contribution. Dissent came from three sources in the next Assembly: one splinter bloc composed of Wetherill, Taylor, and Reune Runyon, the Quaker delegations, and a single member who did not agree significantly with any voting bloc. And those who dissented on military matters in this legislature agreed among themselves on slightly more than half (54 percent) of all the roll calls.

Voting alignments on military affairs and salaries bore a slight resemblance to each other. The members who were inclined to approve low salaries and oppose a support bill tended to come from that cluster which resisted the province's military involvements. But, while Clement and Taylor made such a linkage, many dissenters found it more difficult to begrudge the public official. Those who did so continued a long-standing practice of rewarding one and discriminating against another official. Categorical opposition was most difficult; and, when it came time to vote final approval of a support bill, even those who had dissented and lost on its separate provisions voted for passage. The Quakers found opposition especially difficult and after 1772 had become reliable supporters of high salaries. During the Twenty-First Assembly, nine representatives were inclined to resist military spending, but only one-third--two Baptists and a Presbyterian--consistently voted low salaries for the civil list. Richard Lawrence, who represented Monmouth County in the Twentieth and Twenty-Second assemblies, was exceptional for his consistency on both subjects. Dissenting records often reflected irregular and even idiosyncratic tendencies. Throughout the 1760s, Wetherill had become increasingly stingy and by the end of the decade was voting regularly against high salaries. At the same time he seemed to become more receptive to requests for the military. Robert Hartshorne was moving in the opposite direction: while undeviating in his opposition to the military, he was as likely to vote for high salaries as he was for the lower amounts.

Another category of representatives supported military appropriations and high salaries. This was a diverse lot. Though it agreed on these two issues, it had little else in common. Composed principally of Calvinists and Anglicans, rural and urban members, even rivals, this collection of lawmakers did not form a voting bloc. In the Twentieth Assembly, Rinear Vangieson and Theunis Dey agreed with John Johnston of Perth Amboy and John Brown Lawrence of Burlington on the province's contribution to the war and on salaries. Yet the Dutch Reform Members from Bergen County disagreed with the two urban Anglicans on over half--63 and 53 percent respectively--of all the roll calls. Clearly, support for the military and civil list came from antagonistic quarters. For example, the same Assembly deliberated on the location of Middlesex County's courthouse. One-third of the members who approved the house's military and salary appropriations also backed Wetherill and Runyon in their efforts to remove the courthouse from Perth Amboy. A similar division in this group occurred when the Assembly later considered the robbery of the East Jersey treasury. As the deliberations progressed, they focused on the governor and his apparent efforts to protect Stephen Skinner. This time, half of the members who supported the government joined with the dissenters.

With each addition to the agenda, this diverse and unorganized membership reassembled along a different axis. The divisions on paper money did not correspond to those on military and support bills. In 1768, representatives Johnston, Crane, Vangieson, and Wetherill agreed that the province should emit another £00,000 in currency. Dissent was lodged principally in the western counties. Nor did this division reflect a permanent alignment on the subject. Three years later, seventeen members from both sections endorsed another measure for the printing of paper money. This time, the majority included representatives from the three voting blocs, and a small fragment of one bloc-- comprising only Skinner, Johnston, and Smith--dissented. Again, in 1774, the Assembly passed a bill for issuing Ŀ 100,000 by an equally lopsided margin of twenty-two to seven. The majority also came from all three voting blocs. The minority votes were scattered among the western delegations. Not only did the alignments shift, but they also bore little resemblance to the divisions on other components of the agenda. Representatives who disagreed on paper money in the last Assembly, for example, also made up the majorities that supported the military and civil list.

Indeed, there was no clear division which cut across the several categories of policy. Although discussions of the public welfare linked paper money, debt, the distressed condition of the ploughman, and the predatory attorney, each of these subjects produced a different pattern of response. While these voting patterns seemed to shift with each issue in the manner of a kaleidoscope, they also suggested that there was an underlying and powerful basis for agreement among opposites. In the Twenty-First Assembly, for example, that diverse majority which embraced the motion in support of a currency emission also supported measures to expedite the recovery of debt and to relieve insolvents. But those who had opposed the currency emission also endorsed debt legislation. When the debtor farmers rioted and closed the courts, the legislature acted as a unit, and two-thirds of the membership passed a riot bill and even agreed to the Council's amendments. Only three from the rioting counties disagreed with the action. The same legislators considered the regulation of attorneys. Although the division was not congruent with the voting on rioting and debt, it is significant that a coalition of urban and country members joined to support regulation. But most important, no legislator dissented on the several policy dimensions of currency, debt, riot, and attorneys. When the house turned to a motion for annual elections in the wake of the riots, the lawmakers summarily rejected the idea by a vote of sixteen to six. So, too, the previous Assembly had been grappling with English prohibitions on paper money and the appointment of an agent to represent its interest in London. The vote on the selection gathered support from members of opposite persuasions on paper money, the military, and salaries.

Disagreement took several forms. First, it often focused on aversion of paper money or debt legislation, a military measure, or pay for a specific individual. Some members did disagree on a category of issues. But the differences never assumed a third form of sweeping disagreement over the several categories of public policy. These patterns suggest that the distances were not great and point to the abiding presence of consensus. Indeed, this tendency toward unanimity, such as the nineteen-to-one vote approving an address to the king in 1766, was a recurring phenomenon. Moreover, these voting patterns bear a correspondence to the divisions on social and economic issues. Those who denied high salaries to officials and who rejected military appropriations were also most likely to dissent on social and economic questions. The correspondence was not perfect. Although Theunis Dey tended to support the government, especially in the Twentieth Assembly, he also was a naysayer on domestic improvements. But assemblymen like John Wetherill and Richard Lawrence were inclined to dissent on both categories. In turn, the urban delegations gave support to both. This resemblance in voting behaviors was a tendency suggesting again that differences fell short of the ideological and were temperamental in nature.

These characteristics help to identify different types of assemblymen. At one end of the spectrum stood a handful of representatives from Middlesex and Monmouth counties. Long-standing rivalries with Perth Amboy reinforced rural prejudices and produced a naysaying temperament. Thus, they opposed military appropriations and appeals for raising salaries. In turn, their consistent support for paper money and their opposition to riot legislation suggest a sensitivity to the public's distresses. So, too, they were likely to oppose measures for expediting the collection of debt. And they were inclined to endorse frequent elections and to guard the house's rights to control its own membership from executive manipulation. Perhaps the same attitude moved them to vote that the government's stockpiles of arms be broken up and distributed to the people. Finally, it was these delegations who were most hesitant to embrace reforms for empowering the government to promote commercial arcadia. At the other end of the spectrum were the urban lawmakers from Burlington and Perth Amboy. While they did not reject the Country's principles, they were by temperament more open to the administration and receptive to its requests for military appropriations and for salaries commensurate with the dignity of public office. While recognizing the need for an adequate means of exchange, they also heeded the governor's counsels against emissions in legal tender. And, while appreciating the dignity and rights of the Assembly, they were also reluctant to oppose the governor over control of its membership. So, too, these delegations endorsed riot legislation, opposed annual elections, and voted that the government retain control of its armaments. And this group habitually supported economic and social reforms. But these two clusters of representatives were not irreconcilable. Just as they did at times agree on bounties and trade regulation, they also joined on the necessity for paper money and at times did agree on salaries, debt legislation, the regulation of attorneys, an occasional military appropriation, and the appointment of a provincial agent. Moreover, most members could respond to both persuasions. They supported military appropriations, but often grudgingly, and salaries, but less than what the governor expected. On the one hand, they found annual elections excessive and approved riot legislation; and, on the other hand, they protested the governor's attempt to manipulate the house's membership. So they embraced paper money, but not always predictably, and endorsed the appointment of an agent, the regulation of attorneys, and debt legislation, but not uniformly.[26]

On the floor of the house and in the midst of deliberations, the lawmaker could miscalculate the distance separating him from a colleague, and both could act as if unaware of what they shared. The question was not whether some were contemptuous of provincial liberties or the rights of the house, that some were oblivious to the dangers of opposition or unaffected by public disorders, that some sought to starve the government and its officials, or that any were indifferent to the sanctity of property and contract. Although the lawmakers had to make a choice and vote either "yea" or "nay," they were often responding to dilemmas. And they took a stand after deliberations in which they sought to reconcile shared concerns for provincial liberties with deference toward government and loyalty to the king. Simultaneously, they attended to the administration's recommendations and to the public's petitions for relief and acted upon an abhorrence of the sycophantic courtier and ingrained hesitance to enter into opposition. What they shared was a set of dilemmas. How they responded was shaped by a mixture of economic and social interests, antagonisms emerging from the tensions within commercial arcadia, and contrasting cultural styles. These factors reinforced each other to breed differences in temperament. Often deep-seated propensities toward the manichean encouraged exaggeration and exacerbated differences. And, when this happened, a member who grasped one side of the dilemma projected the other side upon another. What was internal seemed to become external, and what was shared was transformed into dichotomy. Yet boundaries did remain powerful enough to restrain indulgence in dramatic fantasy. Thus, deliberations on salaries turned on how much to pay but not whether to withhold support for the civil list; house majorities came together to approve military appropriations but less than what was requested; and, if the house conceded a right of appointment to the governor, its concession was more symbolic than real. In sum, the voting documents divisiveness but not hard and fast division. And, in its record of inconstancies, it reveals powerful urgings toward unanimity.

This oscillation between polarity and unanimity occurred in part because the lawmakers acted upon beliefs, principles, and prejudices, however formed, wrestled with tensions and ambivalences built within this brittle consensus, often were indifferent to the issue at hand, and sat in an invertebrate legislature lacking organizations for guidance and formal mechanisms for leadership. This condition made them subject to other influences during the course of a session. These members could be persuaded and educated. In 1772, Governor Franklin noted the newcomers and how malleable they were: "The Speaker, & a considerable Number of Members are for trying an Excise; but whether a Majority will be ultimately for this Mode is uncertain, as several of them are changing their Opinions from Side to Side every Day. Hitherto there has not been much Regularity in their Proceedings. They have precipitatly determined one Point contrary to the Inclination of a Majority, owing to several of the new Members not having properly understood the State of the Question."[27] Normally, the governor was able to exercise influence quietly and effectively. Throughout the 1760s, the house had reluctantly approved military appropriations. In the autumn of 1770, it listened to another appeal while digesting news that the Privy Council had rejected its latest currency proposal. On October 23, it decided that "no further Provision be made." Within forty-eight hours, however, Franklin persuaded three Quaker members to reverse their votes. The next year, the issue provoked insults and rivalries between the house and governor. When the Assembly declined to heed his recommendations to supply English troops stationed in the province, Franklin warned that its "rash and imprudent" behavior was "big with Mischief to your Constituents," was an outrage to the "sensible Man," and risked England's censure and possible punishment. As emotions increased, the scene rapidly became a dramatic enactment.[28] Members of all sections, including those who had previously supported the military, joined in opposing Franklin. With only three urban members and Burlington County's Joseph Bullock refusing to join the opposition, Franklin was without influence, and the issue was at impasse. Only the chance removal of English troops broke the drama. The opposition evaporated and enough western representatives resumed their habit of supporting military appropriations.

Unstable voting associations, volatile and dramatic constitutional conflict, and fluctuating alignments on the issues characterized the politics of the last Assembly to meet during the provincial period. Elected in 1772, the Twenty-Second Assembly was a segmented, unorganized collection of strangers.

Sixteen of the thirty members were newcomers. Another seven had sat for no more than three years. Nor was the house given the opportunity to overcome these disadvantages. During the forty months between the beginning of the first and the end of the last session in December 1775, Governor Franklin convened the house only five times and for a total of seven months. Once he prorogued the house for thirteen months, and he later waited for twenty-two months. Moreover, the differences in participation between the activists and backbenchers were considerable. Only four activitists--James Kinsey, John Hinchman, Samuel Tucker, and Hendrick Fisher--sat on between 25 and 37 percent of all the committees appointed. Nineteen backbenchers sat on 12 percent or fewer of the 131 appointed committees. While Kinsey sat on forty-nine committees, Henry Garritse, Jonathan Hand, and Eli Eldridge appeared on only two. Finally, voting blocs remained loose and unstable and bore only slight resemblance to the previous Assembly's alignments. One bloc that included representatives from Middlesex, Monmouth, Bergen, Hunterdon, and Cape May counties tended to vote for low salaries and against military appropriations. At the other end of the spectrum, a heterogeneous group from Essex, Bergen, Somerset, Morris, and Sussex counties and the port of Burlington supported the administration on both counts. Members from the two blocs did, however, tend to agree on debt and currency legislation. The Quakers in the third bloc usually supported high salaries and military appropriations but cast most of the votes against another currency emission. While there was some correspondence between voting blocs and the issues, the disagreements remained less than categorical. Notwithstanding the distance separating the first two blocs, members from both did agree on one in three roll calls.

A domestic scandal unrelated to the imperial relationship sparked the most dramatic confrontation with the governor. In July 1768, the East Jersey Treasurer Stephen Skinner dispatched to the governor that his home had been burglarized and that public funds to the amount of ₤6,570 had been stolen.[29] Reacting promptly, Franklin ordered local authorities to be on the alert for the thieves, posted a reward for information relating to the crime, and began a "very minute" investigation of the affair in consultation with the Council. But he did not assemble the lawmakers and postponed calling the newly elected house until fifteen months after the robbery. When the Twenty-First Assembly met in October 1769, he reported his findings to the lawmakers. They, in turn, congratulated him for his ardor in investigating the crime, drafted legislation requiring the treasurers of both sections to post bond against their behavior, and began their own inquiry. The following year, the house investigation concluded that Skinner had been negligent but not guilty of wrongdoing. While ordering Skinner to replace the stolen funds, it voted him his normal salary.[30] So the issue stood for two years: the thieves remained at large, and the funds were not recovered.

Governor Franklin dissolved the house, called for elections, and met with the Twenty-Second Assembly in the fall of 1772. Suddenly, deliberations on the robbery became emotionally charged and divisive, and the ensuing drama was raised to a constitutional crisis. Under the leadership of James Kinsey, the house first suggested, then demanded, Skinner's immediate removal, proposed special legislation for his prosecution, and finally determined that it and not the governor would name his successor. Franklin first reminded the house that its own investigation had cleared the treasurer of wrongdoing and then with increasing vehemence refused to be bullied into surrendering prerogative rights. From the floor of the Assembly, the matter smacked of Court conspiracy: within months of the robbery, the governor had admitted Stephen Skinner to the Council. Since Cortlandt Skinner, Stephen's brother, was the government's attorney general, the normal process for prosecution had to be circumvented. But the attorney general, Franklin, and the Council opposed such measures. According to the Assembly, Governor Franklin had fallen under the Council's influence, and it concluded that he could not be trusted. When Franklin reported evidence to the house that a band of counterfeiters had been captured and had confessed to the robbery, the Assembly reviewed the evidence and replied that such blackguards could not be believed. According to the governor, the house had fallen under the influence of demagogues: it twisted evidence, was blind to justice, and stood on an irresponsible and groundless position. Its demand that Skinner be removed before being tried violated fundamental principles of English justice. It had embarked on an "unparliamentary" and "despotick" course which, if successful, would destroy the provincial constitution, And, finally, its charges had inflamed the populace.[31] The confrontation between the governor and the house was becoming high drama the likes of which had not been witnessed since the Morris administration. As each side played its role and thereby cued and sustained the other's part, both were assuming equally uncompromising, histrionic postures.

Both parties self-consciously played to the public. The audience had been at first concerned but not riveted on the issue: in October 1769, Gloucester's "principal Inhabitants" had instructed their representatives to investigate the robbery carefully and to inquire into the reasons why New Jersey's legislature did not enjoy the "Indubitable Right" exercised by other colonial legislatures to appoint the treasurer. Suddenly, both parties orchestrated province-wide petition drives. The

215

anti-Skinner group seized the initiative and in the winter of 1774 flooded the Assembly with petitions from both sections, principally the West, and as far removed as Cape May, Burlington, and Middlesex counties. The import of the petitions was that Skinner be removed, then prosecuted, and required to make reimbursement and that in the meantime public funds be deposited in another's care. In response, the friends of the governor mounted their own petition drive advising that in the name of fair play the treasurer's trial be prerequisite to consideration of his removal.[32]

By the winter session of 1774, the confrontation had been raised to a constitutional level involving the power of the purse and appointment. The Assembly and the petitioners echoed that in light of the Treasurer's untrustworthiness public funds be deposited elsewhere, perhaps in the charge of the western treasurer, and warned that treasury funds would be granted in the future on condition of Skinner's removal. Franklin castigated the lawmakers for "so arbitrary an Exercise of your Power" and refused to be swayed by fiscal intimidation or public opinion. At such an impasse, the government's business had ground to a standstill, and the house began consideration of a petition to the crown. Skinner himself had become something of a stage piece: he petitioned and then renewed his petition to the house requesting the opportunity to clear his name. But the house was not willing to let the subject slip through its hands so easily. Finally, in February 1774, Skinner resigned. Still the issue would not disappear. The question of appointing a successor remained. Franklin was already preparing to name Skinner's brother-in-law Philip Kearney, Jr., while the house was preparing to fill the vacancy with John Smyth of Perth Amboy. Had not the Council interceded and pressed Franklin to reconsider, the issue would have been joined again. Finally, Franklin kept face and nominated Smyth to the house.[33]

The majority assembled against the governor during the winter of 1774 was impressive for its size and steadfastness. The house journals record twenty roll calls on the treasury scandal between November 1773 and March 1774. Eighteen of the twenty-nine voting members lined up against Skinner. On February 19, the house considered several resolutions that declared that Skinner was untrustworthy and incapable of handling public funds, that his "Continuance in Office. . .is much to the Dissatisfaction of the good People," that he should be removed, that the governor's "Refusal greatly tends to the Prejudice of his Majesty's Service," that the governor was responsible for the continuing scandal, and that the house should petition the king for redress.[34] Without a single deviation, nineteen members voted to pass these resolutions. They included men who had disagreed regularly on salaries and the military. Indeed, they came from two voting blocs. Edward Taylor, for example, disagreed with John Hinchman and William Winds on nearly half of all the roll calls. That solidarity had not appeared in earlier sessions. Two years earlier, only the barest outlines of that eighteen-man majority could be discerned. Then--just as the script was being read and before the actors had learned their parts--it split in half on whether to receive the treasurer's account, and only eleven regularly agreed on the house's messages to the governor. At that time, the scandal had become a public concern, but it was not yet framed within such a dramatic staging. The alignments were not much different than those on other scandals that periodically reached the house. In the previous Assembly, for example, the lawmakers considered complaints against several lawyers and other officers of the courts. The roll calls document regularities--tendencies to agree--but deviations as well.[35]

James Kinsey of Burlington was instrumental in forging this coalition. The son of a former New Jersey assemblyman who had removed to Pennsylvania and then served conspicuously in that province's legislature, Kinsey spent his youth in Philadelphia where he prepared for the bar. On relocating at Burlington, this wealthy Quaker embarked on a political career and in 1772 was chosen to represent the city in the legislature. Ambitious and industrious, he achieved immediate prominence and by the end of the Assembly had accumulated more committee assignments than any of his colleagues, including Hendrick Fisher. His attack on Skinner and Franklin did not derive from acute Country sensibilities or a suspiciousness of government. In contrast to John Wetherill, he regularly supported military appropriations and high salaries for Governor Franklin, Attorney General Skinner, and the justices of the Supreme Court. But he seemed to recognize that the robbery issues, if properly exploited, provided the means for establishing influence in the house. Thus, he effectively moved his colleagues toward an aggressive posture. It was he who drafted the first message proposing the treasurer's removal. By the next year, he had become the penman of the house's messages to the governor. Incessantly, long into the night, he labored on the house's responses to Governor Franklin.[36]

By the winter of 1774, Kinsey had with the help of William Franklin succeeded in converting a diverse array of representatives into a united opposition. It included all the western delegations with the exception of Kinsey's neighbor Thomas Hewlings. East Jersey was divided, however. Several from Middlesex and Monmouth counties were already predisposed to suspect the government. Others like Theunis Dey and Thomas Van Horne had normally supported the government but were moved to join with Kinsey on the treasury issue. But

217

several other eastern representatives who had endorsed high salaries and military supplies--such as Bergen's John Demarest, Essex's Stephen Crane, and Somerset's Hendrick Fisher--refused to join in the assault on Skinner and Franklin.   Perhaps indicative of the strength of Kinsey's position or his persuasive skills, this minority did not vote as consistently as the majority did.   During the winter session of 1774, only Nathaniel Pettit of Sussex County voted on all twenty roll calls against Kinsey and his followers.

Kinsey's majority was impressive for its size, diversity, and solidarity, but it remained a fragile creation sustained only as long as Kinsey and Franklin delivered the necessary cues.   Once the treasurer had exited, the house drama dissolved.   Within weeks of condemning Franklin, the legislators were sent home. They did not reassemble for nearly a year.   While removed from the scene, they had time to reflect on the hazards of opposition and to turn their attentions elsewhere.   In February 1775, Kinsey sought to revive the issue by moving the adoption of a bill requiring the two treasurers to post a security bond.   But his majority had disappeared.   By a margin of sixteen to six, the house declined to renew the issue.   Of Kinsey's eighteen supporters, seven, including all the western Quakers, had defected.[37]   The vote was significant not only because it revealed the effervescent nature of his coalition but also because it came at a moment when the imperial relationship approached crisis point.

Because the Skinner affair had raised suspicions of the governor, it might be expected that it contributed to the imperial crisis and to the radicalization of the house.   But the lawmakers did not make such a leap.   Instead, they seemed to treat the treasury crisis as just another confrontation between the two branches of government.   In contrast to Governor Morris's dramatically polarized assemblies, the scandal did not directly affect voting on related issues.   Shortly after condemning Skinner and Franklin, the house undertook to set salaries.   Thirteen of Kinsey's eighteen adherents approved a high amount for Franklin.   Although it was more difficult to support Cortlandt Skinner, seven did and two more later joined the majority in favor of a high salary for the attorney general. Throughout this period, the Assembly had acted within limits. It responded cautiously and with uncertainty to an awakening public.   If rioting prodded the legislators to pass debt legislation, it also stirred them to approve a riot bill.   While the public's enthusiasm for liberty was heartening, Robert Ogden's sudden fall from favor served as a reminder of the discomforts and excesses that came with the democracy.   Perhaps this caution explains why the last Assembly chose to record only six divisions related to the looming imperial crisis.

218

Although unanimously apprehensive about English policies, New Jersey's lawmakers, like their counterparts throughout the continent, responded in a variety of ways. The differences did not rise from diametrically opposed opinions but were an expression of interest, social experience, and temperament. In 1765, Cortlandt Skinner and Aaron Leaming, Jr., disapproved of the Stamp Act. The urbane proprietor criticized the new tax for its detrimental impact on the provincial economy. Cape May's self-styled yeoman representative interpreted its passage in broader and more ominous terms as a conscious act of tyranny and a harbinger of worse to come. Skinner and his colleagues disagreed on the proper response to English actions: should protest be confined to the legislature and rest on dutiful remonstrances? should the house petition parliament or the king? how should the petitions be couched? By the time of the Townsend Duties, popular demonstrations had awakened Skinner's innate distrust of the democracy. But, as speaker, he could work comfortably with the legislature as it began to fashion its protest. While preparing to petition the king, the legislators chose to keep their proceedings secret lest the governor interfere. Skinner agreed and refused to leak information to Franklin. The governor found this act a mark of disloyalty: "I had a Right to expect Information of all Matters of a new or extraordinary Nature, which might be agitated in the Assembly." But as voices grew more shrill and the crisis deepened, Skinner found himself increasingly uncomfortable with the politics of protest even within the Assembly. From the speaker's chair, he had presided over the sessions that had pilloried his brother; and, soon after, he watched his colleagues venture beyond the bounds of- his tolerance. In January 1775, the house approved the Continental Congress's boycott on English imports and then moved to petition the king. First the members turned to the speaker, but Skinner's moderately couched and narrowly defined supplication was rejected in favor of a more comprehensive indictment of English misdeeds. Skinner refused to affix his name to the petition, but the lawmakers voted by a ten-to-one margin that he do so. And then only by his own tie-breaking vote was he allowed to record his dissent in the house journals. By 1776, he had declared his loyalty to the crown and fled the province.[38]

The rush of events was equally discomforting for James Kinsey. The Intolerable Acts appalled him. England had demonstrated its "Unjust Cruel & Oppressive" intents, and he warned that acquiescence "Must be of exceeding bad Consequence." Like Skinner, he preferred that the province express itself through established institutions and pressed for reconvening the legislature. But since Skinner and Franklin were reluctant to allow hotheads opportunity to use the

Assembly, concerned Jerseymen chose to meet in a popularly elected convention. When that convention met at New Brunswick, it chose Kinsey, Stephen Crane, and three others to represent the province at the Continental Congress. In January 1775, the Assembly met and listened while Kinsey pressed for participation in the continental boycott. And, with the assistance of Crane and the lobbying efforts of several Essex patriots, he was able to outmaneuver Skinner and the governor. While his differences with Skinner were a matter of public record, Kinsey was also feeling the first twinges of his essentially conservative conscience. Sharing with Skinner inbred apprehensions about popular tumults and perhaps influenced by the meetinghouse's advice to withdraw from activity which "may have a tendency to introduce anarchy & Confusion," Kinsey began to separate himself from the patriots. When Skinner's draft of the house petition to the king was rejected, the lawmakers first turned to Kinsey. His version recommending reconciliation and the establishment of a commission for settling differences between the colonies and England met Governor Franklin's approval but was rejected by the house. Stephen Crane was ready with his own proposal that echoed the sentiments of the Continental Congress but offended both Kinsey and Skinner. Kinsey supported the speaker's refusal to sign the petition and his request to record his opposition to the venture. When the house met the following fall, Kinsey discovered how little influence remained in his hands. The house prepared a message to Governor Franklin which explained that it saw "little Prospect" for the king's "favorable Interposition" in the crisis or for a change of heart in parliament. Kinsey cast the sole dissenting vote. Like many Quakers, he chose to withdraw from politics and resigned his seat in the Continental Congress. During the war, he sought to maintain a position of quiet neutrality but was accused of harboring Tory loyalties. And only after the Revolution was he able to re-enter public life.[39]

The adoption of Crane's petition to the king signaled that the initiative had shifted from Kinsey to a group of Essex politicians. These men who were principally Presbyterian were more daring than Kinsey and more willing to embrace extralegal measures of resistance. Dressed in simple homespun, Stephen Crane absorbed the role of Country patriot and thrived in the crisis.[40] Yet this was a new role. Crane's position did not come from the habit of opposition. In contrast to John Wetherill, who had always been unimpressed by the administration's requests and who was just as ready to enter into opposition, Crane had been a steady supporter of the government. In the Twenty-First Assembly this urban member had voted in 78 percent agreement with Perth Amboy's John L. Johnston. During the treasury crisis, he remained impervious

220

to Kinsey's appeal. On other matters, however, the two representatives agreed 65 percent of the time. After attending the Continental Congress, the two men went separate ways. During the Assembly's last sessions, Crane voted to force the speaker to sign the petition to the king, denied his request to enter his dissent in the house journal, and approved the house's message criticizing the king and parliament. Thus, with independence, he continued to participate in the new state government.

The times bred personal crisis and caused political convulsions. Majorities in the Assembly were unstable and alignments volatile. Caught up in a dilemma between patriotic resistance to tyranny and powerful loyalties to the crown, the lawmakers were at one moment bitterly divided and at another joined in unanimity. Those who agreed to defend provincial rights came from varied backgrounds. Previous political records were not certain prediction of their stand. In 1775, the most steady defenders of provincial rights were three Presbyterians-- Samuel Tucker, William Winds, and Theophilus Elmer--and two Baptists--Eli Eldridge and Jonathan Hand. Although they had joined Kinsey on the treasury affair, they were divided on voting appropriations for salaries and the military. On the other hand, John Demarest, Henry Garritse, and Hendrick Fisher had refused to join in the attack on Stephen Skinner and accepted high salaries, but like Crane they also supported the Assembly's defense of provincial liberties. The times required a delicate balancing between loyalties to the crown and the defense of provincial rights. While supporting the Continental Congress, the house explicitly repudiated all thoughts of independence. Old beliefs and arguments did not die: calls for reconciliation still had powerful appeal. Thus, in the last session, the Assembly continued to vote a high salary for Governor Franklin and assured him that he and his family had no reason to fear for their safety. And, while it self-consciously appealed to the public, the lawmakers found it most difficult to press for elections in a time of crisis. Moreover, that no member--not even Kinsey--could oppose all the Assembly's efforts in defense of provincial rights suggests the underlying basis for agreement that endured in this legislative community.

But the issues provoked instabilities and brittleness. When Governor Franklin met the Assembly at Burlington in November 1775, he had reason to believe that he could still appeal to powerful conservative attitudes. "It seems, indeed, to be the general Opinion of those with whom I converse, that the Majority of people. . .are greatly averse to an Independency."' Petitions of the same nature were being delivered to the legislature. Franklin himself still enjoyed popularity and unlike other royal governors had not taken sanctuary with the English military.

For a moment, his assessment seemed correct. On November 28, the house instructed its representatives at the Continental Congress to oppose all propositions tending toward "Independency" and "to use their utmost Endeavours for the obtaining a Redress of American Grievances, and for the restoring the Union between the Colonies and Great-Britain upon constitutional Principles."[41] Three days later, it was preparing to petition the king for redress of grievances. When the Congress learned of the house's mood, it dispatched three of its members across the river to dissuade the lawmakers. On December 5, John Dickinson of Philadelphia made an impassioned appeal on the floor of the Assembly. Reminding it that numerous attempts to petition had failed, he recounted that the English government had deployed troops that had "without Cause put to Death Some Americans" at Lexington. "Had the Congress then Drawn the sword & thrown away the Scabbard all Lovers of Liberty, all honest and Virtuous Men Would have applauded them." Now England conspired to let loose "The Savages" so that they might "Murder our helpless wives & Children." America had waited patiently but long enough. "Neither Mercy nor Justice was to be Expected from Great Britain." Now "it was Necessary to Convince Great Britain that we would fight, and were not a Rope of Sand." The appeal had immediate affect. The instructions to the congressional delegation were never sent, and the new petition was never completed. Governor Franklin despaired and dismissed the house on December 6.[42]

William Franklin's administration had been a stressful period for the New Jersey Assembly. Challenges from above and below brought out both organizational and ideological brittleness on the floor of the legislature. While English policies provoked an ideological awakening and stimulated articulate, elaborate, and coherent discussions of the relationship between government and the people and between liberty and power, the crisis brought even more brittle ideological responses among the politicians on the floor of the legislature. While an awakened public began to establish networks of communication and organization extending beyond the county to include the entire province, the lawmakers seemed to be ever more disorganized. But, if the centrifugal forces for disunity seemed to overcome the house's proceedings, if the meetings seemed emotionally charged, and if political alignments seemed volatile and segmented, the house was only acting on inherited resources and ingrained habits.

In the months after the last session, resistance turned to rebellion. The lawmakers were forced to choose between republicanism and the crown. Again, the issue provoked

222

realignment and decisions that seemed unrelated to previous habits. John Combs and Edward Taylor had opposed Stephen Skinner, begrudged salaries to the civil list, opposed military appropriations, and voted to resist English tyrannies. Yet both became loyalists.[43] Previous actions had little bearing on the choice: representatives at both ends of the scale made the same decision. As royal government dissolved, Jerseymen wondered whether independence would spell the unleashing of leveling forces in society. In fact, later years proved the opposite--that the legislative community would endure and even flourish.

NOTES

1. For a general discussion of this period, see Gerlach, Prologue to Independence; idem, "Anglo-American Politics in New Jersey on the Eve of the Revolution," The Huntington Library Quarterly, XXXIX (May, 1976), 291-316; idem, "Power to the People"; and Bernstein, "New Jersey in the American Revolution," 1-152.

2. Assembly resolution, Aug. 20, 1772, Votes and Proceedings. Assembly resolutions, Aug. 21, 1772, and Dec. 20, 1773, ibid.; petition from Burlington County, Feb. 9, 1774, ibid.; petition from Gloucester County, Feb. 7, 1774, ibid.; Anton-Hermann Chroust, "The Lawyers of New Jersey and the Stamp Act," The American Journal of Legal History, VI (July, 1962), 286-97. Also Richard D. Brown, Modernization: The Transformation of American Life, 1600-1865 (New York, 1976), 74-93.

3. Petition from Middlesex County, Oct. 23, 1769, Votes and Proceedings; "An Independent Freeholder," Pennsylvania Gazette, Nov. 28, 1771, in N.J.Archs., XXVII, 649; "A Plantation Man," New-York Journal, Oct. 5, 1769, in ibid., XXVI, 514-16; Liberty and Property, Without Oppression (NP, [1769]), 5-8. "A Letter from a Gentleman in Hunterdon County," New-York Weekly Gazette, Mar. 5, 1770, N.J.Archs., XXVII, 80-85; "An Independent Freeholder," Pennsylvania Gazette, Oct. 17, 1771, in ibid., 595-98; Pennsylvania Chronicle, Jan. 11-18, 1768, in ibid., XXVI, 6-7; Thayer, Colonial and Revolutionary Morris County, 128-29; petition from Somerset County, Oct. 16, 1769, Votes and Proceedings.

4. Petition from Monmouth County, Oct. 12, 1769, ibid. Petition from Middlesex County, Oct. 18, 1769, ibid.; Joseph Albert Ernst, Money and Politics in America, 1755-1775: A

Study in the Currency Act of 1764 and the Political Economy of Revolution (Chapel Hill, NC, 1973), 246-51, 260-64, 316-18.

5. "B. C. Caesaria," New American Magazine, July, 1758, in N.J.Archs., XX, 256-61; resolutions of New Brunswick, New-York Journal, Aug. 9, 1770, in ibid., XXVII, 219; "Neo Caesariensis," New-York Journal, Oct. 25, 1770, in ibid., 295-99; Assembly to W. Franklin, June 17, 1765, Votes and Proceedings; Assembly resolution, Nov. 13, 1769, ibid.

6. Countryman's Lamentation, 33.

7. Bernard to Board of Trade, Mar. 30, 1759, N.J.Archs., IX, 171.

8. See Larry R. Gerlach's sketch of Franklin in Governors of New Jersey, 72-76.

9. Assembly resolution, May 31, 1771, Votes and Proceedings. Assembly to W. Franklin, Nov. 26, 1763, ibid.; W. Franklin to Earl of Hillsborough, Jan. 28, 1769, N.J.Archs., X, 99-102; W. Franklin to Council and Assembly, Oct. 11, 1769, ibid., XVIII, 37-38; Assembly to W. Franklin, Oct. 17, 1769, ibid., 42-43; W. Franklin to Council and Assembly, Sept. 28, 1770, ibid., 192; Assembly to W. Franklin, Oct. 18, 1770, ibid., 200.

10. W. Franklin to Hillsborough, Nov. 5, 1770, ibid., X, 202. W. Franklin to Earl of Shelburne, Dec. 16, 1766, ibid., IX, 576-77; Hunterdon County's instructions to John Hart and Samuel Tucker, May, 1771, ibid., X, 269-73; W. Franklin to Council and Assembly, June 10, 1767, Votes and Proceedings; Shy, "Quartering His Majesty's Forces."

11. Assembly to W. Franklin, Apr. 25, 1771, N.J.Archs., X, 256; W. Franklin to Assembly, Apr. 29, 1771, ibid., 257. Leaming to "Dear & worthy Gentlemen," May 26, 1771, Gerlach, ed., New Jersey in the American Revolution, 61-63.

12. W. Franklin to Board of Trade, May 10, 1763, N.J.Archs., IX, 383-86; W. Franklin to Hillsborough, Dec. 24, 1769, ibid., X, 144-45; W. Franklin to Earl of Dartmouth, Jan. 5, 1773, ibid., 389-93; Assembly to W. Franklin, Aug. 26, 1772, ibid., XVIII, 306-8; J. W., An Address to the Freeholders of New-Jersey, on the Subject of Public Salaries (Philadelphia, 1763); Jerome J. Nadelhaft, "Politics and the Judicial Tenure Fight in Colonial New Jersey," The William and Mary Quarterly, 3rd Ser., XXVIII (Jan., 1971), 46-63.

13. Gerlach, Prologue to Independence, 175-76; W.

Franklin to Hillsborough, Nov. 5, 1770, N.J.Archs., X, 202. Also W. Franklin to Assembly, Mar. 26, 1770, Votes and Proceedings; Assembly to W. Franklin, Mar. 27, 1770, ibid.

14. W. Franklin to Hillsborough, Dec. 27, 1771, N.J.Archs., X, 321-23. Also W. Franklin to Hillsborough, Nov. 23, 1768, ibid., 93; W. Franklin to Dartmouth, May 31, 1774, ibid., 458.

15. Gerlach, Prologue to Independence, 98-99. Robert Ogden to Cortlandt Skinner, Aug. 24, 1764, N.J.Archs., IX, 449-50; W. Franklin to Board of Trade, Nov. 13, 1765, ibid., 505-7; W. Franklin to Board of Trade, Dec. 18, 1765, ibid., 524-25.

16. W. Franklin to Assembly, Nov. 30, 1765, Votes and Proceedings. W. Franklin, The Answer of his Excellency . . . ([Philadelphia, 1765]); Assembly to W. Franklin, June 17, 1766, Votes and Proceedings; W. Franklin to Assembly, June 25, 1766, ibid.; Assembly to W. Franklin, June 27, 1766, ibid.

17. Assembly to W. Franklin, June 24, 1767, ibid. W. Franklin to Hillsborough, Jan. 28, 1769, N.J.Archs., X, 101-2; W. Franklin to Hillsborough, June 1, 1771, ibid., 297-99; W. Franklin to Dartmouth, June 28, 1774, ibid., 464-65.

18. W. Franklin to Assembly, Nov. 29, 1771, Votes and Proceedings. W. Franklin to Assembly, Apr. 26, 1771, ibid.; Assembly to W. Franklin, Apr. 26, 1771, ibid.; W. Franklin to Hillsborough, July 20, 1771, N.J.Archs., X, 306-8; W. Franklin to Hillsborough, Apr. 6, 1772, ibid., 334-36.

19. Assembly to king, May 6, 1768, ibid., 18-21; Assembly to W. Franklin, May 20, 1775, ibid., XVIII, 558-62; "Caesariensis," New-York Gazette, Sept. 12, 1765, in ibid., XXIV, 616-18; "Benevolus," Pennsylvania Journal, June 4, 1767, in ibid., XXV, 382-84; resolutions of Burlington County, Pennsylvania Gazette, Sept. 27, 1770, in ibid., XXVII, 260-62; "Z.," Rivington's New-York Gazetteer, Sept. 8, 1774, in ibid., XXIX, 476-78; Assembly resolutions, Nov. 30, 1765, Votes and Proceedings. Randolph G. Adams, Political Ideas of the American Revolution: Britannic-American Contributions to the Problem of Imperial Organization (Durham, NC, 1922); Gerlach, "Power to the People," 7-31.

20. Assembly resolutions, Nov. 28, 1775, Votes and Proceedings; Bailyn, Ideological Origins of the American Revolution, 94-159. Assembly to W. Franklin, Nov. 30, 1775, Votes and Proceedings; resolutions of Sons of Liberty in Hunterdon County, Pennsylvania Gazette, Apr. 3, 1766, in

N.J.Archs., XXV, 64-65; resolutions of Sons of Liberty in Sussex County, New-York Gazette, May 8, 1766, in ibid., 108-11.

21. Leaming to "Dear & worthy Gentlemen," May 26, 1771, in Gerlach, ed., New Jersey in the American Revolution, 61-62; Joseph Borden to "J. L., J. R., and J. L.," New-York Journal, Sept. 27, 1770, in N.J.Archs., XXVII, 255-56. Spicer to James and Drinker, July 8, 1765, Spicer Papers; [Thomas Hopkinson], Liberty . . . (Philadelphia, 1769); "A. Lawyer," New-York Gazette, Oct. 24, 1765, in N.J.Archs., XXIV, 660-62; "An Essay towards discovering the Authors and Promoters of the memorable Stamp Act," Pennsylvania Journal, Sept. 18, 1766, in ibid., XXV, 205-9; Essex County resolutions, New-York Journal, July 26, 1770, in ibid., XXVII, 206-7; "To Mr. Joseph Borden," New-York Journal, Sept. 27, 1770, in ibid., 257-58; "C. D.," Pennsylvania Journal, Apr. 30, 1772, in ibid., XXVIII, 123-25; "Z.," Rivington's New-York Gazetteer, Dec. 1, 1774, in ibid., XXIX, 534-38.

22. "To the Printer," New-York Journal, Sept. 20, 1770, in ibid., XXVII, 244-46; Morgan, "The Puritan Ethic and the American Revolution."

23. Essex County resolves, Oct. 25, 1765, Gerlach, ed., New Jersey in the American Revolution, 19; instructions to Edward Taylor and Robert Hartshorne, Oct., 1769, Holmes Family Papers, Rutgers University Library; "Advertisement," New-York Gazette, Aug. 6, 1770, in Gerlach, ed., New Jersey in the American Revolution, 54. Resolutions of Sons of Liberty in Freehold Township, New-York Gazette, Apr. 10, 1766, in N.J.Archs., XXV, 71-73; Stephen Crane to inhabitants of Monmouth County, June 13, 1774, ibid., X, 459-61; Essex County resolutions, New-York Gazette, Dec. 19, 1774, in ibid., XXIX, 546-47; Gloucester County resolutions, Pennsylvania Gazette, Dec. 21, 1774, in ibid., 549-50; Walter Rutherford to ?, Mar. 21, 1775, Stevens Family Papers, reel 6, 998; Ryan, "Six Towns," 110-14.

24. See Jack P. Greene, "Legislative Turnover in British America, 1696 to 1775: A Quantitative Analysis," The William and Mary Quarterly, 3rd Ser., XXXVIII (July, 1981), 442-63.

25. W. Franklin to Board of Trade, Aug. 8, 1765, N.J.Archs., IX, 491. Smith, History of Nova-Caesaria, 488.

26. The pattern described in Chapter Five continues, but the differences are not as extreme. In the Twentieth Assembly, that third of lawmakers that voted at the antigovernment end of the scale recorded a policy support score of 0, while the third

at the opposite end of the scale recorded a positive score of .4. In the Twenty-First Assembly, the first group left a positive score of .1 and the second .2. In the last Assembly, both groups recorded positive scores again with the first at .1 and the second at .4.

27. W. Franklin to Samuel Smith, Aug. 24, 1772, Samuel Smith Papers, Rutgers.

28. Assembly resolution, Oct. 23, 1770, Votes and Proceedings; W. Franklin to Assembly, Apr. 23, 1771, N.J.Archs., X, 251. W. Franklin to Hillsborough, Nov. 5, 1770, ibid., 202; W. Franklin to Assembly, Apr. 29, 1771, ibid., 256-68.

29. Larry R. Gerlach, "Politics and Prerogatives: The Aftermath of the Robbery of the East Jersey Treasury in 1768," New Jersey History, XC (Autumn, 1972), 133-68.

30. Council to W. Franklin, July 23, 1768, N.J.Archs., XVII, 520. Assembly to W. Franklin, Oct. 17, 1769, ibid., XVIII, 43; "A Hunterdon Freeholder," Pennsylvania Gazette, Feb. 9, 1774, in ibid., XXIX, 246.

31. W. Franklin to Assembly, Sept. 23, 1772, Votes and Proceedings. W. Franklin to Assembly, Sept. 15, 1772, ibid.; Assembly to W. Franklin, Sept. 18, 1772, ibid.; Assembly to W. Franklin, Feb. 9, 1774, ibid.

32. Gloucester County's instructions to Robert Friend Price and John Hinchman, Oct. 3, 1769, Gloucester County, Stewart Collection. Petitions from Middlesex, Cape May, and Burlington counties, Feb. 8, 1774, Votes and Proceedings; petitions from Chesterfield Township and New Brunswick, Feb. 9, 1774, ibid.; petition from Hunterdon County to Franklin, ND, Emley Papers, IV, Hunterdon County Historical Society; "A Somerset Freeholder," Rivington's New-York Gazetteer, Feb. 17, 1774, in N.J.Archs., XXIX, 258-63; "Civis," New-York Journal, Mar. 3, 1774, in ibid., 276-82.

33. W. Franklin to Assembly, Feb. 16, 1774, Votes and Proceedings. W. Franklin to Assembly, Feb. 24, 1774, N.J.Archs., X, 420-24.

34. Assembly resolutions, Feb. 19, 1774, Votes and Proceedings.

35. Oct. 26, 1769, Nov. 3-7, 1769, ibid.

36.   C. Skinner to Philip Kearney, ND, N.J.Archs., X, 412-13; C. Skinner to Kearney, Dec. 5, 1773, ibid., 414.

37.   Assembly roll call, Feb. 9, 1775, Votes and Proceedings.

38.   W. Franklin to Hillsborough, July 11, 1768, N.J.Archs., X, 36. C. Skinner to T. Boone, Oct. 5, 1765, Gerlach, ed., New Jersey in the American Revolution, 16-18; Leaming to "Dear & worthy Gentlemen," May 26, 1771, ibid., 61-64.

39.   James Kinsey to Elias Boudinot, June 14, 1774, ibid., 73-74; Gerlach, Prologue to Independence, 240; W. Franklin to Joseph Galloway, Mar. 12, 1775, N.J.Archs., X, 575; Assembly to W. Franklin, Nov. 30, 1775, Votes and Proceedings.

40.   See Chapter Four.

41.   W. Franklin to Dartmouth, Jan. 6, 1776, N.J.Archs., X, 676-81; Assembly resolutions, Nov. 28, 1775, Votes and Proceedings, in Gerlach, ed., New Jersey in the American Revolution, 164. Petitions from Burlington County, Nov. 23-27, 1775, Votes and Proceedings.

42.   Notes on Delegates' Remarks to the New Jersey Assembly, [Dec. 5, 1775], in Smith, ed., Letters of Delegates to Congress, II, 443-45.

43.   Ryan, "Six Towns," 181.

CHAPTER EIGHT

CONCLUSION

In December 1775, Cortlandt Skinner watched helplessly from the speaker's chair as the patriot enthusiasts outmaneuvered Governor Franklin's last attempts to achieve reconciliation with the crown. The signs were ominous: certainly the impending crisis "will deluge this country in blood." While uncertain "where or what will be the end," he and like-minded provincials dwelt on precedents in Roman and English history. They were surrounded by republican conspirators and demagogues. Passions had been roused and sense and reason overwhelmed. The times were right for a Caesar or a Cromwell. Chief Justice Frederick Smyth worried that liberty had degenerated into "Licenciousness" and that the province teetered on the brink of tyranny by the democracy. True liberty, which "consisteth in the enjoyment of our lives, of our persons and properties in security," was in jeopardy. Daniel Coxe, councilor and West Jersey proprietor, agreed: "Such is the present infatuated Temper of the Times, and the Minds of Men daily increasing in Madness and Phrensey, that they are ready to enter upon the most daring and desperate attempts." With the "prostration of Law and Government," the doors were opened to the "licentious and abandoned to exercise every malevolent Inclination." "Have men of Property not to fear and apprehend, and particularly those who happen and are known to differ in sentiment from the generality?" Such fears were widespread. Burlington's Quakers warned the legislature that "the Unhappy dispute, between Great Britain and her American Colonies. . .is now brought to the most Alarming crisis, and in all Probability will Involve this once Happy Country in all the Horrors of a Civil War." Skinner, Smyth, and Coxe became loyalists, but even those who chose for independence shared their concerns. Within weeks after independence had been declared, Jonathan Elmer addressed his neighbors calling for them to support the new government and "to strive to vindicate the glorious cause of liberty." In the same breath he rallied them to guard against "disorder and licentiousness." Reciting the lessons of history, he warned lest the people fall prey to a "Demagogue, possessed of popular talents and shining qualities, a Julius Caesar, or an Oliver Cromwell."[1]

Independence brought changes in New Jersey's social and political fabric.[2] Until 1776, British policies had roused tempers, provoked disagreements, and caused occasional confrontations, but the divisions had not caused the intensely polarized and disruptive politics witnessed in other colonies. The war, however, turned New Jersey into a battleground, and the new state became one of the most bitterly divided. The struggle for independence became a civil conflict. Nearly five thousand from all social ranks actively supported the crown. Loyalist regiments organized and led by Cortlandt Skinner and Daniel Coxe ravaged the countryside. In response, the state resolved on retribution and in 1778 began the confiscation of twelve hundred loyalist estates. Moreover, the ideology of revolution assumed a momentum of its own. The principle of popular sovereignty inspired a downward revision in the requirements for voting and office holding and thereby expanded the size of the legislative community. Simultaneously, Jerseymen continued to develop statewide political networks which eventually became political parties. Together, the bitterness of the war experience and the emergence of organizations designed to rouse the electorate made for a larger and more politically active citizenry. Habits of indifference and deference were eroded, and new men from lower social ranks appeared in government. Yet conservative fears of a democratic deluge and social cataclysm proved unfounded. A review of the state's political leadership, its relationship to the public, the prevailing rhetoric and ideals, and the policies devised points toward changes which were more evolutionary and gradual than revolutionary. Indeed, statehood signified the maturation of the colonial legislative community.[3]

When Jerseymen read the signs of turmoil as presages of the collapse of government, they lost sight of unmistakable assurances of stability and continuity. In spite of the tumultuous nature of the times, the transition from royal to republican government went smoothly. Months before the last session of the colonial Assembly, Jerseymen had elected a provincial Congress. Twelve current and former assemblymen were sent to the first and ten to the second Congress. And both congresses chose assemblymen Hendrick Fisher and Samuel Tucker as their presiding officers. Well before independence, this extralegal body was adopting measures to raise taxes, issue paper money, and control the militia. In May 1776, Governor Franklin made one last effort to revive royal government by summoning the Assembly. But it never met: the Congress ordered that the summons not be heeded, censured the governor, and ordered his arrest. Then the Congress resolved to establish a government "for regulating the internal police of this colony" and on July 2 approved a new state constitution.[4] Elections were held that summer, and one in five of the new republican legislators were former colonial assemblymen. When the lawmakers met in August to select a governor, they turned to William Livingston.

The choice of Livingston, indeed his continuous re-election until his death in 1790, signified the tone of New Jersey's revolution. Born in New York, Livingston had inherited his family's economic and political fortunes. After receiving his legal education under the tutelage of James Alexander, he entered New York politics and by the time of the Stamp Act crisis had become a spokesman for the dominant legislative faction. In 1772, he had decided to retire from public life and took up residence at Elizabethtown. Certainly he was well received: he enjoyed long-standing friendships with East Jersey's most prominent families, and many had been his legal clients. Perhaps he yearned for retirement and the solitude of arcadia; and, for a time, he devoted his attention to building his new home "Liberty Hall." But England's actions roused his concerns. Conservative by nature, he slowly cast aside his doubts and then plunged into the resistance movement. He soon rose to the fore. In 1774, Livingston and his neighbor Stephen Crane were appointed to the province's first delegation to the Continental Congress. While serving in the Second Congress, he was named brigadier general of the provincial militia. As governor, he rendered able leadership to the state and gave eloquent expression to the American cause. In his first address to the legislature, he reviewed the past decade of tyrannies and injustices. England's leaders, "dissipated in Venality and Riot," had revealed their intent to establish a "System of Despotism concerted for our Ruin." Their "hostile Assaults on our Persons and Properties" and their efforts "to prolong their Luxury and Corruption, by appropriating to themselves the hard-earned Competence of the American World" had roused virtuous Americans to resist this "meditated Bondage" and to rend "the old Fabric, rotten and ruinous as it was." The "whole impartial World" applauded. "Let us unitedly strive to approve ourselves Master-Builders, by giving Beauty, Strength and Stability to the new."[5] Yet he was equally concerned about democracy's excess and feared that it might degenerate into "anarchy and confusion." For him, independence was to preserve the old social order by severing contaminating ties with England. As governor, he promoted the traditional civic virtues. The ideal public servant was one who could "detach himself from all partialities and county-interests, inconsistent with the common weal." What he feared was the unleashing of selfish instincts and the decline of deference. He turned instinctively to scions of the old order such as John Stevens and Elias Boudinot. But, in the course of his administration, he often despaired: "We do not exhibit the virtue that is necessary to support a republican government."[6]

The traditional political leadership and "men of property" believed they had reason for concern. The decision for independence had split the provincial elite: half of the royal

Council and 20 percent of the Assembly had become loyalists. Prominent figures such as Cortlandt Skinner, Daniel Coxe, and David Ogden had fled into exile. Clearly the revolution unleashed democratic impulses. The franchise requirements were so severely reduced that it seemed that men "in meer Rags or Stark naked" could vote. Local officials once appointed by the governor were now chosen by this democracy. The wartime experience had roused a once inert electorate, and emerging political organizations were developing the means to encourage its participation. The state legislature had been transformed. Property qualifications for sitting in the two houses were reduced. Voters seemed to act upon prejudices against "men of education" and preferred "mechanicks" to lawyers. Conservatives grumbled that "there had not been a single gentleman of the Law in the Assembly" and that the majority of the lawmakers were "plain men," who, though possessed "of sufficient honesty and spirit," were "hardly competent to the penning of a common note."[7]

No doubt, revolution had brought disquieting changes. But Jerseymen of conservative temperament were prone to exaggerate. The old elite had been decimated but not obliterated. Large estates of loyalists were confiscated, but they were usually sold in large tracts and purchased by wealthy speculators. Indeed, the social structure--the distribution of wealth--had not been significantly transformed. New faces appeared in politics, but old families remained. Although David Ogden had fled, his son remained and was elected to the new state senate. The legislature's membership lists continued to include such old names as Smith, Morris, Elmer, Eldridge, Dey, Kinsey, Newbold, Cooper, Price, and Leaming. Perth Amboy's proprietors, the most conspicuous bastion of the old order, had been shaken. Not only had many of the proprietors become loyalists, but the town had also lost its seat in the legislature. Yet spokesmen of the proprietary interest, such as William Alexander, James Stevens, and Elias Boudinot, remained prominent fixtures in the new state government. Indeed, after the war, the East Jersey Council of Proprietors revived itself, resumed legal efforts to protect its claims, began to sell lands, and made significant profits.[8]

In fact, voting behavior suggests that ingrained habits of indifference and deference prevailed in the first decades of statehood. While some embraced the implications of popular sovereignty more readily than others, turnout in the 1780s remained low and erratic. In 1787, only 7 percent of Burlington's adult white males bothered to cast a vote for the state legislature. Essex County, however, registered a 66 percent turnout in 1785. But the average for the decade was 30 percent. The pattern did not change in the next decade and did not register an appreciable shift until the next century. And, in the first decade on the nineteenth century, after the emergence of political parties, turnout reached only 51 percent. Moreover, those who lamented the decline of deference exaggerated. Although the social composition of the legislature shifted downward in favor of farmers of moderate economic means, the shift was slight and did not spell either the appearance of men from humbler origins or the demise of the old order. The conservatives' characterization of the legislators did not reflect reality as much as it documented the endurance of prejudices expressed during the colonial period by Governor Morris and his like. In fact, even the so-called Jacksonian revolution would not fundamentally alter the social origins of the state's legislature.[9]

Moreover, this slight shift in the social composition of the legislature was more than offset by the principles and attitudes which the lawmakers brought with them to the capital. The colonial world view of the social and political order remained essentially intact. The issues debated, the vocabulary employed, and the policies created revealed continuities, not change. The vision of commercial arcadia still haunted this legislative community and inspired efforts for agricultural, commercial, and manufacturing improvements. The lawmakers still wrestled with the destructive forces of the marketplace and its unscrupulous "traders and monopolizers." The debates over currency and debt turned on concerns for public morality. And still the lawmakers sought to establish moral reform and invigorate public virtue. The traditional standards of civic virtue had not been forgotten and continued to shape the discussions of state politics. The decision to shed the monarchy had caused personal torment and conflict; but, once done, the legislative community moved effortlessly--almost instinctively-- into a republican world. Resistance to English policy had raised the patriot's understanding of political virtue and dangers of corruption. Independence had been the means to preserve that world and republicanism the logical means to achieve that end. Thus, the Country continued to watch for the predator lurking in the courthouse and state capital and to act upon his fears for American liberty. Echoing the colonial's concerns, "Cato" warned his fellow Jerseymen that this republican experiment would endure as long as "public virtue" remained intact. The times required a selflessness, "a disinterested patriotism," a forswearing of "motives merely selfish or lucrative," and the abolition of favoritism, nepotism, factionalism, and petty squabbling. He concluded his description of the "good Assembly-Man": "As the best calculated laws will be found ineffectual to regulate a people of dissolute morals, he will recommend by his conversation and example, virtue and purity of manners; and discountenance all irreligion and immorality, as equally fatal to the interests of civil society and personal happiness."[10]

Even before independence, Jerseymen had awakened to the need for vigorous programs for realizing commercial arcadia. Now the schemes and ventures seemed to multiply. Petitioners to the legislature and contributors to the public prints promoted measures for the improvement of agriculture, transportation, and trade. In that spirit, the legislature set bounties on wool, flax, and hemp, encouraged the fishing industry, and endorsed projects for road building by private and public means. Improvers of the land called for paper money at loan; and, although their demands often provoked strenuous opposition, the legislature responded with new emissions. Jerseymen were conscious of themselves embarking on a new age and realized that its bounties would only be realized through commerce. "Now is the time," Newark's citizens declared, "for New Jersey to push herself forward, and take her rank among the commercial states in our union." Jealousy and resentment turned toward New York and Philadelphia and their long-standing dominance of the state's economy. Governor Livingston addressed a receptive audience when he urged the legislature to "give proper Encouragement to the Commerce of this State, and to prevent as far as possible our Neighbours from reaping those Profits on our Consumption of foreign Manufactures which might be secured to our Citizens." Again the legislature revived the schemes to encourage the ports of Perth Amboy and Burlington and enacted measures to encourage merchants to migrate to the state by establishing a one-month residency requirement for citizenship, relieving them from taxation, and exempting all foreign goods from duties.[11]

Since the nonimportation movement, Jerseymen were awakening to the need for domestic manufacturing. At first, they seemed to think of household manufacturing, but slowly they were turning to more ambitious projects. During the confederation period, the state's iron furnaces and fulling mills inspired imaginations. The promoters of one project concluded their argument for manufacturing: "we ought to view ourselves as young beginners in the world, whose all is at stake,. . . and. . .it depends upon our virtue and good economy, whether we shall be a prosperous and happy nation, or sink into all the meanness of abject slavery, disgrace and contempt." And another concurred that "unless we manufacture more and import less, we must ever be in a very poor state." In 1791, the legislature had begun to consider the "most probable measures of encouraging the Manufactures of this State" and to deliberate on a proposal to incorporate a Society for the Encouragement of Manufactures and the Useful Arts, when it received news that the new Secretary of the Treasury Alexander Hamilton was considering the establishment of a Society for the Improvement of Useful Manufactures in New Jersey. Hamilton's proposal received the legislature's full and quick endorsement. A bill for issuing a charter to this manufacturing venture passed the lower house by a vote of thirty to four. The charter's provisions were comprehensive and allowed the Society to undertake any venture not prohibited by state law and to acquire lands necessary for the building of canals and improving existing waterways. Although the venture failed, it was a harbinger of the state's future development.[12]

The legislature continued to act upon its ambivalent feelings toward the energies of the marketplace. It shared Governor Livingston's belief that it could distinguish between private interests that produced public improvements and those that were predatory and destructive of community welfare. It would not abide the "licentious Cruelties" of the marketplace. During the war, it responded to speculators and profiteers by establishing a system of price controls. While it recognized that the state lacked the capital for public improvements and therefore had to rely on private capital, it sought to regulate and control road builders by setting limits on the tolls. In the early decades of the nineteenth century, the legislature began to issue more acts of incorporation for manufacturing, internal improvements, and banks but regularly set limits on their fields of enterprise and on the amount of property to be owned. And, in order to insure public responsibility, the Assembly appointed members to the boards of directors and required that reports be regularly submitted to the government for review.[13]

While espousing the principle of popular sovereignty, even the most ardent democrat was not prepared to countenance an alteration of social relationships. His was a revolution to protect the liberty of the propertied, the virtuous and industrious, the improvers of the land. His legislative community understood its world on the same terms as had Jacob Spicer. Thus, it responded to the lower orders and the casualties of this society in much the way as had the previous generation. Although the cries for debt relief had increased, the legislature only made slight alterations in the creditor's power to imprison and in the procedures for collection. More than half of the occupants of the state's jails and prison were debtors. Yet the government refrained from addressing the squalid and desperate condition of these inmates until the second third of the nineteenth century. Nor had attitudes toward the poor changed. Acting on its fears of the "idle and disorderly," the government continued to pass legislation for the regulation of taverns. Drawing its distinctions between the deserving and undeserving poor, it continued to build almshouses and workhouses. The purpose of these institutions was discipline and profit. "A Zealous

235

Columbian" caught the spirit of the times when he proposed the building of workhouses where the poor and criminals could be confined and put to work for the production of woolen and linen goods. Often debtors and paupers became indistinguishable and were confined in the same institutions. So, too, the legislature moved slowly on the matter of slavery. There were nearly eight thousand slaves in the state at the end of the Revolution. And, although the lawmakers agreed to abolish the slave trade, their racist attitudes and fears of domestic unruliness, which were roused by an occasional disturbance, prevented their going farther for nearly two decades. In 1804, the legislature accepted the principle of gradual emancipation but three years later denied free blacks the right to vote.[14]

These same Jerseymen embarked upon the creation of a new government. Once they realized that their world could best be preserved through a republican form of government and once they had embraced the principle of popular sovereignty, they began to discuss the institutions and forms of government according to traditional principles. The new state constitution became a new charter and guarantee of positions long sought but denied during the colonial period. These "Charter-Rights" included the annual election of representatives, the guarantee that the legislature would sit each October, and the prohibition that neither of these rights could be abrogated. Furthermore, districts would be periodically reapportioned according to changes in population. The constitution clearly established the principle of legislative supremacy by giving the lower house the right to initiate money bills. So that the legislature may be "preserved from all Suspicion of Corruption," the constitution declared that "none of the Judges of the Supreme or other Courts, Sheriffs, or other Person or Persons possessed of any Post of Profit under the Government, other than Justices of the Peace, shall be entitled to a Seat in Assembly." These provisions meant a severely circumscribed executive who was annually elected by the legislature. The constitution stripped the governor of the power to summon, prorogue, or dissolve the legislature, to veto its legislation, and to approve its officers. So, too, he lost the power to appoint the attorney general, treasurer, and justices of the peace. And, although the governor remained commander-in-chief of the military, militia appointments were transferred to the legislature.[15]

Of course, "jarring interests," rural-urban antagonisms, denominationalism, and sectionalism continued to divide Jerseymen. At times, disagreements erupted into grand ideological conflict. But the differences did not shatter a fundamental consensus or break continuity with the past. Instead, they were symptoms of manichean and dramatic tendencies witnessed in earlier decades. Jerseymen were still wont to detect conspiracy in their neighbors. They spied "self-interested speculators,. . .lawyers, who glory in the guinea fee,. . .[and] hard hearted creditors," "great men" with their sycophantic and depraved followers, predators who designed to turn the government into an "instrument of oppression." Or they detected the demagogue who worked to rouse "jealousy and discontent" and who manipulated the "degraded and deluded" for his selfish and tyrannical lusts. In the 1790s, political passions ran high, the struggles achieved dramatic intensity, and the divisions became crystallized with the appearance of party organizations and labels.[16] Of course, the cast of characters and the scenario had been rewritten. Americans were no longer re-enacting English political conflicts. Instead, Federalists and Republicans accused each other of betraying the Revolution and subverting the constitution. The French Revolution and the ensuing Anglo-French conflict added ideological intensity and drama to the dispute. Yet the conflict was couched in the same forms and possessed the same manichean and ethereal characteristics found in the provincial period. Republican "Catos" appeared warning of a "secret cabal" of "unprincipled and designing men," former Tories who reassembled the "detestable fragments of monarchical and aristocratical tyranny," and "aristocratical leaders" who grasped for power. A Federalist "Cato" replied charging the opposition with fomenting rebellion. The charge was a common one within the Federalist ranks: the Republicans recruited "the discontented--the ambitious--the unprincipled--and the disappointed of our countrymen." Their objects were obvious--to cause "anarchy and tyranny." "Heaven preserve us from Jacobins, democrats, and Frenchified tories." Such men design to set "Ignorance over Knowledge--Sloth over Industry--Innovation over Experience--Infidelity over Faith--and Associators over Government."[17]

When the two "Catos"--the one Republican and the other Federalist--confronted each other, each responded to the other in much the same manner as their predecessors had during the colonial era. Although the social differences were slight, they translated them into a manichean world. And, in the process, they lost sight of the social and intellectual ties which bound them together. Indeed, the differences seemed rooted in temperament. The issue was not over popular sovereignty or republicanism but the degree to which each could countenance the implications of such principles. Both subscribed to the long-standing vision of commercial arcadia and both sought to build a commonwealth based on civic virtue. While both sought to channel the atomizing energies of the marketplace toward public ends, one was by temperament less inclined than the other to embrace that world. If the one did not dream of an aristocratic restoration, the other was repelled by the thought of a jacobin upheaval. Yet when "Cato" met "Cato," each cast the other into an opprobrious and ridiculous role. Both were projecting what was in themselves upon the other. Such a dramatic and ethereal staging seemed to work best when the issues had little immediate impact upon the actors. Thus, the debate turned on national issues--the policies of the Washington and Adams administrations--and on international affairs such as treaty relations with England and France. But, when the same actors turned to the more mundane and immediate matters of New Jersey's internal policy, that scenario evaporated, differences dissolved, alignments became slippery, and the forces for consensus re-emerged.

Despite appearances, the legislature in the first decades of statehood bore a remarkable resemblance to its colonial antecedent. Annual elections brought a rapid turnover in membership: half the lawmakers served a single year. Voting alignments turned on commercial-agrarian, rural-urban, denominational, and sectional axes, but they shifted with each category of policy. In sum, the legislature remained an institutionally invertebrate and effervescent body. Differences were rooted in temperament rather than contrasting ideologies. Nor did political behavior change significantly with the emergence of parties. While the two parties gave the semblance of ideological distinctiveness, they functioned best as organizations to win elections and advance the ambitions of their adherents. Although they achieved the appearance of ideological consistency on national issues such as Jay's Treaty, they could not maintain solidarity on state policy. Just as the legislature could reach nearly unanimous agreement on the Society for the Improvement of Manufactures, so, too, members from both parties voted together on the state's debt, interest, banking, paper money, incorporation, and education policies. But the social and ideological distances separating both parties were slight. Differences in interest and temperament were not enough to shatter that consensus which bound the lawmakers together in a legislative community. These patterns of behavior continued into the era of the Second Party System. Again, the parties achieved highest coherence when treating with matters of patronage or national issues. While both parties clearly disagreed over the Second Bank of the United States, that division dissolved when the lawmakers treated with local banking.[18]

But the times were also changing. Although independence and statehood marked the ascendance of commercial arcadia, Jerseymen like their fellow Americans were working unwittingly to transform that world. They were not moving at the same pace. Nor were they always conscious of what they were doing. While laboring to preserve one social and political world and while dreaming of ways to realize its full potential, they were stumbling into a very different society. It was as if they were walking backwards. In spite of themselves, they were engaged in the transformation of the American republic. Perhaps for moments, while engaged in the marketplace or factious quarreling, they recognized what they were doing. Often they shrank from what they saw in their hearts and sought to deny what they sensed by projecting that darkness upon their neighbors. But they were becoming accustomed to this world of "jarring interests." Soon they came to recognize the futility of reconciling private interests with the common good by government action. At that point, they also came to embrace a new ideology of liberation. The new age did not dawn suddenly. The developers of the land had not yet become the "greedheads" whom Hunter Thompson discovered in the twentieth century. In the Age of Jackson, the voice of Cato evoking the civic virtues of the past could still be heard. But these Americans were recognizing and accepting a new realism; and, in the process, they were coming to see what James Madison had first spied--that society was nothing more than milling factions and interest groups. So, too, as these Americans discarded older conceptions of civic virtue, they freed themselves from the discomforts that came with factional and party politics. At that point, they found their spokesman in Martin Van Buren. Perhaps these Americans would not recognize what they had wrought until the end of the nineteenth century. Then the corporation seemed to rule the nation: New Jersey had become the epitome of this world and deservedly earned its reputation as "The Home of the Trusts." Woodrow Wilson came to lash out at the "predatory wealth" used for antisocial purposes. And Lincoln Steffens sensed what had happened when he visited the state. The process had begun, he reflected, when the state had welcomed Alexander Hamilton's manufacturing scheme. Eventually, New Jersey succeeded in attracting business but discovered that the corporate leaders "came to rule that State." The state had become "one of the gates through which the flood of privilege broke over this country." Today the visitor will find it difficult to discern the vestiges of New Jersey's past. New Ark's covenanted society has become a wasteland, and the automobile license plates bear silent witness with their "Garden State" labels to history's cruel tragedy.[19]

NOTES

1. C. Skinner to William Skinner, Dec., 1775, Gerlach, ed., New Jersey in the American Revolution, 165-66; Frederick

Smyth to Middlesex County Grand Jury, Apr. 4, 1775, ibid., 129; Daniel Coxe to C. Skinner, July 4, 1775, ibid., 151-52; petition from Nottingham Township, Jan. 30, 1775, ibid., 116; Jonathan Elmer to residents of Cumberland County, Aug. 7, 1776, ibid., 225-27. Also, F. Smyth to Middlesex County Grand Jury, Apr., 1776, ibid., 186-90; and George E. McCracken, "Lieut. Colonel Joseph Barton, Loyalist of Sussex County, New Jersey," Proceedings of the New Jersey Historical Society, LXIX (Oct., 1951), 287-324.

2. For a general discussion of the period before and after 1776, see Gerlach, Prologue to Independence; Bernstein, "New Jersey in the American Revolution"; Leonard Lundin, Cockpit of the Revolution: The War for Independence in New Jersey (Princeton, NJ, 1940); Richard P. McCormick, Experiment in Independence: New Jersey in the Critical Period, 1781-1789 (New Brunswick, NJ, 1950); Carl E. Prince, New Jersey's Jeffersonian Republicans: The Genesis of an Early Party Machine, 1789-1817 (Chapel Hill, NC, 1967); Walter R. Fee, The Transition from Aristocracy to Democracy in New Jersey, 1789-1829 (Somerville, NJ, 1933); Peter D. Levine, The Behavior of State Legislative Parties in the Jacksonian Era: New Jersey, 1829-1844 (Rutherford, NJ, 1977); and Herbert Ershkowitz, The Origin of the Whig and Democratic Parties: New Jersey Politics, 1820-1837 (Washington, DC, 1982).

3. Wallace Brown, The King's Friends: The Composition and Motives of the American Loyalist Claimants (Providence, RI, 1965), 111-26; Gerlach, "Power to the People"; Richard P. McCormick, The History of Voting in New Jersey: A Study of the Development of Election Machinery, 1664-1911 (New Brunswick, NJ, 1953). Also useful in this discussion were John Shy, "The American Revolution: The Military Conflict Considered as a Revolutionary War," in Kurtz and Hutson, Essays on the American Revolution, 121-56; James Kirby Martin, Men in Rebellion: Higher Government Leaders and the Coming of the American Revolution (New Brunswick, NJ, 1973), 44, 113, and passim; Main, Political Parties Before the Constitution; idem, Sovereign States, 312, 323-24, 347.

4. Bernstein, "New Jersey in the American Revolution," 168.

5. William Livingston to the legislature, Sept. 11, 1776, The Papers of William Livingston, ed. Carl E. Prince (Trenton, NJ, 1979-), I, 143-45. Livingston to the legislature, Feb. 25, 1777, ibid., 254-59; Livingston, "The Impartial Chronicle," [Feb. 15, 1777], ibid., 226-39; and Dennis P. Ryan, "William Livingston," in Governors of New Jersey, 77-81.

6. Gordon S. Wood, The Creation of the American Republic, 1776-1787 (Chapel Hill, NC, 1969), 193; Bernstein, "New Jersey in the American Revolution," 230-31; McCormick, Experiment in Independence, 72, 75.

7. Ibid., 81; Bernstein, "New Jersey in the American Revolution," 205-6.

8. Main, Sovereign States, 323-24; Gerlach, "Power to the People," 42-48; Jackson Turner Main, The Upper House in Revolutionary America, 1763-1788 (Madison, WI, 1967), 143-49, 277-78; Toothman, "Trenton," 275-85; Ryan, "Six Towns," 194-301; McCormick, Experiment in Independence, 135-57.

9. Robert J. Dinkin, Voting in Revolutionary America: A Study of Elections in the Original Thirteen States, 1776-1789 (Westport, CT, 1982), 122-24; McCormick, History of Voting, 119-21; Prince, New Jersey's Jeffersonian Republicans, 76-78; Levine, Behavior of State Legislative Parties, 64-90. Also, Chilton Williamson, American Suffrage: From Property to Democracy, 1760-1860 (Princeton, NJ, 1960), 3-181; Richard P. McCormick, "New Perspectives on Jacksonian Politics," The American Historical Review, LXV (Jan., 1960), 288-301; Ronald P. Formisano, "Deferential-Participant Politics: The Early Republic's Political Culture, 1789-1840," The American Political Science Review, LXVIII (June, 1974), 473-87.

10. Quotations in McCormick, Experiment in Independence, 215; and "Cato," New-Jersey Gazette, Jan. 7, 1778, in Gerlach, ed., New Jersey in the American Revolution, 426-27. Any discussion of social and political thought of this period must begin with Wood, Creation of the American Republic. Also see James H. Hutson, "Country, Court, and Constitution: Antifederalism and the Historians," The William and Mary Quarterly, 3rd Ser., XXXVIII (July, 1981), 337-68; and Robert E. Shalhope, "Republicanism and Early American Historiography," ibid., XXXIX (April, 1982), 334-56. For social and economic thought, see Joyce Appleby, "Commercial Farming and the 'Agrarian Myth' in the Early Republic," The Journal of American History, LXVIII (Mar., 1982), 833-49; and idem, Capitalism and a New Social Order: The Republican Vision of the 1790s (New York, 1984). Appleby's argument cannot be ignored, but this essay followed the arguments presented by Lance Banning, The Jeffersonian Persuasion: Evolution of a Party Ideology (Ithaca, NY, 1978); Drew R. McCoy, The Elusive Republic: Political Economy in Jeffersonian America (Chapel Hill, NC, 1980); and Pocock, The Machiavellian Moment, 506-52. For republican ideas, see also Howard Mumford Jones, O Strange New World. American Culture: The Formative Years (New York, 1964), 227-72. Finally, this discussion remains indebted

241

to William Appleman Williams's classic, The Contours of American History (Cleveland, OH, 1961).

11. McCormick, Experiment in Independence, 111, 287. [John Rutherford], "Commercial Projects in New Jersey During the Confederation," Proceedings of the New Jersey Historical Society, 2nd Ser., I (1869), 177-82. Merrill Jensen, The New Nation: A History of the United States During the Confederation, 1781-1789 (New York, 1950), 338-39; and, for a general discussion, see Harry N. Scheiber, "Government and the Economy: Studies of the 'Commonwealth' Policy in Nineteenth-Century America," The Journal of Interdisciplinary History, III (Summer, 1972), 135-51.

12. McCormick, Experiment in Independence, 132; John W. Cadman, Jr., The Corporation in New Jersey: Business and Politics, 1791-1875 (Cambridge, MA, 1949), 33. Jensen, The New Nation, 222. Also see John C. Miller, Alexander Hamilton: Portrait in Paradox (New York, 1959), 300-310.

13. McCormick, Experiment in Independence, 118. Also, ibid., 195-96; Bernstein, "New Jersey in the American Revolution," 362-79; and Cadman, Corporation in New Jersey, passim.

14. Bernstein, "New Jersey in the American Revolution," 399. McCormick, Experiment in Independence, 133, 179-85; James Leiby, Charity and Correction in New Jersey: A History of State Welfare Institutions (New Brunswick, NJ, 1967), 16-32; Coleman, Debtors and Creditors, 134-40. Jordan, White Over Black, 345, 412.

15. New Jersey state constitution, in Gerlach, ed., New Jersey in the American Revolution, 213-16. Idem, "Power to the People," 31-35.

16. McCormick, Experiment in Independence, 194, 292; Fee, Transition from Aristocracy to Democracy, 83.

17. Quotations in McCormick, Experiment in Independence, 292; Fee, Transition from Aristocracy to Democracy, 42, 49, 89, 110, 111, 113, 129, 132, 134. Also see Marshall Smelser, "The Federalist Period as an Age of Passion," American Quarterly, X (Winter, 1958), 391-419; John R. Howe, Jr., "Republican Thought and the Political Violence of the 1790s," ibid., XIX (Summer, 1967), 147-65.

18. Gerlach, "Power to the People," 35-38. Also Levine, Behavior of State Legislative Parties, 76-79 and passim; Prince, New Jersey's Jeffersonian Republicans, 114-15, 149; Fee,

Transition from Aristocracy to Democracy, 210-61; Main, Political Parties, 156-73. Also see Norman K. Risjord, Chesapeake Politics, 1781-1800 (New York, 1978); James H. Broussard, "Party and Partisanship in American Legislatures: The South Atlantic States, 1800-1812," The Journal of Southern History, XLIII (Feb., 1977), 39-58; Coward, Kentucky in the Republic, 132-33; and Lee Benson, The Concept of Jacksonian Democracy: New York as a Test Case (Princeton, NJ, 1961).

19. Hunter Thompson, The Great Shark Hunt: Strange Tales from a Strange Time (New York, 1979), 184; Woodrow Wilson to the National Democratic Club, Apr. 13, 1908, The Papers of Woodrow Wilson, ed. Arthur S. Link (Princeton, NJ, 1966-), XVIII, 263-69; The Autobiography of Lincoln Stephens (New York, 1931), 495-96.

APPENDIX

BIOGRAPHICAL SKETCHES OF REPRESENTATIVES, 1738–1775

These sketches of representatives who sat in the New Jersey Assembly between 1738 and 1775 include family background, religious affiliation, residence, occupation and wealth, and other offices held. Two similar studies have recently appeared: in his Prologue to Independence (359-69), Larry R. Gerlach laid out in briefer form biographical data of assemblymen who sat in the legislature during the fifteen years before independence; and, when this research was nearly completed, Thomas L. Purvis presented an appendix to his dissertation, "The New Jersey Assembly, 1722-1776" (255-312), which gave special attention to each lawmaker's family tree. In contrast to these studies, this collection of biographical sketches has tried to include as full an accounting of wealth and occupations as the sources permitted. And, while it attends to family background, it has not included the detailed genealogical information found in Purvis's dissertation.

The construction of these biographical sketches benefited from but did not always agree with the conclusions drawn by Gerlach and Purvis. In light of the fragmentary, inconclusive, and even contradictory nature of the sources, the differences seem inevitable. The sources do not make for easy certainty about wealth, occupation, or even religion. Moreover, genealogical information is notoriously unreliable, and Purvis may have read those sources uncritically. As Gerlach concluded, "there will always be a paucity of material about the political elite in colonial New Jersey" (359-60). But the research of Gerlach and Purvis was incorporated into these sketches. Sometimes their conclusions corrected judgments; and, as often, they were laid aside. While this study is indebted to their research, it seemed best for the sake of concision that, in general, specific reference to their works need not be made in the following sketches.

A comment on the references to wills is in order. In general, the abstracts of wills in The New Jersey Archives proved an invaluable source, but comparison with the originals revealed that they were not always complete. In such cases, references were made to the originals in the State Library at Trenton.

247

ABBREVIATIONS

A.C. Biographical Directory of the American Congress, 1774-1971 (Washington, D. C., 1971)

Ang.Ch. Nelson R. Burr, The Anglican Church in New Jersey (Philadelphia, 1954)

Brgn. W. Woodford Clayton, ed., History of Bergen and Passaic Counties. . . (Philadelphia, 1882)

Brl. George De Cou, Burlington: A Provincial Capital (Burlington, 1945)

Brl.F. "List of the Freeholders for the City and County of Burlington," P.M.H.B., XXIX (1905), no. 4, 421-26.

Brl.S. R. Morris Smith, The Burlington Smiths (Philadelphia, 1877)

Brl.T.B. Henry H. Bisbee and Rebecca Bisbee Colesar, eds., The Burlington Town Book, 1694-1785 (Burlington, 1975)

C.F. George Norbury MacKenzie, Colonial Familes of the United States of America, 7 vols. (New York, 1907 -1920)

C.G. Lucius Q. C. Elmer, The Constitution and Government of the Province and State of New Jersey, N.J.H.S.C., VII(1872)

C.L.N.J. Edward Quinton Keasby, The Courts and Lawyers of New Jersey, 1661-1912, 3 vols. (New York, 1912)

Cp.My. Lewis Townsend Stevens, The History of Cape May County. . . (Cape May City, 1897)

Cp.My.M.H.G. Cape May Magazine of History and Genealogy

Dem.   Mary Arthur and William H. S. Demarest,
                        The Demarest Family (New Brunswick,
                        1938)

Ec.R.N.Y.   Edward T. Corwin, ed., Ecclesiastical
                        Records.   State of New York,   7
                        vols.(Albany, 1901-1916)

E.J.P.   The Minutes of the General Board
                        Proprietors of the Eastern Dvision,   3
                        vols.   (Perth Amboy, 1949-1960)

Er.G.   Theodore Frelinghuysen Chambers, The
                        Early Germans of New Jersey.   Their
                        History, Churches and Genealogies
                        (Dover, 1895)

Fen.C.   Thomas Shourds, History and Genealogy
                        of Fenwick's Colony (Bridgeton, NJ,
                        (1876)

F.H.A.B.   Friends Historical Society Bulletin

Frgs.   Charles S. Boyer, Early Forges &
                        Furnaces of New Jersey (Philadelphia,
                        1931)

F.W.T.   James H. Levitt,   For Want of Trade:
                        Shipping and the New Jersey Ports,
                        1680-1783 (Newark, 1981)

Glcstr.   Thomas Cushing, History of the Counties
                        of Gloucester, Salem, and Cumberland
                        (Philadelphia, 1883)

G.M.N.J.   Genealogical Magazine of New Jersey

G.P.   Larry R. Gerlach,   Prologue to Inde-
                        endence: New Jersey in the Coming of
                        the American Revolution (New Brunswick,
                        1976)

Hntrdn.M.   George S. Mott,   "The First Century of
                        Hunterdon County, State of New Jersey,"
                        N.J.H.S.P. 2nd ser., V (1877-1879),59-
                        111

Hntrdn.S.   James P. Snell,   History Hunterdon and
                        Somerset Counties (Philadelphia, 1881)

L.C.	Leonard Lundin, Cockpit of the Revolution: The War for Independence in New Jersey (Princeton, 1940)
L.D.S.	The Church of the Latter Day Saints, Genealogical Files, Salt Lake City
L.Gen.	Francis Bazley Lee, Genealogical and Memorial History of the State of New Jersey, 4 vols. (New York, 1910)
Mddlsx.C.	George J. Miller, Ye Olde Middlesex Courts. . . (n.P., 1932)
M.J.	The Journals of Henry Melchior Muhlenberg, trans. Theodore G. Tappert and John W. Doberstein, 3 vols. (Philadelphia, 1942-1958)
Mnmth.	Franklin Ellis, History of Monmouth County (Philadelphia, 1885)
Mnmth.F.	Charles Carroll Gardner, "Eighteenth Century Freeholders in New Jersey, Monmouth County (1748-1755)," G.M.N.J., XVI (Oct., 1941), 83-89, XVII (Jan., 1942), 13-18, (April, 1942), 38-44, (July,1942), 65-69
Mrrs.M.	Manuscript Collections, Morristown Historical Park, 69 reels
Mrrs.T.	Theodore Thayer, Colonial and Revolutionary Morris County (np, 1975)
N.B.G.	William Nelson, New Jersey Biographical and Genealogical Notes. . .N.J.H.S.C., IX (1916)
N.E.H.G.R.	The New England Historical and Genealogical Register
N.J.Archs.	William A. Whitehead, et al., eds., Archives of the State of New Jersey . . .(Newark, 1880-)
N.J.H.S.C.	New Jersey Historical Society Collections

N.J.H.S.P.	New Jersey Historical Society Proceedings
N.J.M.W.	New Jersey Manuscript Wills, State Library, Trenton
Nwt.T	John Clement, Sketches of the First Emigrant Settlers in Newton Township . . .(Camden, 1877)
N.Y.W.	Abstracts of Wills. Collections of the New-York Historical Society, XXX-XXXIII (1897-1900)
Ogdn.	William Ogden Wheeler, The Ogden Family in America (Philadelphia, 1907)
O.H.	Mary Mercy Hawley, Our Heritage (Bishop, CA, 1936)
P.M.H.B.	Pennsylvania Magazine of History and Biography
P.P.	Carl Raymond Woodward, Ploughs and Politicks: Charles Read of New Jersey and His Notes on Agriculture, 1715-1774 (New Brunswick, 1941)
Prth.Amby.	William A. Whitehead, Contributions to the Early History of Perth Amboy . . .(New York, 1856)
Ptsn.	William Nelson and Charles A. Shriner, History of Paterson. . .3 vols. (New York and Chicago, 1920)
R.U.L.	Rutgers University Library
S.C.	Stewart Collection, Glassboro State College
S.G.	Richard Haines, Genealogy of the Stokes Family. . .(Camden, NJ, 1903)
S.H.G.	John E. Stillwell, Historical and Genealogical Miscellany. . .3 vols. (New York, 1903)
S.L.	Lorenzo Sabine, Biographical Sketches

	of Loyalists of the American Revolution, 2 vols. (Boston, 1864)
Slm.C.L.	Robert G. Johnson, "List of Judges, Clerks, Sheriffs, Surrogates, & Attornies of Salem County," N.J.H.S.P., IV (1849), 37-52
Smrst.C.H.Q.	Somerset County Historical Quarterly
Trnt.G.	Genealogy of Early Settlers in Trenton and Ewing. . .(Trenton, 1883)
Trnt.T.	Stephanie Smith Toothman, "Trenton, New Jersey, 1719-1779: A Study of Community Growth and Organization" (Ph.D. diss., University of Pennsylvania, 1977
Wdbrg.	Joseph W. Dally, Woodbridge and Vicinity. . .(New Brunswick, 1873)
Wdbrg.T.B.	Woodbridge Town Book, Satterwaite Collections, Glassboro State College

ANDERSON, John (1704-1793)

Monmouth County: 1763-1768

Father (1665-1736), a Scots immigrant, first settled at New York in 1699 but shortly thereafter bought land in Freehold Township. A justice of the Monmouth County Court, he was appointed to the Council in 1712. Although suspended, he returned and became president of the Council. His estate included slaves, a 300-acre tract, and was evaluated at Ƚ332.

John, a Presbyterian, resided at Lower Freehold. He was deputy surveyor for the East Jersey proprietors, a landowner, and an innkeeper. At one time, he owned a 444-acre tract at Mount Brook which he traded with his brother for a 500-acre tract. Financial difficulties in the late 1760s forced him to sell a 600-acre estate with house, barn, orchards, and 300 acres of cleared meadows. He was appointed justice of the peace and a judge of the county court.

Charles Carroll Gardner, "Monmouth County Andersons," G.M.N.J., XXIII (Jan., 1948), 5-10; William M. Mervine, "John Anderson, Sometime President of His Majesty's Council of New Jersey, and His Descendants," N.J.H.S.P., 3rd ser., VII (1913), 137-46; N.J.Archs., XXVI, 351.

ANTILL, Edward (1701-1770)

Middlesex County: 1738-1739

Edward, the father (1659-1705), migrated from England to New York where he became a merchant and traded with Jamaica and Newfoundland. In addition, he purchased lands in New Jersey and a share of the East Jersey proprietary. He served for a time on Jacob Leisler's council.

Edward, the Assemblyman, was an Anglican. Born in New York, he inherited extensive holdings in New Jersey and took up residence at Raritan Landing and later at New Brunswick. He was a merchant, brewer, land speculator, and lawyer. He lived in a large brick home on a 370-acre farm with orchards. He also was a slaveowner. He left Ł1,000 to his heirs. After serving as justice of the peace and judge of the county court, he was elevated to the Council.

William Nelson, "Edward Antill and some of his Descendants," N.J.H.S.P., 3rd ser., II (1897), 25-55; N.J.Archs., XXVIII, 311-12; N.J.M.W., 4670 L.

BARTON, Joseph (1730-1788)

Sussex County: 1775

Barton was born in New York. A Presbyterian and resident at Newton, Barton owned a share of the East Jersey proprietary. His considerable holdings included twenty-two tracts ranging in size from half an acre to 1,100 acres. In addition, he purchased two gristmills, a sawmill, a potash manufacturing establishment, and a store. In 1766, he purchased his home on an 822-acre tract. A loyalist, he submitted claims for Ł8,522.

George E. McCracken, "Lieut. Colonel Joseph Barton, Loyalist of Sussex County, New Jersey," N.J.H.S.P., LXIX (Oct., 1951), 287-324.

BERRIEN, John (1711-1772)

Somerset County: 1769-1771

Peter, the father (1672-1737), lived in New York, was a wealthy landowner, and married the daughter of an East Jersey councilor.

John, born on Long Island, came to New Jersey in 1717. A Presbyterian and resident at Rocky Hill on a 320-acre estate, he was a merchant, lawyer, surveyor, and trustee of the College of New Jersey. His offices included judge of the county court and the Supreme Court.

C.L.N.J., I, 303-305; "Some Noted Jerseymen of Other States," N.J.H.S.P., V (April, 1920), 107; Elizabeth G. C. Menzies, Millstone Valley (New Brunswick, 1969), 127-28; James Riker, The Annals of Newtown. . .(New York, 1852), 341-44.

BISPHAM, Joshua (1706-1795)

Burlington County: 1749-1751

Joseph, a Quaker, left England in 1737, first resided at Philadelphia and in 1744 purchased land at Moorestown. He worked a 480-acre estate with two slaves. He also owned several other pieces of land. Other public offices were town clerk, township assessor, and county board of freeholders.

William Bispham, Memoranda Concerning the Family of Bispham (New York, 1890); N.J.M.W., 11583 C.

BONNELL, Joseph (1675-1748)

Essex County: 1716-1719, 1722-1725, 1727-1729, 1738-1739, 1743-1744

The father, Nathaniel (1650-1696), was born in New Haven, Connecticut, and was one of the first to move to New Jersey. He sat on the East Jersey Assembly.

Joseph, a Presbyterian, lived at Elizabethtown. He was a wealthy landowner, active in defense of the town's claims against the proprietors, and instrumental in securing the town charter. His estate was valued at Ƅ803 and included a weaver's loom. He was mayor, a loan officer, and a judge of the Supreme Court.

N.J.M.W., 1499-1506 G; Edgar M. Gibby, The Genealogy of the Bonnell Family (pamphlet in the New Jersey Historical Society); Edwin F. Hatfield, History of Elizabeth. . .(New York, 1868), 4.

BORDEN, Joseph (1719-1791)

Burlington County: 1761-1768

Joseph, the father (1687-1765), founded Bordentown, was a store owner, and operated a stage line.

Joseph, the Assemblyman, was an Anglican. He also was a merchant and continued to operate the family's stage line between Philadelphia and New York via Bordentown--at one time with Assemblyman Pontius Steele. He left an estate of lands, silver, china, and three slaves. His estate was valued at ₤6,641. He held several offices: justice of the peace, judge of the county court, delegate to the Stamp Act Congress, and representative to the provincial congress.

N.B.G., 45-48; N.J.M.W., 11364 C; N.J.Archs., XXIV, 654.

BRADBURY, Richard (c.1690-c.1770)

Essex County: 1754-1759

The father, John, came from England and owned a mill on Third River.

Richard, an Anglican, resided in Acquackanonk Township. He died intestate. He also served as a justice of the peace.

N.J.Archs., XVI, 90; XIX, 390; Ang.Ch., 538.

BRICK, John (?-1753)

Salem County: 1742, 1745, 1746-1748, 1749-1751

Father, John, came from England before 1680, bought a large tract at Gravelly Run, and sat in the Assembly.

John, a Quaker, resided at Cohansie. At Gravelly Run, he owned 1,000 acres and built a mill. He also owned several substantial tracts including one at Alloways Creek. He owned six slaves. Offices included justice of the peace and judge of the county court.

N.J.Archs., XXXII, 40-41; William Wade Hinshaw, Encyclopedia of American Quaker Genealogy, 6 vols. (Ann Arbor, MI, 1936-1948), II, 23; L.Gen., III, 328; Fen.C., 42-43, 153; Glcstr., 530.

BULLOCK, Joseph (1723-1792)

Burlington County: 1769-1771

Bullock's father migrated from England to Burlington County around 1700 and became a farmer.

Joseph, a Quaker, lived at New Hanover. A landowner, his estate included farms of 390, 360, and 300 acres and a 400-acre tract in Middlesex County. His estate was valued at ₤2,446.

N.J.M.W., 11430 C; E. M. Woodward and John F. Hageman, History of Burlington and Mercer Counties (Philadelphia, 1883), 276-77.

CAMP, Joseph (1710-1780)

Essex County: 1749-1751

Samuel, the father (1669-1744), was a small farmer at Newark.

Joseph, a Presbyterian, resided at Newark. He bought lands in Clinton Township and built a sawmill. He was active in town affairs in opposition to the proprietors.

William H. Shaw, History of Essex and Hudson Counties, 2 vols. (Philadelphia, 1884), II, 692-93; L.D.S.; N.J.Archs., VII, 405.

CLEMENT, Samuel, Sr. (1710-1765)

Gloucester County: 1754-1760, 1761-1765

Father, Jacob, was born in Haddonfield in 1678 and became sheriff of Gloucester County.

Samuel, a Quaker, resided at Newton Township. He held several tracts of land--one of 350 acres--a share in the West Jersey proprietary, a sawmill, and three slaves. He also sat on the county court.

N.J.M.W., 872 H; L.Gen., I, 292; Nwt.T., 274; Glcstr., 137; N.J.Archs., XVI, 556.

CLEMENT, Samuel, Jr. (1737-1784)

Gloucester County: 1766-1768

The son of Samuel Clement, Sr., and a Quaker, Clement resided at Newton Township. He was a surveyor and West Jersey proprietor and thus owned several tracts of land. His estate was valued at Ł1,748. He also served on the board of freeholders and as county collector.

N.J.Archs., XXXV, 83; L.Gen., I, 292; Glcstr., 122.

COMBS, John (1727-1803)

Perth Amboy: 1772-1775

John Combs's father, Robert (?-1730), migrated from Long Island. John was an Anglican and landowner. He served as a justice of the peace and later became a loyalist.

G.P., 363; Thomas L. Purvis, "The New Jersey Assembly, 1722-1776" (Ph.D. diss., The Johns Hopkins University, 1979), 256.

COOKE, William (c.1680-1760)

Burlington County: 1738-1739, 1740-1742, 1743-1744, 1744, 1745, 1746-1748, 1749-1751, 1751-1754

Father, Thomas, came from Long Island and settled at Shrewsbury in 1676. He served on the East Jersey Assembly.

William, a Quaker born in Monmouth County, resided in Chesterfield Township. A merchant and a large landowner, at his death he owned 5,000 acres, bonds worth Ł827, and a slave which he freed. The estate was valued at Ł3,772. He also sat on the county court.

O.H., 7-8; N.J.M.W., 6615; N.J.Archs., XV, 97.

COOPER, David (1725-1790?)

Gloucester County: 1761-1768

Son of David and second cousin of Joseph, the Assemblyman, Cooper was a Quaker and resident at Woodbury. A slaveowner, he owned several tracts of land at Woodbury, Deptford Township, and elsewhere. Bonds and notes due to him at death came to Ł1,489. His estate was valued at Ł1,693. He was a county collector and justice of the peace.

N.J.Archs., XVI, 556; N.J.M.W., 1931 H; Benjamin B. Cooper Papers, R.U.L., I; Glcstr., 189.

COOPER, Joseph (1691-1749)

Gloucester County: 1730-1733, 1738-1739, 1740-1742, 1743-1744, 1744, 1745, 1746-1748, 1749

Father, Joseph (?-1731), settled at Cooper's Creek and at his death owned several tracts of land. His estate was valued at Ł861. In the same year that he was elected to the Assembly, he was elevated to the Council.

Joseph, a Quaker, was born and resided at Newton Township. His father conveyed to him nearly 1,000 acres. A West Jersey proprietor, he listed in his will a 600-acre tract at Cooper's Creek and two other tracts of 600 and 430 acres. His estate was valued at Ł1,351. In addition to serving as an elder in the Haddonfield Meeting, he served as county collector, member of the board of freeholders, overseer of the poor, and a judge of the county court.

Charles S. Boyer, Pomona Hall, The Home of Joseph Cooper, Jr., ([Camden, 1935]), 1-10; N.J.Archs., XXX, 109; Nwt.T., 92-93; Glcstr., 137.

CRANE, John (1695-1776)

Essex County: 1744, 1745, 1746-1748, 1749-1751

Crane's family had come from Connecticut in the 1660s. His father, Azariah (1649-1730), was active in Newark politics and owned several tracts of land.

John, a Presbyterian, resided at Newark. He owned several tracts of land. He was also a justice of the peace.

Ellery B. Crane, Genealogy of the Crane Family, 2 vols. (Worcester, MA, 1895-1900), II, 308-309; N.J.Archs., XV, 100; Jonathan Crane, "The Crane Family," N.E.H.G.R., XXVII (Jan., 1873), 76-78; L.Gen., I, 33-34.

CRANE, Stephen (1709-1780)

Essex County: 1766-1768, 1769-1771, 1772-1775

The son of Daniel (1670-1724) and descendant of Connecticut immigrants of the 1660s, Stephen Crane was a Presbyterian. He resided at his birthplace in Elizabethtown. A lawyer and landowner, he represented the town in its disputes with the proprietors. He was a justice of the peace, a judge on the county court, a sheriff, and a leader on the town's committees during the political crises of the 1770s. He also served on the Continental Congress and the state Council.

A.C., 449-50; L.Gen., I, 20.

DEACON, John (1702-1760)

Burlington Town: 1751-1754

Father, George, came from England to Salem County in 1677 and later moved to Burlington. Active in Burlington politics, he also served in the Assembly and was president of the West Jersey Board of Proprietors.

John, born in Salem, left an estate valued at ₤306.

N.J.Archs., XXXII, 89; L.Gen., I, 339-40; Thomas P. Hughes et al., American Ancestry, 12 vols. (Albany, 1887-1899), X, 147.

DE HART, Jacob (1700-1777)

Essex County: 1754-1756

Son of Matthias, Jacob was active in Elizabethtown's Anglican community. A merchant engaged in trade with Europe and the Indies, he also listed several tracts of land in his will.

Ang.Ch., 524; N.J.Archs., XIX, 388, 390, XXXIV, 136-37.

DEMAREST, David (1676-1759)

Bergen County: 1738-1739, 1740-1742, 1743-1744, 1744, 1745, 1746-1748

Father, David (1651-1691), was a French Huguenot who resided in New York.

David was born in New York but moved to the Hackensack region in the late 1690s where he became an active member of the Dutch Reform community. He was a substantial landowner with tracts in both Bergen and Essex counties. He was on the board of freeholders and served as justice of the peace, judge on the county court, and sheriff.

Dem., 15, 24-25; N.J.Archs., XXXII, 91; M.J., 341, 406.

DEMAREST, John (1730-1783)

Bergen County: 1769-1771, 1772-1775

The son of Peter (1683-1763), John resided at Old Bridge and attended the Dutch Reform church. He was a landowner. He served as coroner, judge of the county court, and a delegate to the provincial congress. He became a loyalist.

N.J.Archs., XXXV, 118; Dem., 15, 23, 40-41; Brgn., 82

DEY, Derrick (1687-1764)

Bergen County: 1749-1751, 1751-1754

Son of Theunis Dey, Derrick was born in New York and moved to New Jersey in 1708, took up residence in the Preakness area, and attended the Dutch Reform church. In 1717, he purchased 600 acres and lived in a log cabin until 1740 when he constructed a twelve-room brick house. His land holdings were extensive in both East and West Jersey and in New York. A merchant, he moved to New York in the 1750s. In his will, he gave Ł1,000 and New York lots to his two daughters and the rest to his son Theunis. While in New Jersey, he served on the board of freeholders.

"Concerning the Dey Mansion at Preakness," N.J.H.S.P., n.s., VI (Oct., 1921), 251-54; N.Y.W., XXX (1897), 321-22.

DEY, Theunis (1726-1787)

Bergen County: 1761-1768, 1769-1771, 1772-1775

Son of Derrick, Theunis lived at Preakness, was an active member of the Dutch Reform community, and served on the board of trustees of Queens College. He was a substantial landowner and merchant. He also owned slaves. His estate was valued at £1,663. He served on the board of freeholders and was active in community affairs during the revolution crisis.

N.J.M.W., 1873 B; Brgn., 82; Lottye Van Ness, The Van Ness Heritage (Elizabethtown, 1960), 36-40.

DOUGHTY, Daniel (1703-1778)

Hunterdon County: 1743-1744, 1744, 1745; Burlington County: 1761-1768

Father, Jacob, was born in New York (1672), moved to Burlington in 1713, later resided in Hunterdon County, and was elected to the Assembly.

Daniel, a Quaker, owned numerous tracts of land, including 1,212 acres in Hunterdon County and several pieces in Burlington County. In 1750, he purchased Charles Read's 350-acre estate for £1,350 and a share of the East Jersey proprietary. In his will, he gave £600 to his grandchild and £50 per annum to his daughter. He also served on the Hunterdon County court.

Ethan Allen Doty, "The Doughty Family of Long Island," New York Genealogical and Biographical Record, XLIII (July-Oct., 1912), 282-84, 313-14; P.P., 70-75; N.J.Archs., XXXIV, 149; Hntrdn.S., 430.

DUMONT, Peter (1679-1744)

Somerset County: 1738-1739

Father, Wallerand (?-1713), was a French Huguenot who came to New York in 1657 and became active in the Dutch Reform community.

Peter was born in New York, and the family moved to New Jersey in 1699. He purchased a 2,000-acre tract near Raritan Landing from the proprietors and took up residence there. He was an elder in the Dutch Reform church. His will lists several unspecified tracts of land.

John B. Dumont, "Wallerand Dumont and his Somerset County Descendants," Smrst.C.H.Q., I (April, 1912), 106-112; N.J.Archs., XXX, 153.

DUNHAM, Azariah (1718-1790)

Middlesex County: 1775

Father, Jonathan (1693-1777), was a minister of the Seventh Day Baptist church.

Azariah, a Baptist, was born in the Piscataway area and moved to New Brunswick in 1760. His land holdings were extensive. In addition, he was a surveyor for the East Jersey proprietors and a merchant. In his will, he lists seven slaves and a long list of bonds. He gave Ŀ780 to one daughter and Ŀ,161 to another. His estate was valued at Ŀ1,262. In addition to serving as mayor of New Brunswick, he sat on the provincial congress and was appointed colonel of the Middlesex regiment and commissary general.

N.J.M.W., 7527-7558 L; Issac Watson Dunham, Dunham Genealogy (np, [1907]), 254-55; E.J.P., III, 211, 360.

EATON, John (1689-1750)

Monmouth County: 1727-1729, 1730-1733, 1738-1739, 1740-1742, 1743-1744, 1744, 1745, 1746-1748, 1749-1750

Eaton's father came from New England in the 1670s and built a gristmill at what became Eatonville.

John, a Presbyterian, sold his father's mill and moved to Shrewsbury. He also owned lands in Hunterdon County. In his will, he designated that his lands and Ŀ600 be given to his son.

N.J.Archs., VI, 202, XXX, 160; N.B.G., 99-100; Mnmth.F., 40.

ELDRIDGE, Eli (1739-1791)

Cape May County: 1772-1775

Born in Cape May, Eldridge resided in the Middle Precinct. A Baptist farmer, he owned 150 improved and 100 unimproved acres in Cape May County. In addition, he owned two slaves, and his estate was valued at Ł225. He served as sheriff.

N.J.Archs., XXXVII, 121; "Cape May Landowners in Revolutionary Times," Cp.My.M.H.G., I (June, 1934), 157.

ELLIS, Joseph (1700-1757?)

Gloucester County: 1751-1754

Father, Simon (?-1715), lived at Springwell on a 300-acre farm. He also owned two tracts of 200 and 400 acres each at Cooper's Creek and numerous other holdings. His estate was valued at Ł253.

Joseph, a Quaker, also lived at Springwell and died intestate at Newton. His estate inventory included two slaves and Ł628 in bonds and was valued at Ł1,275. He also was a justice of the peace.

N.J.Archs., XII, 672, XVI, 556, XXII, 104, XXIII, 151; Nwt.T., 182-83, 190.

ELMER, Theophilus (1727-1783)

Cumberland County: 1772-1775

A Presbyterian farmer, Elmer resided at Fairfield. His will listed several unspecified tracts of land. He served as coroner, justice of the peace, member of the board of freeholders, sheriff, and a delegate to the provincial congress.

G.P., 368; N.J.Archs., XXXV, 132-33; C.G., 340-41.

EMLEY, John (1691-c.1761)

Hunterdon County: 1738-1739, 1746-1748, 1749-1751, 1751-1754

Father, William (1648-1704), came from England and served on the West Jersey Assembly in the 1680s.

263

John, a Quaker, lived at Bethlehem, speculated in lands, and became a business associate of the East Jersey proprietors and Burlington's Richard Smith. His holdings were numerous and included 300 acres valued at Ŀ1,000, 574 at Ŀ2,009, 141 at Ŀ600, 133 at Ŀ600, and other tracts throughout northern New Jersey. His estate was valued at Ŀ1,466.

Emley Papers, Hunterdon County Historical Society, Box I; O.H., 20, 33; Hntrdn.S., 192-93, 424; N.J.Archs., XXXIII, 132.

FARMER, Thomas (1673-1751)

Middlesex County: 1707-1708, 1709, 1710-1714, 1740-1742, 1743-1744, 1745

Father, Jasper (?-1685), came to Philadelphia two years before his death.

Thomas left Philadelphia in 1703, eventually settled in New York, but later moved to Perth Amboy and then to New Brunswick. He was an Anglican. He spent his life intermittently in both New York and New Jersey. A landowner and intimate of Lewis Morris and the proprietors, he was recognized as "of the best estate in the Province." After election to the Assembly, he removed to New York and, on returning to New Jersey, was appointed to the Council in 1735. Later, he was elected to the lower house. Evidence suggests that he died insane. He also served on the county court of Middlesex County and was mayor of New Brunswick.

William H. Benedict, "Thomas Farmer, First Mayor of New Brunswick, N. J.," N.J.H.S.P., n.s., XIII (Jan., 1928), 45-51; C.L.N.J., I, 276; Prth.Amby., 92-93; Ang.Ch., 492-93; Mddlsx.C., 61; Richard S. Field, The Provincial Courts of New Jersey. . .N.J.H.S.C., III, 126-27.

FISHER, Hendrick (1697-1779)

Somerset County: 1745, 1746-1748, 1749-1751, 1751-1754, 1754-1760, 1761-1768, 1769-1771, 1772-1775

Born in Germany, Fisher came with his father in 1703 and settled at Bound Brook. In 1721, he joined the Dutch Reform church at New Brunswick. A self-styled "mechanic," he owned numerous tracts of land and six slaves. In his will, he gave Ŀ1,065 and lands to his heirs, and his estate was valued at Ŀ4,759. His public life was always busy: he became deacon, elder, and lay preacher in the church and frequently attended church conventions. In addition, he was instrumental in getting a charter for Queens College and, for his services, was named to the board of trustees. Elected to the Assembly in 1740 but disqualified for failure to apply for naturalization, he took his seat in 1745. Later, he was recognized as one of the house's most prominent members. In addition, he served on the county court and as barracks master. During the crisis leading to independence, he was named a delegate to the Stamp Act Congress, sat on committees of correspondence, and was elected to the provincial congress.

A. Van Doren Honeyman, "Hendrick Fisher--The Real German-American," Smrst.C.H.Q., VIII (Jan., 1919), 1-17; N.J.M.W., 608 R; Er.G., 360-62; N.J.Archs., XXVIII, 147-49; Ec.R.N.Y., III, 2211, 2305.

FORD, Jacob (1704-1777)

Morris County: 1772-1775

Father, John, came from Massachusetts and settled at Woodbridge.

A Presbyterian, Jacob was born at Woodbridge but moved to Morris County. First an innkeeper at New Hanover, he extended his interests widely. His landholdings were extensive and included one tract of 2,000 acres. In addition, he invested in several ironworks. But he identified himself as a "merchant." He held the mortgages of many local farmers. In his will, he divided his lands among his heirs and gave L1,000 to his wife. His public career also was active. An elder in the church, he rose rapidly in local politics. Morris County's court first met at his tavern, and later he became a justice of the peace and judge of that court.

N.J.Archs., XV, 91, XVII, 504; L.Gen., IV, 1562-63; Mrrs.T., 28, 57, 90-98, 128; Frgs., 140, 257; Joseph F. Tuttle, "The Early History of Morris County, New Jersey," N.J.H.S.P., 2nd ser., II (1870-1872), 36; N.B.G., 112-13.

GARRITSE, Henry (1721-1805)

Essex County: 1772-1775

Little can be determined about Henry Garritse except that his family came from Holland, that he was a member of the Dutch

Reform church, and that he resided at Acquackanonk. He seems to have been a farmer. He sat in the provincial congress.

G.P., 363.

GIBBON, Grant (1734-1776)

Salem County: 1771, 1772-1775

Father, Nicholas, came from England and settled at Greenwich in the 1720s. He built a gristmill and became a wealthy landowner. He was a sheriff and judge of the county court.

Grant, an Anglican, resided at Greenwich. He became a merchant and lawyer. His public offices included justice of the peace, township collector, township clerk, justice of the county court, and delegate to the provincial congress.

N.J.Archs., XX, 154; Slm.C.L., 45; Mrs. Harry Rodgers, "Abstracts of New Jersey Commissions," Pennsylvania Genealogical Magazine, X (March, 1927), 138; Ang.Ch., 574-75.

GIBBON, Leonard (1705-1744)

Salem County: 1743-1744

Leonard Gibbon, an Anglican, left England with his brother Nicholas and settled at Salem County. The two brothers built a mill at Newport Creek on a 700-acre tract and another near Cohansey. When they divided their lands, Leonard received 2,000 acres. He built a large stone house near Greenwich where he pursued the life of a "gentleman." The inventory of his estate included cattle, wheat, and a slave and was valued at L-585. He sat on the county court.

Ang.Ch., 574-75; N.J.Archs., XXX, 195; Glcstr., 504, 682, 684; Slm.C.L., 42.

HANCOCK, William (1693-1763)

Salem County: 1730-1733, 1738-1739, 1740-1742, 1743-1744, 1744, 1745, 1746-1748, 1749-1751, 1751-1754, 1754-1760, 1761-1763

Father, John, owned a large estate at Alloways Creek.

William, a Quaker, lived at Lower Penn's Neck. He owned several tracts of land there, at Alloways Creek, Elsinboro, and elsewhere. Public service included justice of the peace, judge of the county court, and loan officer.

N.J.Archs., XIX, 392, XXXIII, 174; Slm.C.L., 43-45.

HAND, Jonathan (1731-1790)

Cape May County: 1771, 1772-1775

Little information can be found regarding this Baptist lawmaker. The family came from Connecticut. Jonathan was born in Cape May and became a resident of the Middle Precinct. In that precinct, he owned 232 acres, twenty-eight cattle, fourteen sheep, and a gristmill. His estate was valued at ₤580.

S.C.; N.J.Archs., XXXVI, 99; Ralph D. Smyth, "Joseph Hand of East Guilford (Now Madison), Conn., and his Descendants," N.E.H.G.R., LV, 31; "Notes," ibid., 222.

HART, John (1714-1779)

Hunterdon County: 1761-1768, 1769-1771

Father, Edward, came from Connecticut by way of Newton, Long Island, to West Jersey.

John lived at Hopewell and was a Baptist. He owned several pieces of land, including 79-, 100-, and 193-acre tracts. In addition, he owned mills at Glen Moore and Rocky Hill and several slaves. His public offices included justice of the peace and judge of the county court. During the imperial crisis, he served on committees of correspondence, the provincial congress, and the Continental Congress. After independence, he served in the state legislature.

Allen Johnson and Dumas Malone, eds., Dictionary of American Biography (New York, 1931), VIII, 359; A.C., 1080; N.J.Archs., XXXIV, 233; Louis H. Patterson, "John Hart, The New Jersey Signer," N.J.H.S.P., n.s., X (Oct., 1925), 375-82.

HARTSHORNE, Robert (1721-1801)

Monmouth County: 1769-1771

Father, William (1679-1748), was a justice of the peace and left an estate valued at L386.

Robert, a Quaker, lived at Middletown and Shrewsbury. He was a merchant, wealthy landowner, and a West Jersey proprietor. He became a loyalist.

Arthur Layton Funk, "Richard Hartshorne of Middletown, New Jersey (1641-1722)," N.J.H.S.P., LXVII (April, 1949), 126-40; "Some Early New Jersey Patentees Paying Quit-Rents," ibid., n.s., XV (July, 1930), 385; Mnmth.F., 15; S.H.G., III, 283-89.

HEARD, John (1681-c.1756)

Middlesex County: 1745, 1746-1748

Although a prominent fixture in Middlesex County society, little of substance can be found on John Heard. His family came from New England, and he was born in the County. A Presbyterian and resident of Woodbridge, he owned a gristmill, engaged in trade, and sold liquor. A large landowner, he owned fourteen slaves. His estate was valued at Ł1,089. He served as overseer of the poor, constable, and judge of the county court.

N.J.M.W., 2997-3002 L; F.W.T., 209; Mddlsx.C., 61, 64, 65.

HEWLINGS, Abraham (c.1723-1795)

Burlington Town: 1769-1771

Son of Joseph, Abraham was active in Burlington's Anglican community. He was a wealthy landowner, a West Jersey proprietor, and a merchant. His estate was valued at Ł4,906 .

P.P., 246; Ang.Ch., 498; N.J.Archs., XXXVII, 175-76.

HEWLINGS, Thomas (c.1748-c.1793)

Burlington Town: 1772-1775

Son of Abraham, Thomas was an active Anglican. He

inherited his father's interest in the West Jersey proprietary. His estate was valued at Ь44.

Brl.T.B., 41-42; G.P., 366; N.J.Archs., XXXVII, 177.

HINCHMAN, James (1711-1750)

Gloucester County: 1749-1750

Father, John (?-1721), dealt in real estate and became a wealthy landowner. On his death, he owned three farms and four slaves.

James, a Quaker, lived in Newton Township. He styled himself a "gentleman." In his will, he mentioned only one farm. His slaves were valued at Ь285 and his estate at Ь2,121. He served on the county court.

Nwt.T., 241-44; S.G., 279-80; N.J.Archs., XXIII, 230; N.J.M.W., 458 H.

HINCHMAN, John (1715-1789)

Gloucester County: 1769-1771, 1772-1775

John Hinchman, a Quaker and a resident of the town of Gloucester, owned a share of the West Jersey proprietary, mines, and slaves. His estate was valued at Ь518. He served as township clerk, justice of the peace, sheriff, judge of the county court, and a member of the board of freemen. He became a loyalist.

G.P., 368; N.J.Archs., XXXVII, 112.

HOAGLAND, John (c.1701-c.1766)

Somerset County: 1754-1760, 1761-1766

Father, Hendrick (1679-1746), lived in Long Island and moved to New Jersey in 1719.

John, born in New York, lived at Millstone. He was active in the Dutch Reform church. He farmed a tract of 200 acres and owned several other tracts, including one of 200 acres in Hunterdon County. In addition, he listed six slaves in his will.

269

L.Gen., III, 1268; N.J.Archs., XIX, 391, XXXIII, 201; Hntrdn.M., 73; N.J.M.W., 116-19.

HOLME, Benjamin (1730-1792)

Salem County: 1772-1775

Holme, a Baptist, lived at Elsinboro. This wealthy landowner left an estate valued at Ь1,549. Socially well connected, he won appointments as justice of the peace and judge of the county court. He was sent to the provincial congress.

N.J.Archs., XX, 625-26, XXXVII, 181; Fen.C., 90-91.

HOLMES, James (1702-1762)

Monmouth County: 1751, 1751-1754, 1754-1760, 1761-1762

Holmes, a Baptist and a New York merchant, had taken up residence at Upper Freehold. In 1758, he owned 700 acres in that district, and his will indicated that he owned additional lands at Perth Amboy. His estate was valued at Ь5,890.

N.J.Archs., XIX, 390, XXXIII, 199; Mnmth., 615; G.P., 365.

HOPKINS, Ebenezer (1718-1757)

Gloucester County: 1745, 1746-1748

A Quaker, Hopkins was born in London. He inherited property in New Jersey and arrived there in 1723. A resident of Newton Township, he pursued several occupations: watchmaker, carpenter, and leatherworker. In addition, he was an agent of London's Pennsylvania Land Company. His estate was valued at Ь945. He was active in the meetinghouse and served as county collector.

Hopkins Family File, Gloucester County Historical Society; Rebecca Nicholson Taylor, "Ebenezer Hopkins, 1718-1757," F.H.A.B., XXI (Spring, 1932), 20-26; N.J.Archs., XXXII, 164.

HUDE, James (1695-1762)

Middlesex County: 1727-1729, 1730-1733, 1738-1739

Father, Adam (?-1746), left Staten Island to live at Woodbridge. In 1710, he was elected to the Assembly and in 1718 was appointed to the county court.

James, a Presbyterian, lived at New Brunswick where he became a merchant. He owned two slaves. His estate was valued at Ł4,583. He was appointed to the county court and later was elevated to the Council.

L.Gen., IV, 1665; Wdbrg., 156; N.J.M.W., 216-218 I; Prth.Amby., 373-74.

HUDE, Robert (1691-1749)

Middlesex County: 1740-1742, 1744

The brother of James Hude, Robert also was a Presbyterian and a resident at New Brunswick. He owned lands at Woodbridge, and his estate was valued at Ł496. He served on the county court.

N.J.Archs., XV, 99, XXX, 249-50; Prth.Amby., 373-74.

JOHNSTON Family

The first Johnston, Dr. John (1661-1732), left Scotland and took up residence in Perth Amboy. The Johnstons were Anglicans. And they made their fortunes through proprietary interests and trade, especially with the West Indies. Dr. John was the first to be elected to the Assembly, and the following two generations followed his example.

JOHNSTON, Andrew (1694-1762)

Perth Amboy: 1727-1729, 1738-1739, 1740-1742, 1743-1744

The son of Dr. John, Andrew was born in Perth Amboy, resided in his youth in New York, married the daughter of Stephanus Van Cortlandt, and began his career in trade. In 1718, he returned to Perth Amboy where he continued a profitable trade with the West Indies. He inherited his father's proprietary right. In the Peapack patent, he owned 10,000 acres and began to develop tenant farms. In addition, he owned 600 acres in Monmouth County, twenty tenant farms in Hunterdon, and other tracts in Somerset and Essex counties, as well as in Perth Amboy. He served as mayor of Perth Amboy, colonel of the Middlesex militia, treasurer of the eastern division, president of the board of proprietors, trustee of the new college at Princeton, and councilor.

Edith H. Mather, "Andrew Johnston and his Ancestors," Smrst.C.H.Q., III (July, 1914), 161-73; N.J.Archs., XXV, 328-29, XXXIII, 223; F.W.T., 125; Prth.Amby., 68-72.

JOHNSTON, John (1719-1760)

Perth Amboy: 1751-1754, 1754-1760

The grandson of Dr. John, nephew of Andrew, and son of John who sat in the Council, John profited at trade and land speculation. He built an ironworks at Glen Brook.

Frgs., 106, 212.

JOHNSTON, John (1737-1820)

Perth Amboy: 1763-1768

Son of Andrew, John also was a merchant.

G.P., 363.

JOHNSTON, John L. (1748-1825)

Perth Amboy: 1769-1771

Grandson of Dr. John and son of Lewis, John L. was a merchant and East Jersey proprietor. He was also a justice of the peace. He became a loyalist.

G.P., 363.

JOHNSTON, Lewis (1704-1773)

Perth Amboy: 1738-1739, 1740-1742, 1749-1751

The son of Dr. John and brother of Andrew, Lewis was educated at Leiden and practiced medicine. In addition, he was a merchant, a member of the board of eastern proprietors, and an agent for the western proprietors.

Lewis Johnston Papers, R.U.L.; N.J.Archs., XXXIV, 277.

KEARNEY, Philip (1704-1775)

Middlesex County: 1746-1748

Father, Michael, migrated from Ireland first to Virginia, then to New York, Philadelphia, and finally New Jersey. A resident of Perth Amboy, he became provincial secretary, judge of the county court, and eastern treasurer. He married the daughter of Lewis Morris.

Born in New York, Philip resided in Perth Amboy. He was an Anglican and son-in-law of Robert L. Hooper, the province's chief justice. As an eastern proprietor, he owned numerous and large tracts of land at Perth Amboy, Woodbridge, Sussex County, and Philadelphia. In addition, he owned shares in English joint stock companies. He also practiced law.

Michael J. O'Brien, "The Ancestry of Major-General Philip Kearny," American Irish Historical Society Journal, XI (1912), 160-68; N.J.Archs., XXXIV, 281-83; L.C., 13; Prth.Amby., 90-91.

KEASBY, Edward (1726-1779)

Salem County: 1763-1768

Father, Edward, was born in Salem, the son of an English immigrant.

Edward, although born a Quaker, became a Baptist. A resident of Salem, he became a wealthy landowner. His will lists several tracts in Salem and provided that ₤5,000 be given to his two daughters. His estate was valued at ₤20,374. Offices held included board of freeholders, justice of the peace, and delegate to the provincial congress.

C.L.N.J., III, 386; N.J.Archs., XXXIV, 283; Glcstr., 394.

KINSEY, James (1731-1803)

Burlington Town: 1772-1775

James Kinsey was the third generation of Quaker politicians. His grandfather had served in the New Jersey Assembly; and his father, after moving to Philadelphia, became a member of the Pennsylvania legislature and eventually its presiding officer.

Born in Philadelphia, James studied law and practiced in New Jersey and Pennsylvania. On removing to Burlington, he continued that practice and speculated in land. His inventory included tracts in Sussex, Middlesex, and Burlington counties and in Pennsylvania. During the imperial crisis, he sat at the Continental Congress but was later charged with loyalty to the crown. In 1789, however, he returned to public life and became Chief Justice of the state Supreme Court.

C.G., 275-76; Issac Sharpless, "John Kinsey, 1693-1750," F.H.A.B., VIII (Nov., 1917, and May, 1918), 2-10, 46-53; N.J.Archs., XXXIX, 258-59; A.C., 1239.

LADD, John (1695-1770)

Gloucester County: 1754-1760

Father, John, migrated from England to Burlington about 1678. He was a wealthy landowner and master of slaves.

John, a Quaker, lived at Woodbury. He was a surveyor and land speculator. As a western proprietor, his holdings were extensive: in addition to his home estate of 1,367 acres, he claimed other tracts ranging in size from 150 to 1,270 acres. In addition, he owned a sawmill and engaged in trade with Philadelphia's Israel Pemberton. His offices included justice of the peace, county clerk, and councilor.

Ladd Papers, S.C.; N.J.Archs., XVII, 612-13, XXXIV, 292; N.B.G., 154-55; L.Gen., II, 746.

LAWRENCE, John Brown (1726-1796)

Burlington Town: 1761-1768

The grandfather, Elisha, had settled in Monmouth County and became a leading opponent of the eastern proprietors. He represented the county in the legislature.

John Brown, an Anglican, resided in Burlington where he practiced law. After service in the Assembly, he was appointed to the Council. He was also the town's mayor.

During the imperial crisis, he served on a committee of safety but was later accused of being a loyalist.

S.L., II, 3; N.J.Archs., X, 302; John Roger McCreary, "Ambition, Interest and Faction: Politics in New Jersey, 1702-1738" (Ph.D. diss., University of Nebraska, 1971), 144.

LAWRENCE, Richard (1720-1798)

Monmouth County: 1761-1768, 1772-1775

Son of William, Richard was a Quaker. A resident of Shrewsbury, he was a substantial landowner and owned tracts in Perth Amboy and Rhode Island.

S.H.G., III, 416; N.J.Archs., XLII, 249.

LAWRENCE, Robert (1692-1788)

Monmouth County: 1743-1744, 1744, 1745, 1746-1748, 1749-1751, 1751-1754, 1754-1760

Father, William (1658-1740), lived in Middletown. He served as justice of the peace, judge of the county court, and assemblyman.

Robert, the uncle of Richard, was a Quaker and a resident of Upper Freehold. He owned several tracts. In 1731, he owned 375 acres in Upper Freehold; and, in 1758, he had increased his holdings to 796 acres. In addition, he owned 110 acres in Franklin Township. He also was a lawyer. A leader of the antiproprietary interest, he was regularly elected to the Assembly.

S.H.G., III, 394-400, 408; Mnmth., 614-15; Mnmth.F., 67; Ralph Voorhees, "The Raritan and Its Early Holland Settlers," Our Home, I (Aug., 1873), 337-44.

LEAMING, Aaron, Sr. (1688-1746)

Cape May County: 1727-1729, 1730-1733, 1738-1739, 1740-1742

Born on Long Island, this Quaker moved to Cape May and soon became one of the county's wealthiest landowners. In addition, he owned a sawmill, and his will listed several slaves. His estate was valued at £1,174 . He practiced law in the local courts and served as a justice of the peace.

S.H.G., I, 430-36; N.J.Archs., XXX, 294; "An Appraisal of the Personal Estate of Aaron Leaming," April 16, 1747, Spicer-Leaming Papers, Historical Society of Pennsylvania.

LEAMING, Aaron, Jr. (1715-1780)

Cape May County: 1740-1742, 1743-1744, 1745, 1746-1748, 1749-1751, 1751-1754, 1754-1760, 1761-1768

Although his father was a Quaker, Aaron Leaming, Jr., became a Baptist. A resident of the Middle Precinct, he pursued numerous business ventures. His extensive landholdings ranged in size from 180 to 1,735 acres. In the Middle Precinct, he owned 1,567 acres, ninety-seven cattle and horses, nineteen sheep, and three slaves. This estate put him at the top of the tax list. In total, he owned between thirty and forty slaves. Also, he owned two sawmills. In addition, he was a lawyer and surveyor. At his death, the estate was valued at ₤181,000.

S.H.G., III, 437-38; "Diaries of Aaron Leaming," Cp.My.M.H.G., I (June, 1932), 69-82; N.J.Archs., XXXIV, 299-302; Leaming Papers, S.C.

LEONARD, Samuel (1676-1758)

Perth Amboy: 1722-1725, 1743-1744, 1744

Father, Samuel, sat in the East Jersey Assembly and in the governor's Council.

Samuel, an Anglican, was an eastern proprietor and owned extensive landholdings. He also sat on the county court.

N.J.Archs., XV, 99, XXXII, 196; E.J.P., III, 445.

LEONARD, Thomas (1685-1759)

Somerset County: 1722-1725; 1740-1742

Leonard's family came from Massachusetts. Thomas, a Presbyterian, owned considerable property. His will lists tracts ranging in size from 100 to 10,000 acres and city lots in Perth Amboy. In addition, he owned a gristmill. Public offices included judge of the county court and councilor. He also was a trustee of the college at Princeton.

N.J.Archs., XXXII, 196-97; Fanny Leonard Koster, Annals of the Leonard Family (New York, 1911), 191-92; Constance M. Greiff, Mary W. Gibbons, and Elizabeth G. C. Menzies, Princeton Architecture: A Pictorial History of Town and Campus (Princeton, 1967), 23-24.

LOW, John (1702-1774)

Essex County: 1740-1742, 1745, 1746-1748, 1751-1754

The son of Cornelius, John was born in New York and moved to Newark. He was active in the Dutch Reform church. He was a merchant shopkeeper and traded with Boston. In addition, he held land titles challenged by the proprietors. In 1765, he sold 300 acres in Essex County for £1,200 and moved to Albany, New York. He was colonel of the Essex militia and commissioner of supply for provincial tropps.

N.Y.W., XXXIII (1900), 256-57; J. P. Ricks, "Notes on the Low Family," Maryland Genealogical Bulletin, VII (April, 1936), 15; N.J.Archs., XVIII, 210-11.

MEHELM, John (1733-1809)

Hunterdon County: 1772-1775

Mehelm, a Presbyterian, came from Ireland and first settled in Pennsylvania where he taught school before removing to Tewksbury. There he prospered as a merchant, landowner, mill owner, and lawyer. He was a justice of the peace and a delegate to the provincial congress.

Hntrdn.M., 92-93; Hntrdn.S., 204.

MICKLE, John (1687-1744)

Gloucester County: 1722-1725, 1727-1729, 1738-1739, 1740-1742, 1743-1744, 1744

Father, Archibald, was an Irish Quaker who first settled at Philadelphia in 1682. In 1690, he bought land at Newton Township and settled there. At death, he owned several tracts, including one of 760 acres and was rated the second wealthiest resident of the township.

John, a Quaker, lived at Newton Creek. He owned a share

in the western proprietary and in his will listed several tracts of land and eight slaves. His estate was valued at Ŀ62 3. He also sat on the county court.

Nwt.T., 139-41; N.J.M.W., 308 H.

MICKLE, William (1706-1777)

Gloucester County: 1750-1751, 1751-1754

The son of John, the Assemblyman, William was a Quaker. A Greenwich landowner, he also held an interest in the western proprietary. He listed several tracts in his will--the largest of which was 350 acres. His estate was valued at Ŀ38 0.

"Records of the Haddonfield Monthly Meeting," G.M.N.J., IV (July, 1928), 11, 14; N.J.Archs., XXXIV, 345; Nwt.T., 141.

MIDDAGH, Peter (1700-?)

Hunterdon County: 1754-1760

Peter's father moved from New York and settled on the Raritan. Peter was born at Somerville and was baptised in the Dutch Reform church. He later moved to Readington.

John Neafie, "The Somerset Middagh Family," Smrst.C.H.Q., VI (April, 1917), 112-17; idem, "Middagh Memoranda," N.J.H.S.P., 3rd ser., IX (Jan., 1914), 58.

MILLER, Ebenezer (1702-1774)

Salem County: 1754-1760, 1761-1768, 1769-1771

Son of Joseph, who came from Connecticut in 1698, Ebenezer was a Quaker and resided at Greenwich. He was a surveyor and held an interest in the western proprietary. In his will, he listed several holdings--the largest of which was 427 acres. His estate was valued at Ŀ186 . He also served on the county court.

L.Gen., II, 782-83; N.J.Archs., XIX, 393, XXXIV, 347.

MOORES, John (1700-1745)

Middlesex County: 1745

Moores's family came from Massachusetts. John, a Presbyterian, resided at Woodbridge. He listed several unspecified tracts and three slaves in his will.

[John Moore], "A Moore Family of Middlesex County, N. J.," N.J.H.S.P., n.s., XI (Jan., 1926), 53; N.J.M.W., 1685-1688 L.

MOORES, John (1725-1774)

Middlesex County: 1772-1774

The son of John, the Assemblyman, John Moores was a Presbyterian and resident of Woodbridge. He owned a mill and several tracts of land and left Ŀ100 to his wife. He served as township assessor and moderator.

N.J.M.W., 5125-5126 L; Wdbrg.T.B.

MOTT, William (1699-1760)

Hunterdon County: 1743-1744, 1744, 1745, 1746-1748, 1749-1751, 1751-1754

Father, Gershom, moved to Monmouth County from Long Island about 1685. Appointed sheriff and then elected to the Assembly in 1709, he was part of the "Scotch" proprietary faction and an outspoken opponent of Lewis Morris. His estate was valued at Ŀ497.

William moved to Trenton. His religion is difficult to establish: his parents were Baptists, but his brother was a Quaker. He grew wheat on a 35-acre farm, and he owned a mill. His will listed three slaves. Ranked as one of the community's wealthiest men, he left an estate valued at Ŀ,794. He was also a justice of the peace.

Trnt.T., 227-28, 246, 289; S.H.G., III, 76-80, 88; N.J.M.W., 501 J; Dennis P. Ryan, "Six Towns: Continuity and Change in Revolutionary New Jersey, 1770-1792" (Ph.D. diss., New York University, 1974), 56.

NEVILL, Samuel (1697-1764)

Middlesex County: 1743-1744; Perth Amboy: 1744, 1745, 1746-1748, 1749-1751; Middlesex County: 1754-1760, 1761-1764

Editor of the London Morning Post, Nevill inherited lands and proprietary rights in East Jersey and migrated in 1736. An Anglican and resident of Perth Amboy, he pursued several public lives: in addition to being a lawyer, an active member of the board of East Jersey proprietors, editor of the New American Magazine, and compiler of New Jersey's laws, he was also a justice of the peace, judge on the Supreme Court, and mayor of Perth Amboy.

Prth.Amby., 120-24.

NEWBOLD, Barzillai (1710-1757)

Burlington County: 1751-1754, 1754-1757

Father, Michael (1667-1721), migrated from England to Burlington County and died a wealthy landowner in Chesterfield Township.

Barzillai, an Anglican, resided at Mansfield Township. Although a blacksmith, he was a wealthy landowner. In his will, he listed tracts in Burlington and Morris counties. His estate was valued at Ƚ1,437. His public offices were local in nature and included overseer of the poor and a seat on the board of freeholders.

Brl., 199-202; N.J.M.W., 5933-5936 C; Charles Platt, Jr., Newbold Genealogy in America (New Hope, PA, 1964), 4-8; Brl.F., 423.

OAKE, William (1708-1779)

Middlesex County: 1744

Oake's family came from Long Island around 1700. William settled at New Brunswick and was a member of the Dutch Reform church. He was a merchant and owned a tavern. His offices included justice of the peace, judge of the county court, and the town's mayor.

N.J.Archs., XX, 151; N.B.G., 172; William H. Benedict, "Early Taverns in New Brunswick," N.J.H.S.P., n.s., III (July, 1918), 129-46.

OGDEN Family

The Odgens came from Long Island and resided at Newark and Elizabethtown. They were principally merchants and land speculators. Originally Presbyterian, some joined the Anglican church.

OGDEN, John (1709-1795)

Essex County: 1760, 1761-1768, 1769-1770

Father, David (1697-1734), was born in Newark and was an Anglican.

John, also a Newark resident, built the Bloomingdale Furnace in Bergen County and ventured into several mining properties. In addition, he speculated in land and owned a general store in Newark. He also was a lawyer. Financial difficulties eventually forced him to resign his seat in the legislature. Active in local politics, he served as town moderator, member of the board of freeholders, justice of the peace, and judge on the county court.

L.Gen., I, 97-98, 364; Frgs., 41; Records of the Town of Newark, N.J.H.S.C., VI, passim; N.J.Archs., XVI, 89, XVII, 502.

OGDEN, Josiah (1679-1763)

Essex County: 1716-1719, 1722-1725, 1738-1739

Son of David, an Assemblyman, Josiah was reared a Presbyterian but broke with the church and helped establish the Anglican church at Newark. He invested with other family members in the Ringwood Furnace in Bergen County and in several land schemes in Morris County. He was also a merchant and lived in a large three-story house in Newark.

Ogdn., 52-54; Frgs., 12, 17-18; N.J.Archs., XXIV, 212-13, XXXIII, 312; David Lawrence Pierson, Narratives of Newark . . . , 1666-1916 (Newark, 1917), 159-61.

OGDEN, Robert (1716-1787)

Essex County: 1751-1754, 1754-1760, 1761-1765

Son of Robert (1687-1733), Robert lived in Elizabethtown where he became an active member of the Presbyterian church, practiced law, and entered trade. He also owned a tannery. Active in local affairs, he represented the town's land claims against the proprietors. He was appointed justice of the peace and judge of the county court. A friend of Governor Jonathan Belcher and later speaker of the house, his political position seemed secure until the Stamp Act crisis. Although a delegate to the Stamp Act Congress, he refused to endorse its proceedings and soon after suffered so grievously at the hands of his neighbors that he resigned from the house.

Ogdn., 78-84; Theodore Thayer, As We Were: The Story of Old Elizabethtown (Elizabeth, 1964), 91-94; N.J.Archs., XXVIII, 112.

PAXSON, Henry (1719-1778)

Burlington County: 1754-1760, 1769-1771, 1772-1775

Paxson, a Quaker, was born in Pennsylvania and came to New Jersey in the 1730s. He lived in Northhampton Township where he established himself as a hatter. He owned some land (his will is not specific), a tannery, and one slave. His estate was valued at Ł1,586. He served as justice of the peace and a judge on the county court.

N.J.M.W., 10639-10648 C, 10830 C; N.J.Archs., XVII, 455.

PEACE, Joseph (1695-1744)

Hunterdon County: 1740-1742

Peace's religious affiliation cannot be established. A resident of Trenton, he invested in numerous schemes, including an ironworks and gristmill at Bordentown, another grist mill at Trenton, and numerous land ventures--one of which was a 2,500-acre tract in Morris County. He served as county collector and loan officer.

American Weekly Mercury, Aug. 2-9, Aug. 28-Sept. 4, 1740; Trnt.T., 245, 259-260; N.J.Archs., XXX, 372-73.

PEARSON, Issac (c.1687-1749)

Burlington Town: 1727-1729, 1730-1733, 1738-1739, 1740-1742, 1743-1744, 1744

A Quaker born in Philadelphia, Pearson described himself in his will   as a silversmith.   He was also a clockmaker.   As a West Jersey proprietor,   he came to own considerable land, including tracts in Burlington County and   at Rancocas Creek where he established an ironworks with Mahlon Stacy.   He   listed one slave in his will.   He was active in local government and served as assessor for the poor, member of the board of freeholders, and alderman.

Frgs., 128-29; Brl., 195; Brl.T.B., 14-26; N.J.M.W., 4309-4312 C; N.J.Archs., VI, 202.

PETTIT, Nathaniel (1737-1811)

Sussex County: 1772-1775

The Pettit family came from Long Island in the 1680s.

A resident of Newton, Pettit was an active member of the Anglican   community.   This farmer also served on the board of freeholders and was   appointed justice of the peace and judge of the county court.   He became a   loyalist.

Richard I. Shelling, "The Protestant Episcopal Church in Sussex County,   New Jersey, 1770-1784," N.J.H.S.P., L (Jan., 1932), 58; Ang.Ch., 555; G.P., 369.

PRICE, Robert Friend (1730-1782)

Gloucester County: 1769-1771, 1772-1775

A Quaker and resident at Gloucester, Price listed lands of unspecified   size in his will.   He also provided for the freedom of one slave.   His estate was valued at £2,068.   He was sheriff, justice of the peace, and judge of the   county court.

N.J.M.W., 1363 H; G.P., 368.

READ, Charles (1715-1774)

Burlington Town: 1751-1754, 1754-1760

Read's grandfather had first lived in Burlington and then

moved to Philadelphia where he became active in local politics. His father was a prosperous merchant and prominent in Pennsylvania politics.

Read, an Anglican, was born in Philadelphia and received his education in England. After returning to Philadelphia, he moved to Burlington. His economic activities were numerous: in addition to land speculations, he invested in sawmills and ironworks, including the Taunton, Etna, Atison, and Butso furnaces. He owned estates in Springfield Township, Morris County, and Burlington. He also held numerous public posts: county clerk, collector, provincial secretary, councilor, justice of the Supreme Court, major in the militia, and commissioner of supply to the provincial military. In addition, he actively promoted the college of New Jersey, the American Philosophical Society, and the library companies of Philadelphia and Burlington. In 1773, he foresook the province and reestablished himself in North Carolina.

P.P.; Frgs., 154-170.

READING, George (1725-1792)

Hunterdon County: 1761-1768

The Readings had come from London in 1683 and settled in Gloucester County. Both his grandfather and father were prominent politicians and wealthy landowners.

George, a Presbyterian, inherited extensive holdings and an interest in the West Jersey proprietary. A resident of Amwell, he also owned an ironworks and was a lawyer. In 1769, he publicly announced his indebtedness, sold a 180-acre tract of timber, meadows, and orchards in Gloucester County, and then published his intention to apply for relief. Early in the Revolution, he moved to Pennsylvania and later migrated to Kentucky.

Trnt.G., 195-97; N.B.G., 181; N.J.Archs., XXVI, 372-73.

REEVES, Joseph (c.1690-c.1747)

Salem County: 1738-1739

Son of Mark, Joseph was a Quaker and landowner whose estate was valued at Ł59. He served on the county court.

L.Gen., II, 817; N.J.Archs., XV, 97, XXX, 394.

RODMAN, Thomas (1716-1796)

Burlington Town: 1767-1768

Father, John (?-1756), a physician, came from Long Island to Burlington in 1725. He owned numerous tracts, including 1,300 acres in Burlington, two farms in Hunterdon County, and land in Pennsylvania. In addition, he served in the Assembly and Council.

Thomas, a Quaker, was a silversmith and West Jersey proprietor. His estate was valued at Ŀ407. His public services included the board of freeholders, commissioner of roads, justice of the peace, judge of the county court, and sheriff.

Charles Henry Jones, Genealogy of the Rodman Family (Philadelphia, 1886), 19-20, 29; Walter Hamilton Van Hoesen, Crafts and Craftsmen of New Jersey (Rutherford, NJ, 1973), 228; Brl.T.B., 28-41; N.J.Archs., XVII, 278; N.J.M.W., 11689 C.

ROLPH, John (1700-1750)

Essex County: 1740-1742

Rolph's family came from Massachusetts in the 1680s. John resided at Elizabethtown and was a Presbyterian. He was appointed justice of the peace. His estate included one slave and was valued at Ŀ1,410.

N.J.M.W., 1805 G; Rolph Family File, New Jersey Historical Society; N.J.Archs., XV, 100.

ROY, John (1712-1780)

Somerset County: 1772-1775

The son of Joseph, Roy was born on the Isle of Jersey, came to Boston, and then transplanted to New Jersey, first at Woodbridge and then at Basking Ridge. He was a Presbyterian. He seemed to be a modest farmer, and his estate was valued at Ŀ473. He served on the county court and was elected to the provincial congress.

N.J.M.W., 638 R; Roy Family File, New Jersey Historical Society.

RUNYON, Reune (1711?-1776)

Middlesex County: 1765-1768, 1769-1771

The Runyons were Huguenots who settled on the Raritan River. Reune, a Baptist, resided at Piscataway. He was a modest landowner. Public service included justice of the peace, judge of the county court, barracks master, and township clerk.

Thomas S. Griffiths, A History of Baptists in New Jersey (Highttown, NJ, 1904), 256; N.J.Archs., XXXV, 337; G.P., 364; Calvin I. Kephart, "Runyon-Runyan Family (New Jersey)," National Genealogical Society Quarterly, XXIX (Dec., 1941), 129-130.

SHARP, Issac (c.1710-1770)

Salem County: 1769-1770

Sharp's grandfather owned proprietary shares in East and West Jersey. His father, Issac (?-1735), was an Irish Quaker who came to New Jersey in 1703 and owned considerable land in both sections, including 1,050 acres in Gloucester County. He served in the Assembly but later returned to Ireland where he died.

Issac had been born in New Jersey but returned to Ireland with his father. He returned to New Jersey in 1730 and settled at Pilesgrove. He was a Quaker. His land speculations were scattered throughout the province, and he invested in mills and ironworks. At his death, he owned two slaves. He was a justice of the peace and judge of the county court.

N.B.G., 188; "Notes," P.M.H.B., XX (1896), no. 1, 134; N.J.Archs., XXVI, 445-46, XXVIII, 8-9; "Cumberland County Ratables, 1751," G.M.N.J., XIV (Jan., 1939), 37; E.J.P., III, 446; N.J.M.W., 1615 Q; Slm.C.L., 42-45.

SHEPPARD, John (1730-1805)

Cumberland County: 1772-1775

The son of Moses, the Assemblyman, John was a Quaker.

A resident of Greenwich, he was a merchant and in addition to his store owned a wharf and ferry. His estate was valued at $4,565. He was also on the board of freeholders.

Glcstr., 687; N.J.M.W., 1313 F.

SHEPPARD, Moses (1698-1753)

Salem County: 1744

Father, Thomas (?-1721), owned considerable land, including 250 acres at Shrewsbury, and was elected to the Assembly in 1709.

Although the Sheppards were Quakers, many, including Moses, became Baptists. A resident of Fairfield Township, he owned some land, and his estate was valued at Ŀ404 . He was a justice of the peace and judge of the county court.

Fen.C., 180-81, 215; Glcstr., 687; N.J.Archs., XXXII, 289.

SHINN, Thomas (c.1690-1753)

Burlington County: 1742, 1743-1744, 1744

Father, Thomas (?-c.1694), was born in England and settled at Burlington where he owned land and slaves.

Thomas was born in Springfield and lived there most of his life. He was active in the Quaker meetinghouse. He owned slaves to whom he promised freedom in his will. In addition to an inn, he owned several tracts of land, and his estate was valued at Ŀ1,893 . He was a justice of the peace and judge of the county court.

Josiah H. Shinn, The History of the Shinn Family in Europe and America ([Chicago], 1903), 64-68, 81-83; N.J.M.W., 5325-5334 C; Frgs., 131; N.B.G., 190-91.

SKINNER, Cortlandt (1727-1799)

Perth Amboy: 1763-1768, 1769-1771, 1772-1775

Father, William (1687-1758), fled Scotland in 1715 for Philadelphia. He became a missionary for the Society for the Propagation of the Gospel and settled at Perth Amboy in 1723.

He married the daughter of Stephanus Van Cortlandt of New York.

Cortlandt, an Anglican, was born in Perth Amboy and undertook his legal education in New York. On returning to his birthplace, he practiced the law. He profited from his legal work and from his share in the eastern proprietary. As a loyalist, he claimed losses of ₺7,000 to the English claims commission. He was also attorney general.

S.L., II, 305-6; L.C., 73-74; Hugh Edward Egerton, ed., The Royal Commission on the Losses and Services of American Loyalists, 1783 to 1785 (New York, 1915), 113-15.

SMITH Family

The Smiths were Quakers who came from England in the 1690s. They owned shares in the West Jersey proprietary and soon established themselves through trade with the West Indies and land speculation as one of Burlington's wealthiest families.

Brl.S.

SMITH, Benjamin (1704-1755)

Hunterdon County: 1738-1739, 1740-1742

The son of Daniel, who was Burlington's representative to the Assembly, Benjamin moved to Trenton in the 1730s. He became a merchant and in addition owned several tracts in Trenton, Amwell, Hanover, and Bethlehem townships, and nearly 1,000 acres in Morris County. He also owned a mill at Amwell. And he listed a slave in his will. He sat on the county court.

Trnt.T., 217, 224; N.J.M.W., 370 J; Pennsylvania Gazette, April 19, 1744, Sept. 3, 1747.

SMITH, Daniel (1696-1769)

Burlington Town: 1745, 1746-1748, 1749-1751

Son of Daniel, the Assemblyman, Daniel Smith amassed considerable wealth through the West Indian trade. His estate was valued at ₺1,126. Offices held were assessor for the poor, board of freeholders, tax assessor, road surveyor, and justice of the peace.

Brl.S., 96-99; N.J.Archs., XVI, 89; N.J.M.W., 8593 C; Brl.T.B., 14-34.

SMITH, Joseph (?-1792)

Burlington Town: 1769-1771

This Quaker merchant also served as West Jersey Treasurer.

Brl.S., 193.

SMITH, Richard (1699-1751)

Burlington Town: 1730-1733, 1738-1739, 1740-1742, 1743-1744, 1744, 1745, 1746-1748, 1749-1751

Richard's father, Samuel, had also represented the town in the Assembly. Richard prospered through the West Indian trade and owned several lots, wharves, and warehouses in Burlington. In addition, he owned a country estate at "Greenhill" and numerous other tracts. He listed a slave in his will and left nearly £2,000 to his heirs. He also served on the county court.

Brl.S., 101-3, 136; Samuel Smith Papers, R.U.L.; N.J.M.W., 4875-4878 C.

SMITH, Samuel (1721-1776)

Burlington Town: 1754-1760, 1761-1766

In addition to trade, Samuel engaged in land speculation and developed his properties into tenant farms. He also owned lands in Pennsylvania. He left £6,000 to his heirs. In 1766, he was elevated to the Council. He was the West Jersey Treasurer in addition.

Brl.S., 117; N.J.M.W., 10183-10186 C.

SMITHS unrelated

SMITH, James (1700-1773)

Middlesex County: 1749-1751

Smith's family came from Massachusetts in the 1670s. This Presbyterian resident of Woodbridge appeared to be a slaveowning farmer of moderate wealth. He served as the town's constable and surveyor and was appointed justice of the peace.

N.J.M.W., 5013-5014 L; Mddlsx.C., 64; N.J.Archs., XV, 100; Wdbrg., 175.

SMITH, Richard (1690-1740)

Salem County: 1740-1741

Smith's family had come from England in the late 1670s. Richard was a Quaker and resided at Elsinboro. In addition to the 600 acres that he farmed, he owned numerous other tracts, including one in Virginia. He listed five slaves in his will. His estate was valued at ₤1,073. He served on the county court.

Slm.C.L., 41-42; N.J.Archs., XXX, 442.

SMITH, Shobal (1692-1768)

Middlesex County: 1751-1754

The father, Samuel (1644-1719), left Barnstable, Massachusetts, and settled at Woodbridge in 1676 on 103 acres.

Smith was a Quaker and was active in the Woodbridge meetinghouse. He lived on a 110-acre farm and owned several other tracts of similar size in the neighborhood. He gave over ₤,300 to his heirs. He served as town moderator and constable.

C.F., IV, 462-63; Wdbrg., 71, 197, 210; Wdbrg.T.B., 61; N.J.Archs., XXVI, 232, XXXIII, 398; Louise Aymar Christian, "Nathaniel Fitz Randolph of Woodbridge, N. J., Quaker and his Descendants," N.E.H.G.R., III C (Oct., 1943), 330-33; "Death Records at Rahaway and Plainfield Meeting," G.M.N.J., XXVII (Jan., 1952), 45.

SMYTH, Andrew (c.1727-1763)

Perth Amboy: 1760, 1761-1763

Born in Monmouth County, Smyth resided in Perth Amboy.

He was an Anglican. A merchant and eastern proprietor, he died intestate.

N.J.Archs., XXXIII, 399; G.P., 363.

SPICER, Jacob (1716-1765)

Cape May County: 1744, 1745, 1746-1748, 1749-1751, 1751-1754, 1754-1760, 1761-1765

Spicer's grandfather (?-1699) had come from England to Long Island in 1645 and in 1687 moved to Gloucester County. His father, Jacob, Sr., (1668-1741) settled in Cape May in 1691. A substantial landowner, he held title to two 400-acre tracts. He sat on the county court and in the legislature.

Although Jacob, Jr., was born a Quaker, he became a Baptist. A resident of the Lower Precinct, this entrepreneur speculated widely. In 1751, the county's list of tax ratables enumerated 2,342 acres, fifty cattle and horses, and thirty-nine sheep. In 1756, he bought an interest in the West Jersey Society, which gave him rights to mines, minerals, hunting, and fishing. In addition, he owned lands scattered throughout the province, including several tracts of cedar, and in New York and North Carolina. He also operated a fishery. And, according to his diary, he was a merchant who traded principally with Philadelphia. He also sat on the county court and was coeditor of New Jersey's Grants, Concessions, and Original Constitutions.

N.J.Archs., XIX, 393; William A. Ellis, ed., "Diary of Jacob Spicer, 1755-6," N.J.H.S.P., LXIII (Jan., April, and July, 1945), 37-50, 82-117, 175-88; John R. Stevenson, "Samuel Spicer and His Descendants," ibid., 2nd ser., XIII (1891-1895), 41-58; "Cape May County Ratables," G.M.N.J., XIV (Jan., 1939), 32; "Memorandum Book of Jacob Spicer, 1757-1764," Cp.My.M.H.G., I (1934), no. 3, 109-18, 162-89, no. 4, 162-173; N.J.M.W., 253 E; New Jersey Deeds, State Library, 277-280 R.

STACY, Mahlon (1686-1742)

Burlington County: 1727-1729, 1730-1733, 1738-1739, 1740-1742

Father, Mahlon (?-1704), came from England and was a founder of Trenton. A West Jersey proprietor, he owned 3,500 acres and a mill. He was engaged in trade with the West Indies.

Mahlon, Jr., was a Quaker. While he continued to own land in Trenton, he moved to Northampton Township where he invested in ironworks at Mt. Holly with Issac Pearson. His will also notes a mill and a slave. His estate was valued at Ł1,903.

Trnt.T., 60, 91, 104-5; N.J.Archs., XI, 544; Elizabeth B. Satterthwaite, "Mahlon Stacy--Quaker Founder of Trenton," N.J.H.S.P., n.s., IX (April, 1924), 150-54; N.J.M.W., 3519-3520 C.

STEELE, Pontius (1707-1770c)

Perth Amboy: 1745, 1746-1748

Steele's grandfather was a Huguenot who first came to the West Indies in the 1670s and then moved to Boston and New York before settling in Monmouth County in the 1690s. His father, Gabriel (1685-1738), owned several tracts, including a large estate in Woodbridge Township. He also was a merchant and established a ferry at Perth Amboy.

Born in Monmouth County and active in Shrewsbury's Anglican community, Steele later moved to Perth Amboy. He was a merchant and operated a stage line between Perth Amboy and Burlington with Joseph Borden. He served on the county court.

Maud Burr Morris, "Four Generations in America of the Huguenot Family of Steele," New York Genealogical and Biographical Record, XLIV (Jan., 1913), 61-69, 107-15; N.J.Archs., XXIV, 142; American Weekly Mercury, April 17-24, 1740.

STEVENS, John (1716-1792)

Perth Amboy: 1751-1754, 1754-1760, 1761-1763

The son of an English immigrant who settled at New York before moving to New Jersey, Stevens was an Anglican. He switched his residence between New York and Perth Amboy. He was a merchant engaged in the West Indian trade, an eastern proprietor with extensive lands, and an investor in copper mines. He sat in the Council, was elected to the provincial congress, was sent to the Continental Congress, and served at the Constitutional Convention of 1787.

L.Gen., I, 189-92; A.C., 1752-53; L.C., 91.

STILLWELL, Nicholas (1714-1771)

Cape May County: 1766-1768, 1769-1771

Father, William, came to Cape May from New York in the 1690s.

Nicholas, a Baptist, resided at Great Egg Harbor. He operated an inn, a ferry, and owned ships. His will lists slaves worth Ł 240. And his estate was valued at Ł 4,839. He was a justice of the peace and sat on the county court.

Benjamin Marshall Stillwell, Early Memoirs of the Stillwell Family (New York, 1878), 276, 285; N.J.M.W., 313 E.

STOKES, Samuel (1711-1781)

Burlington County: 1757-1760

Father, Joseph (1680-1760), owned lands in Chester and Evesham townships.

Samuel, a Quaker, inherited lands and lived in Chester Township. He remained a farmer of modest means. His estate was valued at Ł 324.

Joseph Stokes, Notes on My Stokes Ancestry (np, 1937), 16-21; S.G., 8, 12, 19; N.J.Archs., XXXV, 376.

SYKES, Anthony (1717-1783)

Burlington County: 1772-1775

Sykes's family had come from England. He was a Quaker and resided at Chesterfield Township. According to his will, he owned numerous tracts in Burlington, Hunterdon, and Monmouth counties, several cedar swamps, and sawmills. His estate was valued at Ł 1,221. He also served on the board of freeholders.

N.J.M.W., 10912 C.

TAYLOR, Edward (1712-1783)

Monmouth County: 1769-1771, 1772-1775

The Taylors had come from England in the 1680s.

Edward, the son of George (1684-1758), was a Baptist. He lived at Middleton on his father's estate. In addition to purchasing a share in the East Jersey proprietary, he operated a tavern and store, was engaged in trade with New York, and invested in a stage line between Philadelphia and New York. He also owned a mill and several slaves. Public service included the board of freeholders, township assessor, and the provincial congress. He wavered in his loyalties during the Revolution and was required to post a $1,000 bond as guarantee that he would not oppose the state government.

S.H.G., III, 50-51; Mrrs.M., reel 55; N.J.M.W., 5103-5105 M; Asher Taylor, "A Genealogy of the Taylor Family, of Monmouth County," The Jerseyman, VIII (May, 1902), 10, IX (Feb., 1903), 1-6; N.J.Archs., XX, 378-79; N.J.M.W., 5103-5105 M.

TUCKER, Samuel (1721-1789)

Hunterdon County: 1769-1771, 1772-1775

Tucker, a Presbyterian, lived at Trenton where he was engaged in trade with Thomas Riche of Philadelphia. That trade included slaves and extended from the West Indies to New England. In addition to a large brick home and several lots in Trenton, he owned lands throughout the county and in Somerset and Morris counties. He provided for the freedom of his slaves in his will. His estate was valued at Ь5,977. He was a justice of the peace, judge of the county court, sheriff, and a delegate to both the provincial and Continental congresses.

N.J.Archs., X, 270-71, XXXVI, 233-35; Trnt.T., 344, 389; C.G., 265.

VAN BUSKIRK, Lawrence (1686-1752)

Bergen County: 1727-1729, 1730-1733, 1738-1739, 1740-1742, 1743-1744, 1744, 1745, 1746-1748, 1749-1751

Van Buskirk's father, Lawrence, Sr., had represented Bergen County in the Assembly.

Lawrence, Jr., was an active Lutheran. A resident at Mingackqua, he was a wealthy landowner. At his death, he owned six slaves and gave his heirs Ь1,410. He was appointed a justice of the peace.

M.J., I, 284, 307, 331, 344; N.J.M.W., 109 F; Ec.R.N.Y., IV, 2381, 2430.

VANDERVERE, Cornelius (1697-1782)

Monmouth County: 1738-1739, 1740-1742

Born in New York, Vandervere came to New Jersey in the 1720s. He was Dutch Reform and resided at Middletown. He worked a farm inherited from his father, owned another at Shrewsbury, and listed fourteen slaves in his will. The estate was valued at Ŀ 700. He also served on the county court.

N.J.M.W., 4938-4944 M; N.J.Archs., XVI, 310; Mnmth.F., 18.

VANGIESON, Rinear (1704-1784)

Bergen County: 1754-1760, 1761-1768

Vangieson's family came from New York in the 1660s. A member of the Dutch Reform church at New Barbadoes, he owned several large tracts. He served on the board of freeholders and was commissioned a justice of the peace and judge of the county court.

N.J.Archs., XIX, 391; Ptsn., 266-67.

VAN HORNE, Thomas (1722-1744)

Sussex County: 1772-1774

Father, Cornelius (1695-1744), was a New York merchant who owned extensive holdings in New Jersey. The family moved to New Jersey in 1710 and settled in Monmouth County.

Thomas inherited his father's farm but sold it in 1757 to buy land in Mansfield Township. He was a Presbyterian. Public service included the board of freeholders, justice of the peace, and judge of the county court.

Elsie O. Hallenbeck, Our Van Horne Kindred (Amsterdam, NY, 1959), 12-13; N.J.Archs., XI, 83, XXXIV, 545.

VAN MIDDLESWARDT, John (1704-1770)

Somerset County: 1740-1742, 1743-1744, 1744, 1745, 1746-1748, 1749-1751, 1751-1754

Van Middleswardt's family came from New York in the 1680s. He resided at Raritan Landing and was a member of the Dutch Reform church. He managed a 650-acre farm, which he worked with slaves. He also served on the county court.

N.J.M.W., 386 R; N.J.Archs., XV, 99, XVI, 90; Cornelius C. Vermeule, "Raritan Landing That Was," N.J.H.S.P., LIV (July, 1936), 198.

VAN NESTE, Abraham (1713-1780)

Somerset County: 1768

Abraham was born in Somerset County, the son of George, an Assemblyman, and was a member of the Dutch Reform church. A resident of Millstone, he was a local merchant, landowner, and an operator of mills. He noted one slave in his will and gave Ь3,000 to his heirs. He was a justice of the peace and a delegate to the provincial congress.

N.J.Archs., XXXV, 414; Mrrs.M., 61.

VAN NESTE, George (1676-1747)

Somerset County: 1730-1733, 1738-1739

Van Neste's family had come from New York in the 1680s. He was Dutch Reform and lived on a 504-acre farm on the Raritan River.

N.J.Archs., XXX, 501; C.F., II, 737.

VAN VEGHTEN, Derrick (1699-1781)

Somerset County: 1743-1744, 1744

Father, Michael (?-1734), came from New York to the Raritan region about 1685 and became a large landowner.

Derrick inherited 2,000 acres. He was active in the Dutch Reform community in the Raritan Valley region. He owned several large tracts, including one of 1,200 acres in Somerset County, lands in Bergen County, and some at Albany. The inventory of his estate included twenty-two horses, twenty-two cattle, fourteen hogs, and twenty-five slaves.

James Brown Van Vechten, The Van Vechten Genealogy (Detroit, 1954), 41-42, 338, 360-62; N.J.M.W., 694 R; Katharine Hubbell Birdsall, "The Historical Van Veghten House," Smrst.C.H.Q., I (April, 1912), 92-94; Er.G., 549; Cornelius C. Vermeule, "Raritan Valley, Its Discovery and Settlement," N.J.H.S.P., n.s., XIII (July, 1928), 295.

VAN VORST, Cornelius (1700-1760)

Bergen County: 1751-1754

Van Vorst's family came to New Jersey early in the seventeenth century. Cornelius was Dutch Reform. One of the county's wealthiest, he was a merchant, landowner, and manager of a ferry. He was a member of the board of freeholders and a justice of the peace.

N.J.Archs., XVII, 502; G.P., 466; Brgn., 81-82.

VREELAND, George (1710-1795)

Essex County: 1743-1744, 1744; Bergen County: 1754-1760

Father, Enoch, purchased a farm at New Brunswick for L665 in 1732.

George moved, first to Acquackanonk Township in Essex County. He left the Dutch Reform church and became an Anglican. By 1758, he was at Monachquay in Bergen County. He was a farmer, land speculator, and slaveowner. He owned several large tracts in Bergen County and on Staaton Island. He gave ₤500 to each of his four daughters, and his estate was valued at ₤1,125. In Essex County, he served as a justice of the peace and judge of the county court. In Bergen County, he served on the board of freeholders and the county court.

N.J.M.W., 2572-2574 B; Louis Beach Vreeland, Annals of the Vreeland Family (Charlotte, NC, 1956), 28; Ptsn., 114-15; N.J.Archs., XV, 100, XVI, 89, XVII, 502, XIX, 390; Ang.Ch., 232-33, 538, 550-51.

WETHERILL, John (1703-1784)

Middlesex County: 1749-1751, 1751-1754, 1754-1760, 1761-1768, 1769-1771, 1772-1775

Wetherill's family came from England in the 1680s. John was born in Middlesex County and was a Presbyterian. A prosperous farmer residing in the New Brunswick area, he owned three farms and several other tracts ranging in size from 100 to 300 acres. Some of his titles were contested by the proprietors. He also owned seven slaves. His estate was valued at Ł 411. He was elected to the provincial congress.

N.J.M.W., 6503-6510 L; "List of the Freeholders of Middlesex," N.J.H.S.P., 2nd ser., II (May, 1894), 94; William H. Benedict, New Brunswick in History (New Brunswick, 1925), 364.

WILLETS, John (1685-1777)

Cape May County: 1743-1744

The Willets family came from New York.

John was a Quaker, residing at Peck's Beach. His estate was valued at Ł 645. He sat on the county court.

L.D.S.; N.J.Archs., VI, 202, XVI, 430; Cp.My., 54-56.

WINDS, William (1727-1789)

Morris County: 1772-1775

Born on Long Island, Winds moved at an early age to New Jersey. He lived at Rockaway and became an active Presbyterian. At his death, he had established himself as a wealthy landowner. His public service included justice of the peace, captain of the provincial troops during the last war with France, colonel of the militia, delegate to the provincial congress, and an officer during the war for independence.

J. F. Tuttle, "Biographical Sketch of Gen. William Winds," N.J.H.S.P., VII (1853-1855), 13-37; Mrrs.T., 126, 130-32, 135-36; N.J.Archs., XXXVII, 257.

WOOD, Richard (1694-1759)

Salem County: 1751-1754

The Wood family came from Rhode Island in the 1680s. A Quaker, Richard resided at Gravelly Run and was a large landowner. He sat on the county court.

Fen.C., 398-99; Glcstr., 687; Joseph S. Sickler, The History of Salem County (Salem, [1937]), 123.

WRIGHT, Samuel (1719-1781)

Burlington County: 1745, 1746-1748

The son of John, Samuel was born at Wrightstown. He was a Quaker, residing in New Hanover. He owned some land and a brickyard.

John Wesley Haines, Richard Haines and his Descendants (Medfordlakes, NJ, 1961), 77; N.J.Archs., XXXV, 458; Brl.F., 426.

YARD, Joseph (1707-1763)

Hunterdon County: 1754-1760

Father, William (?-1742), came from England to Philadelphia in the 1680s. Then he moved to Trenton in 1700. He was a major landowner in the area.

Joseph, an active Presbyterian, lived at Trenton. He also owned a house in Philadelphia. In his will, he gave all but Ƚ525 to his wife and children. He was a commissioner of supply to the New Jersey troops and served on the board of freeholders.

N.J.Archs., VIII, pt. 2, 140, XIX, 394, XXXIII, 493; Trnt.G., 317-18.

YOUNG, Henry (1691-1767)

Cape May County: 1730-1733, 1738-1739, 1744

Young was born in England. Impressed into the English navy, he jumped ship on the coast of New Jersey about 1713.

He resided in Upper Township and may have been a Baptist. He was a surveyor for the western proprietors and came to own extensive tracts of land. His estate was valued at ₤ 1,106. He was a justice of the peace, judge of the county court, and a colonel of militia.

N.J.M.W., 274 E; P.P., 300; I. Gilbert Young, Fragmentary Records of the Youngs (Philadelphia, 1869), 36; Cp.My., 54-56; Emma Steelman Adams, "Tombstone Inscriptions in the Baptist Graveyard at Cape May Court House, N. J.," P.M.H.B., XXXVI (1912), no. 2, 235.

76, 81-85, 92; votes on economic issues, 43, 51; votes on Morris and Belcher administrations, 138, 146; votes on Franklin administration, 195, 211, 214

Burr, Aaron, 161

Camp, Joseph, 33, 256

Cape May County: representatives 38-39; votes, 85, 87; votes on economic issues, 53; votes on slavery, 53; votes on Morris and Belcher administrations, 150; votes on Franklin administration, 195, 214

Clements family, 37-38

Clements, Samuel, Jr., 257

Clements, Samuel, Sr., 256-57; Assembly role, 64; votes on military, 175, 208; votes on salaries, 208

Combs, John, 223, 257

Constitution of 1776, 236

Continental Congress, 110-11, 222

Converse, Philip, 109

Cooke, William, 37, 257; Assembly role, 66, 72, 73; votes, 91; votes on Morris and Belcher administrations, 142-43, 144

Cooper family, 37-38, 64, 194, 232

Cooper, David, 258; Assembly role, 64

Cooper, Joseph, Jr., 38, 258, Assembly role, 64

Cooper, Joseph, Sr., 38

Coxe, Daniel, 229, 232

Crane, John, 258-59; votes, 76; votes on Morris and Belcher administrations, 140

Crane, Stephen, 32, 109-11, 259; Assembly role, 73, 92, 194; Continental Congress and, 220-21, 231; Franklin administration and, 194, 196, 209, 218

Cumberland County: representatives from, 38

Currency: Assembly policy, 14, 103-104; votes on, 51; in Morris and Belcher administrations, 123-24, 149; in Great War for Empire, 162, 164-66, 169, 174, 176; in Franklin administration, 185-89, 196, 209-10, 213, after independence, 233-34, 238

Deacon, John, 259; votes, 153

Debt: Assembly policy, 10; votes on, 51-52; in Franklin administration, 185-87, 196, 210, after independence, 233, 235-36, 238

De Hart, Jacob, 259-60; votes, 169

Demarest, David, 33, 260; Assembly role, 64; votes, 92; votes on economic policy, 43; votes on Morris and Belcher administrations, 139-41, 150

Demarest, John, 260; votes on economic policy, 52; votes on Franklin administration, 218, 221

Dey family, 5, 34, 232

Dey, Derrick, 34, 260-61; votes, 153

Dey, Theunis, 34, 261; votes on economic policy, 54; votes on Franklin administration, 196, 209, 211, 217

Doughty, Daniel, 39, 261; Assembly role, 72; votes, 91

Dumont, Peter, 261-62
Dunham, Azariah, 262; Assembly role, 66
Dutch Reformed: from East Jersey, 25, 30, 33; number in
    Assembly, 74; votes, 76, 81-87, 93; votes on Franklin
    administration, 195, 209; votes on slavery, 53
East Jersey: votes, 75; votes on Franklin administration, 217-
    18; West Jersey compared to, 25, 35
East Jersey proprietors, 30, 31-33; in Morris administration,
    122, 123; after independence, 232
Eaton, John, 31, 65, 301-302; Assembly role, 72; votes, 81;
    votes on Belcher administration, 139
Economic policy, 6; bounties, 14-15, 43, 187, 196; fishing, 43;
    hunting, 9; local improvements, 6-7, 9; timber, 9, 43;
    trade, 9, 12-14, 43, 187; transportation, 8-9, 53, 187;
    in Franklin administration, 185-87, 193, 196, 211; after
    independence, 234-35
Eldridge family, 232
Eldridge, Eli, 263; Assembly role, 66, 214; votes on Franklin
    administration, 221
Elizabethtown, 31-33; Intolerable Acts and, 111 votes, 92; votes
    on slavery, 53
Ellis, Joseph, 263
Elmer family, 232
Elmer, Jonathan, 229
Elmer, Theophilus, 263; votes on Franklin administration, 221
Emley, John, 40, 263-64; votes, 76, 81, 85, 91-92
Ernst, Joseph, 108
Essex County: elections, 232; Intolerable Acts and, 110-11;
    representatives from, 31-33, 81, 87; votes, 146; votes
    on Franklin administration, 194, 214, 220; ;
Farmer, Thomas, 29, 264; votes, 76
Federalists, 237-38
Fisher, Hendrick, 34, 264-65; Assembly role, 61-63, 65, 66, 72-
    74, 214; in provincial congress, 230; votes, 87, 91, 92;
    votes on economic policy, 43, 51, 54; votes on Morris
    and Belcher administrations, 139-40, 143, 153; votes on
    Great War for Empire, 174, 179; votes on Franklin
    administration, 218, 221;
Fithian, Philip, 3, 41, 54-55
Fitz-Randolph family, 30
Ford, Jacob, 41, 265
Franklin, Benjamin, 3
Franklin, William, 188-9; administration, 188-94; on Assembly
    politics, 4, 190, 194-95, 213-14; on currency, 188-89;
    on economic improvements, 14, 187; on independence,
    221-22, 230; on military, 189, 213; on salaries, 190; on
    treasury robbery, 214-18
Frelinghuysen, Theodore, 61
Garritse, Henry, 265-66; Assembly role, 66, 214; votes on
    Franklin administration, 194, 221

Gerlach, Larry, 26
Gibbon family, 194
Gibbon, Grant, 39, 266
Gibbon, Leonard, 39, 266
Gipson, Lawrence H., 168
Gloucester County: representatives from, 34, 37-38; votes, 87
Greene, Jack P., ix, 95
Hamilton, John, 125
Hancock, William, 8, 38, 266-67; Assembly role, 64; votes on
    economic policy, 43; votes on Indian treaty, 179; votes
    on Morris and Belcher administrations, 139-40; votes on
    Great War for Empire, 176, 179;
Hand, Jonathan, 267; Assembly role, 66, 214; votes on Franklin
    administration, 221
Hart, John, 40, 267; votes on slavery, 53
Hartshorne family, 31
Hartshorne, Robert, 31, 267-68; votes on Franklin
    administration, 209
Hartz, Louis, xvi
Heard, John, 30, 268; votes, 92; votes on Morris and Belcher
    administrations, 139-40
Heathcoate family, 28
Henretta, James, 5
Hewlings family, 36
Hewlings, Abraham, 268; on Franklin administration, 194
Hewlings, Thomas, 268-69; on Franklin administration, 194, 217
Hinchman family, 37-38
Hinchman, James, 269
Hinchman, John, 269; Assembly role, 64-65, 73, 214; votes on
    Franklin administration, 196, 208, 217
Hoagland, John, 269-70; votes on Great War for Empire, 174
Holme, Benjamin, 270
Holmes family, 31
Holmes, James, 31, 270; votes on Indian treaty, 179; votes on
    Belcher administration, 139-40, 153; votes on Great War
    for Empire, 174-75
Hopkins, Ebenezer, 270; votes on Morris and Belcher
    administrations, 139
Hude family, 29-30
Hude, Adam, 30
Hude, James, 30, 271; Assembly role, 65
Hude, Robert, 30, 271
Hunterdon County: appointments in, 101-102; representatives
    from, 39-40; role of representatives in Assembly, 64;
    votes, 87, 92; votes on economic policy, 53; votes on
    Franklin administration, 214
Indians: conference, 165; treaty, 179
Johnston family, 28-29, 271
Johnston, Andrew, 28-29, 271-72; Assembly role, 65, 92
Johnston, John (1661-1732), 28

administration, 195, 208, 211, 214, 217

Middletown, 30-31

Military: Assembly policy on militia and military supply, 102, 104, 122, 163; votes before Great War for Empire, 139-40; votes on Great War, 161-68, 174-79; votes in Franklin administration, 196, 208-213; votes on quartering troops, 166, 187-88, 189, 190, 192, 208

Miller, Ebenezer, 278; votes on bounties, 43; votes on Indian treaty, 179; votes on military, 208

Monmouth County: representatives from, 30-31; votes 81, 85, 87, 91-92; votes on economic policy, 43, 53; votes on military, 208; votes on slavery, 53; votes on Morris and Belcher administrations, 139; votes on Franklin administration, 195, 211, 214, 217

Moores, John (1700-1745), 30, 279

Moores, John (1725-1774), 279

Moraley, William, 3

Morality legislation: Assembly policy, 15, 187, 193; votes on, 51-52; after independence, 233

Morris County: votes in Franklin administration, 214

Morris family, 232

Morris, Lewis, 27-28, 29, 30, 32, 147-49; before appointed governor, 107; appointment and administration, 29, 121-25; on assemblymen, 109, 153; on governor's powers, 95; on reforms, 122; on trade, 12-13

Morris, Robert Hunter, 29, 122, 124, 149

Mott, William, 40, 279; Assembly role, 66; Lewis Morris and, 144; votes, 81, 91; votes on Morris and Belcher administrations, 139, 140, 150, 152-53

Nevill, Samuel, 29, 280; Assembly role, 65, 92, 142-43, 150; votes 76; votes on Morris and Belcher administrations, 138

Newark: representatives from, 31-33; votes, 76, 81, 92; votes on slavery; votes on Franklin administration, 195

Newbold family, 232

Newbold, Barzillai, 37, 280; votes, 85

New Brunswick, 4; representatives from 29-30; votes, 76, 81, 92; votes on currency, 51; votes on economic policy, 43

New York: New Jersey and, 25, 27-28, 234

Oake, William, 30, 280

Ogden family, 32-33, 93, 281

Ogden, David, 232

Ogden, John, 10, 32, 194, 281; resigns, 191; votes, 87

Ogden, Josiah, 32, 281; votes, 76

Ogden, Robert, 32, 281-82; Assembly role, 65, 92; resignation, 191, 194-95; Stamp Act and, 109; votes, 85; votes on Belcher administration, 146, 153; votes on Great War for Empire, 169

Partridge, Richard, 36

Paxson, Henry, 37, 282; Assembly role, 73; votes on economic

306

policy, 52

Peace, Joseph, 282

Pearson, Issac, 36, 37, 282-83; votes, 76; votes on Morris administration, 138, 146

Pemberton family, 35, 36

Pemberton, Israel, 38

Pennsylvania: New Jersey compared to, 99

Perth Amboy: Middlesex County and, 9; representatives from, 25, 27-29, 148; trade, 13; votes, 76, 81-87, 92; votes on currency, 51; votes on economic policy, 43; votes on slavery, 52; votes on Morris and Belcher administration, 138, 151, 152, 153; votes on Great War for Empire, 169; votes on Franklin administration, 194-95, 211

Pettit, Nathaniel, 41; votes in Franklin administration, 218

Philadelphia: New Jersey and, 25, 234

Pocock, J. G. A., 105

Poverty: Assembly policy, 10-11; votes on 51-52; after independence, 235-36

Presbyterians: in East Jersey, 25, 32-33; in West Jersey, 35, 39; number in Assembly, 74; votes on military, 208; votes on salaries, 209; votes on slavery, 53; votes on Great War for Empire, 169; votes on Franklin administration, 195, 221

Price family, 232

Price, Robert Friend, 283; votes on economic policy, 52; votes on military, 208

Provincial Congress, 230

Quakers: Belcher and, 149; independence and, 229; in East Jersey, 30-31; in West Jersey, 25, 34-36; number in Assembly, 74; slavery and, 12; Spicer and, 178; votes, 76, 81-87, 91-93; votes on economic policy, 52; votes on military, 139; votes on Morris and Belcher administrations, 150; votes on Great War for Empire, 162-63, 169, 174, 175-76, 180; votes on Franklin administration, 195, 208, 209, 214, 218

Read, Charles, 4, 36-37, 73, 94, 283-84; Assembly role, 65-66, 92; Ladd and, 175; votes, 85; votes on Great War for Empire, 169

Reading, George, 40, 284

Reading, John, 167

Reeves, Joseph, 284

Republicans, 237-38

Riots: in Morris and Belcher administrations, 124-25, 139, 140; in Franklin administration, 196, 210

Rodman, John, 36

Rodman, Thomas, 36, 285

Rolph, John, 285

Roy, John, 285

Runyon, Reune, 286; votes on military, 208

Salaries: in Morris and Belcher administrations, 124, 139, 141,

145, 149; in Franklin administration, 188-90, 196, 208-12, 218, 221
Salem County: representatives from, 34, 38-39, 64; votes, 87
Schuyler family, 28, 34
Servants: Assembly policy, 11-12; drafting of, 166
Sharp, Issac, 39, 286
Sheppard family, 38-39
Sheppard, John, 38-39, 286-87
Sheppard, Moses, 38, 287
Shinn, Thomas, 37, 287
Shirley, William, 164
Shrewsbury, 30-31
Skinner family, 29
Skinner, Cortlandt, 29, 287-88; Assembly role, 92, 194; Franklin administration and, 219; independence and, 229, 232; robbery of East Jersey Treasury and, 215; Stamp Act and, 219; votes on currency, 210
Skinner, Stephen: robbery of East Jersey Treasury, 190, 214-18; votes on his removal, 209
Slavery: Assembly policy, 11-12, 187, 193; population, 3-4; votes on, 51, 52-53; after independence, 236
Smith family, 35-36, 288; in Assembly, 194; independence and, 232
Smith, Benjamin, 39-40, 288
Smith, Daniel, 35-36, 41, 288-89; votes in Morris and Belcher administrations, 150
Smith, James, 30, 289-90; votes, 92
Smith, Joseph, 289; votes in Franklin administration, 208, 210
Smith, Richard (Burlington), 35, 289; Assembly role, 72; Belcher and, 138; college at Princeton and, 93; votes, 76; votes on Morris and Belcher administrations, 138, 142, 146, 150
Smith Richard (Salem), 290
Smith, Samuel, 289; Assembly role, 65; votes, 85; votes on Great War for Empire, 175-76
Smith, Shobal, 30, 290; Assembly role, 64; votes on Belcher administration, 153
Smith, William, 62
Smyth, Andrew, 290-91
Smyth, Frederick, 229
Smyth, John, 216
Society for the Improvement of Useful Manufactures, 234-35, 238
Somerset County: representatives from, 33-34, 72; votes, 81, 91; votes on Great War for Empire, 174; votes on Franklin administration, 195, 214
Sons of Liberty, 185
Spicer family, 2
Spicer, Jacob, 1-2, 5, 10, 25, 112, 291; Assembly role, 64-65, 73, 101; Belcher and, 64; Leaming and, 9; military and, 102; Quakers and, 178; votes, 81; votes on economic

on slavery, 53; votes on Great War for Empire, 178, 179; votes on Franklin administration, 211

Willets, John, 298

Wilson, Woodrow, 239

Winds, William, 41, 298; votes in Franklin administration, 217, 221

Wood, Richard, 299

Woodbridge, 30

Wright, Samuel, 299; votes in Morris and Belcher administrations, 139, 140

Yard, Joseph, 299; votes in Great War for Empire, 174

Young, Henry, 41, 299–300

Zemsky, Robert, xiii

LIBRARY OF DAVIDSON COLLEGE

Books on regular loan may be checked out for four weeks. Books must be presented at the Circulation Desk in order to be renewed.

A fine is charged after date due.

Special books are subject to special regulations at the discretion of the library staff.